TWO *LIVES*
OF
SAINT CUTHBERT

TWO *LIVES*
of
SAINT CUTHBERT

A Life by an
Anonymous Monk of Lindisfarne
and
Bede's *Prose Life*

TEXTS, TRANSLATION, AND NOTES

by

BERTRAM COLGRAVE

Reader in English of the
University of Durham

GREENWOOD PRESS, PUBLISHERS
NEW YORK

CONTENTS

PREFACE

To edit the two most important Lives of St Cuthbert is almost a pious duty for one who lives under the shadow of Durham Cathedral. But it is something more than that. These Lives of St Cuthbert throw considerable light on the secular history of the golden age of Northumbria. They also illustrate one of the most important periods in the history of the English Church, when, after having passed through its infancy, it was faced with the alternative of clinging to the attractive, but undoubtedly moribund, Celtic forms, or accepting the doctrines and practices of the youthful and progressive Roman Church. At the Synod of Whitby, Oswiu and his councillors chose the latter alternative. Cuthbert, like very many more, accepted the changes, but remained Celtic at heart to the end, in spite of the words which Bede puts into his mouth on his death-bed (p. 284 below). It would be difficult to find two more typical representatives of the Roman and Celtic outlook respectively than Wilfrid and Cuthbert: the one proud, capable, determined, a born fighter, a magnificent organiser, patron of the arts, rivalling the king himself in his pomp and ceremony— and Cuthbert, humble, simple, spiritual, ascetic, beloved by all both high and low, but looking always to the past rather than to the future.

If any further apology is required for editing these Lives of St Cuthbert, let it be that probably the greatest lack in the whole field of English ecclesiastical history is a critical edition of the works of Bede. This great need can only be supplied by the co-operation of many scholars, and if this present volume helps to fill a portion of the gap, it will have fulfilled its purpose. The juxtaposition of the two Lives provides an example of Bede's attitude towards his sources and how he made use of them. It is, for instance, an interesting comment on his methods, that although it is quite clear that Bede has followed the Anonymous Life closely throughout, the verbal likenesses between the two are so small as to be negligible.

The editing of these Lives has been a work of considerable labour, but of much interest. Every editor of any part of Bede's work is faced first of all by an extraordinary wealth of MSS, scattered through all the libraries of western Europe. Hardy (*Catal.* 1, 300) mentions twenty-six MSS of Bede's Prose Life and one of the Anonymous Life. But a search through the libraries of Great Britain and the Continent has produced thirty-eight MSS of the former and seven of the latter. All these I have collated and, with the exception of six (M, Bn, Go, W, Bo, Va), I have seen the originals myself. But this study, though at times laborious, has brought its own reward. It has brought to light a number of particularly interesting MSS which have not received the notice they deserve, particularly Go (Gotha, 1.81) with its unedited Lives of Celtic Saints, Du (Durham A.iv.35) which has since been acquired by the Durham Chapter Library and restored to its original home, and Bn (Berne, Stadtbibliothek 392) with the marks of the editor of the *editio princeps* of Bede's Prose Life still upon it. The study has also provided Ad$_2$ (B.M. Add. 39943), one of the greatest treasures in the British Museum, with a much fuller history, and has incidentally shown the source of the Cuthbert paintings on the stalls in Carlisle Cathedral. And finally the seven MSS of the Anonymous Life have provided some interesting early variations of place-name forms for the north of England. Two of these MSS (O$_1$ and T) had been used by the Bollandists in the *Acta Sanctorum,* but the place and personal name-forms were very carelessly transcribed. Though Cadwallader Bates took the trouble in the summer of 1892 to go to Trier and Arras to see two of the MSS of the Anonymous Life (T and A) and to give the correct form of most of the place-names (see *Arch. Ael.* N.S. XVI, 1894, pp. 81 ff.), the errors of the Bollandist edition have been widely copied. The other five MSS of the Anonymous Life add a certain amount of fresh material in this respect.

Needless to say, in the course of my work, I have incurred a very heavy debt of obligation to many, which I gladly and gratefully acknowledge: to the Librarians and staffs of the various libraries in which MSS of the Lives are found, and particularly to the Librarians and staffs of the Durham Cathedral Chapter Library, the Durham University Library, the Cambridge University Library, the Libraries of Trinity College and Corpus Christi College, Cambridge, the Bodley Library, Oxford, the MS Department of the British Museum, the Lincoln Cathedral Chapter Library, and the Bibliothèque Nationale, Paris. I am very grateful to Professor Bruce Dickins of Leeds University, Dr C. E. Wright of the MS Department of the British Museum, and Mr R. A. B. Mynors of Balliol College, Oxford, who have all read some part of the introduction or notes and have made many valuable suggestions. My thanks are also due for help of various kinds given by Mr H. W. Acomb, Durham University Librarian; Professor H. M. Chadwick, Elrington and Bosworth Professor of Anglo-Saxon in the University of Cambridge; Sir Allen Mawer, Provost of University College, London; the Rev. Dr W. Telfer, Dean of Clare College, Cambridge; and Dom André Wilmart, Farnborough.

But above all my thanks are due to P. Paul Grosjean, S.J., Bollandiste, Brussels, who has seen the proofs and made many helpful suggestions; to my colleague, the Rev. Dr Edward Pace, Reader in Divinity of the University of Durham, who has taken endless trouble over the translation, advising on difficult points and thoroughly revising it and often giving timely encouragement when it was most needed; and to Dr W. Levison, late Professor of Mediaeval and Modern History in the University of Bonn, now Honorary Fellow of the University of Durham, who has read the proofs, has given in generous measure from his vast stores of learning, and has taken the greatest interest in my work on St Cuthbert almost since it began. I have been fortunate in my helpers. If I have not always taken their advice it was because I had committed myself to certain principles to which I felt bound to adhere. For the mistakes I have made the responsibility must be mine alone.

And finally my thanks are due to the Syndics of the Cambridge University Press for undertaking the publication of this volume and to the staff for its unfailing patience and vigilance.

BERTRAM COLGRAVE

Hatfield College, Durham
St Cuthbert's Day, 1939

LIST OF ABBREVIATIONS

A.E.E.	G. Baldwin Brown, *Arts in Early England*. 6 vols. London, 1903–37.
AA.SS.	*Acta Sanctorum*, ed. J. Bollandus and others. Antwerp, Brussels, 1643, etc.
A.S.C.	*Two Saxon Chronicles parallel*, ed. J. Earle and C. Plummer. 2 vols. Oxford, 1892–9.
Anal. Boll.	*Analecta Bollandiana*. Brussels, 1882, etc.
Arch. Ael.	*Archaeologia Aeliana*: or Miscellaneous Tracts relating to Antiquity. Newcastle, 1822, etc.
Archiv.	*Archiv der Gesellschaft für ältere deutsche Geschichtskunde*. Frankfort-on-Main and Hanover, 1820, etc.
B.H.L.	*Bibliotheca Hagiographica Latina*, ed. Socii Bollandiani. Vols. 1, 2 and supp. Brussels, 1898–1911.
Bede, L.T.W.	*Bede, his Life, Times and Writings*, ed. by A. Hamilton Thompson. Oxford, 1935.
Bede, Opp.	*Venerabilis Bedae Opera*, ed. J. Giles. 12 vols. London, 1843–4.
Bright.	W. Bright, *Chapters on Early English Church History*. 3rd ed. Oxford, 1897.
Cabrol.	F. Cabrol et H. Leclercq, *Dictionnaire d'Archéologie chrétienne et de Liturgie*. Paris, 1924, etc.
Cat. Gén.	*Catalogue général des manuscrits des bibliothèques publiques de France*. Paris, 1849, etc.
Cath. Enc.	*Catholic Encyclopaedia*. 15 vols., index and supp. New York, 1907–14.
Catt. Vett.	*Catalogi veteres Librorum Ecclesiae Cathedralis Dunelm.*, Surtees Soc. vol. VII, 1837.
D.C.B.	*Dictionary of Christian Biography*, ed. W. Smith and H. Wace. 4 vols. London, 1877–87.
D.N.B.	*Dictionary of National Biography*, ed. Leslie Stephen. 63 vols. and 10 supps. London, 1885, etc.
Du Cange.	C. Dufresne Du Cange, *Glossarium mediae et infimae latinitatis*, ed. L. Favre. 10 vols. Niort, 1883–7.
E.H.R.	*English Historical Review*. London, 1886, etc.
E.R.E.	*Encyclopaedia of Religion and Ethics*, ed. J. Hastings. 13 vols. Edinburgh, 1908–26.
Eddius.	*The Life of Bishop Wilfrid by Eddius Stephanus*: text, translation and notes, by B. Colgrave. Cambridge, 1927.
Eyre, St Cuthbert.	C. Eyre, *The History of St Cuthbert*. Second ed. London, 1858.

Gougaud, *C.C.L.*	L. Gougaud, *Christianity in Celtic Lands*. London, 1932.
Greg. Dial.	*Gregorii Magni Dialogi*, ed. U. Moricca. Fonti per la storia d' Italia. Rome, 1924.
Haa.	*Historia abbatum auctore anonymo*, ed. Plummer. See *H.E.*
Hab.	*Historia abbatum auctore Beda*, ed. Plummer. See *H.E.*
H.E.	*Baedae Historia Ecclesiastica gentis Anglorum: Venerabilis Baedae opera historica*, ed. C. Plummer. 2 vols. Oxford, 1896.
H.L.	*Palladii Historia Lausiaca*, ed. D. Cuthbert Butler. Cambridge, 1898.
H. and S.	A. W. Haddan and W. Stubbs, *Councils and Ecclesiastical Documents relating to Great Britain and Ireland*. 3 vols. (4 parts). Oxford, 1869–78.
H.Y.	*Historians of the Church of York and its Archbishops*, ed. J. Raine. Rolls Series. 3 vols. 1879–94.
Halm.	*Sulpicii Severi Opera*, ed. C. Halm, Vienna Corpus, vol. I. 1866.
Hardy.	*Descriptive Catalogue of MSS relating to the History of Great Britain*, ed. T. D. Hardy. Rolls Series. 3 vols. in 4. 1862–71.
Jaager.	*Bedas Metrische Vita sancti Cuthberti*, ed. W. Jaager. Palaestra, 198. Leipzig, 1935.
Kurz.	B. P. Kurz, *From St Antony to St Guthlac*. University of California Publications in Modern Philology, vol. XII, no. 2, 1926, pp. 104–46.
L.I.S.	*Lives of Irish Saints*, ed. C. Plummer. 2 vols. Oxford, 1922.
Liber Vitae.	*Liber Vitae Ecclesiae Dunelmensis*, ed. J. Stevenson. Surtees Soc. vol. XIII, 1841, and facsimile, Surtees Soc. vol. CXXXVI, 1923.
M.G.	*Monumenta Germaniae historica*, ed. G. H. Pertz, etc. 1826, etc.
Mab. *AA.SS.*	*Acta Sanctorum ord. S. Benedicti*. 6 saecula in 9 vols., ed. J. Mabillon. Venice, 1733–8.
Mawer.	A. Mawer, *The Place-names of Northumberland and Durham*. Cambridge, 1920.
Metr. Life.	*The Life of St Cuthbert in English Verse*, ed. J. T. Fowler, Surtees Soc. vol. LXXXVII, 1891.
Migne.	*Patrologiae cursus completus. Patrologia latina*. 221 vols. 1844–64.
N.E.D.	*A New English Dictionary on Historical Principles*, ed. J. A. H. Murray, etc. Oxford, 1888–1935.

Neues Archiv.	*Neues Archiv der Gesellschaft für ältere deutsche Geschichts-kunde.* Hannover, 1876, etc.
O.E.N.	H. M. Chadwick, *The Origin of the English Nation.* Cambridge, 1907.
Opp. Min.	*Venerabilis Bedae opera historica minora,* English Historical Society, ed. J. Stevenson. London, 1841.
Redin.	Mats Redin, *Studies in Uncompounded Personal Names in Old English.* Uppsala Universitets Årsskrift, Uppsala, 1919.
Reg. Benedict.	*Sancti Benedicti regula monasteriorum,* ed. D. Cuthbert Butler. Editio Altera. Freiburg, 1927.
Ryan, *Monast.*	John Ryan, *Irish Monasticism.* London, 1931.
St Ciaran, Irish Life.	*The Latin and Irish Lives of Ciaran,* translated and annotated by R. A. S. Macalister. London, 1927.
St Samson of Dol.	*Life of St Samson of Dol,* translated by T. Taylor. London, 1925.
Schenkl.	H. Schenkl, *Bibliotheca patrum Latinorum Britannica.* Vienna, 1890–1905. [*Sitzungsberichte der Wiener Akademie der Wissenschaften* (Phil.-hist. Kl.), vols. CXXI-CXXVII, CXXXI, CXXXIII, CXXXVI, CXXXVII, CXXXIX, CXLIII, CL.]
Script. rerum Merov.	*Monumenta Germaniae Historica. Scriptores rerum Merovingicarum.* 7 vols. 1885, etc.
Stevenson, C.H.	*The Church Historians of England,* ed. J. Stevenson, vol. I, pt 2. London, 1853.
Stubbs, *Dunstan.*	*Memorials of St Dunstan,* ed. Wm Stubbs. Rolls Series. 1874.
Surtees Soc.	Surtees Society Publications. Durham, 1834, etc.
Symeon, H.D.E.	Symeon of Durham, *Historia Dunelmensis Ecclesiae,* ed. T. Arnold. Rolls Series. 2 vols. 1882–5.
V.A.	*Vita sancti Cuthberti auctore anonymo.*
V.M.	*Vita sancti Cuthberti metrica auctore Beda.*
V.P.	*Vita sancti Cuthberti prosaica auctore Beda.*
V.S.H.	*Vitae sanctorum Hiberniae,* ed. C. Plummer. 2 vols. Oxford, 1910.
Vit. Col.	*Vita sancti Columbae auctore Adamnano.*
Vit. Col. Fowler.	*Adamnani Vita sancti Columbae,* ed. J. T. Fowler. Oxford, 1894.
Vit. Col. Reeves.	*Vita sancti Columbae Auctore Adamnano,* ed. W. Reeves. Dublin, 1857.
Vit. Tr.	*The Tripartite Life of St Patrick,* ed. Whitley Stokes. Rolls Series. 2 vols. London, 1887.

INTRODUCTION

O F all the English saints none figures more prominently in the history of the north of England than St Cuthbert. Reginald of Durham says[1] that the three most popular saints of his day were Cuthbert of Durham, Edmund of Bury, and Aethilthryth of Ely; and he goes on to prove that Cuthbert was the greatest of the three. The saint's incorruptible body became the centre of a cult which, within a few centuries, had reached all parts of England and many parts of western Europe. Bede in his Prose Life puts into the mouth of the dying saint (c. 39) prophetic words which, though they seem peculiarly out of place on the lips of the humble-minded Cuthbert, were nevertheless destined to come true: "For I know that, although I seemed contemptible to some while I lived, yet, after my death, you will see more clearly what I was and how my teaching is not to be despised."

Undoubtedly Bede's reputation had something to do with the widespread respect in which St Cuthbert was held, for the writings of the Jarrow monk, including his two Lives of St Cuthbert, were in constant demand from the eighth century onwards, not only in England but on the continent. Cuthbert, the disciple of Bede, who afterwards became abbot of Wearmouth and Jarrow, writes to Lull, bishop of Mainz (754–86), to say that he is sending him copies of the Life of St Cuthbert in prose and verse.[2] There are fourteen MSS of the Prose Life still preserved in continental libraries, the majority of which were written abroad; besides these there are several recorded in mediaeval catalogues and elsewhere and since lost,[3] while eight of the Metrical Life also remain on the continent.[4] That this popularity abroad was not entirely due to Bede seems to be evidenced by the fact that of the seven MSS of the Anonymous Life which still remain, it is almost

1 *Libellus*, c. 19, Surtees Soc. 1, 1835, pp. 37 ff.
2 *M.G.* Epistolae selectae, 1, Berlin, 1916, p. 250, no. 116.
3 See pp. 39 ff.   4 Jaager, pp. 25 ff.

certain that every one was written on the continent. In the ninth century his name appears in the Martyrologies of Florus of Lyons, of Wandalbert, of Rhabanus Maurus, of Ado of Vienne, of Usuard, in Notker's Martyrology of Saint-Gall and in the Codex Epternacensis of the Hieronymian Martyrology.[1] Alcuin in the same century could also say of him in an epigram:

> Laudibus ac celebrat quem tota Britannia crebris,
> Et precibus rogitat se auxiliare piis.[2]

When in Fulda the Church of the Saviour was consecrated in 819, "in absida occidentali, ubi martyr Bonifacius quiescit", amongst other saints venerated "in crypta eiusdem absidae" were Cuthbert and Bede.[3]

In England many churches were dedicated to St Cuthbert, not only in the northern counties, but also as far afield as Leicestershire, Derbyshire, Nottinghamshire, Shropshire, Warwickshire, Herefordshire, Bedfordshire, Norfolk, Dorsetshire, Somersetshire and Cornwall.[4] In the *Historia de Sancto Cuthberto* an anonymous author relates how Cuthbert appeared to King Alfred at Glastonbury and tells how the same king's dying commands to his son Edward were to love God and St Cuthbert.[5] Aethelstan on his way to Scotland, probably in 934, came to Chester-le-Street in order to bestow lands upon the saint and also treasures, some of which still survive. These are merely a few examples of the widespread cult which finally led to the building of the noblest of the English cathedrals and the establishment of a see at Durham more powerful in temporal authority and richer in estates than any other in the country.

The chief authorities for the life of the saint are the two works that follow, the Life written by an anonymous monk of Lindisfarne, and Bede's Prose Life. The latter was not Bede's first attempt at writing a Life of St Cuthbert, for he had previously written a metrical version which was, as he explained

1 *AA.SS.* Nov. II, p. 154.
2 *De clade Lindisfarnensis monasterii*, ll. 177–8: Dümmler, *M.G. Poetae atini*, I, p. 233.
3 Hrabani Mauri carm. 41, II, l. 4: Dümmler, *loc. cit.* II, p. 208.
4 A. Hamilton Thompson, "Churches dedicated to St Cuthbert", *Transactions of the Architectural and Archaeological Society of Durham and Northumberland*, 1936, pp. 151 ff.   5 Symeon, *H.D.E.* I, p. 207.

in the Prologue to the Prose Life, "somewhat shorter indeed, but similarly arranged" (p. 147). The models for this twofold treatment of the subject were Sedulius' *Carmen* and *Opus paschale*, both of which were very familiar to Bede.[1] Both Bede's versions are based upon the Anonymous Life, but both, in addition to filling out the concise account of the anonymous writer, have extra information to give.

Many, perhaps most, lives of the saints written in the traditional form give a brief account of the birth of the saint and of portents connected therewith and with his early years; then follow a series of miracles associated with his life, his death natural or violent, and the miracles which took place at his tomb. The story is diversified by a list of his virtues, by an account of his triumphant resistance to the assaults of devils and temptations of various kinds; usually there is a model sermon and a farewell oration from the saint's deathbed. But though all three of the Cuthbert Lives follow in outline the regular development of the typical saint's life, there is something fresh about them, something which makes us realise that Cuthbert is a human being and not merely a wonder-worker.

This fact is true of both the Lives that follow, for, though the author of the Anonymous Life confines himself to the shortest possible space in his description of an event, he often achieves a conciseness and clarity in relating an incident which compares favourably with Bede's more diffuse account.[2]

The Anonymous Life gradually builds up a complete picture of the saint. While a youth he is good-natured and thoughtful, as his dealings with the precocious and not very attractive infant described in the first miracle show (I, 3); he is polite to strangers (I, 4), kind to animals (I, 6), and pursues the ordinary avocations of the youth of his day (I, 5, 6); in later life he is devoted to his foster-mother (II, 7), kind and cheerful towards all, as for instance to his friend Hildmer when the latter is in distress (II, 8); even in his life on Farne, there are human touches

---

1 Cf. Levison, *Bede, L.T.W.* p. 126. E. R. Curtius, "Dichtung und Rhetorik im Mittelalter," *Deutsche Vierteljahrsschrift für Literaturwissenschaft und Geistesgeschichte*, XVI, 1938, pp. 439 ff.
2 Cf. for instance, *V.P.* cc. 5, 34, 41, with *V.A.* I, 6, IV, 10, IV, 15. See also below, p. 15.

in his attitude towards the birds (III, 5), in the way in which he provides for his own simple requirements, and even in the miracle by which he obtains the necessary timber for the humblest of his buildings (III, 4). The list of Cuthbert's virtues, borrowed almost wholesale from the description of another saint, nevertheless reflects his personality in a most interesting way in at least one instance; for in one of these passages (III, 7) the writer, borrowing from the Evagrian *Life of Antony*, has made a significant change. Evagrius, translating Athanasius, says of Antony (c. 13) that he "never through an excess of hilarity burst into laughter"; but the anonymous author, omitting this phrase, substitutes the statement that "at all hours he was happy and joyful".

In such ways an impression of reality is obtained which is generally missing from the typical saint's life. Still another reason for this impression of reality is the constant reference to places and people known to his original readers or hearers and also well known to us to-day. Chester-le-Street and Carlisle, Iona, Coldingham, Coquet Island and Whitby, Melrose and Farne, the rivers Leader, Teviot and Tweed, can all be visited to-day; while Trumwine, Eata and Eadberht, Boisil and Aidan, Aldfrith and Ecgfrith, all of whom are mentioned, are familiar historical characters. All this is true, though to a less extent, of Bede's Prose Life, for Bede often deliberately omits the name of a person or place which he thinks may not be familiar to the wider circle of readers for whom his Life was probably intended. But in both, the careful documentation adds an air of verisimilitude to even the most remarkable of the miracles.

We get details in each of them of the daily life of the monk, much slighter it is true than we could have wished, but sufficient to enable us to construct some sort of a picture of the daily round of worship and work, the chapter meetings, the midday rest, the simple meals, the dress, the constant evangelistic journeys, the visits of guests, the hermit life to which occasionally the more saintly ones aspired, the burial rites and the elevation of the relics.) In the fuller account of the Prose Life the picture is correspondingly more complete, and Bede's gift of picturesque writing is seen at its best in such incidents as the scene by the

river Tyne (c. 3), Cuthbert's entry into Melrose (c. 6), the
angelic visitor at Ripon (c. 7), the death of Boisil (c. 8) and
particularly the long account of Cuthbert's death which, though
attributed to Herefrith, bears the unmistakable stamp of Bede's
own style. In both Lives the appeal to witnesses, many of
them still living when the Lives were written, helps to give the
impression of veracity, though, as we shall see later, this method
of vouching for the truth of a story was in the regular tradition
and did not necessarily mean much.

This is not the place to give more than the briefest outline
of the period in which Cuthbert lived. But it is clear that he
belongs to the Celtic rather than to the Roman tradition, and
that, in spite of his dying attacks upon the Celtic "heretics",[1]
he lived and died after the manner of the typical Irish monk.
The date of his birth is uncertain, but it must have been within
a year or so of 634, just about the time of that dark period in
Northumbrian history, when Edwin was slain by Cadwallon,
king of the Britons, and when, with the help of Penda and his
Mercians, the Northumbrian army was completely destroyed
at Heathfield. This was in October 633, six years after Edwin's
conversion. For "one hateful year" Cadwallon "occupied the
provinces of the Northumbrians, not ruling them like a vic-
torious king but ravaging them like a furious tyrant".[2] Paulinus
fled to Kent taking with him Edwin's widow Aethilburg and
her little daughter Eanfled who was afterwards to marry Oswiu,
king of Northumbria. In 634 Oswald with his little force
defeated a great British army under Cadwallon at Heaven-
field. It was symbolical that a vision of St Columba appeared
to him on the night before the battle[3] bidding him be of good
courage. When the great victory had been won and Oswald
was established as king over all Northumbria, he applied to
Iona for a Christian teacher.

So while Cuthbert was an infant, Aidan in 635 established
a monastery at Lindisfarne near Oswald's royal city of Bamburgh
and became bishop of Northumbria. It was natural that he
should have chosen an island see in the Iona tradition rather
than York with its memories of Paulinus. Aidan travelled over

[1] *V.P.* c. 39.   [2] *H.E.* III, 1.   [3] *Vit. Col.* I, 1.

the countryside on foot, preaching the gospel and reconverting those who had lapsed into heathenism. It is possible that Cuthbert may have heard the great preacher while he was still an infant in the charge of his parents. When the child was eight years old, he was given over to the care of his foster-mother, Kenswith, or Coenswith, in the village of *Hruringaham*. This was just about the time when the seven happy years of Oswald's reign were ended by the attack of the heathen Penda of Mercia who defeated and slew Oswald at the battle of Maserfield in 642. Oswald had been king over all Northumbria, both Deira and Bernicia, but his death led to the dividing up of the two kingdoms, Deira reverting to the house of Aelle and refusing to acknowledge Oswald's younger brother Oswiu. So Oswini became king of Deira while Oswiu ruled Bernicia only. This division of the two kingdoms of course prevented any really efficient opposition to Penda and until 655 the latter repeatedly harried both kingdoms; we read of his devastations as far north as Bamburgh,[1] and it was perhaps during one of these raids that Cuthbert was engaged on the military service mentioned in the Anonymous Life (I, 7). In 651 Oswini, king of Deira, was murdered with the connivance, if not by the definite orders, of Oswiu, and twelve days afterwards Aidan also died. This was the year too when Cuthbert entered Melrose. Four years afterwards, in 655, Penda vowed to destroy the nation of the Northumbrians, but Oswiu, with a small army, defeated and slew him near the river Winwaed. From 655 to 658 Northumbrian authority reached to the Severn and the Thames. Oswiu was a Christian like his brother Oswald, and the period of his supremacy gave Christianity time to settle down and take root once more all over the north and midlands. In 658 Mercian power was re-established under Wulfhere, Penda's son.

Meanwhile, Oswiu's son, Alhfrith, who was now ruling with his father as under-king of Deira, had come under the sway of Agilberht and the young priest Wilfrid recently returned from Rome. He seems to have been converted by them to an enthusiasm for the Roman form of Christianity.

1 *H.E.* III, 16.

Before this he had given some land to Eata, abbot of Melrose, to found a monastery at Ripon. The latter had gone there taking Cuthbert with him as guest master,[1] but when Wilfrid returned from Rome and had won Alhfrith's heart somewhere about 660, Alhfrith drove out Eata and his Celtic monks and gave the monastery to Wilfrid. In 664 the famous Synod of Whitby was held when Oswiu and his counsellors accepted the Roman form of the faith. For the time Wilfrid and his party had conquered and in the same year Wilfrid became bishop of all Northumbria and went to Gaul to be consecrated. Eata, who had apparently in the meantime accepted the Roman Easter and the outward forms, at any rate, of the Roman practice, became abbot of Lindisfarne in place of Colman who, unable to accept the Roman customs, had retired to Iona. Cuthbert accompanied Eata to Lindisfarne. But Wilfrid delayed in Gaul, and when he returned home in 666 he found that Chad, one of Aidan's twelve pupils, had meanwhile been consecrated to the vacant see. For three years Chad remained bishop while Wilfrid lived in retirement, until Archbishop Theodore of Canterbury in 669 restored Wilfrid to his see, and sent Chad to be bishop of Mercia at Lichfield. Wilfrid remained in charge of the diocese and occupied himself in building and rebuilding churches at York and Ripon and elsewhere, living in great state and prosperity, in striking contrast to the simple ascetic monks of the island of Lindisfarne. In 671 Oswiu died and was succeeded by Ecgfrith, not by Alhfrith, for the latter had rebelled against his father some time after 664 and disappears from history. During all these events Cuthbert was living quietly at Lindisfarne as prior.

In the second year of Ecgfrith's reign (673) Bede was born, and three years[2] afterwards Cuthbert retired to Farne Island. In 678 Theodore in accordance with his policy of dividing up the great dioceses obtained the consent of Ecgfrith, but not of Wilfrid himself, to the division of the great Northumbrian diocese. It was decided to construct three new dioceses, one to consist of Bernicia with an episcopal seat either at Lindisfarne or Hexham; another in Deira with a seat at York; and another

1 *V.P.* c. 7.   2 Symeon, *H.D.E.* II, p. 27; but see Bright, p. 302, n. 6.

in Lindsey which had been lately wrested by Ecgfrith from Wulfhere of Mercia. Wilfrid went to Rome to complain of this treatment and laid a petition before Pope Agatho. Bosa, one of Hilda's pupils, was thereupon appointed bishop of Deira; Eata, Cuthbert's friend and abbot, superintended Bernicia; while Eadhaeth, a friend and companion of Chad, became first bishop of Lindsey.

Wilfrid returned from Rome in 680 bearing the decision of the pope, on the whole favourable to himself; his great diocese was to be divided up, but the recently appointed bishops were to be deposed, and Wilfrid was to choose his own assistants. Ecgfrith however refused to accept the pope's decision and put the outraged Wilfrid into prison, releasing him in the following year and sending him into an exile which lasted for the rest of Ecgfrith's life.

In 680 Hilda of Whitby died, and in the following year the monastery at Jarrow was founded and soon after Bede went there as a monk. In this year too Eata gave up Hexham to Tunberht, a kinsman of Bede's beloved abbot, Ceolfrith, and went to Lindisfarne. Thus the great diocese was divided up still further. Tunberht, for some reason which Bede does not explain, was deposed in 684 and Cuthbert consecrated in his place at Easter 685. No one in all these arrangements seems to have paid the slightest heed to Pope Agatho's decision of 679. In order that Cuthbert might stay in Lindisfarne, Eata went back to Hexham. Only a few weeks later, while Cuthbert was making his first episcopal visitation, Ecgfrith was killed at the battle of Nechtansmere, and Northumbria by this defeat lost its supremacy beyond the Forth, and for a time in Strathclyde too. Ecgfrith's illegitimate brother Aldfrith came to the throne in his place, a man of scholarly interests, himself a writer and learned in all the learning of the Irish. But Cuthbert, worn out by his asceticism, soon realised that he was no longer able to perform the arduous labours of constant preaching and visitation which were the duty of a bishop, and, shortly after the Christmas of 686, he returned to his island where he died on March 20th, 687.

Meanwhile Wilfrid, after an exile of over five years, returned to the north through the influence of Archbishop Theodore and was received in a friendly way by Aldfrith, who was evidently prepared to make a fresh start. Nothing further was heard of Pope Agatho's decision, and Wilfrid was content to accept the see of Hexham made vacant by the death of Eata. Shortly afterwards Bosa seems to have been expelled from York to make way for Wilfrid, while Eadhaeth, who had been at Ripon possibly as bishop, left that too. All this was during Cuthbert's episcopacy at Lindisfarne, and it looks very much as though Wilfrid, in the early days of his reconciliation, had been trying to rush the king into gradually giving into his charge once more the whole of the Northumbrian diocese. And chance played into Wilfrid's hands. For having obtained Hexham by the death of Eata, and York and Ripon by the departure of Bosa and Eadhaeth, Cuthbert's retirement in 686 enabled him to obtain the see of Lindisfarne. Now in the Prose Life (c. 40) we learn how serious troubles arose at Lindisfarne after the death of Cuthbert, which ceased on the election of Eadberht to the bishopric; it is difficult not to associate this with Wilfrid's government of the see; Wilfrid can hardly have loved the monastery which was the centre whence the Celtic "heresy" had spread over the north and over which had ruled Colman, his chief antagonist at the Synod of Whitby, whom he had succeeded in driving out of England. From Lindisfarne, too, had come at least three of the bishops who had usurped part or the whole of his diocese, namely, Chad, Eata and Cuthbert, and possibly Eadhaeth, the friend of Chad.[1] It seems likely, therefore, from what we know of the character of Wilfrid, that he would not have dealt very gently with his old foes. But Aldfrith, though he may have been carried off his feet at first by the overwhelming personality of Wilfrid, soon saw his mistake, even if he had ever intended to make Wilfrid's appointment permanent. At the end of 687 John of Beverley was appointed to Hexham, and, in the following year, Eadberht, a man of the same pious simplicity as Cuthbert, was appointed to the see of Lindisfarne. Needless to say the old trouble blazed up again between Wilfrid and the king of Northumbria, and in 691-2 still another quarrel arose and

1 *H.E.* III, 28.

Wilfrid departed for a third period of exile. But with his later history we are not here concerned.

The reign of Aldfrith (685–705) seems to have covered the two most brilliant decades of what has rightly been called "the golden age of Northumbria". This golden age is the period covered by the life of Bede (673–735). It was a time of great activity, when literature and the arts flourished. To this period, above and beyond the works of Bede and the Anonymous Life of Cuthbert, belong other Latin works, such as Eddius' Life of Wilfrid, the anonymous monk of Wearmouth's biography of his abbot Ceolfrith, and the oldest legend of Gregory the Great, which probably came from Whitby. To this period also belong such wonderful works of art as the Lindisfarne gospels now in the British Museum. This codex is probably only one survivor of many others of the same kind. For we read also of the gospel book presented to Ripon by Wilfrid[1] and of the two gospels dating from Wilfrid's time which were still preserved in York cathedral in the sixteenth century.[2] Another form of art which developed at this time, and in all probability reached its highest point during the period, was the construction of tall sculptured stone crosses of which the most famous are those still standing at Ruthwell and Bewcastle, and the Acca cross once more in its ancient home, at Hexham. A closely connected art is seen in the carved coffin in which the body of St Cuthbert was placed, now preserved in the Chapter Library at Durham, and the Franks' casket in the British Museum. Church building went on apace, as the remains still to be seen at Hexham, Ripon, Corbridge, Monkwearmouth, Jarrow, Escomb and elsewhere, all show; and the theory has even been put forward with some plausibility that the greatest poem of our pre-conquest literature, *Beowulf*, emanated from the court of Aldfrith.[3] But, however great may have been the artistic, literary, and general cultural outlook of the time, it is the great men and women who have left the most impressive mark on the history of this period, and of these St Cuthbert rightly takes his place in the very forefront.

1 *Eddius*, c. 17.   2 *H.Y.* III, p. 387.   3 See p. 329.

SOURCES, DATE AND AUTHORSHIP

The main source of the Anonymous Life, so far as the actual facts of Cuthbert's life are concerned, is the tradition at Lindisfarne, the saga which grew up around the name of the saint, much of it probably during his lifetime or very soon after his death. The author or authors of the Life simply put into writing the floating tradition. As Delehaye has pointed out, there are two main sources in all hagiographical literature. The first is the people, whose imagination perpetually creates fresh products of its fancy, and attaches wonders drawn from the most diverse sources to the name of its favourite saints; while the second source is the writer, whose duty it is to put the floating traditions into literary shape; he takes the material given him, but his ideas and standards determine its permanent form.[1] In this determination our writer, like the average writer of saints' lives of this period, was much influenced by earlier models such as Evagrius' translation of Athanasius' *Life of St Antony*, Sulpicius Severus' *Life of St Martin* or the *Actus Silvestri*.

Who this author was is unknown. Bede in his introduction to the *Ecclesiastical History* says: "What I have written concerning the most holy father and bishop Cuthbert, whether in this volume or in my little book concerning his acts, I took in part from what I have previously found written about him by the brethren of the church at Lindisfarne, yielding simple faith to the story I read; and in parts I ventured to add with care such facts as I myself had learned from the unimpeachable testimony of faithful men." From this statement it looks as though Bede himself was not aware of the author's name or perhaps considered it to be a composite work; but, in any case, it is clear that the author or authors belonged to Lindisfarne. Thus Aidan is referred to as "our bishop" (i, 5), and Lindisfarne is "our island" (iii, 1; iv, 15), or "our monastery" (iv, 7, 16, 17), or "our church" (i, 3; ii, 8; iv, 1). If the work is the composite effort of the Lindisfarne brethren, nevertheless the first person singular is constantly used. The theory, first propounded by

---

1 Cf. H. Delehaye, *Les Légendes hagiographiques*, Brussels, 3rd ed. 1927, pp. 11 f.

Heinrich Hahn,[1] that Herefrith was the author is scarcely
tenable. In the first place it is highly improbable that Herefrith
who was apparently at Melrose with Boisil[2] should have been
under the impression that Cuthbert received the tonsure at
Ripon,[3] that he should not have mentioned the death of Boisil
and his prophecy of Cuthbert's future bishopric,[4] nor the story
of how Cuthbert cured Aelfflaed,[5] both of which incidents are
peculiar to Bede and based on Herefrith's testimony. But to
my mind the most convincing proof of all is that the man
who gave Bede such an affecting account of Cuthbert's last
days, if he was the author of the other Life was there content
to describe the saint's passing in a few perfunctory sentences.
Hahn's argument that Herefrith's account in Bede has verbal
borrowings from the account in the Anonymous Life, is easily
answered by pointing out that Herefrith's account is over
twelve times as long and contains only seven words borrowed
from the Anonymous Life; while in the very sentence in which
these verbal borrowings occur[6], is a phrase of seven words
borrowed (scarcely by Herefrith) from Gregory's *Dialogues*.
The most specious of Hahn's arguments, that Herefrith's name
is never mentioned in the Anonymous Life, might be made the
basis of an argument that the Life was written by Baldhelm or
Cynimund,[7] both of whom are mentioned by name as witnesses
in the Prose Life but not in the Anonymous Life.

The authorship of the earlier Lindisfarne Life must probably
always be a matter of conjecture. The writer was a monk at
Lindisfarne and was apparently a well-read, well-educated man.
He was familiar with the *Epistola Victorii Aquitani ad Hilarium*,
with the Evagrian *Life of Antony*, with Sulpicius Severus' *Life
of St Martin*, with the *Actus Silvestri*, with some of the works of
Ambrose, probably with Gregory's *Dialogues*, and above all
with the Scriptures. For the information about the miracles
performed by the saint, he was indebted to the general body of
tradition preserved in the church and particularly to certain
people whom he quotes by name, such as Plecgils, Tydi,

1 *Bonifaz und Lul.* Leipzig, 1883, pp. 175 ff.
2 *V.P.* c. 8.   3 *V.A.* II, 2.   4 *V.P.* c. 8 and note.
5 *V.P.* c. 23 and note.   6 *V.P.* c. 39 *ad fin.*   7 *V.P.* cc. 25, 36.

Aethilwald, Aelfflaed, and Walhstod, as well as various other priests, deacons, trustworthy men and faithful witnesses whom he does not mention by name. But this quoting of authorities is only part of the regular routine of the writing of mediaeval saints' lives. This feature goes back to Athanasius' *Life of Antony*, in the preface to which the writer declares that he is writing only what he has learned on the authority of Antony himself. But many of the stories which follow of fights with devils, of visions, and miracles of healing are to say the least of a highly imaginative order. In the same way Adamnan mentions eyewitnesses in his *Life of St Columba* to various miracles as in the marvellous story of the pestiferous rain.[1] Günter quotes many other instances of this constant appeal to witnesses in the lives of saints, even when the events witnessed to are incredible in the highest degree.[2] It is therefore clear that too much emphasis must not be placed upon this appeal to credible witnesses.

The date of the Anonymous Life is fixed within a few years. It must have been written at least a year after the Translation. The miracle recorded in IV, 17 is related as taking place in "this present year", which would seem to imply that the other miracles recorded as taking place after the Translation (IV, 15, 16) did not take place in the same year but at least a year before. Now the Translation took place in 698, so we may take the earliest date for the composition of the Life as 699. The latest date is given by the reference in III, 6 to "Aldfrith who is now reigning peacefully". Aldfrith died in 705. It therefore narrows down the date of composition to between 699 and 705.

There is no question as to the authorship of the Prose Life, and even if we did not possess Bede's own Prologue in which he proclaims himself as the author, it could easily be recognised as an authentic work of Bede. In the Preface to the *Ecclesiastical History*, Bede explains that his chief source is the Anonymous Life, but in the Prologue to the Prose Life he does not mention it. He explains instead the elaborate precautions he took to

1 *Vit. Col.* II, 4.
2 H. Günter, *Die Christliche Legende des Abendlandes*, Heidelberg, 1910, pp. 175 ff.

make the Life an authentic account of the saint, which included showing his notes to the brethren at Lindisfarne, and particularly to Herefrith (a delicate position indeed for Herefrith, if he were really the author of the Anonymous Life). But the real source of the work is the Anonymous Life itself. Of the forty miracles recorded in the Prose Life, only eight are peculiar to Bede (cc. 3, 8, 19, 23, 31, 35, 36, 46), and of these eight, two (cc. 31, 35) are mentioned by the earlier writer but passed over (IV, 18). Generally speaking he omits the names of witnesses given by the Lindisfarne monk. The only exceptions are Bishop Trumwine (c. 1) and Aethilwald, late bishop of Lindisfarne (c. 30). On two other occasions he mentions the name of a witness when the Lindisfarne monk does not give one. On both occasions he has heard the account of the miracle at first hand (cc. 5, 27). But when he tells a fresh miracle not related in the other Life, he refers to his witnesses, though not in every case by name (cf. cc. 3, 19, 46). He also distinguishes between eyewitnesses and those who had heard the details from others, just as he does in the *Ecclesiastical History* (cf. cc. 5, 6, 23).

The arrangement of the work follows the Anonymous Life almost exactly for the first three books, but in the long fourth book Bede changes the order of the miracles considerably (the order of Bede's chapters as compared with the fourth book of the *V.A.* is 24, 26, 29, 30, 32, 33, 25, 27, 28, 34, 36, 38, 39, 42, 41, 44, 45). The resulting change of order is an improvement, and this, together with the addition of various incidents such as his entry into the monastery at Melrose, adds clarity to the work. But the chief addition in the Life is the long and vivid account of the death of Cuthbert supplied from information given by Herefrith. The whole story is alleged to be in the very words of Herefrith, but the verbal reminiscences from Possidius' *Life of St Augustine*, Gregory's *Dialogues* (a favourite work of Bede), and also from the Anonymous Life, prove that Bede has at any rate worked carefully over Herefrith's account.

A comparison between the two accounts of almost any of the miracles common to both, illustrates how closely Bede follows his original. But it is amusing to notice how carefully he avoids using the same words and phrases. Jaager has col-

lected the few verbal borrowings that exist[1] but they are almost
negligible. It did not seem worth while to note them in the
text and I have not done so. Occasionally Bede changes an
incident considerably, sometimes by no means for the better.
Compare for instance the two accounts of how Cuthbert was
divinely provided for when he was travelling over the deserted
country near Chester-le-Street; the simple account in the
Anonymous Life (I, 6) compares very favourably with Bede's
account (c. 5) where the whole motivation of the story has
been changed. Or again, the story of his announcement of
his coming death to the anchorite Herbert of Derwentwater
(c. 28) where Bede has enlarged the simpler account of the
Anonymous Life by mere unnecessary verbiage. It would be
difficult to find a better illustration of Plummer's statement
in which, comparing the two Lives of Cuthbert, he says:
"He seems to take delight in altering the language for the
mere sake of alteration...he amplifies the narrative with
rhetorical matter which can only be called padding."[2] Another
incident in which Bede has completely missed the point of the
story is the account of the revelation which Cuthbert had of
Hadwald's death (c. 34). Bede also suppresses many interesting
proper names of persons and places, perhaps, as has been suggested, in order to make the account more easy to read in the
services of the church or the refectory. In fact, even in the
Anonymous Life, certain MSS (notably B and H) have omitted
many of the proper names for the same reason. But probably
Bede's account was written in the first instance for a wider
circle of readers than the Anonymous Life and was therefore
intended to be somewhat less personal. He has however added
one place-name, Derwentwater, the home of the anchorite
Herbert (c. 28). Besides this the historical interest of some of
Bede's additions is considerable. We have already mentioned
the long account of the death of Cuthbert; to Bede we owe also
the interesting description of the attitude of the simple people
of Northumbria to the new religion (c. 3), the story of the entry
of Cuthbert to Melrose, and of the death of Boisil (cc. 6, 8),
and the vivid and interesting story of the brethren who forgot

1 Jaager, pp. 135–6.   2 H.E. I, p. xlvi.

to cook and eat the goose on Farne (c. 36), the death and burial of Bishop Eadberht (c. 43), and the account of Cuthbert's successors on Farne (c. 46). Plummer has declared that "it cannot be said that Bede has bettered his original",[1] but it is only fair to Bede to note the improvement in lucidity and arrangement, in vivid and picturesque writing and in his attempts to make what Levison calls an "aretalogy" into a reliable and trustworthy account of the saint.[2]

In addition to the use made of the Anonymous Life, Bede was also indebted, as the text and the notes will show, to Gregory's *Dialogues*, to Possidius' *Life of St Augustine*, and to the Evagrian *Life of Antony* as well as to the Scriptures for many quotations.

The date of the Life is apparently somewhere about 721. It is dedicated to Bishop Eadfrith who died in that year. In the book usually called *De temporum ratione* which he wrote in 725, he speaks of it as having been written "some years ago".[3] One would therefore gather that it cannot have been written much before 721.[4]

---

1 *H.E.* I, p. xlvi.   2 Levison, *Bede, L.T.W.* p. 129.
3 *Opp.* VI, p. 329. Cf. also T. Mommsen, *Chronica Maiora*, § 570: *M.G. Auctores antiquissimi*, XIII, pp. 316–17.
4 Cf. Plummer, *H.E.* I, p. cxlviii.

MANUSCRIPTS

A. THE ANONYMOUS LIFE

1. O₁. St Omer 267.[1] 9¼ × 6 in. 83 ff. 25 lines to the page. Single column. This MS is in an insular hand of the late ninth or early tenth century and, like O₂, belonged to and was probably written at the Abbey of Saint-Bertin. It contains more than one hand. It is bound in calf and has on it the arms of Benoît Ier de Béthune, that is, Benoît de Béthune des Plancques, the abbot who, about the year 1677, had many of the monastery MSS rebound. It contains works by St Augustine, St Jerome and St Cyprian, and hymns to St Bertin and St Martin, the latter with music. The Anonymous Life occupies ff. 67 b–83 b.

2. O₂. St Omer 715. Tom. I.[2] 20 × 14 in. 187 ff. 48 lines to the page. Double columns. This volume forms part of a twelfth-century legendary once belonging to and probably written at the Abbey of Saint-Bertin. It originally contained at least 208 ff. It was adorned with many illuminated initials for the sake of which some 20 ff. have been removed, while many other initials have been cut out. The fifty-seven saints' lives cover most days from December 31st to April 9th. The Anonymous Life occupies ff. 164–168 b, but two folios have been lost between 165 and 166. The other three volumes which are also numbered 715 form a quite separate legendary which originally belonged to the cathedral library of St Omer.

3. A. Arras 812 (1029).[3] 7¼ × 5 in. 154 ff. 18 lines to the page. Single column. This late tenth-century MS originally belonged to the Benedictine monastery of St Vaast at Arras, and is mentioned in the eleventh-century catalogue of the

1 *Anal. Boll.* XLVII, Brussels, 1929, p. 246. *Cat. Gén.* (4º), III, Paris, 1861, p. 135.

2 *Anal. Boll.* XLVII, pp. 254 ff. *Cat. Gén.* (4º), III, p. 316. *Script. rerum Merov.* VII, p. 672. *Archiv*, VIII, 1843, p. 414.

3 *Cat. Gén.* (4º), IV, Paris, 1872, p. 322. It is numbered 1029 in the catalogue made by Caron in 1860, and 812 in the General Catalogue. Stubbs, *Dunstan,* p. xxxviii. *Script. rerum Merov.* V, p. 575 and n. 2; VII, p. 555.

monastery.[1] It now contains part of the Anonymous Life
(ff. 1–22 b, 25–26 b, 23 b–24 b), some nine chapters being missing,
and some of the later chapters being out of order; it is followed
by a Life of St Guthlac of which the first part is missing. This
is followed by an imperfect Life of St Dunstan, and a Life of
St Filibert, abbot of Jumièges, of which the end is missing.
It originally also contained the Life of St Aichard, another abbot
of Jumièges. Apparently this Life was still at St Vaast in the
seventeenth century, for it is mentioned in the seventeenth-
century list of contents on the first folio and was used by the
Bollandists for their text of the Life of St Aichard in *AA.SS.
Sept.* v. pp. 85–100. Since that time several folios have been
lost and some of the remaining folios have been rebound in
the wrong order.

4.   H. British Museum, Harleian MS 2800.[2] 18¾ × 10¾ in.
262 ff. 50 lines to the page. Double columns. The three
Harleian MSS numbered 2800–2802 together form a great
legendary from the Premonstratensian monastery at Arnstein
in Nassau. The first volume dates from about 1200 and is
beautifully written with many elaborately illuminated initials.
It consists of 128 items, being lives of saints from the beginning
of January to June 8th, the Anonymous Life appearing on
ff. 248–251 b. Harl. 2800–2802 and Brussels 207–208, 98–100,
and 206 together formed two copies of a great legendary
which was written in the diocese of Trier. Of the 128 items
in Harl. 2800 there are only five which are not found in one
of the Brussels volumes.

5.   B. Brussels, Royal Library 207–208.[3] 19⅜ × 13½ in.
284 ff. 44 lines to the page. Double columns. This forms the
first of three volumes corresponding with the three volumes

1 G. Becker, *Catalogi Bibliothecarum Antiqui*, Bonn, 1885, p. 143.
2 *A Catalogue of the Harleian MSS in the Brit. Mus.* II, London, 1808, pp. 712 f.
Script. rerum Merov. VII, pp. 537 ff. and 603 ff. Frieda Hoddick, *Das Münster-
maifelder Legendar*, Dissertation, Bonn, 1928, pp. 36 ff. W. R. Tymms and
M. D. Wyatt, *The Art of Illuminating*, London, 1860, Saec. XII, Tab. 1 and 3.
H. Shaw, *A Handbook of the Art of Illumination*, London, 1866, pp. 15 ff.
3 *Cat. Cod. Hag. Bibl. Reg. Brux.* pars I, tom. I, Brussels, 1886, 135 ff.
Script. rerum Merov. VII, pp. 537 ff. and 563. Hoddick, *op. cit.* pp. 36 ff. J. Van
den Gheyn, *Catalogue des manuscrits de la Bibliothèque royale de Belgique*, V,
Brussels, 1905, pp. 60 ff. (no. 3132, tom. I).

in the Harley collection above. All three volumes are at Brussels, 207–208 (January–June 8th), 98–100 (June 8th–Sept.), and 206 (Oct.–Dec.). B contains altogether 125 items; a few Lives are missing from the Harley volume which are present in the Brussels volume, and the later lives of this volume are in a somewhat different order. The MS is beautifully written in a thirteenth-century hand, and the initial letters of each life are large and often ornate, worked in various colours, even in gold. The second and last folios have the red stamp of the Bibliothèque Nationale of Paris, and on the first folio is stamped "Bibliothèque de Bourgogne". The Anonymous Life occupies ff. 158–163.

6. T. Trier, Public Library 1151 (Kentenich 422, tom. 1).[1] $13 \times 9\frac{5}{8}$ in. 223 ff. 40 lines to the page. Double columns. This is one of four volumes of a legendary preserved in the public library at Trier. This legendary originally consisted of nine volumes, and together they form the most comprehensive of all the legendaries written on German soil. Of these nine volumes the first (January) and the fifth (August) are preserved in Paris at the Bibliothèque Nationale; the second volume (February, March and April), the third (May), the fourth (June and July), and the seventh (October) are in the Trier public library; the sixth (September) and the eighth (November) are in the priests' seminary at Trier. The ninth volume has been lost. According to Levison,[2] the legendary was composed, if not in the Benedictine monastery of St Maximin at Trier, at any rate for the monks, about the year 1235. The first volume contains seventy-one lives and passions and other kindred items of which the Anonymous Life occupies ff. 135–142.

7. P. Paris, Bibliothèque Nationale, Fonds Latin 5289.[3] $16\frac{7}{8} \times 11\frac{7}{8}$ in. 76 ff. 40 lines to the page. Double columns. This MS, which consists of a series of lives and passions of the saints, is in a fourteenth-century hand. It begins with the Lives

---

1 M. Keuffer and G. Kentenich, *Verzeichnis der Handschriften der Stadt-Bibliothek zu Trier*, VIII, Trier, 1914, pp. 221 ff. B. Krusch, *Neues Archiv*, XVIII, pp. 618 ff. M. Coens, *Anal. Boll.* LII, 1934, pp. 193 ff.

2 *Script. rerum Merov.* VII, pp. 536 f. and 685 ff.

3 *Cat. Cod. Hag. Lat. Paris*, I, Brussels, 1889, p. 538. *Script. rerum Merov.* VII, p. 636.

of St Vaast and St Amantius of Rodez and consists altogether
of thirty different items of which all except two are found in
both B and H. It is carelessly written. The MS has been wrongly
bound at some time, and at present the Anonymous Life
begins on f. 55b, then continues on ff. 49b–52b and ends on
ff. 56–58b.

B. BEDE'S PROSE LIFE

1. C$_1$. Corpus Christi College, Cambridge, 183.[1] $11\frac{1}{2} \times 7\frac{7}{8}$ in.
96 ff. 26 lines to the page. Single column. This MS, written
in a very beautiful English hand, contains the Prose Life
(ff. 1b–56), followed by two chapters from the *H.E.* (IV, 31
and 32), the Metrical Life, a list of English bishops and kings,
the Mass and Office of St Cuthbert, together with a list of
difficult words in the Metrical Life with interpretations partly
in Anglo-Saxon. The work of two scribes is distinguishable.
On the reverse side of the first folio is a full-page picture,
now badly oxidised, which is said to represent Aethelstan
presenting the book to St Cuthbert. In the *Historia de Sancto
Cuthberto* we learn that Aethelstan travelling to Scotland gave
to the see which was then at Chester-le-Street "unam sancti
Cuthberti uitam, metrice et prosaice scriptam".[2] It is quite
possible that it may have been this very MS. James declares that
it can hardly be doubted that the book is from Durham Priory.
That it belonged to the priory at some time is possible, though
it is not mentioned in the 1391 or 1415 catalogues of the
priory, but it was almost certainly not written in the north,
nor can James be correct when he attributes it to the ninth
century. If this were so, then the picture could hardly represent
Aethelstan unless it were added some years afterwards, which
seems unlikely. But furthermore, as Armitage Robinson has

1 For further discussion of the date and origin of this MS, cf. Plummer,
H.E. I, p. cxlvii, note 1; M. R. James, *A Descriptive Catalogue of the MSS in the
Library of Corpus Christi College, Cambridge*, I, Cambridge, 1912, pp. 426 ff.;
J. Armitage Robinson, *The Saxon Bishops of Wells*, London, 1918, pp. 7, 12 ff.,
and *The Times of St Dunstan*, Oxford, 1923, pp. 53 f.; E. G. Millar, *English
Illuminated MSS from the Xth to the XIIIth Century*, Paris-Brussels, 1926, pp. 3,
71 and plate 3 a. Judging by the dates of the latest bishops mentioned, the book
must have been written between 934 (the accession of Aethelgar of Crediton)
and 937 or 938 (the death of Aelfheah of Wells).
2 *Symeon of Durham*, ed. Hinde, Surtees Soc. LI, 1867, p. 149.

pointed out, several tenth-century bishops are mentioned in the list of bishops at the beginning of the MS. As the only lists of bishops brought up to date are those of Wells, Sherborne, Crediton, and Dorchester, and as the last bishop of Wells mentioned is Aelfheah who died in 937 or 938, Robinson suggests that the book was promised in 934 when Aethelstan was in the north, was then ordered at Glastonbury and presented to St Cuthbert's shrine in 937. The list of bishops is in the same handwriting throughout and presumably by the same scribe as the earlier part of the MS. At any rate the hands are contemporary. The MS must therefore be dated as early tenth.

2. C_2. Trinity College, Cambridge, O.1.64.[1] $6\frac{1}{4} \times 4\frac{1}{4}$ in. 88 ff. 24 lines to the page. Single column. This MS is written in a beautiful twelfth-century hand. It once belonged to the cathedral church of Coventry and contains only the Prose Life (ff. 2–87b) with the same two chapters from Bede's *H.E.* as C_1. The MS was meant to be copiously illustrated, a space for a picture and for ornate initials being left at the beginning of each chapter. But no sketches have been begun except for the two full-page drawings on ff. 9b and 10 both illustrating chapter II, the healing of Cuthbert's knee by an angel.

3. C_3. Trinity College, Cambridge, O.3.55.[2] $9\frac{1}{2} \times 6$ in. 69 ff. 37 lines to the page. Single column. This MS is written in a fine hand of the mid-twelfth century. It comes from Durham Priory and is noted in the 1391 catalogue,[3] identifiable by the catchword of the second folio "sime ea quae paruuli" (but see Cl, p. 31 below). It contains a list of relics[4] formerly in Durham Priory; a list of bishops of Lindisfarne and Durham down to William (1143–53), with Hugo[5] (d. 1195) in a slightly later hand; the preface to Bede's Metrical Life; the Prose Life

---

1 M. R. James, *The Western MSS in the Library of Trinity College, Cambridge*, III, Cambridge, 1902, p. 66. Schenkl, no. 2382.

2 See M. R. James, *loc. cit.* III, p. 241, and *Symeon of Durham*, ed. Hinde, Surtees Soc. LI, 1867, pp. lxxviii ff. and Schenkl, no. 2415. See also pp. 34–5 below.

3 *Catt. Vett.* p. 30.

4 A list of relics occurs in Dj$_2$ which is almost identical with the list here except that *Caput Ceolwulfi* in C_3 appears as *Caput Edwoldi* in Dj$_2$, and the last three items in C_3 (*Dens Sancti Blasii, Ossa Gereonis, Ossa sanctarum virginum XI milium Coloniae*) are missing in Dj$_2$. The office of St Cuthbert is substantially the same in both and the music almost identical.

5 For similar lists of bishops cf. O$_8$, Ad$_1$, Dj$_2$ and Go.

(ff. 5*b*–25*b*), followed by the usual two chapters from the *H.E.* (IV, 31 and 32), 23 miracles[1] and a part of the *Brevis Relatio*. The codex also contains the office for the deposition of St Cuthbert with music, the office and hymn to St Oswald, and the life of St Aidan. The name of Symon Garstell in a sixteenth-century hand appears on folio 4. Other names which occur in this MS are those of W. Ellvyt in a fifteenth-century hand, and Thomas Hersley, Henry Dalton and Humfrey Radcliff, all in sixteenth-century hands.

4. O_1. Digby 175 (1776), from the Bodleian Library, Oxford.[2] $10\frac{5}{8} \times 7\frac{1}{4}$ in. 46 ff. 34 lines to the page. Single column. A nicely written MS of the late eleventh or early twelfth century. There is more than one hand, though that in which the Prose Life is written is the same throughout. The MS apparently derives from the same scriptorium as Bodley 596 (O_4) and may well be a Durham book. It belonged once to Thomas Allen of Gloucester Hall.[3] It contains the Prose Life (ff. 1–23, later foliation), but the first quire is missing and the Life actually begins towards the end of chapter 8: then follow the usual two chapters from the *H.E.* and one other miracle; the Metrical Life; and Bede's Lives of St Aidan and St Oswald from the third book of the *H.E.* Each of these three last pieces is imperfect.

1 These posthumous miracles which gradually came to be attributed to the saint are found in varying numbers attached usually to MSS of Bede's Prose Life of St Cuthbert though occasionally occurring by themselves (as in B.M. Cotton. Nero A. ii or York Dean and Chapter Library, xvi.i.12; see also Hardy, I, p. 303). These miracles probably formed part of an oral saga tradition which arose apparently in the tenth century and was written down about the twelfth. None of these miracles is found in MSS dating before the twelfth century, though occasionally the two chapters from the *H.E.* are present. The earlier twelfth-century MSS, such as O_2, O_5, or O_9, contain only six or seven, together with the two chapters from Bede, while in the latter part of the century we find up to twenty-five miracles often followed by the *Brevis Relatio* (*B.H.L.* 2031), a collection varying in length but at its longest consisting of thirty-eight chapters partly historical and partly miraculous. These miracle stories seem to have been used considerably by Symeon of Durham and less obviously by Reginald. See further Symeon, *H.D.E.* I, pp. 229–61; II, pp. 333–62; also *Symeon of Durham*, ed. Hinde, Surtees Soc. LI, 1867, pp. xxxix ff. and 158–201.

2 Cf. W. D. Macray, *Cat. codicum manuscript. Bibl. Bodl.* pars IX, Oxford, 1883, p. 187.

3 Allen left his MSS to Kenelm Digby who afterwards left them to the Bodleian (cf. O6). See *D.N.B. s.v.* Thomas Allen.

5. O₂. Bodley 109 (1962), from the Bodleian Library, Oxford.[1] 8½ × 5⅝ in. 80 ff. 21 lines to the page. Single column. A MS perhaps of the eleventh century. It has a few feebly coloured capitals, but most of the capital letters and chapter headings are missing. It contains the Metrical and Prose Life of St Cuthbert (the latter only as far as chapter 29, ff. 28–77). The handwriting is peculiar and unpleasing, varying a good deal in size, and certainly the work of more than one scribe. The MS originally belonged to Sir Henry Savile and was presented by him to Bodley in 1620.

6. O₃. Fairfax 6 (3886), from the Bodleian Library, Oxford.[2] 13½ × 8½ in. 299 ff. 47 lines to the page. Double columns. This MS, belonging to the second half of the fourteenth century, was written at Durham. The scribe up to page 159b was Petrus "plenus amoris".[3] It is mentioned in the 1391 Durham catalogue[4] and can be identified by the catchword of the second folio ('ramine et prudencia'). It consists of three main parts. The first part contains four different Lives of St Cuthbert, the first being the so-called Irish Life;[5] the second Bede's Metrical Life; the third the Prose Life (ff. 13–29b) with the usual

1 Madan and Craster, *A Summary Cat. of Western MSS in the Bodl. Library*, II, i, Oxford, 1922, p. 134.

2 *Summary Catalogue of Western MSS in the Bodleian Library*, Oxford, 1936, pp. 773 ff. (new edition of the 1697 catalogue). Schenkl, no. 289.

3 Cf. Plummer, *H.E.* I, p. cxxxviii. The name "plenus amoris" if it is the name of a scribe (Fulleylove?) occurs at least half a dozen times and always in the hexameter "Nomen scriptoris est...plenus amoris". It may be just padding to fill the line and to rhyme with "scriptoris".

4 Cf. *Catt. Vett.* p. 55.

5 The so-called Irish Life of St Cuthbert or, more accurately, *Libellus de Ortu Sancti Cuthberti* professes to give an account of the early years of the saint's life of which nothing is said in Bede, nor in the Anonymous Life. It contains twenty-nine chapters and seems to have been written in the late twelfth century and, in all probability, at Melrose. The main part of the Life is apparently a reproduction of the early life and miracles of a certain St Lugaid of Lismore (d. 592) or Mulucc, as he is called in the *Libellus*. St Cuthbert is identified with this saint, and the miracles related of the Irish saint are there attributed to him. After chapter 23, the writer, having reached the end of his Irish source, identifies Cuthbert with St Adamnan of Hy (d. 704), the biographer of St Columba. The writer also devotes three chapters to explaining why women were not allowed in St Cuthbert's churches. For a full account of this work see Miss M. Hope Dodds' article entitled "The Little Book of the Birth of St Cuthbert", in *Arch. Ael.* fourth series, VI, Newcastle, 1929, pp. 52 ff. and H. H. E. Craster, *E.H.R.* XL, 1925, p. 507.

chapters from the *H.E.*, and twenty-two miracles, followed by the Life[1] by Reginald, a twelfth-century monk of Durham (*B.H.L.* 2032). The second part consists of lives of other saints: the Lives of Eata and Oswald by Reginald of Durham; the Life of Aidan and the abbots of Wearmouth by Bede; an anonymous Life of Bede;[5] the Life of Ebba by Reginald of Durham; and the Lives of Godric and Bartholomew by Galfridus (probably Geoffrey of Coldingham). The third part consists of various historical pieces relating to Durham, including Symeon of Durham's chronicle of the church of Durham with the continuations by Geoffrey of Coldingham, Robert de Greystanes, and others. It ends with a passage concerning Richard de Bury in a fifteenth-century hand. See also under H_2, pp. 28 f.

7. O_4. Bodley 596 (2376), from the Bodleian Library, Oxford.[2] $9\frac{7}{8} \times 7$ in. 214 ff. 38 lines to the page. Single column. This is a composite volume and consists of three parts, of which the first is connected with Westminster Abbey and consists of English and Latin pieces of the early fifteenth century. The second part is John Lydgate's Life of Our Lady, of the fifteenth century. The third part (ff. 175–214) contains the Prose Life of St Cuthbert with the exception of part of the last chapter; four leaves are lost between ff. 200b and 201; then follows part of the Metrical Life. All this part is in one hand and is followed by part of the *Historia de Sancto Cuthberto*[3] in a second hand, one leaf of the latter being lost. Each of the hands is of the early twelfth century, and this section of the MS is written in single column with about 38 lines to the page. The third part of the volume up to this point was probably written in Durham. Then follows the Life of St Julian, bishop of Le Mans (*B.H.L.* 4544), together with an Office of St Julian, both in a later hand.[4]

---

1 Printed in the Surtees Soc. I, 1835, pp. 1–292.

2 Madan and Craster, *A Summary Cat. of Western MSS in the Bodl. Library,* Oxford, II, i, pp. 335 ff. and information received from Mr R. A. B. Mynors.

3 The last paragraph of this piece occurs only here (see H. H. E. Craster, "The Red Book of Durham", *E.H.R.* XL, 1925, pp. 504 ff.) and in Paris, Fonds Latins 5362 (P1); see below, p. 35.

4 W. H. Frere, *Bibliotheca Musico-liturgica*, Lambeth and Oxford, vol. I, 1901, pl. 6.   5 *B.H.L.* 1070.

The third part formed a volume in the library of St Augustine's Abbey at Canterbury and is mentioned in the fourteenth-century catalogue.[1] The library shelf mark occurs on f. 175. Dr Craster suggests that this is from the same scriptorium as O_1.

8. O_5. Digby 20 (1621), from the Bodleian Library, Oxford.[2] $6\frac{1}{2} \times 4\frac{1}{2}$ in. 227 ff. 36 lines to the page. Single column. This MS consists of three separate books bound together, written in seven or eight different hands. The other contents are various astronomical and theological tracts. All three of these originally belonged to T. Allen.[3] The Prose Life (ff. 194–222 b), which forms the third part of the volume, is followed by the usual chapters from the H.E. together with five other miracles. This part is written in a small but well-formed hand of the early twelfth century, in single column with 36 lines to the page. After the preface one folio is missing and two other folios are missing between ff. 224 and 225. The first initial of the Prose Life contains a miniature of a scribe at work. It represents a monk in a green robe seated on a pile of large books dipping his pen into an ink-horn behind him, while the other hand is on the sheet of parchment before him which rests on a stand. There are other initials in green, red and purple with some ornamentation. Judging by its appearance it seems very probable that this part of the volume was written in Durham.

9. O_6. Digby 59 (1660), from the Bodleian Library, Oxford.[4] $7\frac{7}{8} \times 4\frac{7}{8}$ in. 153 ff. 27 lines to the page. Single column. A nicely written MS in a hand of the late twelfth century. It contains the Prose Life (ff. 1–45 b), the usual two chapters from the H.E., and seven other miracles, followed by ten chapters from the Brevis Relatio. It also contains an anonymous Life of Bede;[6] Ailred of Rievaulx's Life of Edward the Confessor; and four visions extracted from the H.E. This MS once belonged to T. Allen.[5]

1 M. R. James, *Ancient Libraries of Canterbury and Dover*, Cambridge, 1903, pp. 238 and 517.
2 W. D. Macray, *Cat. cod. man. Bibl. Bodl.* pars IX, Oxford, 1883, p. 15.
3 See note 3, p. 22 above.
4 W. D. Macray, *op. cit.* p. 63.
5 See note 3, p. 22 above.   6 *B.H.L.* 1070.

10. O_7. Fell 3, from the Bodleian Library, Oxford. $12\frac{3}{4}$ × $8\frac{1}{4}$ in. 115 ff. This MS, in a late eleventh-century or early twelfth-century hand, is written in single column with about 40 lines to the page up to f. 101 b. Then it continues in double column with 48 lines to the page. It consists of a series of lives and passions of the saints, thirty in all, including Eddius Stephanus' Life of St Wilfrid. The Prose Life (ff. 57–76) is followed by the usual two chapters from the H.E. The MS once belonged to Salisbury, whence it was borrowed by Archbishop Ussher in 1640 and afterwards deposited in the Bodleian Library. This, together with five other MSS, was subsequently borrowed by Dr Fell, Bishop of Oxford (d. 1686), and on his death returned to the library in the form of a bequest.[1]

11. O_8. Laud Misc. 491 (1093), from the Bodleian Library, Oxford.[2] $7\frac{1}{2}$ × $5\frac{1}{4}$ in. 173 ff. 21–22 lines to the page. Single column. A well-written MS dating from some time between 1153 and 1195. It contains the Prose Life (ff. 1–66 b), followed by the two chapters from the H.E.; a series of twenty-four miracles; and part of the Brevis Relatio. In addition to this there is the Preface to the Metrical Life; the Lives of St Oswald and St Aidan from Bede; a metrical prayer to St Cuthbert;[3] and a list of the bishops of Lindisfarne and Durham as far as Hugo (d. 1195) (cf. p. 21 n. 5). Hugh Puiset's name is entered in the original hand and the years of his episcopate are added in a second hand. It has some very elaborate initials including some peculiar capital I's. The MS was probably written at Durham though it is not mentioned in the old catalogues. It once belonged to Leonard Pylkington, fourth prebendary of the seventh stall at Durham from 1567 to 1592.[4]

12. O_9. University College, Oxford, 165.[5] $7\frac{3}{4}$ × 5 in. 202 ff. 24 lines to the page. Single column. An excellently written

---

1 Eddius, p. xiv.
2 H. O. Coxe, Cat. Cod. MSS Bibl. Bodl. II, 1858–85, cols. 352 ff.
3 Jaager, p. 32.
4 See D.N.B., s.v. and Rites of Durham, ed. J. T. Fowler, Surtees Soc. CVII, 1903, pp. 100 and 281.
5 H. O. Coxe, Cat. Cod. MSS qui in Collegiis Aulisque Oxoniensibus hodie asservantur, pt. I, Oxford, 1852, p. 45.

MS of the first half of the twelfth century, now kept in the Bodleian Library. It consists of 202 ff. and contains the Prose Life (ff. 1–130b), followed by the usual two chapters from the H.E., seven miracles, and a Hymn to St Cuthbert.[1] This MS is beautifully illustrated throughout by delicate pen drawings in coloured ink, without washes of colour. These illustrations bear some resemblance to the miniatures in Ad₂ and it is quite possible that they derive from the same source. It is very likely that the MS came originally from the Durham Scriptorium,[2] though it is not mentioned in the old catalogues, and there may well have been a tradition of pictorial illustration of Cuthbert books at Durham. It possesses several marks of ownership[3] but was finally, in 1666, in the possession of William Rogers of Painswick, Gloucestershire, who gave it to University College, Oxford.[4]

13.   V. British Museum, Cotton. Vitellius A.xix.[5] $8\frac{5}{8} \times 5\frac{1}{2}$ in. 114 ff. 22 lines to the page. Single column. A carefully written MS of the tenth century. On f. 8b is a purple panel on which is roughly scratched a figure, presumably St Cuthbert, with halo and ecclesiastical robes, in the act of blessing. It contains the Prose Life (ff. 1b–7, 9–84b), followed by two chapters from the H.E. On ff. 7b and 8 are two poems in an eleventh-century hand. Cotton has written his name on f. 9. The MS also contains the Metrical Life. There is a gloss in a contemporary hand throughout, a few words being in Anglo-Saxon. There is also a gloss which adds various proper names, given in the Anonymous Life, but omitted by Bede in the Prose Life. These names seem to be eleventh-century additions. There are also marginal notes throughout in a hand of the seventeenth century.

1 Printed from this MS by J. Raine in *Miscellanea Biographica*, Surtees Soc. VIII, 1838, pp. 91–117.

2 E. G. Millar, *English Illuminated MSS from the Xth to the XIIIth Century*, Paris-Brussels, 1926, pp. 37 and 87 and pl. 54a.

3 Namely, M. Lelonde; Joh. Theyer de Cowpers Hill iuxta Glouc.; Fulconis Wallwyn, ex dono John Daniell, Bachelor of Musick; Willielmi et Thomae Leigh.

4 Rev. J. T. Fowler, "On the St Cuthbert Window in York Minster", *Yorkshire Archaeological and Topographical Journal*, IV, 1877, pp. 249 ff.

5 *A Cat. of the MSS in the Cott. Lib. in the Brit. Mus.* London, 1802, p. 381.

14. H. British Museum, Harleian MS 1117.[1] 10 × 7$\frac{1}{8}$ in. 66 ff. 22 lines to the page. Single column. An eleventh-century MS of which the glosses are probably contemporary. There are several different hands in the course of the MS, but the Prose Life is in the same hand throughout and is probably copied from V (see p. 46 below). The contents include verses on the death and translation of St Edward of Shaftesbury; the Prose Life (ff. 2–40b), with the usual two chapters from the *H.E.*; the antiphonae for St Cuthbert's, St Benedict's, and St Guthlac's days; and the Metrical Life of St Cuthbert. The music for the office of St Benedict is marked in the Chartres notation, a form of notation found specially in MSS from the south of England.[2] It contains the name of John Anstis on f. 1b.[3]

15. H$_1$. British Museum, Harleian MS 1924.[4] 8$\frac{1}{4}$ × 5$\frac{1}{2}$ in. 71 ff. 27 lines to the page. Single column. A twelfth-century MS, almost certainly originally a Durham book, though it is not apparently mentioned in any of the older catalogues. It contains part of the Prose Life only. Chapters 41 and 42 and 44–46 are missing. The Life occupies ff. 1–48b. The rest of the contents are eight miracles belonging to the posthumous miracles of the saint. According to a reference in the Harleian Catalogue, the book was annotated by Richard Bell, prior of Durham and afterwards bishop of Carlisle from 1478 to 1495. There seems to be no verifiable reason for this attribution, but the mark at the head of several folios ∴ $\overline{IHC}$ ∴ *maria* ∴ is the unmistakable sign of Thomas Gascoigne and most of the notes are certainly his.[5]

16. H$_2$. British Museum, Harleian MS 4843.[6] 13 × 9$\frac{1}{4}$ in.

---

1 *A Cat. of the Harl. MSS in the Brit. Mus.* I, London, 1808, p. 556.

2 H. Sunyol, *Introducció a la Paleografía musical*, Montserrat, 1925, p. 179 and pl. 62.

3 John Anstis was a seventeenth- to eighteenth-century heraldic writer and Garter King at Arms. See *D.N.B. s.v.*

4 *A Cat. of the Harl. MSS in the Brit. Mus.* II, London, 1808, p. 349.

5 See *D.N.B. s.v.* I owe this information to Mr R. A. B. Mynors. Mr N. P. Ker has discovered that four odd leaves in MS Digby 41, ff. 91, 91*, 92, 101, containing a list of Durham relics and notes in Thomas Gascoigne's handwriting, originally belonged to this MS. See *British Museum Quarterly*, XII, 1938, p. 133.

6 *A Cat. of the Harl. MSS in the Brit. Mus.* III, London, 1808, p. 211. Symeon, *H.D.E.* I, p. xix. *Reginald of Durham*, ed. J. Raine, Surtees Soc. I, 1835, pp. xvii ff. H. H. E. Craster, "The Red Book of Durham", *E.H.R.* XL, 1925, p. 506.

276 ff. 44–46 lines to the page. Single column. A paper MS
of the early sixteenth century, much of which seems to be
a transcript from O₃. On f. 276b is the inscription "*Calamo
Dompni Willelmi Tode Pingitur* [?] *iste libellus*", and near the
end of the MS is a sermon on death which ends with the
words "*Amen. dompnus Willelmus Tode anno Christi 1528*"
(f. 262). William Tode or Tod was the first prebendary of the
fifth stall in Durham in 1541.[1] The MS contains the Prose Life
(ff. 13b–30), followed by the two chapters from the *H.E.*;
twenty-two other miracles and the *Brevis Relatio*; the Metrical
Life; the *Libellus* of Reginald of Durham; twelve miracles
connected with Farne Island, apparently not found elsewhere;[2]
the so-called Irish Life; the Life of William Carilef; and of
Bartholomew (as in O₃); a list of churches in England dedicated
to St Cuthbert;[3] inscriptions beneath the figures of kings and
bishops in front of the entrance to the choir;[4] a poem on the life
of St Cuthbert, and the history of Durham down to the battle of
Neville's Cross; and some verses on St Cuthbert by Johannes
Alt dedicated to Prior Castell of Durham (1494–1519).[5] On
the last folio of the MS occur the names of William Hacfurth
and Johannes Eyrsdon in sixteenth-century handwriting.

17. Ar₁. Arundel 222 in the British Museum.[6] 9 × 6½ in.
166 ff. About 28 lines to the page. Double columns. This is
a nicely written thirteenth-century MS. It contains the Prose
Life (ff. 1–34b) and the usual two miracles from the *H.E.*,
William of Malmesbury's *De gestis pontificum Anglorum*, and
the miracles of St Andrew by Gregory of Tours.

18. Ar₂. Arundel 332 in the British Museum.[7] 7½ × 4¼ in.
234 ff. 40 lines to the page. Double columns. This MS is in

1 Cf. *Wills and Inventories*, Surtees Soc. II, 1835, p. 269 and note. *Rites of Durham*, Surtees Soc. CVII, 1903, pp. 99 and 280.
2 See Craster, *loc. cit.* p. 506, n. 2.
3 See *Transactions of Durham and Northumberland Archaeological Association*, VII, pt. ii, Durham, 1936, pp. 169ff., for a longer Durham version.
4 Other versions of this are found in MS Harl. 367, f. 76, and in Durham Cosin's Library, B.II.2, printed in the *Rites of Durham*, *op. cit.* pp. 137ff.
5 For an account of both these sets of verses see Jaager, pp. 11 and 13.
6 *Cat. of MSS in the Brit. Mus.* New Series, I, pt. i (Arundel MSS), London, 1834, p. 64. W. Stubbs, *Willelmi Malmesbiriensis Gesta regum*, I, Rolls Series, 1887, pp. cxxf. and *Neues Archiv*, XXVIII, 1903, pp. 249f.
7 *Cat. of MSS in the Brit. Mus.* New Series, I, pt. i (Arundel MSS), London, 1834, pp. 97f.

a hand of the thirteenth century and contains various theological and mathematical tracts, including some by Johannes de Sacro Bosco (John Holywood).[1] Then comes the Prose Life (ff. 74–101 b), followed by the usual two chapters from the *H.E.*, twenty-two miracles of St Cuthbert and the *Brevis Relatio*. The first few lines of the Prose Life are missing as a result of certain folios containing the "Irish" Life having been cut out. Then follow Bonaventura's *Summa de fide Christiana*, and various verses on theological and medical subjects. There is a note preceding the Prose Life in a seventeenth-century hand to the effect that the "Irish" Life has been cut out. The book once belonged to William Hertylpulle, a Durham monk, and afterwards to the Durham Library. It probably comes from the Durham Scriptorium, and with the exception of the fly-leaves of the codex is in the same hand throughout. It does not seem to be mentioned in the old Durham catalogues.

19. Oth. British Museum Cotton. Otho D.viii.[2] 9 × 5½ in. Approx. 269 ff. 38 lines to the page. Double columns. This is a late twelfth-century legendary which was almost destroyed in the great fire of 1731. The scraps preserved, which were carefully backed and pasted together, show a table of contents and a calendar followed by the legendary consisting of twenty-four lives and passions of saints. The Life appears on ff. 148–168 b. Certain other items in a later hand appear after the legendary, including the Annals of Nicholas Trivet to the year 1307, a catalogue of English kings and the Ramsey Chronicle from 1341 to the death of Richard II, and a "cronicon lyrice a Bruto ad annum Domini 1388", all now in a fragmentary condition.

20. Cl. British Museum, Cotton. Claudius A.i.[3] 9 × 7 in. 152 ff. 34 lines to the page. Single column. This is a mixed codex containing pieces of various dates. It once contained 154 ff., though two of these are now missing. The first piece is Fridegoda's Life of St Wilfrid followed by thirteenth- and

1 See *D.N.B. s.v.*

2 *A Cat. of the MSS in the Cott. Lib. in the Brit. Mus.* London, 1802, p. 369, where the codex is described as "The remains of a MS on vellum in small folio, which once consisted of 267 [actually 269] leaves, now burnt to a crust and preserved in a case". See also W. Levison, *Script. rerum Merov.* VII, p. 602.

3 *A Cat. of the MSS in the Cott. Lib. in the Brit. Mus.* p. 188.

fourteenth-century letters. The second part consists of lives of saints, eleven items in all, followed by the Prose Life (ff. 123 b–152 b) together with the two chapters from the *H.E.* written in a twelfth-century hand. It is headed by a title in Joscelin's hand and has notes by him throughout. It is a curious coincidence that the catchword of the second folio of the life (f. 126) is "sime ea quae paruuli", the same as C_3 (see p. 21 above), but it is not likely that this was ever the second folio of the MS. There is indeed no doubt that C_3 and not this MS is the one mentioned in the 1391 Durham catalogue.

21. Ad₁. British Museum, Add. 35110.[1] $11\frac{1}{2} \times 7\frac{1}{2}$ in. 187 ff. 32 lines to the page. Double columns. This MS of the late twelfth century is described on f. 2b as "Liber fratrum heremitarum ord. Sci. Augustini de Novo Castro" (Newcastle-upon-Tyne), and was probably written at Durham. It contains a Life of St Augustine from various sources, the Prose Life (ff. 30b–61), followed by twenty-two miracles and the *Brevis Relatio.* Then comes a list of bishops of Lindisfarne and Durham ending with Hugo (*d.* 1195), the Life of St Columba by Adamnan,[2] Bede's Lives of King Oswald and St Aidan, and Ailred of Rievaulx's Life of Edward the Confessor. The MS once belonged to Sir Henry Savile, Provost of Eton, and afterwards to Sir Thomas Phillipps (no. 26075); and was acquired by the British Museum in 1897.

22. Ad₂. British Museum, Add. 39943.[3] $5\frac{3}{8} \times 3\frac{7}{8}$ in. 150 ff. originally. 23 lines to the page. Single column. This exquisite MS of the late twelfth century has been very often described and its miniatures reproduced. It possesses forty-five full-page miniatures and the remains of one other, out of a probable

---

1 *Cat. of Additions to the MSS in the Brit. Mus. in the years 1894–1899*, London, 1901, pp. 160ff. Cf. also p. 21 n. 5 above.

2 Gertrud Brüning, "Adamnans Vita Columbae und ihre Ableitungen", Dissertation, Bonn, 1916, *Zeitschrift für Celtische Philologie*, XI, pp. 219f. Neither Reeves nor Fowler seems to have known of the existence of this MS.

3 *Cat. of Additions to the Brit. Mus. 1916–20*, London, 1933, pp. 262ff. See also James Raine, *St Cuthbert*, Durham, 1828, p. iv. Rev. J. T. Fowler, *Yorkshire Archaeological and Topographical Journal*, IV, 1877, pp. 249 ff. W. Forbes-Leith, *The Life of St Cuthbert*, Edinburgh, 1888 (reproductions of some of the miniatures). J. A. Herbert, *Illuminated MSS*, London, 1911, p. 140. E. G. Millar, *English Illuminated MSS*, Paris-Brussels, 1926, pp. 36f. and 87, and pl. 52. Schenkl, no. 4757.

total of fifty-five. The removal of some of the miniatures has led of course to gaps in the text as well. The MS was doubtless executed in the Durham Scriptorium and is mentioned in the old Durham catalogues of 1391 and 1416, where it is described as "Vita Sancti Cuthberti et miracula ciusdem curiose illuminata. ii fo. dubiorum".[1] The 1416 catalogue notes that it had been in the possession of Richard le Scrope, archbishop of York, who was executed in 1405. It is usually supposed that the miniatures were intended to serve the artist who was commissioned to design the famous Cuthbert windows in York Minster, but there is little evidence of his having used them. On the other hand, the paintings illustrating the life of St Cuthbert on the backs of the stalls of Carlisle Cathedral show very clear and obvious signs of the influence of the miniatures from this MS. There is no doubt in my mind that the artist had the MS before him when he was painting the stalls.[2] In the early eighteenth century it was in the possession of John Forcer of Harbour House, Durham (see p. 54 below). It afterwards came into the possession of the Lawson family of Brough Hall who were related by marriage to the Durham Forcers; it was bought by Mr H. Yates Thompson in 1906 in the sale of Sir John Lawson's library and was acquired by the British Museum in 1920. The MS contains the Prose Life (ff. 2b–82b); the usual two miracles from the H.E.; and twenty-five other miracles followed by the Brevis Relatio. It also contains an account of the early provosts of Hexham.[3]

23. Du. Durham Cathedral Chapter Library, A.iv.35.[4] 6 × 4 in. 158 ff. 24 lines to the page. Single column. This MS of the late twelfth century is beautifully written and almost certainly comes from the Durham Scriptorium. It contains the Prose Life (ff. 3–65b), twenty-one miracles and the Brevis Relatio, as well as the Lives of St Oswald and St Aidan. The book is mentioned in the 1391 and 1416 Durham cata-

---

1 Catt. Vett. pp. 29, 107.
2 For further details see: B. Colgrave, "The St Cuthbert Paintings on the Carlisle Cathedral Stalls", Burlington Magazine, LXXIII, 1938, pp. 17ff., and "The history of MS. B.M. Add. 39,943". E.H.R. LIV, 1939, Oct.
3 Printed by J. Raine, Priory of Hexham, I, Surtees Soc. XLIV, 1864, App. p. vii.   4 Durham University Journal, XXX, 1936, pp. 1 ff.

logues,[1] where it is described as "Liber de Vita Sancti Cuthberti, Sancti Oswaldi et Sancti Aydani, ii fo. gacionis. Est liber specialis et preciosus cum singnaculo deaurato". It has several beautifully designed and illuminated initials in the text. A remarkable feature of this MS is that its edges are decorated with paintings of St Oswald, crowned and bearing his sceptre, on the top edge; St Cuthbert in his robes on the fore-edge; and St Aidan on the bottom edge. The painting of the edges is of doubtful date but possibly fourteenth-century and doubtless some of the earliest fore-edge painting known. The MS was bought for the Durham Chapter Library in 1936 and has recently been rebound, though the older sixteenth-century binding has been preserved in the Library.

24. Li. Lincoln Cathedral Chapter Library, B.1.9.[2] $15\frac{1}{4}$ × 11 in. 181 ff. 47 lines to the page. Double columns. This is a well-written MS of the thirteenth century, one of two volumes of lives and passions of the saints, which together cover the whole year. Both volumes once belonged to Michael Honywood, dean of Lincoln from 1660 to 1681,[3] and are mentioned in the catalogue of his own books, where they are described as "*Vitae Sanctorum per Aurelianum,*[4] 2 vols. Fol. H 11.12". The MS has Honywood's initials on f. 1. It consists of fifty-eight items in all, including a number of English and British saints. The Prose Life occurs on ff. 106–114. It is not complete, various chapters having been omitted to shorten it while preserving the main thread of the Life.[5]

25. Cm. Cambrai, Bibliothèque Publique 816(721).[6] 11 × $8\frac{1}{8}$ in. 443 ff. 36–39 lines to the page. Double columns. A paper MS of the fifteenth century. It bears the mark of the library of the Abbey of the Holy Sepulchre of Cambrai where

1 *Catt. Vett.* pp. 30, 107.

2 R. M. Woolley, *Catalogue of the MSS of Lincoln Cathedral Chapter Library,* Oxford, 1927, pp. xix, 102 ff. *Script. rerum Merov.* VII, pp. 598 f.

3 See *D.N.B. s.v.*

4 Possibly the description *per Aurelianum* is due to the second Life of St Martialis written by the Pseudo-Aurelianus (*B.H.L.* vol. II, no. 5552) which is found in the second volume of the legendary, Lincoln, B.I.16 (Woolley, *op. cit.* p. 111).

5 The missing chapters are 5, 7, 8, 11–15, 21, 26–28, 30–33, 35, 43, 45, 46.

6 *Cat. Gén.* XVII, Paris, 1891, xi, pp. 301 ff. *Script. rerum Merov.* VII, pp. 570 f.

the compilation was probably made during the fifteenth century, a period when studies seem to have flourished greatly in the monastery. It is a compilation of lives, passions and translations of saints, ninety-five in number, the first seven being lives of saints of the name of William. The Prose Life (ff. 153–175) is followed by an account of the translation of St Cuthbert in 1104 and the *Brevis Commemoratio* of Bede (*B.H.L.* 1071). There is more than one handwriting, a distinct change taking place after f. 224*b*.

26. Dj₁. Dijon, Bibliothèque Publique 574(334).¹ 12¾ ×9½ in. 116 ff. 36 lines to the page. Double columns. A MS of the twelfth century (before 1171). It is bound in calf and bears the arms of the Abbey of Cîteaux. It contains Bede's *Ecclesiastical History*, the Prose Life (ff. 81–99*b*) followed by the usual two miracles from the *H.E.*, nine other miracles and seventeen chapters from the *Brevis Relatio*. The last three items are concerned with Thomas à Becket and are written in single column in a slightly later hand.

27. Dj₂. Dijon, Bibliothèque Publique 657(396).² 10¼ × 7 in. 66 ff. 47 lines to the page. Double columns. A MS of the early thirteenth century. The handwriting is English in appearance and the MS possibly came from the Durham Scriptorium, though it does not seem to be mentioned in the old catalogues. The book bears the arms of the Abbey of Cîteaux, and in the catalogue drawn up in 1480 by the well-known Abbot Jean de Cirey this MS is mentioned, though Dj₁ is not. It contains the Prose Life of St Cuthbert (ff. 1*b*–17*b*), the usual chapters from the *H.E.*, and twenty-two other miracles followed by the *Brevis Relatio*. It also contains the Lives of St Aidan and St Oswald from Bede, as' well as the offices for the feasts of St Cuthbert and St Oswald; a catalogue of relics in the church at Durham; a list of the bishops of Lindisfarne and Durham down to Philip (*d.* 1208); a Life of St Godric and a Life of St Bartholomew, both by Galfridus.³ The catalogue

1 *Cat. Gén.* v, Paris, 1889, p. 142.   2 *Ibid.* v, pp. 191 f., and p. 21 n. 5 above.
3 The name is no longer legible in the MS but it is clearly legible in the other MSS (O₃ and H₂) where the latter Life occurs. For further particulars concerning this Galfridus see Symeon, *H.D.E.* i, p. xl. It was this MS which was used by the Bollandists for those Lives.

of relics and the offices for the feasts of St Oswald and St Cuthbert bear a close relationship to those in C₃ (see p. 21 above).

28. La. Laon, Bibliothèque Publique 163 *bis*.[1] 12¼ × 8¾ in. 193 ff. 30 lines to the page. Double columns. A twelfth-century MS. The codex bears the stamp of the Abbey of Vauclair. It contains four books of the Dialogues of Gregory; the Prose Life (ff. 91–123 *b*) followed by the usual chapters from the *H.E.*; and twenty-six chapters of miracles, consisting of the same seventeen chapters from the *Brevis Relatio* and nine other miracles as the rest of the Bz group; a *Brevis Commemoratio* of Bede; Bede's Lives of St Aidan and St Oswald; and Eadmer's Life and Miracles of St Dunstan (*B.H.L.* 2346).

29. P₁. Paris, Bibliothèque Nationale, Fonds Latin 5362.[2] 9 × 6 in. 126 ff. 26 lines to the page. Single column. A twelfth-century MS. The first three folios are badly discoloured and illegible in places. It contains the Prose Life (ff. 1–51 *b*) followed by the usual chapters from the *H.E.*; and another miracle which forms the last part of the *Historia de Sancto Cuthberto* of which the last paragraph occurs only here and in O₄. It also contains the Lives of Edmund, Oswald, Birinus, Aethelwold, Aethilthryth; the Translation of St Swithin and the Lives of St John, abbot of Reome, St Margaret and St Austreberta. It will be seen that the majority of these are English saints and the handwriting too is English, so that it is probable that the MS is from England.

30. P₂. Paris, Bibliothèque Nationale, Fonds Latin 2475.[3] 12¾ × 9 in. 208 ff. 32 lines to the page. Double columns. A thirteenth-century MS. It contains some writings of Anselm followed by his Life; a Life and Miracles of St Dunstan; the Prose Life (ff. 142–167) followed by the Life and Translation of St Aelfheah; Eadmer's Life of St Odo and Abbo of Fleury's Life of St Edmund; lections for the feast of St Alban; a Life of Bede (*B.H.L.* 1070); and the Metrical Life of St Mary of Egypt. The MS is probably of English origin.

---

1 *Cat. Gén.* (4°), I, Paris, 1849, p. 122.
2 *Cat. Cod. Hag. Lat. Paris*, II, Brussels, 1890, pp. 354 ff.
3 *Ibid.* I, Brussels, 1889, pp. 127 f.

31. P₃. Paris, Bibliothèque Nationale, Fonds Latin 5348.[1] 14 × 10 in. 151 ff. 36 lines to the page. Double columns. A thirteenth-century MS. It contains the Prose Life (ff. 32–57) followed by the usual two chapters from the *H.E.*; the Life and Miracles of St Leonard and St Brendan, St Dunstan and St Anselm, together with various extracts from Bede's *H.E.* concerning other saints, as for example St Germanus of Auxerre. The MS is probably of English origin.

32. M. Montpellier, Library of the School of Medicine, Codex 1, Tomus quintus.[2] 20 × 13¾ in. 183 ff. 46 lines to the page. Double columns. This is the second volume of a great Clairvaux legendary which consisted of eight volumes written in the late twelfth century. When the Clairvaux library was broken up at the end of the eighteenth century, the first volume of this great legendary was lost, the third left at Troyes and the rest deposited in the Library of the School of Medicine, and inscribed in the catalogue in the wrong order. Thus this volume was originally volume II and consisted of lives of saints whose festivals fell in February and March. This legendary is far and away the most outstanding of those written in France. The Prose Life appears on ff. 142–167, followed by twenty-eight chapters of miracles identical with the rest of the Bz group of MSS, and the *Brevis Commemoratio* of Bede. The thirty-four other items are all concerned with the lives, passions and miracles of saints whose feasts occur in February and March.

33. Bn. Berne, Stadtbibliothek 392.[3] 9½ × 6 in. 52 ff. 30–37 lines to the page. Single column. This is a twelfth-century codex. It once belonged to the Abbey of St Victor in Paris and contains the shelf number BBB7 on the first folio. It came later on into the possession of Jacques Bongars (1554–1613), and so through the hands of Jacques Gravisset to the University Library at Berne in 1631. Only part of the St Cuthbert Life is contained in it. The Prose Life originally occupied from

1 *Cat. Cod. Hag. Lat. Paris*, II, Brussels, 1890, p. 295.
2 *Anal. Boll.* XXXIV/V, 1915/16, pp. 237f. *Script. rerum Merov.* VII, pp. 547ff., 626ff.
3 H. Hagen, *Catalogus codicum Bernensium*, Berne, 1875, p. 360. See also p. 52 below and B. Colgrave and I. Masson, "The Editio Princeps of Bede's Life of St Cuthbert, and its Printer's XII Century 'Copy.'" *The Library*, XIX, 1938, pp. 289ff.

ff. 2–35b as shown by the fifteenth-century index on f. 16, but now ff. 24–35 are missing. It must have been complete in 1563, for it was this MS which Hervagius used in that year for printing the first edition (see p. 51 below). The Life now reaches only as far as c. 28 and is very carelessly written. It is followed by the account of the Translation, after which come some extracts from Augustine's *City of God*. From the index we learn that there were originally 97 folios, the rest of the codex being devoted to a "hystoria regum britanniae maioris ab eorum exordio".

34. Go. Gotha, Herzogliche Bibliothek I.81.[1] $12\frac{1}{2} \times 9\frac{1}{4}$ in. 230 ff. 48 lines to the page. Double columns. This codex, written in a clear hand of the second half of the fourteenth century, consists of 43 lives of saints, all of them, except two, being of English or Celtic extraction. The Prose Life occupies ff. 64–80b. It is followed by four miracles, four chapters from the *Brevis Relatio* and a list of bishops of Lindisfarne, Chester-le-Street and Durham. The lives are roughly grouped as follows: first of all is a series of kings, then a series of bishops, followed by a group of saints connected with south-west England and south Wales, and lastly a series of women, queens and abbesses. A few of the lives have got out of order. The separate group devoted to the south-west suggests that the MS itself derives from somewhere in that district.

The MS is a very remarkable one and contains the lives of a number of English, Welsh and Cornish saints which do not occur elsewhere and which, until attention was called to this MS, were only known by the epitomes in John Capgrave's *Nova Legenda Angliae*.[2]

35. W. Wolfenbüttel, Herzogliche Bibliothek 2738 (76, 14 Aug. fol.).[3] $11\frac{1}{4} \times 7\frac{3}{4}$ in. 184 ff. 71 lines to the page. Double

1 Fr. Jacobs and F. A. Ukert, *Beiträge zur ältern Litteratur*, III, 2, Leipzig, 1843, pp. 271–2, where there is only a summary and somewhat inaccurate account of the MS. I have not seen this MS myself but I am greatly indebted to Professor Max Förster of Munich for a description on which the above account is based. Cf. also p. 21 n. 5 above.

2 As this MS is at present (June 1938) being examined by the Bollandists I refrain from giving a list of contents. The Bollandists intend in due course to publish such a list together with a selection of the more important texts.

3 O. v. Heinemann, *Die Handschriften der Herzogl. Bibliothek zu Wolfenbüttel*, Abt. II, Augusteische Handschriften, III, Wolfenbüttel, 1898, pp. 396ff. Cc. 2, 8–40 and the beginnings of cc. 41 and 42 are missing.

columns. This codex consists of two parts bound together; the first part on parchment is twelfth century, while the second part on paper dates from the fifteenth century. The first part is written in a very small hand. It contains a number of important historical pieces concerned chiefly with Metz and Cologne.[1] Only a few fragments of the Prose Life are found in this codex, on ff. 34b–36. The two parts of the codex seem to have been first united in the seventeenth century when they received their present binding.

36. Bo. Bollandist Library, Brussels, 353.[2] $9\frac{3}{4} \times 6\frac{3}{4}$ in. 169 ff. 32 lines to the page. Single column. The earlier part of this codex is in a hand of the late twelfth or early thirteenth century. It contains the Prose Life (ff. 1–34) followed by the same set of miracles as in the rest of the Bz group. The latter part of the codex contains a Life of Bishop Odo of Cambrai, and extracts from patristic writings in a contemporary hand. There is also a Life of St Rombaut (ff. 105–111) in a late fourteenth-century hand. The codex was presented to the Bollandists in 1844 by Charles, Comte de l'Escalopier.

37. Vn. Vienna, Nationalbibliothek 9394.[3] $11\frac{1}{4} \times 8\frac{1}{4}$ in. 264 ff. 42–44 lines to the page. Double columns. This codex of the fifteenth century is partly on vellum and partly on paper. It formerly belonged to the private library of the Emperor of Austria, to whom it was given along with other MSS in 1803. It is written by various hands. It is a legendary containing altogether fifty items of which the Prose Life occupies ff. 95–97. Only a small part of the Life is found in this codex, sufficient extracts from chapters 36–40 to form a summary account of the death and burial of the saint. The legendary comes from the monastery of Rouge-Cloître near Brussels, and is probably the one mentioned in a catalogue of the library of that house still preserved in the Emperor of Austria's collection, MS 9373.

38. Va. Vatican Library, Codices Reginae Sueciae 483.[4] $8\frac{3}{4} \times 6$ in. 180 ff. 27 lines to the page. Single column. This codex, written in a beautifully clear hand of the thirteenth

---

1 Cf. *M.G. Script.* IV, 1841, p. 253. Many of the pieces referred to above are printed in this volume.

2 *Anal. Boll.* XXIV, 1905, p. 452.   3 *Ibid.* XIV, 1895, pp. 257ff.

4 A. Poncelet, *Cat. Cod. Hag. Lat. Bibl. Vat.* Brussels, 1910, p. 330.

century, contains a Life and Miracles of St Dunstan; the Prose Life (ff. 59–99b) followed by the same selection of miracles as in the rest of the Bz group; the *Brevis Commemoratio* of Bede; the Lives of St Aidan and St Oswald from Bede; the prayer of St Anselm; finishing up with an altercation between a Jew and a Christian concerning the Catholic faith, dedicated to Alexander Bishop of Lincoln. This MS once belonged to Paul Petau (1568–1614),[1] a counsellor in the Parliament of Paris (1588), who possessed a large number of MSS which had originally belonged to French churches and monasteries.[2]

LOST MANUSCRIPTS

1. In the 1561 catalogue of MSS from Fulda, of which the most important copy is still at Fulda, there is an entry under IV.2.14: "Idem (Beda) de s. Gutberto." This may possibly be the Prose Life. The other Life of St Cuthbert entered under IV.4.14 is the Metrical Life (Karl Christ, *Die Bibliothek des Klosters Fulda im 16. Jahrh.* Beiheft LXIV zum Zentralblatt für Bibliothekswesen, Leipzig, 1933, pp. 257, 258; cf. pp. 143, 301).

2. In the 1461 catalogue of the Stiftsbibliothek St Gallen appears the entry under R.14, "Beda de vita Cudeberti". This is probably the Prose Life, as in the same catalogue a Metrical Life of St Cuthbert is distinguished by the addition of "metrum" (P. Lehmann, *Mittelalterliche Bibliothekskataloge Deutschlands und der Schweiz*, I, Munich, 1918, p. 114). In a catalogue of the middle of the ninth century of the library of St Gallen occurs, "Item de miraculis Gudberti episcopi et Althelmi de laude uirginum liber 1". But this is probably the same book as the one described in the 1461 catalogue (Gottlieb, 1387), where it is clearly the Metrical Life that is referred to (P. Lehmann, *op. cit.* pp. 74, 108).

3. In a tenth-century catalogue at Bobbio occurs the entry "296. libros de vita patrum…ex his habetur vita Gutbercti" (G. Becker, *Catalogi Bibliothecarum Antiqui*, Bonn, 1885, p. 68).

1 I am indebted to Dom André Wilmart, O.S.B., for this information.
2 On the MSS of Paul Petau see L. Delisle, *Le Cabinet des manuscrits de la Bibliothèque impériale*, I, Paris, 1868, pp. 287ff.

4. In the same catalogue, in the "Breve de libris Theodori presbyteri"[1]: "572. de vita sancti Gutberti liber" (G. Becker, *op. cit.* p. 72).

5. In a tenth-century catalogue at Lorsch appears, under item 38, "item regula sancti Benedicti et vita sancti Chutberti et hymni et amnales (*sic*) in uno codice". And again item 280, "item vita sancti Cuthberti et regula sancti Benedicti et annalis in uno codice". The same MS appears also in another catalogue of the same monastery and apparently of the same date (G. Becker, *op. cit.* pp. 82, 100, 121).

6. A late twelfth-century catalogue of Whitby gives a "vita Cuthberti" among its items. This catalogue is contained in the Whitby register and quoted by Young in his history of Whitby (G. Young, *A History of Whitby and Streoneshalh Abbey*, II, Whitby, 1817, pp. 918–920 and G. Becker, *op. cit.* p. 227).

7 and 8. In a twelfth-century catalogue of Durham books occur two "Vitae Sancti Cuthberti", one under the heading of "Libri Willelmi de Nunnewick", the other under the heading of "Libri Thomae Prioris" (*Catt. Vett.* pp. 8, 9).

9. In the Durham catalogue of 1391 under "Vitae Sanctorum" appears the entry: "E. Liber de Vita et miraculis Beati Cuthberti. Tractatus ex quatuor libris historiae gentis Anglorum. ii. fo. de vita et virtutibus" (*op. cit.* p. 30).

10. In the 1395 catalogue under "Legendae seu Vitae Sanctorum" appears the entry: "M. Vita Sancti Cuthberti. Vita Sancti Oswaldi Regis et Martiris. Vita Sancti Aydani, cum quibusdam Miraculis ejusdem Sancti Patris Cuthberti. ii. fo. facere quia" (*op. cit.* p. 55). The same entry occurs also in an undated fourteenth-century list of books used in the refectory (*op. cit.* p. 80).

11. In the same catalogue is a list of books belonging to Henry Helaugh, sent to Stamford in 1422, of which one of the items is: "Vita Sancti Cuthberti. ii. fo. principium" (*op. cit.* p. 116).

12. On a fly-leaf of one of the MSS in the Durham Chapter Library (A.iii.16) is the entry: "Hii sunt libri magistri Roberti

---

1 See Giov. Mercati, "Prolegomena de fatis bibliothecae monasterii S. Columbani Bobiensis", *Codices e Vaticanis selecti quam simillime expressi*, XXIII, Rome, 1934, pp. 34 ff.

de Aedingtona repositi apud Sanctum Victorem....Liber de vita et miraculis sancti Cuthberti." The date of this entry is probably about 1200.

13. In a catalogue of books of Durham College, Oxford (*ca.* 1400), preserved in the Durham Muniments (Durham, Repertorium Magnum, 2ª, 6ᵃᵉ, Ebor. No. 5) occurs the entry: "Vita Sancti Cuthberti".

14 and 15. John Boston, a fifteenth-century monk of Bury, in his *Catalogus Scriptorum Ecclesiae* records two copies of the Prose Life, one at Bury St Edmunds and one at Exeter. He got the latter from the *Registrum Librorum Angliae*, an early Franciscan Bibliography of the English monastic houses, which is still extant in Bodley Tanner 165 and Peterhouse (Cambridge) 163, and in which the Exeter copy is the only MS of the Life recorded. To this, as his custom was, he added a reference to his own library at Bury (John Boston, *Catalogus Scriptorum Ecclesiae*, partially published in D. Wilkins' edition of Thomas Tanner's *Bibliotheca Britannico-Hibernica*, London, 1748, p. xxix. I am also indebted to Mr R. A. B. Mynors for further information).

16. In a catalogue dating from the thirteenth century of an anonymous English library in B.M. Harl. 50, f. 48*b* occurs as item 54, "Vita Cuitberti", possibly the Prose Life (H. Omont, "Anciens catalogues de Bibliothèques anglaises", *Centralblatt für Bibliothekswesen*, IX, 1892, p. 204).

17. In a catalogue of MSS from Corbie dating from about 1200 occurs the entry: "264, sancti Cu(t)berti et alia passio Sebastiani. vita Alexis. passio Blasii. vita Thebaldi. passio Viti, Modesti, Crescentie, Cirici et Iulite" (G. Becker, *op. cit.* p. 284).

18. In a fourteenth-century MS catalogue of the library of the monastery of Rievaulx occurs: "1. Beda de vita sancti Cuthberti et Cuthbertus de transitu sancti Bede in uno volumine" (Edward Edwards, *Memoirs of Libraries*, I, London, 1859, p. 337).

19. Montfaucon gives a list of books of Alexander Petau in the Vatican Library which includes "Cutberti episcopi miracula", 1285, 113, 115, 118 (B. de Montfaucon, *Bibliotheca bibliothecarum manuscriptorum nova*, I, Paris, 1739, pp. 42, 75).

Only one now remains in the Vatican Library (presumably the first of these). It is MS Reg. Suec. 483 (Va), cf. Montfaucon, *op. cit.* p. 42.

20. Montfaucon quotes a MS catalogue in the Royal Library, Paris (Bibliothèque Nationale), no. 10284, which gives a list of MSS in the monastery of St Victor at Paris. In this is the entry: "Cuthberti vita et miracula". It is possible that this may be Bn, which was once in this monastery (see p. 36 above. Montfaucon, *op. cit.* II, p. 1370).

21. In a catalogue of the cathedral library of Cologne dated 833 occurs the entry 88: "Vita sancti Chutberti in quaternione uno" (Anton Decker, *Die Hildebold'sche Manuskriptensammlung des Kölner Domes*, Festschrift der 43. Versammlung Deutscher Philologen und Schulmänner dargeboten von den höheren Lehranstalten Kölns, Bonn, 1895, p. 227. As to the date of the catalogue, see Paul Lehmann, "Erzbischof Hildebald und die Dombibliothek von Köln", *Zentralblatt für Bibliothekswesen*, XXV, 1908, pp. 153–8).

22. In a fourteenth-century catalogue of Melsa (Meaux Abbey near Beverley) (Brit. Mus. Cotton. Vit. C. 6) occurs the entry: "vita beati Gregorii Papae in quo vitae sanctorum Silvestri, Cuthberti, Martini, Albani, Germani, Leonardi et Hugonis Lincolniensis" (*Chronica Monasteria de Melsa*, ed. E. A. Bond, Rolls Series, III, 1868, p. xcvi).

23 and 24. A catalogue of MSS of the monastery at Glastonbury dated 1247 contains on folio 103: "Vita sancti Cuthberti". And below: "Item vita sancti Cuthberti" (*Johannis Glastoniensis Chronica*, ed. T. Hearne, Oxford, 1726, p. 437).

25 to 27. In the edition of the Prose Life published by the Bollandists the editor states that three MSS have been used all of which have apparently since been lost (see p. 53); these are a very ancient MS belonging to themselves, a MS from Bonnefontaine and a third from Utrecht, which is described as being "contractus" (*AA.SS. Mart.* III, p. 95. Cf. also Levison in *Script. rerum Merov.* VII, pp. 539ff.; but see Addenda below).

28. Mabillon in his edition used a MS from Compiègne which has also apparently now disappeared (Mab. *AA.SS. Saec.* II, p. 841. Cf. also Levison, *Script. rerum Merov.* VII, p. 543).

THE RELATIONSHIPS OF THE MANUSCRIPTS

A. THE ANONYMOUS LIFE

The seven MSS of the Anonymous Life divide themselves into three main groups, consisting of O_1, O_2 and A (group X) on the one hand, and H and B (group Y) on the other. Midway between these two groups stand T and P. The distinction between groups X and Y is very strongly marked. H and B both go back to a common ancestor, a legendary composed apparently some time in the twelfth century in the diocese of Trier.[1] The compiler of this parent legendary treated his exemplar in a summary manner, occasionally missing out a whole sentence, particularly in order to avoid the name of a person or place which he presumes will be of no interest to his hearers or readers. Thus in II, 3, p. 78, he omits the sentence giving the name of Plecgils as a witness to a miracle. And again in IV, 3, p. 114, the name of Aldfrith's *gesith* and the region where he lived are both omitted, and also the name *Bedesfeld*, IV, 4, p. 116; *Medilwong*, IV, 6, p. 118; and the name of his foster-mother Kenswith and the village of *Hruringaham* in II, 7, pp. 88, 90. In IV, 12, p. 128 the name of Walhstod is omitted in both MSS; and the name of the river Tweed near which Sibba, thane of Ecgfrith, lived in IV, 7, p. 120. ⁄

On the other hand, T and P both agree in many respects with the Y group, and there are about one hundred and fifty variations of spelling, word-order, or syntactical forms in which T and P agree with H and B against the X group. The main feature of agreement common to this group is the fact that they all omit the first part of the preface entitled "*De prohemio oboediendi*", beginning with the second part, the "*De praefatione scribendi*". T and P agree together comparatively rarely against H and B, while far more frequently P agrees with H and B where T does not. P is therefore nearer to the Y group than T. It must be noted, however, that P is a carelessly written MS

1 *Script. rerum Merov.* VII, p. 537.

and has many readings peculiar to itself which are often no more than obvious scribal errors, though not all its variants come under this head. T, also, has a fair number of peculiar readings of its own. It seems likely that P and T go back to an exemplar or exemplars closely associated with the exemplar from which H and B were derived.

O_1, O_2 and A form a distinct and closely connected group. In the first place they all have the first part of the preface entitled, "*De prohemio oboediendi*", and all agree in many places in variants differing from the other four MSS. At first sight O_1 and A seem to be more closely connected. They agree frequently in their readings when O_2 has some other reading. Thus in I, 2, p. 62, both read *uoluisset* where O_2 reads *uoluit*. In I, 6, p. 70, both read *Kuncacester*, while O_2 reads *Kunnacester*. In the same chapter, p. 70, both read *panne linea*, while O_2, with all the other MSS, reads *panno lineo*. In IV, 13, p. 130, there is a form *incorruptibilem* in O_1, which occurs also in A, while O_2 with the rest has the more correct form *incorruptibile*. In IV, 14, p. 132, the form *eleuatis eum* occurs in O_1, a form which probably occurred in the original exemplar of this group. This will not make sense and A, seeing the difficulty, has changed it to *eleuantis eum*. A further attempt at correction occurs in O_2 in the form of *eleuatus enim*, while the rest have what was probably the correct reading, *eleuantes eum*. But a closer study will show that many of these readings are later corrections, as for instance the reading *panno lineo* mentioned above: and the many obvious mistakes which O_1 and O_2 have in common prove conclusively that they go back to the same exemplar.

It seems possible that A may have had a slightly more correct exemplar than O_1 or O_2. Thus in IV, 5, p. 116, both O_1 and O_2 read *Uel*, where A and all the other MSS read *Luel*, the first letter having been lost in the exemplar to which O_1 and O_2 originally go back. In the same way in IV, 9, p. 124, O_1 and O_2 have *Lues* where A reads *Luel* with the rest. Further, in IV, 8, p. 122 O_1 and O_2 read *mirabile* where A, with the rest of the MSS, reads more correctly *miserabile*. In II, 3, p. 78, O_1 reads *Plecgilf*, while A reads *Plecgils*, a much more likely form. And, again, both O_1 and O_2 agree in the omission of *querens* in IV, 9,

p. 124, while A with the rest of the MSS correctly inserts it. It is clear therefore that these three MSS go back to the same exemplar, though not directly. It was an exemplar in which the runic letters *p*, *þ* and *æ* were used, for all these letters occur in all three MSS in proper names and place names. The differences are sufficiently explained by suggesting that O_1 and O_2 are both copies of one exemplar, which was probably itself a copy of the archetype. A is perhaps a second copy of the archetype which has survived. The considerable omissions which occur in both O_2 and A are due to losses which were sustained in the later history of the MSS.

O_1 has been chosen as the basis of the text of the Anonymous Life, because it is the oldest MS. Had A been complete it would probably have been a more satisfactory MS to use as a basis. But of the complete MSS none can rival O_1 in nearness to the original and in correctness, as a study of the variants will speedily show. In editing this MS and also the MS on which the edition of the Prose Life is based, I have preserved the spelling and capitals of the original except where noted in the footnotes. Capitals have also been added in the case of proper names and titles of God. The punctuation of the Anonymous Life represents that of O_1.

B. BEDE'S PROSE LIFE

The thirty-six MSS of the Prose Life (not counting the Wolfenbüttel and Vienna fragments) divide themselves into two main groups, A and B, one of which (A) consists of C_1, V, H, Ar_1, O_7, P_1, and P_3; while the other group consists of the other twenty-nine. The first of these groups omits passages which are shorter or longer in extent. In chapter 5, p. 168, the words *uiam repetiit ieiunus* are omitted in each of these MSS. Other omissions found are chapter 3, p. 164, *relatione didici sese haec*, though the passage has been inserted above in V and in the text in Ar_1; chapter 7, p. 178, *aliquando quidem palam*; chapter 8, p. 182, *celauit, ipsum uero abbatem suum non ea*; chapter 10, p. 190, *ac uillo satagebant extergere*; chapter 16, p. 212, *imitaretur ipse quod ageret*; chapter 18, p. 218, *tibracis quas pellicias habere solebat, sic menses perduraret integros. Aliquando etiam calciatus.* These are the chief passages in which the above seven MSS of the A group vary from the rest. In Ar₁ a MS of the B group has been used to fill in omissions and in most cases, though not all, the correction is made in a later hand either by erasing a line or two of the original text and filling in the passage, together with the original omission, in a closer hand, or else by adding it in the margin or at the bottom of the page.

In this smaller group there are two distinct subgroups consisting of (Am) C₁, V, H, Ar₁, on the one hand; and (An) O₇, P₁, and P₃ on the other. There are certain omissions in the first subgroup (Am) which do not occur in the other (An). The most important is the passage in chapter 35 where in the Am group the whole passage between *biberet* in line 6 and *biberet* in line 18 has been omitted. Other passages are chapter 25, p. 240, *rogauitque obnixe ut ad benedictionem dandam*, where it is omitted in each MS of the Am group except Ar₁ and there it is added in a different hand. In chapter 37, p. 276, the words *Ex quo autem ingrediens* are omitted in this group, though again they appear in Ar₁ in a different hand.

Within this smaller group of four (Am) a still closer relationship can be established between V and H. V has been glossed sporadically throughout in a hand which is apparently contemporary, and the same gloss appears in a contemporary hand in H also. Of the ninety words glossed in V, with the exception of two Anglo-Saxon glosses all occur in H, while there are in addition a few extra glossed words in H, mostly in the last few chapters. The text of H follows V with the utmost faithfulness even in its mistakes, as for instance in chapter 24, p. 234, where *quo* becomes *co*, destroying the sense; or *aliquit* in chapter 24, p. 236; or *conuertemini* for *confortemini* in chapter 27, p. 244. In one place there is a not very successful attempt at correction in H, where in chapter 16, p. 212 V reads *exscitat* for *excitat*. This appears in H as *exsuscitat*. It seems very probable, in fact almost a certainty, that H is a copy of V. Ar₁ follows V and H generally when they differ from C₁, but its variations in word-order and spellings are so considerable as to make it highly improbable that Ar₁ is derived from the same exemplar as V.

The second subgroup (An), consisting of O₇, P₁, and P₃, also has omissions of some length which do not occur in Am. Thus in chapter 7, p. 178, the passage *erat quem suscepi pascere non pasci ueniens. En,* does not occur in this group, nor do the words *libenter ea quae dicerentur audirent* in chapter 9, p. 186; in addition there are several omissions of two or three words peculiar to the group as in chapter 7, p. 178, *autem uelate*; or in chapter 12, p. 196, *illam porro uolantem*; or chapter 22, p. 230, *non parum*; or chapter 27, p. 246, *in orationibus et uigiliis*; and further on in the same chapter, p. 246, *et illi*; and chapter 40, *sancta illa.* In addition there are about seventy other places where the group differs from the rest of the MSS in word-order, or in the omission of a single word, or in differences of spelling. There are three omissions in O₇ which are not found in P₁ and P₃, viz. chapter 11, p. 192, *quam putabant*; chapter 15, p. 204, *non integra...Domini* (ten words); and chapter 37, p. 274, *iussi...mihi* (ten words). There are besides a considerable number of minor differences between each of the three MSS both in word-order and word-form which preclude the possibility that any one was copied from another of the same group. In view of the very considerable number of minor differences between each of these three, it is probable that they derive from three different exemplars which probably in their turn derive from the same one.

It will be seen that all the earliest MSS with the exception of O₁ belong to the A group. This is unfortunate, because it seems that the text of this group is less faithful to the original than that of the B group, judging by its frequent and serious omissions noted above and its treatment of unfamiliar words such as *uagitibus* in chapter 1, p. 156, or *iusum* in chapter 5, p. 170, or its numerous mistakes in syntax which are correct in the other group such as *ut* for *ne* in chapter 6, p. 174, *donabat* for *donare* in chapter 7, and many other places noted in the text. It seemed therefore safer to use a MS of the B group as a basis for the text even though it was of later date, and particularly of the Bx subgroup, most of which were probably written in Durham and have the Durham tradition behind them. The earliest MS of this group, O_1, late eleventh or very early twelfth, is incomplete; it was therefore necessary to fall back on the best of the early twelfth-century group, namely O_9, which has consequently been used as the basis of the text; the B group consists, then, of all the other MSS—namely C_2, C_3, O_1, O_2, O_3, O_5, O_6, O_8, O_9, H_1, Cl, Bn, Ad_1, Ad_2, Du, Dj_2, Ar_2, Go, H_2, O_4, P_2, Li, Oth, Dj_1, La, M, Bo, Va, Cm. W and Vn are only fragments and cannot be classified.

The MSS of this group bear much resemblance to one another and it is not easy to divide them into smaller groups, and practically impossible to trace back their relationship with one another with any accuracy. Two minor groups stand out fairly clearly, however. Of these the most distinctive is the group (By) consisting of O_4, P_2, Li, and Oth. These agree together in over one hundred and twenty places, occasionally agreeing with one or other of the other MSS, but in the great majority of cases differing from all the rest. The differences consist in changes of word-order, insertions or omissions of one or two words, and variations such as chapter 6, p. 172, *seruus* for *famulus*; chapter 9, p. 186, *dicendi* for *docendi*; and occasionally mistakes occur in all four but in no other MS; such as chapter 34, p. 262, *angelorum* for *angelicis*; or chapter 3, p. 160, *peccatorem* for *pauperem*. It is clear that all four of these derive originally from the same exemplar but not directly, for Oth and P_2 in some twenty-five instances agree together against O_4 in word-order, in the insertion or omission of words, and in occasional slips such as *candentia* for *cadentia* in chapter 5, p. 170. It is very probable that both Oth and P_2 are derived from the same exemplar, for when they differ from one another the differences are all easily attributable to scribal errors. The exemplar of these two is probably copied from the MS from which O_4 and Li also derive. The occasional agreement between this group (By) and the group (An) would tend to show some remote connection between the two groups.

Another minor group of the B class (Bz) consists of Dj_1, La, M, Bo, Va, Cm. The chief distinguishing mark of this group is the omission in chapter 18, p. 218, of a sentence of

eleven words—*Fodiamus in medio...potabit nos.* In addition
there are some half-dozen cases where the group agrees in a
word-order different from the rest of the MSS; and there are
five or six cases of agreement in the omission, insertion, or
variation of a word as opposed to the rest of the group. Another
connection between the group is that in Dj_1, La, M, Bo, and
Va the Prose Life is followed by a series of twenty-eight
miracles consisting of the usual two chapters from the *H.E.*
as well as nine chapters of miracles and seventeen other chapters
from the *Brevis Relatio*, all in the same order, an order which is
found in none of the other collections of miracles in any of the
English or foreign MSS. Cm contains only the account of the
Translation. It is probable that this group goes back to an
exemplar carried across to the Continent in the mid-twelfth
century; there is not sufficient evidence to show that any one
of the group was the exemplar. Four of them (Dj_1, La, M, Cm)
belonged to Cistercian houses and it is quite possible that the
other two (Bo and Va) were also copied in a Cistercian house
on the Continent, most likely in North or Central France.

There is also an interesting connection between O_3 and H_2.
There is a series of marginal notes in both which agree closely
throughout. The handwriting of each seems to be contemporary
with the MS and in H_2 at any rate seems to be the same as that
of the text. There are twenty-six of these glosses in O_3, and
all of them occur in H_2. These glosses are practically all names
of places and persons which Bede omits to give, but which
are taken from the corresponding incident in the Anonymous
Life. In three instances the names of the places or persons given
in both glosses are not derived from the Anonymous Life but
from some other source, possibly oral tradition. H_2, in fact,
is pretty certainly an early sixteenth-century copy of O_3 made
in Durham by William Tode (see p. 29). There is nothing in
the text to prove it was not a transcription; though there are a
considerable number of differences, these consist exclusively
of omissions on the part of the scribe of H_2, variations in
word-order and spelling. Many of these marginal notes are
found in C_3, also a Durham book.

Of the nineteen MSS which belong to the Bx group, four

(Ad$_2$, C$_3$, O$_3$, Du) are definitely known to come from the Durham scriptorium and are noted in the fourteenth-century Durham catalogues; and no less than thirteen of the others (H$_1$, H$_2$, Ar$_2$, Cl, Ad$_1$, Dj$_2$, C$_2$, O$_1$, O$_2$, O$_5$, O$_6$, O$_8$, O$_9$) may be presumed, with varying degrees of probability, to have come from the Durham scriptorium, judging by their appearance, the form of the initial letters, their contents, connections or history. It is probable that all this group go back to a very early exemplar brought to Durham by the followers of St Cuthbert in the tenth century and used as a basis for the earlier copies made in the monastic scriptorium. The text must have been a good one and not far removed from the archetype.

The groups of MSS therefore divide themselves up as follows:

Am: C$_1$, V, H, Ar$_1$.

An: O$_7$, P$_1$, P$_3$.

Bx: C$_2$, C$_3$, O$_1$, O$_2$, O$_3$, O$_5$, O$_6$, O$_8$, O$_9$, H$_1$, Cl, Bn, Ad$_1$, Ad$_2$, Du, Dj$_2$, Ar$_2$, Go, H$_2$.

By: O$_4$, P$_2$, Li, Oth.

Bz: Dj$_1$, La, M, Bo, Va, Cm.

All the differences between O$_9$ and the following representative MSS have been shown in the footnotes to the text:

Am: C$_1$, V, H.

An: P$_1$.

Bx: C$_3$, O$_3$, O$_8$.

By: O$_4$.

Bz: M.

Although O$_9$ has been used as the basis of the text for reasons stated above (p. 48), yet occasionally the readings, especially from the A group, which are to be found in the footnotes, show variants, word-order and spellings which are probably older and nearer to the original than those of O$_9$ which appear in the text.

PREVIOUS EDITIONS

A. THE ANONYMOUS LIFE

1. The Anonymous Life was first printed by the Bollandists in the *Acta Sanctorum Martii*, III, Antwerp, 1668, 117–24. The text was based upon O₁ (St Omer 267) and upon T (Trier 1151). The text omits the chapter headings and lists of chapters but preserves the division into chapters and books, adding new titles to each of the four books. There are a good many mistakes in the text and practically all the place-names and some of the personal names are very badly mangled owing to the confusion of the Old English runic "wen" (ƿ) with a "p", and of the insular "s" with "r". Hence arise such extraordinary forms as *Kenspid* for *Kenswith*, *Medilpong* and *Mudpieralegis* for *Medilwong* and *Niudwera regio*, *Opide* for *Twide* and many others.

2. The Anonymous Life was reprinted from the Bollandist text by Joseph Stevenson in his *Venerabilis Bedae Opera Historica Minora*, English Historical Society, London, 1841, pp. 259–84. He preserves the division into books and inserts the Bollandist titles, but numbers the chapters concurrently with the exception of the last chapter which he does not number at all. He corrects one or two of the most obvious mistakes in place and personal names and suggests the right reading in other places.

3. The life was again reprinted from the Bollandist text by J. A. Giles in an appendix to the sixth volume of his collected edition of Bede's works, *Patres Ecclesiae Anglicanae*, vol. VII, *Bedae Opera*, vol. VI, edited by J. A. Giles, London, 1843, pp. 357–82. It preserves the division into books but not the chapter divisions. All the mistakes of the Bollandist text are preserved and there are a few of his own as well.

B. BEDE'S PROSE LIFE

1. Bede's Prose Life of St Cuthbert was first printed in the collected edition of Bede's works printed at Basle by Johannes Hervagius in 1563 (Tertius Tomus, cols. 209–54). The edition was printed directly from a manuscript which by a fortunate

chance still exists and can be recognised. It is Bn (Berne, Stadtbibliothek 392). The MS must have been complete then, but has since lost the latter portion from c. 28 onwards. Bn still has upon it, plainly visible, the ink marks of the corrector of the press and the compositor's chalk marks with the numbers of the columns and even the signatures, all corresponding with the 1563 edition, at the side. It also contains on the face of it and in the margin, the spelling and other alterations which the corrector for the press saw fit to make, such as the change of small letters into capitals in proper names and the names of the Deity.[1] Probably the MS was borrowed from the Abbey of St Victor in Paris to which it once belonged before it came into the possession of Jacques Bongars (1554–1613). The MS is not a good one and there are several omissions, e.g. c. 1 from *mestumque...coepit*; c. 7 *aperte...replicat*; c. 10 *situm*, and c. 16 *tangendo...tantum*. All these of course are also omitted in the Basle edition.

2. A reprint of the Basle edition of Bede's works appeared in Cologne in 1612 (Tomus Tertius, cols. 152–85) and this was itself reprinted at Cologne in 1688 (Tomus Tertius, cols. 152–85).

3. The first edition of Laurentius Surius' *De probatis sanctorum historiis* published in Cologne in 1571 also contained an edition of the Prose Life (vol. II, pp. 299–327). It was based principally on the Basle edition and still preserves the omissions in c. 1 and c. 10 (see above), but the others have been filled up by reference to some other MS, though it is not possible to tell, in the absence of any information, what MS it was. Various mistakes found in the Basle edition remain uncorrected, such as c. 11 (p. 306) *laterent* for *taberent*; c. 6 (p. 303) *benigne* for *benignius*; and the insertion of *in* before *patriam*, the last word but one of c. 11 (p. 306); and *prehenderat* for *prendiderat* in c. 12 (p. 307). It is fairly obvious that for the most part the editor has relied upon the Basle edition, only referring to the MS very occasionally. On the other hand quite a number of variations, almost certainly mere misprints, occur, as for example *primitiva* for *primitus* in c. 1 (p. 300); *nullus* for *nullius* in c. 3 (p. 301);

1 For further details see: B. Colgrave and I. Masson, "The Editio Princeps of Bede's Life of St Cuthbert, and its Printer's XII Century copy". *The Library*, XIX, 1938, pp. 289 ff.

praecedunt for *praecellunt* in c. 7 (p. 304); *pisce* for *pisciculo* in c. 12 (p. 307); and *superaddere* for *supradicere* in the prologue (p. 299). The Life appeared also in the four later editions of Surius; second edition published in Cologne, 1578 (II, pp. 331–59); third edition published in Venice, 1581, entitled *De vitis Sanctorum* (II, 93 v.–102 v.); fourth edition published in Cologne, 1618, entitled *De probatis sanctorum Vitis* (III, pp. 214–28); fifth edition published in Turin, 1875 (III, pp. 378–413).[1]

4. The Life was reprinted from the Cologne, 1618 edition, by J. Colgan, in *Acta Sanctorum ueteris et maioris Scotiae seu Hiberniae sanctorum insulae*, Louvain, 1645 (Primus Tomus, pp. 659–79).

5. The Bollandist edition of the Prose Life appeared in the *Acta Sanctorum Martii*, III, Antwerp, 1668, pp. 97–116. The editors used three MSS, one a very ancient MS in the possession of the Bollandists which now seems to have disappeared (Jaager, p. 25), the second a MS which belonged to the Cistercian monastery of Bonnefontaine near Reims, the third from Utrecht which was incomplete (see p. 42 above and Addenda below). None of these MSS is now in existence. There is a list of chapter headings which differs slightly from those in any of the MSS known to me. They also used "the Life found amongst the works of Bede and edited separately by others" (p. 95). It is clear from this that they are referring to the Basle edition or the first Cologne reprint, for a few of the original mistakes of the Basle edition still persist, and probably to Surius' edition too, for many of the variant readings or mistakes introduced by Surius find their way into the Bollandist edition, including all those mentioned above under the account of Surius' edition. Though a list of chapter headings is given at the beginning of the work, these are not preserved in the body of the text and there is an arbitrary division into twelve chapters with new chapter headings.

6. J. Mabillon's edition appeared in the *Acta Sanctorum Ordinis Sancti Benedicti* (Paris, 1669, Saec. II, pp. 877–915; Venice, 1733, Saec. II, pp. 843–78). He follows the two editions of Surius and the Bollandists and also a MS from Compiègne

1 For Surius' methods of working see Paul Holt, "Die Sammlung von Heiligenleben des Surius", *Neues Archiv*, XLIV, Berlin, 1922, pp. 341–64.

which has since been lost (see above, p. 42). He made good use of this MS in correcting many though not all of the mistakes of Surius and the Bollandists. It is clear from some of the alterations in the text that the Compiègne MS was one of the Bz group, a group connected with the north of France (p. 48 f.). The chief evidence for this is the omission in c. 18, p. 858 of a sentence of eleven words: *Fodiamus in medio...potabit nos*, which Mabillon has deliberately omitted though it appears in both the editions he was using. The text is an improvement on these and he divides it up into proper chapters, inserting the chapter headings from his MS.

7. The next edition of the Life was the important edition of Bede's *Ecclesiastical History* and other historical works begun by John Smith, a canon of Durham, and finished by his son George, and published in Cambridge in 1722 (*Historiae Ecclesiasticae Gentis Anglorum, auctore Beda, una cum reliquis eius operibus historicis*, ed. J. Smith, Cambridge, 1722, pp. 225–64). For this edition five MSS were used: C_1 (Corpus Christi College, Cambridge, 183), which he calls Benedictinus, after the earlier name of the college; H (Harl. 1117); O_1 (Digby 175); O_2 (Bodl. 109); and lastly Ad_2 (Add. 39943). The latter, he explains, belongs to a certain "William Forcer Esquire of Durham". He describes it as being "most beautifully and elegantly adorned with pictures which illustrate the story contained in each chapter". In the copy of the Basle edition of Bede's works (see above) which is now in the Cosin Library at Durham (E. 1.16), Thomas Rud, the librarian of the Chapter Library at Durham in the early eighteenth century, has collated the text of Bede's Prose Life with a MS which he states belongs to "John Forcer". These collations prove beyond all doubt that this MS is Ad_2. John Forcer, who died in 1725, belonged to a Roman Catholic family who for many years lived at Harbour House near Plawsworth, Durham. There was no William Forcer living at the time, and in fact the name William never occurs in the Forcer family in the seventeenth or eighteenth centuries (R. Surtees, *History of Durham*, 1, London, 1816, p. 65). It becomes certain, then, having regard to Smith's description of his MS, that he has made a mistake in the name, that he meant

John Forcer, and that the MS he is referring to is therefore Ad₂.
In addition he used the Cologne edition, that is, the reprint of
the Basle edition and Mabillon's text. He has produced in this
way a conflate text, noting variant readings in the footnotes,
sometimes from the MSS, sometimes from the editions he was
using. He does not state which is which but puts them all
under the heading *Vulgg*. He gives no separate list of chapter
headings but headings appear under the separate chapters.

8. Joseph Stevenson was the next to publish the Life in his
Venerabilis Bedae Opera Historica Minora, English Historical
Society, London, 1841, pp. 45–137. He maintains that he has
used H (Harl. 1117) and V (Cotton. Vit. A. xix), the latter being
in addition to the MSS which Smith used, but as H is probably
no more than a transcript of V it could not greatly help. He
also refers to O₂, O₃, O₄, O₆, O₈. But, as he himself says in the
introduction (p. viii), it is Smith's edition which he has principally followed. In fact his edition is little more than a reprint
of Smith.

9. The next edition was that of J. A. Giles in the fourth
volume of his collected edition of the works of Bede published
in 1843, pp. 202–357. It contains the text and a translation. He
mentions (p. vi) another MS, Ar₁ (Arundel 222), but he seems
to have made little use of it. The text is again that of Smith
with only a few slight variations.

10. Mabillon's text was reprinted in a slightly improved form
in Migne's *Patrologia latina*, xcIV, 1862, cols. 733–90.

TRANSLATIONS

The Anonymous Life was translated by W. Forbes-Leith
under the title of *The Life of St Cuthbert*, privately printed,
Edinburgh, 1888. In this work the miniatures from Add. 39943
(Ad₂) were reproduced in colour. Bede's Prose Life was translated by J. A. Giles in his edition (see above). This was reprinted
in the Everyman's Library, No. 479, in 1910. Another translation
by Joseph Stevenson was printed in *The Church Historians of
England*, I, pt. 2, London, 1853, pp. 546–603.

SCRIPTURAL QUOTATIONS

The Scriptural quotations in the Anonymous Life differ but little from the Vulgate. There are a few differences of word-order as in Mal. 1. 2, 3 (I, 3). One or two differences are probably due to loose quotation such as the quotation from Luke 10. 7 (II, 5), and from Romans 8. 32 (III, 7); the quotation from Romans 8. 30 (I, 3) in O₁ reads "Quos *ante* predestinauit" though the *ante* for *autem* occurs only here and is possibly a scribal error, an easy confusion between aū and añ. In the quotation from Matth. 6. 33 (II, 5) a text of the Celtic type has been used (see *Novum Testamentum secundum editionem S. Hieronymi*, ed. J. Wordsworth, etc., Oxford, 1889, etc.).

In Bede's Prose Life, however, the majority of the quotations do not conform to the text of the Vulgate. This may be partly due to Bede's habit of loose quotation and his way of fitting in the text to suit the syntax of his sentence, as for instance 1 Cor. 13. 11 (c. 1); Ps. 33. 18 (c. 3); Eph. 6. 16, 17 (c. 17); Ps. 113. i, 8 and ii, 1 (c. 18); and 1 Cor. 16. 13 (c. 27). But in a certain number of instances, it is clear that Bede has been using a text which is not the ordinary Vulgate text, but which, in the Old Testament, corresponds more or less with the reading given by Sabatier (*Bibliorum Sacrorum Latinae Versiones Antiquae*, ed. Pierre Sabatier, 3 vols., Paris, 1751) as the Itala or Versio Antiqua, or which in the New Testament can in several instances be identified from Wordsworth's edition (see above) as a text of the Celtic type. We may therefore, partly following Plummer (*H.E.* II, 392), divide Bede's quotations into six classes: (1) those which are certainly taken from the Vulgate; (2) those quotations from the Old Testament which correspond with the Itala or Versio Antiqua as given by Sabatier; (2a) those quotations from the New Testament which are taken from a text of the Celtic type; (3) those of which the source is doubtful because in these passages the Vulgate and the other versions do not differ; (4) those of which the source is doubtful but is apparently not the Vulgate; (5) those in which the quotation seems to be conflate in character and to derive partly from the Vulgate and partly from some other version:

(1) Certainly from the Vulgate: Ps. 26. 13 (Prol.); Prov. 6. 6 (c. 20); Ps. 59. 3 (c. 40); 1 Kings 3. 20 (c. 45).

(2) Certainly from the Itala or Versio Antiqua: Ps. 8. 3 (c. 1); Ps. 32. 18, 19 (c. 5); Ps. 39. 5 (c. 12); Ps. 83. 8 (c. 17); Ps. 34. 10 (c. 26); Ps. 146. 2 (c. 40); Ps. 102. 3 (c. 45); Ps. 102. 4, 5 (c. 46).

(2a) Certainly from a text of the Celtic type: 1 Cor. 13. 11 (c. 1); John 1. 47 (c. 6, where the reading of the original was probably *uir* as in V and H); Matt. 26. 41 (c. 27).

(3) The Vulgate reading does not differ from the older version (in the Old Testament) or from texts of the Celtic type (in the New Testament): 2 Peter 2. 16 (c. 1); Matt. 25. 29 (c. 2); Ps. 33. 18 (c. 3); Matt. 6. 33 (c. 5); Num. 6. 3 (c. 6); 2 Cor. 12. 2 (c. 7); 2. Cor. 12. 9 (c. 8); Matt. 17. 9 (c. 10); Eph. 6, 16, 17 (cc. 14 and 17); Ps. 35. 9 (c. 18); Ps. 89. 9 (c. 24); 2 Cor. 7. 10 (c. 26); Luke 2. 10, 1 Cor. 16. 13 (c. 27); 2 Tim. 4. 6–8 (cc. 28, 37, 38); Luke 4. 39 (c. 29).

(4) The source is doubtful but apparently not the Vulgate: Lam. 3. 27, 28 (c. 1); 1 Sam. 3. 7 (c. 1); Gal. 5. 6 (c. 8); Ps. 113. i, 8 and ii, 1 (c. 18); Eccles. 11. 8 (c. 24).

(5) The quotation seems to be conflate in character: Isa. 43. 2 (c. 14); Ps. 76. 11 (c. 45). The references are in each case to the Vulgate.

VITA SANCTI CUTHBERTI
AUCTORE ANONYMO

ANONYMOUS LIFE OF
ST CUTHBERT

VITA SANCTI CUTHBERTI
AUCTORE ANONYMO

Incipiunt capitula Libri Primi In uita Sancti Cudberti[1].

I. De prohemio oboediendi[2]

Epistola
Victorii
Aquitani
ad
Hilarum
de cursu
paschali

Praeceptis[3] *tuis utinam* sancte episcope Eadfride, et totius familiae *tam effectu*[4] *ualeam parere quam uoto.* Est enim mihi[5] *et hoc opus arduum, et meae intellegentiae facultas exigua. Ego* autem *quod ad me pertinet, etiamsi delicatae*[6] *materiae* [7]*superer quantitate*[8] *satis habeo iussioni*[9] uestrae *possibilitatis meae non oboedientiam*[10] *defuisse, quae tamen etsi ministerium minime expleret iniunctum, certe debitum exsoluit obsequium.* V*osque deprecor, ut si*[11] *quippiam secus quam*[12] *uoluistis proueniret inbecillitatem meam adque*[13] *onus inpositum aequo iure perpendentes inperfecti laborem negotii officii magis aestimaretis*[14] *quam merito. Maximum enim indicium erga* uos *meae reuerentiae est imperiis uestris amplius me inpendere*[15] *uoluisse quam possim. Quod si dignum aliquid* uestrae *lectioni*[16] *confecero,*

---

1 *ins.* episcopi O₂. *There is no list of chapters in A.*   2 *There are no separate chapter numbers nor headings throughout* O₂. O₁ *has* prefatio *only.*
3 æ *and* œ *are sometimes written in full in* O₁, *sometimes represented by* ę.
4 affectu O₁O₂A. eff. Eddius.   5 michi O₂.

✠

The Life of St Cuthbert
The Chapters of Book I

CHAPTER I. *A prologue concerning obedience*

I would that the result of my obedience to your commands,
O holy bishop Eadfrith, and to the commands of the whole
community might be as good as my intentions. For this is a
great task for me and my powers of understanding are small.
But, so far as I am concerned, even if I am overwhelmed by the
amount of sacred material at my disposal, yet I am satisfied
that I have not failed in obedience to the commands you laid
upon my powers which, although ill able to perform the task
you have allotted me, have at any rate fulfilled the duty I owe
you. And I beg you, if anything has turned out otherwise
than you wished, that balancing fairly my weakness against the
task imposed, you will judge the labour of my imperfect
enterprise in terms of duty rather than of merit. For what
greater proof could there be of my respect for you than my
wish to devote myself to your commands, even though they
exceed my powers? But, if I produce anything worthy of your

6 dilicate A.   7–8 super quantitatem O_1O_2, super quantitate A.   9 *alt. from*
iussione O_2.   10 obedientiam O_1.   11–12 quispiam secusque O_1O_2A.
13 atque O_2.   14 est...O_1.   15 imp...O_2.   16 electioni Eddius;
electione Victorius (*but here also occur various readings* lectioni *and* lectione).

id erit profecto diuini muneris. Tum etiam beniuolentia uestra
inertes quoque ad profectum excitat, nec dubitatur ipsorum
fide perficiendum, quorum *est adortatione*[1] *susceptum, cum
mihi*[2] *quoque fiducia*[3] *sit peragere posse quod praecipitis, cui
id tam confidenter iniungitis. Quis namque non intellegat*[4],

f. 68
Ath. Vit.
Ant.
Preface

uestris orationibus | *iam praesumptum esse, quod etiam per me
creditis adimplendum?* Magna namque *cum laetitia suscepi
uestre*[5] *caritatis imperium. Etenim ingens mihi*[6] *lucrum est
atque utilitas, hoc*[7] *ipsum quod recordor* sancti Cuðberti[8].
Est siquidem perfecta uia ad uirtutem, illum scire quis fuerit.
Ideo *ut breuiter dicam, omnia quae de eo sermo referentium*[9]
iactauit credite[10], *et minima uos aestimate*[11] *de maximis audisse
quia*[12] *non ambigo, nec eos potuisse omnia cognoscere.*

II. *De prefatione scribendi*

Sulpicius
Seuerus
Vita S.
Martini
c. I.

Igitur[13] [14]*uitam sancti* Cuthberti [15] *scribere exordiar*[16], *ut se*[17]
uel[18] *ante episcopatum*[19]*uel in episcopatu*[20] *gesserit, quamuis
nequaquam ad omnes*[21] *illius potuerim peruenire* uirtutes,
adeo[22] *ea in quibus ipse tantum sibi conscius fuit nesciuntur,
quia*[23] *laudem ab hominibus non requirens*[24], *quantum*[25] *in ipso
fuit, omnes uirtutes suas latere uoluisset*[26], *quamquam*[27] *etiam
ex his*[28] *quae nobis comperta*[29] *erant*[30] *plura omisimus*[31], *quia
sufficere credimus, si tantum excellentiora notarentur*[32], *simul
et legentibus consulendum fuit, ne quod*[33] [34] *his pararet*[36] *copia*[35]
congesta[37] *fastidium. Obsecro* itaque[38] *eos qui lecturi sunt ut
fidem dictis adhibeant, neque me quicquam nisi* quod[39] *compertum et probatum sit*[40], *scripsisse*[41] *arbitrentur, alioquin tacere*

---

1 adhortatione O₂.   2 michi O₂.   3 fidutia O₁.   4 *changed* to
intelligat O₁.   5 vestrae O₂.   6 michi O₂.   7 *capital
letter in* O₁.   8 Cudberti O₂. Cuðberhti A.   9 referentem
O₁O₂A.   10 cred. iact. O₂.   11 est... O₁.   12 *om.* O₁O₂A.
13 H *begins here with* Incipit uita uenerabilis Cuthberti episcopi. T *begins
here with* Incipit uita Sancti Cuthberti edita a uenerabili Beda presbitero.
B *begins here with* Incipit uita sancti Cuthberti episcopi. P *begins
here. om.* igitur HTB. 14–16 Sci. Guthberti vit. scrib. exordior H. Sci.
Cudberti vit. scrib. exordior T. Sci. Cuthberti vit. scrib. exordior B.
15 Cuthberhti A.

reading, it will assuredly be by the help of divine grace. Moreover, your kindness arouses even the idle to go forward, and
without doubt the task will be carried to completion by the
faith of those through whose exhortation it was begun; for
even I have confidence that I can accomplish the behest which
you so confidently impose. Who will fail to understand that
the task undertaken was one which you believe even me capable
of carrying through with the help of your prayers? So with
great joy I undertook your loving command. For this record
of St Cuthbert is of great gain and value to myself. Indeed it
is in itself a ready path to virtue to know what he was. So, to be
brief, even though you believe all the claims that popular report
has made for him—and you may well do so—yet be sure that,
even then, you have heard very little about matters that are
very great, for I am certain that none could know them all.

CHAPTER II. *Preface to the writing*

I will therefore undertake to write the life of St Cuthbert and
how he lived both before and after he became bishop; yet I have
not been able to find out all his miracles by any means; for those
which he alone was aware of are unknown, because, as he did
not seek the praise of men, he desired that all his miracles should
be hidden so far as this was in his power. Yet we have omitted
many, even, of those which were known to us, because we
believed that it would be sufficient if only the more outstanding
ones were noted, and at the same time, we had to consider our
readers, lest too plentiful an abundance might produce in them
a feeling of distaste. So I beseech my readers to believe my
report and not to think that I have written anything except
what has been received on good authority and tested. Nay,

17 *changed to* quae O₁.   18 *om.* O₂.   19–20 *om.* T. epyscopatu B. que
O₂HB.   21 ad om. neq. HB.   22 *ins.* tamen HB. tamen P.   23 quae
O₁A. qui O₂. que HB.   24 requirebat O₂. querens T.   25 *capital letter
in* O₁.   26 uoluit O₂HBP. uoluisse T.   27 *changed to* quasquam A.
28·h *above* O₁.   29 conp... T.   30 sunt P.   31 omissimus O₁A.
32 notantur O₂HB.   33 quam O₁O₂A.   34–35 copia his HB.
36 pareret P.   37 congestaret HB.   38 igitur HB.   39 *om.* HB.
40 *om.* HB.   41 scriptitasse P.

Actus
Siluestri.

quam *falsa dicere*[1] *maluissem. Verum quoniam ad omnium operum eius* numerum, *nec littera nec sermo*[2] *proficere*[3] *potest*[4], *ad ea quae gesta sunt accedamus.*

f. 68*b*

III. [5]*De eo quod infans de illo prophetauit*[7, 6]

Primum quidem ponimus quod in prima aetate[8] accidisse relatu multorum didicimus, ex quibus est sanctae memoriae episcopus Tumma, qui spiritalem[9] Dei electionem[10] predestinatam[11] a[12] sancto Cuðberhto[13] audiens didicit, et presbiter nostrae aecclesiae[14] Elias[15] dicentes, Dum ergo puer esset annorum octo[16], omnes coaetaneos[17] in agilitate et petulantia superans[18], ita ut sepe postquam fessis menbris[19] requiescebant alii, ille adhuc in loco ioci quasi in stadio triumphans aliquem secum ludificantem[20] expectaret[21]. Tunc congregati sunt[22] quadam die multi iuuenes in campi planicie[23], inter quos ille inuentus est, ioci uarietatem, et scurilitatem[24] agere ceperunt[25]. Alii namque stantes nudi uersis capitibus contra naturam deorsum ad[26] terram, et[27] expansis cruribus erecti[28] pedes ad coelos[29] sursum prominebant[30]. Alii sic, alii uero[31] sic fecerunt[32]. Interea quidam infans erat cum eis ferme trium annorum qui[33] incipiebat constanter ad eum dicere[34], Esto stabilis, et relinque uanitatem ioci amare, et iterum negligenti[35] eo uerba precepti[36] eius plorans et lacrimans quem pene[37] nullus consolari potuit. Postremo tamen interrogatus quid sibi esset, clamare cepit[38], O sancte[39] episcope [40]et presbiter[41] Cuðberhte[42], hec[43] tibi et tuo[44] gradui[45] contraria[46] nature[47] propter[48] agilitatem non conueniunt. Ille uero non plene

1 dic. falsa O_1O_2AT.   2 serm. nec litt. HTBP.   3 profecisse P.
4 possit TP.   5-6 *om.* A. HBP *omit all chapter headings.*
7 prophetauerit T.   8 eta... BP.   9 spiritualem O_2P.
10 dilectionem P.   11 prae... O_2.   12 in T.   13 Gutberto H.
Cuthberto BP. Chudberto T.   14 ecclesie TP. ecclesiac B.
15 Helias O_2AT. *om.* HB. Helyas P.   16 octo ann. T. viiiº B.
17 coet... HTBP.   18 superauit HBP.   19 membris O_2AT.
20 ludentem T.   21 exspectans O_1O_2. expectans AT.   22 *om.* HBP.
23 planiciem O_1A. planitiae O_2.   24 scurril... HBP.

I would rather hold my peace than state what is false. But since, assuredly, neither the written nor the spoken word can do justice to all his numerous works, let us start upon an account of his deeds.

CHAPTER III. *How a child prophesied concerning him*

First we record an incident of his early youth, known to us through the reports of many, among whom are Bishop Tumma of holy memory, who learnt from St Cuthbert's own lips that God's choice of him to a spiritual office had been predetermined, and Elias also, a priest of our church. These tell the story thus. When he was a boy of eight years, he surpassed all of his age in agility and high spirits, so that often, after the others had gone to rest their weary limbs, he, standing triumphantly in the playground as though he were in the arena, would still wait for someone to play with him. At that time many youths were gathered together one day on a piece of level ground and he too was found among them. They began thereupon to indulge in a variety of games and tricks; some of them stood naked, with their heads turned down unnaturally towards the ground, their legs stretched out and their feet lifted up and pointing skywards; and some did one thing and some another. Now among them there was a certain child scarcely three years old who began to call out to him repeatedly: "Be steadfast and leave this foolish play." Seeing his commands disregarded, he thereupon wailed and wept and became almost inconsolable. At last being asked what was the matter with him, he began to cry out: "O holy Bishop and priest Cuthbert, these unnatural tricks done to show off your agility are not befitting to you or your high office". Cuthbert did not clearly under-

---

25 coep... O₂H.   26 in B.   27 *om.* T.   28 *ins.* per HBP.
29 caelos O₂. celos A. coelum H. celum TBP.   30 *ins.* et HB.
31 *om.* HB.   32 faciebant HBP.   33 *om.* O₁O₂AP.
34 dic. ad eum HTBP.   35 negligente HP. negligenter B.
36 praecepti O₂A.   37 fere HB.   38 coep... O₂H.   39 *ins.* Cuthberte B.
40–41 *om.* HB.   42 Cuþberht A. Cutberte T. Cuthberte HBP.   43 haec O₂H.   44 tui O₁A.   45 *ins.* et T.   46 contrariae HB. contraire P.
47 naturae O₂HB.   48 propter nature P.

intellegens[1], adhuc[2] tamen[3] ioci uanitatem[4] derelinquens, consolari infantem cepit[5]. Reuertensque[6] ad domum
f. 69   suam, prophetiae[7] uerba[8] in mente retinens[9], | sicut sancta
Luke 2. 51   Maria *omnia uerba* praedicta de Iesu[10] memorans *conseruabat.* Videte fratres quomodo iste antequam per laborem operum suorum[11] agnoscatur[12], per prouidentiam[13] Dei electus ostenditur. Sicut de[14] patriarcha per prophetam dicitur[15],
Mal.   *Iacob dilexi, Esau autem odio habui.* Samuhel[16] quoque et
1. 2, 3   Dauid, utrique in infantia electi inueniuntur. Hieremias[17] uero propheta[18], et Iohannes baptista, in officium[19] Domini
Jerem. 1. 5   *a uulua* matris[20] *sanctifica*ti leguntur. Sicut doctor gen-
Rom.   tium adfirmauit[21] dicens, *Quos autem*[22] *predestinauit*[23], *hos*
8. 30   *et uocauit,* [24]*et reliqua*[25].

IIII. *De eo quod*[26] *angelus sanauit eum*[27]

In eadem aetate[28] alio miraculo[29] Dei electione[30] predesti-natum[31], Dominus magnificauit[32] eum. Dum ergo esset puer iam ut dixi adhuc laicus, in[33] infirmitate premente eum[34] acriter detinebatur[35]. Nam quia[36] genu tumente[37] adstrictis[38] neruis claudicans, [39]pede altero[40] terram non[41] tangens[42] foris deportatus[43] iuxta parietem in solis ardore iacens, uidit hominem honorabilem et mirae[44] pulchritu-dinis[45] super equum ornatissimum in albis uestimentis sedentem, de longinquo ad se uenire[46]. Qui uero[47] adpro-pinquans[48] ei, salutansque[49] uerbis pacificis, interrogauit si uoluisset tali hospiti[50] ministrare. Ille etiam[51] intrepida[52] mente corporis infirmitatem reuelans[53] ait, Si Deus uoluis-set et me nodibus[54] infirmitatis[55] [56]pro peccatis non obligasset[57], in honorem eius ministrare hospitibus piger

1 *changed to* intelligens O₁, intelligens O₂HTBP. *ins.* nec HB.   2 *om.* O₂.
3 *om.* HB.   4 *ins.* non HBP.   5 coep... O₂AH.
6 Reuersusque HB.   7 prophetie TP.   8 *ins.* retinet P.
9 *om.* P.   10 Ihesu B.   .   11 suor. oper. B.
12 agnosceretur O₂.   13 prouidentia O₁.   14 *om.* P.
15 dicentem P.   16 Samuel AHTBP.   17 Iheremias BP.
18 pro. uer. HB.   19 offitio P.   20 *om.* P.   21 affirmat
O₂HTBP.   22 ante O₁.   23 prae... O₂.
24-25 *om.* O₂P.   26 *ins.* eum T.   27 eum san. A. *om.* T.
28 et... HP.   29 *ins.* ex HBP.   30 electioni O₁O₂.

stand, but he nevertheless gave up his vain games and began to console the child; and returning home, he kept in mind the prophetic words, just as St Mary kept in her memory all the words which were prophesied about Jesus. Behold, brethren, how even before he is recognised by the performance of his works, he is shown by the providence of God to be elect; even as it is said concerning the patriarch by the prophet: "Jacob have I loved but Esau have I hated." Samuel and David also are both found to have been chosen in their infancy. The prophet Jeremiah too and John the Baptist are said to have been sanctified for the work of the Lord from their mother's womb. So the teacher of the Gentiles affirmed, saying: "Whom he did-predestinate, them he also called" and so forth.

CHAPTER IV. *How he was healed by an angel*

While he was still the same age, the Lord by another miracle honoured him as one who had been predestined by the election of God. For when he was a boy, as I have said, and still of the laity, he was laid up with an infirmity which pressed cruelly upon him. His knee swelled, his sinews contracted, and he became so lame that one foot was unable to touch the ground. Once, when he had been carried outside and was lying near the wall in the warmth of the sun, he saw a man of noble appearance and of wondrous beauty, clad in white robes, come riding up to him from afar, upon a magnificently caparisoned horse. When he drew near, he saluted the boy with words of peace and asked him if he was willing to minister to him as a guest. Cuthbert, showing him his bodily infirmity, answered fearlessly, "If it had been God's will and if He had not bound me with the bonds of infirmity on account of my sins, I would

31 prae... O₂. predestinato HB. predestinata P.   32 magnificabat P.
33 *om.* HTBP.   34 *om.* P.   35 deten... T.   36 *om.* HTBP.
37 *ins.* et HBP.   38 ast... HBP.   39–40 pene P.   41 *om.* B.
42 attingens HTBP.   43 deportatur HBP. *ins.* et HBP.   44 mire HP.
45 pulcr... HT. pulcrh... B.   46 uenisse HTBP.   47 *om.* T.
48 app... O₂HBP. propinquans AT.   49 *ins.* eum HTBP.
50 hospite HB.   51 uero iam HB. iam TP.   52 trepida P.
53 releuans HBP.   54 nodis HBP.   55 infirmitatibus T.
56–57 non obl. pro pecc. meis HB. non obl. pro pecc. P.

non essem. Deinde itaque[1] uir ille post haec[2] uerba |
descendens[3] de equo, considerato genu eius quod a nullis
medicis ut dixerat ante curatum erat, precepit[4] ei dicens,
Coquere[5] farinam tritici, simul et lac, et cum[6] calido
unguens[7] linire debes. Puer autem post discessum uiri,
precepto[8] oboediens[9] angelum Dei esse intellexit. Post
paucos dies secundum fidem eius sanatus[10] est, gratias[11]
agebat[12] Deo miseranti[13] qui sanitatem integre[14] sicut
[15]cecato[17] Tobie[18],[16] per angelum suum curantem dederat.
Et ab[19] hoc tempore ut ille probatissimis uiris reuelauit,
angelorum auxilio deprecatus Dominum in maximis
angustiis suis non est defraudatus[20].

V. De eo quod animam episcopi ad coelum[21]
eleuari uidit[22]

Alio quoque tempore in adolescentia sua, dum adhuc
esset in populari uita, quando in montanis iuxta fluuium
quod[23] dicitur Ledir[24], cum aliis pastoribus pecora domini
sui pascebat, *pernoctans in uigiliis* secundum morem eius,
mente fideli, pura fide[25], uberrimis orationibus, uidit
uisionem quam ei Dominus reuelauit, hoc est coelo[26]
aperto[27] non reseratione elementorum, sed spiritalibus[28]
oculis intuens, sicut beatus Iacob patriarcha[29] in Luza[30]
quae cognominabatur[31] Bethel, *angelos ascendentes et descen-*
dentes[32] *uid*erat, et[33] inter manus eorum[34] animam sanctam,
quasi in globo igneo ad coelum[35] efferri[36]. Remque[37]
illam[38] tam mirabilem, statim suscitatis[39] pastoribus, ut
uiderat indicauit[40], prophetans[41] quoque eis animam esse
sanctissimi episcopi[42], aut alterius magne[43] persone[44] ut
rei effectus probabat[45]. Nam etenim[46] post paucos dies,

Marginal references:
f. 69b
Tob. c. 11
Sulp. Seu. Ep. III. 14
Gen. 28. 12

---

1 *om.* HBP.   2 hec TBP.   3 descens O₁.   4 prae... O₂.
5 coque HTBP.   6 *om.* T.   7 ungens HB. inungens P.
8 prae... O₂.   9 obed. HTBP.   10 saluatus HTBP.
11 *ins.* ergo HB.   12 agens P.   13 miserante HTB.
14 integrae A.   15–16 Tob. caec. H.   17 caec... O₂.
18 Tobiae O₂.   19 ob HB.   20 fraudatus B.
21 cel... T.   22 *om. chapter heading* A.   23 qui BP.
24 Ledyr B.   25 fid. pur. P.   26 celo T. coelum H. celum BP.

not be slow to minister to guests in his honour." The man thereupon descended from his horse and examining his knee, which, as Cuthbert had already explained, no doctor had tended, gave him these instructions: "You must cook wheat flour with milk, and anoint your knee with it, while it is hot." After the man had gone, the boy obeyed his command, perceiving that he was an angel of God. After a few days he was healed according to his faith, and gave thanks to God who had shown him pity and had completely cured him through the ministration of his angel, even as He had healed Tobias when he was blind. And from that time, as he revealed to men who can be fully trusted, whenever he prayed to the Lord in the times of his greatest distress, he was never denied the help of angels.

CHAPTER V. *How he saw the soul of a bishop being borne to heaven*

On another occasion, also in his youth, while he was still leading a secular life, and was feeding the flocks of his master on the hills near the river which is called the Leader, in the company of other shepherds, he was spending the night in vigils according to his custom, offering abundant prayers with pure faith and with a faithful heart, when he saw a vision which the Lord revealed to him. For through the opened heaven—not by a parting asunder of the natural elements but by the sight of his spiritual eyes—like blessed Jacob the patriarch in Luz which was called Bethel, he had seen angels ascending and descending and in their hands was borne to heaven a holy soul, as if in a globe of fire. Then immediately awaking the shepherds, he described the wonderful vision just as he had seen it, prophesying further to them that it was the soul of a most holy bishop or of some other great person. And so events

27 apertum HBP.   28 spiritualibus O₂TP. spiritalis B.   29 pat. Jac. P.
30 Lusa P.   31 cognomibatur A. cognominatur P.   32 desc. et asc. HTB.
33 *capital letter in* O₁.   34 *ins.* uidit P.   35 caelum O₂. celum ATBP.
36 deferri P.   37 rem namque HTB. regem P.   38 *om.* HTB.
igitur P.   39 sciscitans HB.   40 indicans P.   41 *capital letter in* O₁.
prophauit P.   42 *ins.* dixit HB.   43 magnae O₂H. persone P.
44 personae O₂H. magne P.   45 probauit HTBP.   46 *om.* HBP.

celeberrime[1] obitum sancti[2] episcopi nostri Aegdani[3], eadem hora noctis qua ille uiderat uisionem, longe lateque nuntiatum[4] esse audierunt.

f. 70   VI. *De eo quod Dominus eum[5] pascebat in uia[6]*

Unum adhuc miraculum[7] quod in iuuentute sua ei[8] contigit, non omitto. Pergenti namque[9] eo ab austro ad flumen quod Uuir[10] nominatur, in eo[11] loco[12] ubi[13] Kuncacester[14] dicitur, et[15] transuadato eo[16] ad habitacula[17] uernalia et aestualia[18], propter imbrem[19] et tempestatem[20] reuersus est[21]. Nam[22] quia[23] illo tempore hiemali[24] desertis habitaculis sibi et equo eius fatigato causa itineris et famis ab hominibus ibi[25] consolationem non inuenit, itaque[26] distrato[27] equo trahens[28] in domum et alligans ad parietem, expectans[29] serenitatem, oransque[30] sibi[31] ad Dominum, uidit equum capud[32] sursum[33] eleuantem ad tecta domun-

Psa. 128. 6   culi[34] partemque *foeni[35] tectorum* auide adprehendens[36] traxit ad se. Et[37] [38] cum quo[40] statim[39] panis calidus et[41] caro[42] inuolutus[43] in panne[44] linea[45] diligenter deorsum cadens emissus[46] est. Ille uero consummata oratione probauit[47], animaduertitque[48] sibi esse cibum[49] a Deo predestinatum[50] per emissionem angeli, qui sepe in angustiis suis adiuuauit[51] eum, gratias[52] agens Deo, benedixit et

1 Kings   manducauit. Iamiamque diuino *cibo[53]* saciatus[54] et suf-
19. 8   fultus, *in fortitudine* eius glorificans Dominum prospere proficiscebat[55].

---

1 caeleberrimum O₂. celeberrimi TP. celeberrimae B.   2 *om.* P.
3 Aedani H. Edani TBP.   4 nunciatum H.   5 eum Dom. T.
6 in uia pasc. AT.   7 mir. adh. O₂.   8 *om.* HTBP.
9 igitur P.   10 Iuur HB. Wir P.   11 eum HP.   12 locum HP.
13 qui P.   14 Kunnacester O₂. Concalestir H. Cuncacestir T.
Concalestyr B. Concarestir P.   15 *capital letter in* O₁.
16 *om.* O₂.   17 habicula A.   18 aestatualia O₁. estualia HTBP.
19 ymbrem TB.   20–21 diuertit P.   22 et P.   23 *om.* HTB.
24 hiemale T. hyemali BP.   25 sibi HB.   26 *capital letter in* O₁.
tamen P.   27 distracto O₂HB. destrato P.   28 *om.* B.

proved; for a few days afterwards, they heard that the death of our holy bishop Aidan, at that same hour of the night as he had seen the vision, had been announced far and wide.

CHAPTER VI. *How the Lord gave him food by the wayside*

There is still another miracle that I must not omit, which happened to him in his youth. Coming from the south to a river which is called the Wear, on reaching a place called Chester-le-Street, he crossed it and turned aside on account of the rain and tempest to some dwellings used only in spring and summer. But it was then winter time and the dwellings were deserted, so that he found no man to succour him and his horse, wearied as they were by their journey and by lack of food. So he unsaddled his horse and led it into the dwelling-place and, fastening it to the wall, he waited for the storm to cease. As he was praying to the Lord, he saw his horse raise its head up to the roof of the hut and, greedily seizing part of the thatch of the roof, draw it towards him. And immediately there fell out, along with it, a warm loaf and meat carefully wrapped up in a linen cloth. When he had finished his prayer, he felt it and found that it was food provided beforehand for him by God through the sending forth of his angel who often helped him in his difficulties. And he thanked God, blessed it and ate it: and now being satisfied and supported with divine food, and glorifying the Lord, he set forth prosperously in the strength of it.

29 exspectabat O_2. 30 *capital letter in* O_1. 31 *om.* HTBP.
32 caput O_2HTBP. 33 suum HP. 34 domuncula O_2. domuncule P.
35 feni TBP. 36 app... HB. sumens P. 37 *om.* HTB.
38–39 ecce P. 40 *ins.* et T. 41 cum P. 42 claro T. carne P.
43 *changed to* inuoluta O_2. 44 *changed to* panno O_2. panno HTBP.
45 *changed to* lineo O_2. lineo HTBP. 46 elapsus P. 47 *om.* HB.
48 *om.* que HB. aduertitque T. 49 cybum P. 50 prae... O_2.
destinatum HTBP. 51 adiuuabat HTBP. 52 *ins.* igitur HB.
itaque T. 53 cybo P. 54 satiatus AP. *ins.* est HBP.
55 profectus est HB. proficiscebatur TP.

VII. *De mirabilibus pretermissis*[1]

Cetera uero opera iuuentutis floride[2] pullulantia[3], silentio
pretereo[4], ne fastidium lectori ingererem[5,6], anhelans perfecte[7] aetatis[8] *pacatissimum fructum* in uirtutibus Christi
sub scruitio[9] Dei singulariter intimare. Omitto namque
quomodo[10] in castris contra hostem cum exercitu sedens,
ibique habente[11] stipendio[12] paruo[13], tamen[14] omne spa-
tium[15] habundanter[16] uiuens[17] | diuinae[18] auctus[19] est sicut
Danihel[20] et tres pueri cibo[21] regali non contenti, seruili
tamen[22] [23]et eo[24,25] paruissimo[26] mire saginati sunt.
[27]Nec[29] non[30,28] pretereo[31] quomodo animam[32] praefecti[33]
in obitu suo ad coelum[34] eleuari uidit. Taceo quoque
quam mire demones[35] effugauit, et insanientes uerbo
orationis suae[36] sanauit.

Heb.
12. 11

f. 70b
Dan. c. 1

Explicit liber I

1 *om. chapter heading* A.   2 floridae O_2H.   3 pululentia O_1A.
4 prae... O_2.   5 inger. lect. T.   6 ingererer O_1O_2. ingerer A.
7 perfectae H.   8 et... HTBP.   9 servicio H.   10 quo. nam. P.
11 habens P.   12 stipendium P.   13 paruum P. parua T.
14 *ins.* per P.   15 spacium HT.   16 abundanter P.
17 uiuuens O_1. conuiuans P.   18 diuinitus T.   19 actus T.

CHAPTER VII. *Concerning miracles which have been omitted*

The rest of the abundant works of the flower of his youth,
I pass over in silence, lest I should engender a distaste in the
reader, for I am eager to describe, one by one, the peaceable fruits
of his maturity, manifesting the power of Christ in the service
of God. I omit, therefore, how when dwelling in camp with
the army, in the face of the enemy, and having only meagre
rations, he yet lived abundantly all the time and was strengthened
by divine aid, just as Daniel and the three children, refusing
the royal food, flourished wonderfully on slaves' food and
that, too, very small in amount. And I omit as well how he
saw the soul of a reeve carried up to the sky on his death. I also
refrain from telling how wonderfully he put demons to flight
and healed the insane by his prayers.

End of Book I

20 Daniel HTB.   21 cybo P.   22 tantum HB.   23-24 *om.* HB.
25 A *breaks off here.*   26 *ins.* cibo HB.   27-28 *om.* HB.
29 haec O_1O_2.   30 nunc P.   31 prae... O_2. *ins.* etiam HB.
32 anima O_1O_2.   33 perfecti P. pre... T.   34 caelum O_2. celum TBP.
35 daem... O_2.   36 sue TBP.

Incipiunt capitula libri II[1]

I. De primordio uite[2] eius sub seruitio Dei.

II. De eo quod angelo ministrauit et tribus panibus a Deo donatus est.

III. De seruientibus illi animalibus marinis, et sanato fratre temptante[3].

IIII. De delphina carne sibi largiente Deo[4] et prophetia eius.

V. De eo quod aquila capiebat piscem per prophetiam serui Dei.

VI. De prophetia qua praeuidit inludere[5] diabolum[6] auditores eius.

VII. De eo quod nutricis suae habitacula ab urente flamma[7] imperio suo custodiuit.

VIII. De eo quod sanauit mulierem a demonio[8] uexatam[9].

I. De primordio uite eius sub seruitio[10] Dei[11]

Ath. Vit.
Ant.
cc. 5, 6

Bene ergo *disponens duriori*[12] *se uite*[13,14] *lege*[15] [16]in monasterio[17] *constringere*[18], a populari uita reuertens[19], religiosa[20] tamen atque[21] immaculata ad meliora proficiens, *sanctum laborem tolleranter*[22] *ferebat, quia*[23] *uoluntariae*[24] *seruitutis longum in Dei opere studium consuetudinemque in naturam*[25] *uerterat. Inedie*[26] *autem et uigiliarum in tantum patiens*[27] *erat, ut incredulitatem*[28] *uiribus uinceret. Pernoctabat*[29] *in oratione sepissime, nonnumquam* etiam[30] *bidui*[31] *triduique*[32] *sic permanens,*

f. 71
Heb.
12. 11

quarta demum die[33] *reficiebatur,* recordatus[34] Pauli | apostoli dictum, *Omnis* quidem[35] *disciplina in praesenti*[36] *quidem*[37] *uidetur non*[38] *esse gaudii sed meroris*[39]*. Postea autem fructum*

---

1 HTBP *omit list of chapters.* secundi O₂.   2 uitae O₂.   3 *om.* O₂.
4 Domino O₂.   5 illudere O₂. *ins.* a O₂.   6 diabolo O₁O₂.
7 flammina O₁.   8 daem... O₂.   9 vexatum O₁.   10 seruicio T.
11 Incipit liber secundus O₂.   12 durioris P.   13 uit. se HB.
14 uitae O₂.   15 *om.* HB.   16–17 monasterii se T.
18 constringens T.   19 *ins.* per HB.   20 *capital letter in* O₁.
religiosus P.   21 adque O₁. et HB.   22 toler... O₂.

The chapters of Book II

CHAPTER I. *Of the beginning of his life in the service of God*

So having arranged to bind himself by the more rigid rule of life in a monastery, leaving his secular life, pious and undefiled though it was, he advanced to better things and patiently bore the holy labour for, by long-standing zeal for voluntary bond-service in the work of God and by custom, it had become part of his nature. He was able to endure such fastings and such watchings that his strength silenced unbelief. He very often spent the whole night in prayer, sometimes even enduring a second and a third night, and refreshed himself only on the fourth day, remembering the words of the Apostle Paul, "Now no chastening for the present seemeth to be joyous but grievous; nevertheless afterwards it yieldeth the peaceable fruit

tolerabiliter P.   23 quam O₁O₂.   24 uoluntarie TBP.   25 natura O₁.
26 inediae O₂HB.   27 paciens H.   28 credulitatem HBP.
29 pernoctando HB.   30 *ins.* post HTBP.   31 biduum HTBP.
32 triduumque HTBP.   33 die demum P.   34 *ins.* beati P.
35 enim P.   36 pre... T.   37 *ins.* non HB.   38 *om.* HB.
39 maer... O₂. memoris O₁.

pacatissimum[1] *exercitatis*[2] *per eam* [3]*iustitie*[4] *reddit*[5]. O fratres conuersatione eius[6] dignum me[7] esse[8] non usurpo[9], quin immo nullius[10] sermone explicari[11] potest[12]. *Erat*

Actus
Siluestri

enim aspectu angelicus, sermone[13] *nitidus*[14]*, opere sanctus, corpore integer, ingenio optimus, consilio magnus, fide catholicus, spe patientissimus*[15]*, caritate*[16] *diffusus,* sed uirtutum tramitem enodabo.

II.   [17]*De eo quod angelo ministrauit et tribus panibus a Deo donatus est*[18]

Fuit igitur miraculum aliud, in quo primum sanctus homo Dei[19] Cuðberhtus[20] a Domino glorificatus est, postquam[21] seruitutis Christi iugum tonsuraeque Petri formam in modum corone[22] spineae[23] capud[24] Christi cingentis[25] Domino adiuuante susceperat, in cenobio[26] quod dicitur Hrypae[27], sicut nostri fidelissimi testes et adhuc uiuentes indicauerunt. Ministrare namque hospitibus aduenientibus statim neophitus[28] [29]a familia[30] electus est, inter[31] quos quidem[32] quadam die in matutina hora hiemali[33] et niuali

Gen. 18
1, 2

tempore, *apparuit ei* angelus *Domin*i in forma stabilis uiri perfectaque[34] aetate[35], sicut patriarchae[36] Abrahe[37] *in ualle Mambre*[38] angeli in forma uirorum[39] *apparuerunt*[40]. Deinde ergo[41] suscepto[42] eo secundum morem eius benigne, putans adhuc hominem esse, et[43] non angelum, lauatis manibus et pedibus linteaminibusque[44] tergens et manibus suis[45] humiliter propter frigorem[46] fricans et calefaciens pedes eius[47], et[48] ut horam diei tertiam[49] ad capiendum[50] cibum[51] expectaret[52], nolentem rennuentemque[53] |

f. 71 b

causa itineris diligentissime inuitabat. Et[54] postremo[55] tamen adiurando in nomine Domini nostri Iesu Christi,

---

1 *ins.* reddit B.   2 *ins.* reddit HP. reddet T.   3 A *begins again here.*   4 iustitiae O₂. iusticie TBP.   5 *om.* HTBP.
6 *ins.* explicare P.   7 me dig. HTBP.   8 *ins.* referre HB.
9 *ins.* enarrare T.   10 nullus T. nullo P.   11 explicare O₁O₂A.
12 posse O₂.   13 nomine H. *om.* B.   14 *ins.* nomine B.
15 pacientissimus HB.   16 karitate O₂.   17–18 De primordio uite eius sub seruicio Domini nostri T.   19 Dei homo HB.
20 Cuthbertus HBP. Cutbertus T.   21 *capital letter in* O₁.
22 coronae O₂HB.   23 spinee T.   24 caput O₂HTBP.
25 cingentes O₁O₂A. 26 coen... O₂. 27 Hyrpae O₁. Hyrpe O₂.

of righteousness to them that are exercised thereby". O brethren, I do not assume that I am worthy to tell his life, nay rather, no man's words can describe it. For he was angelic in appearance, refined in conversation, holy in works, unblemished in body, noble in nature, mighty in counsel, orthodox in faith, patient in hope, wide in charity. Let me, nevertheless, make clear the course of his miracles.

CHAPTER II. *How he ministered to an angel and was given three loaves by God*

Now this was another miracle in which Cuthbert the holy man of God was first glorified by the Lord, after he had by the Lord's help taken upon him the yoke of bondservice to Christ and the Petrine tonsure after the shape of the crown of thorns that bound the head of Christ, in the monastery which is called Ripon. This miracle our most trustworthy witnesses who are still alive have testified to. For while a neophyte, he was at once elected by the community to minister to guests on their arrival. Among these, on the morning of a certain day when the weather was wintry and snowy, an angel of the Lord appeared to him in the form of a well-built man in the flower of his age, just as angels appeared to the patriarch Abraham in the valley of Mamre in the form of men. Then having received him kindly in accordance with his wont, still thinking him to be a man and not an angel, he washed his hands and feet and wiped them with towels, and, having in his humility rubbed his guest's feet with his own hands to warm them on account of the cold, he invited him most urgently to wait until the third hour of the day to take food; but he was unwilling and refused on account of his journey. Finally Cuthbert adjured him in the

Hripe HTB. Rhipe P.   28 neophytus B.   29–30 *om.* HB.
31 *capital letter in* O₁.   32 *om.* HB.   33 hyemali O₂BP.
34 perfectaeque HB.   35 aetatis HB. et... TP.   36 patriarche TP.
37 Abrahae O₂H. Habrahe B.   38 Mambrae O₂. Manbre B.
39 *changed from* uiuorum A.   40 aparuerunt O₁.   41 *om.* HB.
42 accepto HBP.   43 *om.* HTBP.   44 linth... AH. lynth... B.
om. que BP.   45 *om.* O₁O₂.   46 frigus BP.   47 *om.* O₂P.
48 *capital letter in* O₁.   49 terciam HTBP.   50 capiendam P.
51 cibus O₁O₂. escam P.   52 exsp... O₂.   53 renitentemque HB.
renuentemque P.   54 ad HTP.   55 posttremo A. postremum HTBP.

consentiendo[1] superabat. Facto[2] iam signo diei[3] hore[4] tertiae[5] et oratione consummata[6], mensam statim adposuit[7] [8]praeparato[10] cibo[11] desuper quem habebat[9]. Panis enim ut[12] casu aliquo euenit[13], non erat in diuersorio nisi tamen[14] micas pro benedictione[15] panis[16] congregatas[17] super mensam constituit[18]. Ille etiam homo Dei reuertens ad monasterium querens[19] panem[20], et non[21] inuento eo, adhuc enim coquebant[22] panes in fornace[23], reuersus[24] uero[25] ad hospitem quem solum reliquerat[26] manducantem[27], et[28] non inuenit eum ibi[29], nec[30] uestigia pedum eius[31]. Iam enim [32]niuis[34] erat[33] super faciem terrae[35]. Obstupefacto[36] ergo sibi[37], mensam remouit ad cubiculum[38], intellegens[39] eum[40] angelum Dei esse[41]. Et primo in[42] introitu eius, nares odore[43] panis suauissimi[44] replete[45] sunt, et inuentis quoque[46] tribus panibus calidis, gratias agens[47] Domino quod[48] in eo impletum[49] est dictum Domini, *Qui recipit uos, me recipit. Et*[50] *qui recipit me*[51] *recipit eum qui me misit*[52]. Et iterum, *Qui recipit prophetam in nomine prophetae, mercedem prophetae accipiet.* [53]*Et qui*[55] *recipit iustum in nomine iusti, mercedem iusti accipiet*[54]. Et ab hac iam die frequenter esurienti[56] eo Dominus cibauit[57] eum, ut professus est fidelibus fratribus non propter iactantiam, sed propter[58] aedificationem[59] multorum, ut[60] Paulus de semetipso multa locutus est.

Matth.
10. 40, 41

III.   *De seruientibus illi animalibus marinis*
[61] *et sanato fratre temptante*[62]

Et[63] hoc dicendum puto quod relatu multorum bonorum[64] agnoui. [65]Ex quibus est[67] Plecgils[68] presbiter eo tempore quo fuit in monasterio quod nobiscum dicitur Mailros[69],[66].

1 consentientem HTBP.   2 *ins.* uero HB.   3 *om.* H. tercie BP.
4 horae O₂AH.   5 terciae HT. *om.* BP.   6 consumata O₁A.
7 app... O₂HTBP.   8–9 *om.* HB.   10 pre... T.   11 cybo P.
12 *om.* O₁O₂AT.   13 *om.* T.   14 tantum HBP.
15 benedicto O₁O₂A.   16 pane O₁O₂A.   17 congregans HTBP.
18 *ins.* preparato desuper cibo quem habebat HB. posuit T.
19 quaer... O₂H.   20 panes HB.   21 *om.* HB.
22 coquebantur HBP.   23 furno O₂.   24 *capital letter in* O₁.
25 *om.* HTBP.   26 relinquerat O₁. *om.* HTBP.   27 *ins.* reliquerat HTBP.   28 *om.* HBP.   29 *om.* HB.   30 *ins.* in niue HBP.

name of our Lord Jesus Christ and so won his consent. When the signal was given at the third hour of the day and prayer was over, he at once set out a table and spread thereon such food as he had. Now by some chance there was no bread in the guesthouse, save that he had placed some crumbs on the table as a blessed gift of bread. Thereupon the man of God went back to the monastery to seek a loaf; but failing to get any (for they were still baking in the oven) he returned to the guest whom he had left eating alone; but he did not find him nor even his footprints although there was snow over the surface of the ground. He was amazed and removed the table to the storehouse, realising that it was an angel of God. And immediately at the entrance, his nostrils were filled with the odour of the choicest bread and, finding three warm loaves, he gave thanks to God, because in him was fulfilled the saying of the Lord: "He that receiveth you receiveth me, and he that receiveth me receiveth him that sent me", and, again "He that receiveth a prophet in the name of a prophet shall receive a prophet's reward; and he that receiveth a righteous man in the name of a righteous man shall receive a righteous man's reward." And frequently from that day, when he was hungry, the Lord fed him, as he used to declare to faithful brethren, not boastfully, but for the edification of many, just as Paul told many things about himself.

CHAPTER III. *How the sea animals ministered to him and how a brother who tested him was healed*

And this incident I think should also be related, which I learned from the account of many good men, among whom is Plecgils a priest, at the time when he was in the monastery which we

31 eius ped. HBP.   32-33 ninxerat HB.   34 nix P.   35 terre TP.
36 obstupefactus HBP.   37 eo O_2. *om.* HTB. ipse P.
38 *ins.* ibat HBP.   39 intelligens HTBP.   40 *om.* HTB.
41 esse Dei B.   42 *om.* HB.   43 *om.* HB.   44 *ins.* odore HB.
45 repletae O_2H.   46 *om.* HTP.   47 agebat HB. egit T.   48 quia HTBP.
49 repletum HB.   50 *om.* T. que P.   51 me rec. P.
52 misit me HB.   53-54 *om.* HBP.   55 *om.* T. O_2 *breaks off here.*
56 esuriente TP.   57 cybauit P.   58 ob HB.   59 ed... HTBP.
60 *ins.* sanctus HBP.   61-62 *om.* T.   63 De T.   64 *om.* T.
65-66 *om.* HB.   67 *om.* P.   68 Plecgilf O_1. Pleggils T. Pleggilis P.
69 Meilros TP.

f. 72   Accersitus[1] est a sanctimoniali[2] | uidua matreque omnium
in Christo[3] Æbba[4]. Veniens ergo[5] ille ut inuitatus est
ad cenobium quod dicitur Colodesbyrig[6], manensque[7]
ibi aliquod[8] dies non deserens relaxando sue[9] constitu-
tionis[10] propositum, cepit[11] nocte maritima loca circuire[12]
morem consuetudinis cantandi et uigilandi seruans. Quo[13]
conperto[14], a quodam[15] clerico familie[16], qui[17] incipiebat
occulte de longinquo obsequi[18] eum temptando[19], scire
uolens quomodo uitam nocturnam transegeret[20]. Ille uero
homo Dei Cuðberht[21], inobstinata[22] mente adpropin-
quans[23] ad mare usque ad lumbare in mediis fluctibus[24],
[25]iam[27] enim[26] aliquando usque[28] ad ascellas[29] tumultuante
et fluctuante tinctus est. Dum[30] autem de mare[31] ascendens,
et in arenosis locis[32] litoris[33] flectens genua[34] orabat[35], uenerunt statim post uestigia eius duo pusilla[36] animalia maritima humiliter proni[37] in terram[38], lambentes[39] pedes eius[40],
uolutantes[41] tergebant pellibus suis, et calefacientes[42] odori-
bus[43] suis. Post seruitium[44] autem et[45] ministerio[46] impleto[47]
accepta ab eo benedictione, ad cognatas[48] undas maris[49]
recesserunt[50]. Ille iam[51] homo Dei in galli cantu reuertens[52]
ad orationem communem[53] cum fratribus ad[54] aecclesiam[55]
Dei, clericus[56] uero familiae[57] supradictus in scopulosis
locis[58] latens, uisu pauidus et tremebundus[59], tota nocte
coangustatus [60]prope mortem accederat[62],[61]. Crastina
autem die prosternens se ante pedes hominis Dei[63], flebili
uoce ueniam indulgentiae[64] deprecauit[65]. Cui homo Dei
prophetali sermone[66] respondit, Frater mi, quid est tibi?
Numquid propius adpropinquasti[67] mihi[68] temptando

1 accitus HTBP.   2 sancto moniali P.   3 *ins.* nomine HB.
4 Ebba HTBP. *ins.* abbatissa famularum Dei HTB. *ins.* abbatissa
famulantium Deo P.   5 itaque HTBP.   6 Colodesburc H.
Colodesburg T. Colodesburch B. Colodesbuc P.   7 mansit HBP.
8 aliquot HB.   9 sui T. suae H.   10 institutionis P.
11 coepit H. *capital letter in* O₁. *ins.* namque HBP.   12 circum-
ire P.   13 quod HBP.   14 ut compertum est HB. compertum
est P.   15 *om.* HB.   16 familiae H.   17 *om.* HB.
18 sequi HBP.   19 *om.* HB.   20 transigeret HB. transiret P.
21 *om.* HB. Cudbertus T. Cuthbertus B.   22 peruigili HB.
simplici T. obstinata P.   23 app... HBP.   24 fructibus P.
25–26 stetit HB.   27 *capital letter in* O₁.   30 tum P.
28 utque O₁.   29 *gloss above* vel ina A.

call Melrose; Cuthbert was sent for by the nun Aebbe, a widow, and the mother of them all in Christ. He came to the monastery which is called Coldingham, in response to the invitation, and remaining there some days, did not relax his habitual way of life but began to walk about by night on the seashore, keeping up his custom of singing as he kept vigil. When a certain cleric of the community found this out, he began to follow him from a distance to test him, wishing to know what he did with himself at night. But that man of God, approaching the sea with mind made resolute, went into the waves up to his loin-cloth; and once he was soaked as far as his armpits by the tumultuous and stormy sea. Then coming up out of the sea, he prayed, bending his knees on the sandy part of the shore, and immediately there followed in his footsteps two little sea animals, humbly prostrating themselves on the earth; and, licking his feet, they rolled upon them, wiping them with their skins and warming them with their breath. After this service and ministry had been fulfilled and his blessing had been received, they departed to their haunts in the waves of the sea. But the man of God, returning home at cockcrow, came to the church of God to join in public prayer with the brethren. The above-mentioned cleric of the community lay hidden amid the rocks, frightened and trembling at the sight and, being in anguish all night long, he came nigh to death. The next day he prostrated himself before the feet of the man of God and, in a tearful voice, prayed for his pardon and indulgence. The man of God answered him with prophetic words: "My brother, what is the matter with you? Have you approached nearer me, to test me, than

31 mari HTBP. 32 har... HB. *om.* O₁. 33 litt... HB.
34 gen. flect. HBP. 35 oraret HTB. *ins.* et ecce P. 36 pussilla O₁A.
37 prona HBP. 38 terra P. 39 lambentia HBP. 40 *om.* O₁.
ins. et se HB. 41 uolutantia HBP. 42 calefaciebant HB. calefacientia P.
43 aloribus P. 44 seruicii H. seruitii B. 45 *om.* HB.
46 ministerium HTBP. 47 impletum HTBP. 48 cognitas T.
incognitas HB. 49 maris undas P. 50 recessere B. 51 uero HB.
52 est *in marg.* O₁. reuersus est HTBP. 53 *om.* P. 54 in HTBP.
55 ecclesia P. eccl.... T. 56 *capital letter in* O₁. 57 familie AT.
om. HB. 58 *cm.* HTBP. 59 *ins.* et HB. 60–61 fere mortuus
erat HB. 62 deuenerat T. accesserat P. 63 *ins.* humiliter et HB.
ins. humiliter TP. 64 indulgentie TB. 65 deprecatus est HTBP.
66 uoce HBP. 67 app... HBP. 68 michi T.

f. 72b   quam debuisti? Et[1] tamen hoc tibi | confitenti[2] uno modo indulgetur, si uotum uoueris, numquam te esse quamdiu[3] uixero[4] narraturum. Frater autem sic uouens et perficiens, benedictus et saluatus ab eo exiit[5]. Post uero obitum[6] eius multis fratribus narrans seruitionem[7] ani-

Dan. c. 6   malium, sicut leones in ueteri[8] legimus[9] Danihelo[10] seruire[11], et quod spiritalibus oculis latitantem eum et

Acts c. 5   probantem, sicut[12] uiderat[13] Petrus[14] Annaniam[15] et Saphiram[16] spiritum sanctum temptantem[17], mirabiliter defamauit[18].

IIII. *De delfina[19] carne sibi largiente Domino et prophetia eius[20]*

Alio quoque tempore de eodem monasterio quod dicitur Mailros[21], cum duobus fratribus pergens et nauigans ad terram Pictorum, ubi dicitur[22] Niuduera regio[23] prospere peruenerunt. Manserunt autem ibi aliquod[24] dies in magna penuria, nam famis[25] premebat eos et tempestas maris potestatem iterum[26] nauigandi prohibuit[27]. Ille uero homo Dei pernoctans iuxta litora[28] maris in oratione, peruenit ad eos mane in die Epiphanie[29] Domini. Nam etenim[30] post diem[31] nataliciae[32] Domini pergere ceperunt[33]. Suadens autem, dixit eis, Eamus et queramus[34] petentes a Deo

Matth.   secundum id quod promisit dicens[35], *Petite et dabitur uobis[36]*.

7. 7   [37]*Querite et inuenietis. Pulsate et aperietur uobis[38]*. Puto enim quod aliquid nobis [39]Dominus[41] donauerit[40], ad celebrandum diem in quo magi cum muneribus adorauerunt eum, et in quo spiritus sanctus in specie columbe[42] baptizato[43] in Iordane super eum descendit, et in quo aquam in Chana[44] Galileae[45] uertit in uinum, ad confirmandam

---

1 hoc O₁A.   2 confitendi P.   3 quam T.
4 dixero T. uixeris B.   5 exiit ab eo HBP.   6 ob. uero HTBP.   7 seruitium HTBP.   8 *ins.* testamento P.
9 legemus T.   10 Daniheli H. Daniel T. Danieli BP.
11 seruisse HBP.   12 *om.* P.   13 *ins.* sicut P.   14 Pet. uid. B.
15 Ananiam HBP.   16 Saphyram TBP.   17 temptantes P.
18 diff... HBP.   19 delphina A. delfino T.   20 eius prop. T.
21 Mauros P.   22 *om.* O₁A.   23 Niudpæralegio O₁A.

you should have done? nevertheless, since you admit it, you shall receive pardon on one condition; that you vow never to tell the story so long as I am alive." The brother made the vow and kept it afterwards and departed with his blessing, healed. But after Cuthbert's death he told many brethren how the animals ministered to the saint, just as we read in the Old Testament that the lions ministered to Daniel, and related how Cuthbert, to his amazement, had seen him with his spiritual eyes, when he was lying hid and testing him, just as Peter detected Ananias and Sapphira when they were tempting the Holy Spirit.

CHAPTER IV. *Concerning the dolphin flesh which the Lord provided for him and concerning his prophecy*

At another time also, he went from the same monastery which is called Melrose with two brothers, and, setting sail for the land of the Picts, they reached the land called the region of the Niduari in safety. They remained there some days in great want, for hunger afflicted them and the tempestuous sea prevented them from continuing their voyage. But the man of God, after spending the night near the shore in prayer, came to them in the morning of the day of the Epiphany of the Lord, for they had started out after Christmas. Thereupon he urged them saying: "Let us go and seek, asking God to fulfil his promise when he said: 'Ask and it shall be given you, seek and ye shall find, knock and it shall be opened unto you.' For I think that the Lord will give us something to celebrate the day on which the Magi worshipped him with gifts and on which the Holy Ghost in the form of a dove descended upon him at his baptism in Jordan, and on which he turned water into wine in Cana of Galilee to confirm the faith

Niuduera iregio P. 24 aliquot HB. 25 fames HTBP.
26 itineris O₁. 27 *changed to* prohibita est A. *ins.* eis P.
28 litt... HTBP. 29 Epiphaniae H. Epyphaniae B. 30 *om.* HB. et
T. statim P. 31 *om.* O₁O₂A. 32 natalicii HB. natalicium TP.
33 ceperant HB. 34 quaer... H. 35 dixit T. 36 *ins.* et caetera HB.
37-38 *om.* HB. 39-40 donabit TP. 41 *om.* HB.
42 columbae H. 43 baptyzato B. *ins.* eo HB. 44 Cana T.
45 Galilee TP. Galylee B.

fidem[1] discipulorum suorum[2]. Tunc itaque surgentes exierunt. Ille autem precedens eos quasi preuiator, usque ad mare peruencrunt. Et statim uidentes[3] tres partes delfini[4] carnis[5] | quasi humano[6] manu cum cultella[7] sectas[8], et[9] aqua mundatas inuenerunt. Homo igitur Dei prouolutis[10] genibus gratias agens Domino, dixit sociis suis, Tenete portantes et benedicite Dominum. Ecce enim[11] tres partes tribus uiris [12]tribusque[14] noctibus et diebus sufficiunt[13]. Quarta[15] uero die serenum erit mare ad nauigandum. Illi namque[16] portauerunt[17] et[18] coxerunt, mirabilemque[19] suauitatem[20] carnis degustauerunt. Manentes[21] autem tribus diebus[22] ualida tempestate, quarta[23] die secundum uerbum eius in serenitate nauigantes prospere portum salutis tenuerunt, sicut nobis[24] unus e duobus fratribus supra[25] nomine Tydi[26] qui presbiter est adhuc uiuens[27] coram multis testibus indicauit, glorificans[28] Deum quod eadem misericordia tunc homini Dei, qua et olim in deserto Helie[29] carnes largitus est. Et eodem spiritu imbutus tempestatem et serenitatem praeuidit, quo et Paulus apostolus in actibus apostolorum nauigantibus prophetauit.

f. 73

I Kings 17. 6

Acts c. 27

V. *De eo quod aquila capiebat piscem per[30] prophetiam serui Dei[31]*

Supradictus autem presbiter Tydi[32] aliud miraculum quod multis cognitum est indicauit. Alia[33] die[34] proficiscebat[35] iuxta fluuium Tesgeta tendens in meridiem inter montana docens rusticanos et[36] baptizabat[37] eos[38]. Habens quoque puerum in comitatu eius[39] secum ambulantem, dixit [40]ad eum[41], Putasne quis tibi hodie prandium preparauit[42]? Cui[43] respondente,[44] nullum in illa uia[45] scire cognatum

1 om. B.   * 2 ins. fidem B. ins. In eodem quoque die sancto Augustino testante (attestante TP) de quinque panibus et duobus piscibus saturauit Dominus quinque milia hominum HTBP.   3 om. HB.   4 delphini O₁A. delfine P.   5 carnes T. om. P.
6 humana AHTBP.   7 cultello HTBP.   8 factas P.
9 in P.   10 prouolutus P.   11 ins. hae H. ins. he B.
12–13 suff. trib. dieb. et trib. noct. P.   14 om. que HBP.
15 quarto T.   16 itaque HB.   17 deportantes HB.

of his disciples." They then arose and went out. He went in front of them as though he were the forerunner, until they came to the sea. And immediately they looked and found three portions of dolphin's flesh as though they had been cut by a human hand with a knife and washed with water. So the man of God, kneeling down, gave thanks to the Lord and said to his companions: "Take them and carry them away and bless the Lord. For behold three portions are sufficient for three men for three days and three nights; but on the fourth day, the sea will be calm for sailing." So they took them away and cooked them and enjoyed the wonderful sweetness of the flesh. They remained three days amid a fierce tempest and on the fourth day, according to his word, they prosperously reached a port of safety after a calm voyage. So one of the two brethren mentioned above named Tydi, who is a priest and still alive, declared to us before many witnesses; and he glorified God because He then bestowed flesh upon the man of God with the same mercy as He had once bestowed it in the desert upon Elijah, and because, inspired by the same Spirit, Cuthbert foresaw the tempest and the calm, just as the Apostle Paul did in the Acts of the Apostles when he prophesied to the voyagers.

CHAPTER V. *How an eagle caught a fish in accordance with the prophecy of the servant of God*

Now the above-mentioned priest Tydi spoke of another miracle which is known to many. On a certain day, he was going along the river Teviot and making his way southward, teaching the country people among the mountains and baptizing them. Having a boy walking with him in his company he said to him: "Do you think that someone has prepared you your midday meal to-day?" He answered that he knew of none of their

18 *om.* HB.   19 et mirabilem T.   20 *ins.* que P.   21 manente T.
22 *ins.* in HB.   23 *ins.* uero P.   24 *om.* HBP.   25 supradictis HTBP.
26 Tydius HB. Tidi T.   27 *ins.* nobis HB.   28 *capital letter in* O₁.
29 Heliae H. Helye TBP.   30 secundum T.   31 *ins.* excelsi T.
32 *om.* HB.   33 alio HTBP.   34 -e *above* O₁.   35 proficiscebatur HTBP.
36 *om.* HBP.   37 baptyzabat B. baptizansque P.   38 *om.* O₁.
39 *om.* P.   40-41 ei HB.   42 preparauerit HTB. ministrabit P.
43 qui HB.   44 respondit HTBP. *ins.* se HB.   45 *ins.* se P.

et nec ab alienis[1] incognitis aliquid[2] genus misericordiae sperantem[3], seruus autem[4] Domini, iterum[5] ait [6]ad eum[7], Confide fili, Dominus[8] prouidebit uictum speran-

Matth.
6. 33

tibus[9] in se, qui[10] dixit, [11]*Quaerite ergo*[13] *primum*[12] *regnum Dei et iustitiam*[14] *eius, et haec omnia adicientur*[15] *uobis.* Et[16] ut impleatur prophetae dictum, | *Iunior fui, etenim*[17] *senui,*

f. 73 b
Psa. 36. 25
Luke
10. 7

et non[18] *uidi iustum derelictum,* et reliqua. *Dignus est*[19] nam-que[20] *operarius mercede sua*[21]. Ergo post talia[22] uerba intuens in celum[23], uidit aquilam uolantem in aere[24], dixit[25] puero suo, Haec est aquila cui praeceperat[26] Dominus ministrare nobis hodie cibum[27]. Post paululum autem iter agentibus illis, uiderunt aquilam super ripam fluminis sedentem. Currens[28] etiam ad aquilam[29] puer secundum praeceptum[30] serui Dei, hesitans[31], inuenit piscem grandem, portantique ad eum integrum, dixit puero, Cur piscatori nostro ieiunanti partem ad uescendum non dedisti? Tunc uero[32] puer, sicut praeceperat[33] homo[34] Dei, partem piscis aquilae[35] dedit. Alteram autem secum portantes [36]inter homines[37] assauerunt et manducauerunt. Aliisque[38] dederunt, et satiati[39] [40]adorantes Dominum[41] gratiasque[42] agentes [43]in uoluntate Dei[44], ad montana ut[45] supra[46] diximus[47] pro-

Matth.
28. 19

ficiscebant[48] *docentes*[49] et *baptizantes*[50] *eos*[51], *in nomine patris et filii, et spiritus sancti.*

VI. *De prophetia qua praeuidit*[52] *inludere*[53]
diabolum[54] *auditores eius*

Eo[55] tempore ibi inter[56] montana[57] baptizans[58] ut diximus[59] in uilla quadam[60], uerbum Domini [61]secundum morem eius diligenter[62] docuit[63]. Prophetali[64] spiritu Dei[65] prae-

1 *ins.* et P.   2 aliquod HTBP.   3 sperare HBP.   4 *om.* T.
5 *om.* HB.   6–7 ei HB.   8 *ins.* autem HB.   9 speranti HTBP.
10 *capital letter in* O₁.   11–12 primum querite HBP.   13 *om.* T.
14 iusticiam HTBP.   15 addic... T.   16 *om.* P.   17 et HTB.
18 *ins.* inde HTBP.   19 *om.* TP.   20 enim HB. *ins.* est TP.
21 merc. sua oper. HBP.   22 alia O₁.   23 coelum H.
24 *ins.* et P.   25 *add* que TB.   26 praecepit HB. precepit P.
27 cybum P.   28 cucurrens O₁A.   29 eam HB.   30 pre... T.
31 *om.* HB.   32 *om.* HB.   33 pre... T.   34 uir O₁A.

kindred along that way and he did not hope for any sort of kindness from unknown strangers. The servant of God said again to him : "My son, be of good cheer; the Lord will provide food for those who hope in him, for he said, 'Seek ye first the Kingdom of God and his righteousness and all these things shall be added unto you' in order that the saying of the prophet may be fulfilled: 'I have been young and now am old, yet have I not seen the righteous forsaken', and so forth. 'For the labourer is worthy of his hire.'" After some such words he looked up to heaven and saw an eagle flying in the sky and said to his boy: "This is the eagle which the Lord has instructed to provide us with food to-day." After a short time, as they went on their way, they saw the eagle settling on the bank of the river. The boy ran towards the eagle in accordance with the command of the servant of God, and stopping, he found a large fish. The boy brought the whole of it to him, whereupon Cuthbert said: "Why did you not give our fisherman a part of it to eat since he was fasting?" Then the boy, in accordance with the commands of the man of God, gave half of the fish to the eagle while they took the other half with them, and broiling it in the company of some men, they ate it, and gave some to the others and were satisfied, worshipping the Lord and giving thanks. Then they set out according to God's will to the mountains, as we have said above, teaching and baptizing the people in the name of the Father and of the Son and of the Holy Ghost.

CHAPTER VI. *Concerning his prophecy wherein he foresaw the devil deluding his hearers*

At that time, while baptizing there among the mountains, as we said, he was diligently teaching the word of the Lord at a certain village in accordance with his custom, and there, by

35 aquile TBP.   36–37 *om.* HB.   38 aliosque O₁.   39 saciati HB.
40–41 *om.* HB.   42 *om.* que HB.   43–44 Domino HB.
45 sicut B.   46 *om.* HB.   47 prediximus HB.
48 proficiscebantur HTB.   profecti sunt P.   49 *ins.* eos HBP.
50 baptyzantes B.   51 *om.* HBP.   52 uidit T.   53 ill... T.
54 diabolo O₁A.   55 eodem P.   56 in HTBP.   57 montanis HB.
58 baptyzans B.   59 dixi HTB.   60 quidam O₁.   61–62 *om.* HB.
63 *ins.* et T.   64 *add* que HB.   65 Dei spir. B.

uidit[1] temptantem diabolum, et uerbi[2] Domini[3] auditum[4] retardare uolentem, inludentis[5] fantas iam predicens, inter alia uerba ait, O fratres karissimi[6], si aliqua temptatio exorta foris repente extiterit, uos tamen *stabiles estote*, nec[7] foras currentes a[8] uerbi Dei auditione tardamini[9], per inlusionem[10] proibiti[11]. Post haec[12] iterum cepto ordine [13]euangelii[15] uerba exponens[16],[14], audierunt[17] accensa[18] domu[19] strepitum[20] ignis uociferantesque homines. Tunc itaque[21] homines[22] exceptis paucis quos manu retinuit, instabiliter[23] currentes | prosiluerunt[24], et ad domum quasi inflammatam usque peruenerunt dissipantes[25] parietes eius, extinguere flammam[26] uolentes[27]. Deinde ergo[28] extimplo[29] nec saltim uestigia fumi quod[30] ignem[31] praecedit[32], [33]et[35] sequitur[34], uidentes[36] et agnoscentes se inlusos[37] esse[38] secundum praedictum[39] serui Dei[40] [41]per fantasiam diaboli[42] ad domum unde uenerunt[43] reuersi sunt, prouolutis[44] genibus[45] [46]ante pedes praedicatoris[48]. Orante [49]iam eo[50] pro illis per inlusionem[51] Satane[52] fallatos[53],[47], ueniam indulgentie[54] perpetrauerunt[55], confitentes se[56] multifariam fallacis[57] astutie[58] seductionem spiritalem[59] [60]per uisibilia fantasia[62],[61] intelligere[63]. Igitur unusquisque[64] per doctrinam eius[65] bene emendatus et confirmatus gaudens[66] ad [67]domum suam[68] reuersi sunt[69].

VII. *De eo quod nutricis suae habitacula[70]* *[71] ab urente flamma imperio suo[72] custodiuit*

Eodem tempore inuitatus est sanctus homo Dei, a quadam muliere [73]quae dicitur Kenspið[75], adhuc uiuens[76],[74]

I Cor.
15. 58

f. 74

1 pre... T.   2 uerbum HB.   3 Dei P.   4 *om.* HB.
5 ill... HBP. *add* que T.   6 carissimi AP.   7 ne HB.
8 *om.* P.   9 tardemini HB.   10 ill... HTBP.
11 prohibiti AHTBP.   12 hec TBP.   13–14 exponens euangelica uerba P.   15 euangelica HTB.   16 exponente T.   17 *capital letter in* O₁.   18 accensae HBP. accensam T.   19 domus HBP. domum T.   20 crepitum HB. crepitus P.   21 *om.* HB.
22 omnes HB.   23 *om.* HB.   24 prosilierunt HBP.
25 disipantes T. *add* que HB. dissipauerunt P.   26 flammas T.
27 uolebant HB.   28 *om.* HB.   29 extymplo B.
30 qui AP. quae HB. quidem T.   31 ex igne A. *om.* T.
32 procedit A. praecedere solet HB. pre... T.   33–34 *om.* HB.

the prophetic Spirit of God, he foresaw the devil tempting them and trying to hinder the hearing of the word of the Lord. So foretelling the illusion of the deceiver, he said amongst other things: "O beloved brethren, if any temptation should suddenly arise outside, be steadfast and do not run out and be prevented from hearing the word of God, nor be hindered by an illusion." Afterwards, when he had resumed his exposition of the Gospel, they heard the noise of fire from a burning house and men shouting. Then the men, with the exception of a few whom he had kept back with his hand, sprang up and ran out recklessly and came to the house which appeared to be in flames, and demolished the walls, seeking to extinguish the flames. Then, seeing no trace of the smoke which precedes and follows fire, at once they realised that they had been deceived, according to the prediction of the servant of God, through an illusion of the devil; and returning to the dwelling whence they had come, they fell on their knees before the feet of the preacher. He prayed for those who had been deceived by an illusion of Satan and they won pardon and indulgence on confessing that they realised that it was one of the manifold spiritual seductions of fallacious cunning brought about by imaginary sights. And one and all of them, being greatly improved and strengthened by his teaching, returned home rejoicing.

CHAPTER VII. *How by his commands he preserved the dwellings of his nurse from a blazing fire*

At the same time the holy man of God was invited by a certain woman called Kenswith, who is still alive, a nun and widow

---

35 *capital letter in* O₁.   36 *capital letter in* O₁.   37 delusos HB. ill... TP.
38 *om.* HB.   39 uerbum HB. pre... T.   40 Dei serui B.
41–42 *om.* HB.   43 uenerant HB.   44 prouoluti P. *add* que HB.
45 *ins.* eius HB.   46–47 *om.* HB.   48 pre... TA. *ins.* et P.
49–50 illo P.   51 ill... TP.   52 Sathane TP.
53 seductos T. deceptis P.   54 indulgentiae AHB.   55 impetrauerunt
HTBP.   56 *ins.* per HB.   57 *om.* HB.   58 astucie T. astutiae HB.
59 spiritualem P.   60–61 quoque HB.   62 fantasmata P.
63 intellere O₁. intellegere A.   64 *om.* HB.   65 *ins.* unus quisque HB.
66 est sicque HB.   67–68 sua HB.   69 reuertitur P.
70 habitaculum T.   71–72 ab igne orando T.   73–74 *om.* HB.
75· Coensuid T. Coesuid P.   76 uiuente P.

sanctimonialis[1] uidua, quae[2] enutriuit eum ab octo annorum[3] usque ad perfectam aetatem[4] in qua seruitium[5]
Dei arripuit. Ideo namque eam matrem appellauit, et sepe
uisitans eam, uenit quadam die ad uillam in qua habitabat,
[6]quae[8] dicitur Hruringaham[9,7], tunc[10] ardente domu[11]
quae[12] in extrema parte uici ad orientem posita uidebatur.
Et de[13] eodem[14] climate[15] flante maximo uento ignis
excitatus est. Mater uero pauida ad domum ubi manebat
cucurrit, et ut auxilium Dei petere dignetur[16] a globeis[17]
ignis[18] circumdantibus habitacula eorum[19] seruare[20] popos-
cit[21]. Ille iam[22] intrepida mente matri [23]stabilitatem inti-
mauit dicens[24], *Noli timere*, hec[25] enim flamma tibi non
nocet[26]. Et procidens[27] ante ianuam pronus in terram[28],
orauit [29]in silentio[30]. Et[31] statim [32]etiam[34] deprecante[35]
eo[33] uentus[36] ingens extitit[37] ab occidente, et omnem |
magnitudinem flamme[38] a domibus innocenter abegit. Et
sic euidenter in se[39] esse Dei uirtutem uidentes[40] [41]protec-
tione[43] eius innoxii seruati sunt[42]. Gratias[44] agentes,
benedixerunt Dominum[45].

Gen. 15. 1

f. 74*b*

VIII. *De eo quod sanauit mulierem a daemonio*[46] *uexatam*

Fuit quidam uir religiosus[47] specialiter carus homini Dei
[48]nomine Hildmaer[50,49], cuius uxor a demonio vexabatur
nimis. Illa namque multum uastata et usque ad exitum
mortis coangustata, frendens dentibus gemitum lacrima-
bilem[51] emittebat. [52]Supradictus uero[53] uir de amara
morte nihil[54] dubitans ad monasterium nostrum proficiscens, uocauit ad se sanctum[55] Cuðberhtum[56], nam[57]
etenim[58] illo[59] tempore aecclesiae[60] nostrae[61] praepositus[62]
erat, indicans ei uxorem suam pene usque ad mortem

---

1 sancta monialis O1. sanctimoniali HBP.   2 que TBP.
3 *ins.* spatio HB. annis TP.   4 etat...TBP.   5 seruicium H.
6–7 *om.* HB.   8 que T.   9 ʰruringaham A. runingaham T.
rimingaha P.   10 *ins.* autem HTBP.   11 domo HTBP.   12 que
TBP.   13 *om.* T.   14 eadem T.   15 clima O1T. clymate B.
16 dignaretur P. *ins.* quod HB. *ins.* et T.   17 globis HTBP.
18 igneis HBP.   19 eius HB.   20 seruarentur HB. seruari T.
21 deposcit P.   22 uero HB.   23–24 dicebat HB.   25 haec AH.

who had brought him up from his eighth year until manhood, when he entered the service of God. For this reason he called her mother and often visited her. He came on a certain day to the village in which she lived, called *Hruringaham*; on that occasion a house was seen to be on fire on the eastern edge of the village and from the same direction a very strong wind was blowing, causing a conflagration. His mother, in great fear, ran to the house in which he was and begged him to deign to ask help of God in order that their dwellings might be preserved from the masses of flame surrounding them. With fearless mind, he urged her to be steadfast, saying: "Fear not, for the flame does not harm you." And falling prone upon the earth before the door, he prayed in silence and immediately, even while he was praying, there arose a mighty wind from the west and drove away the whole volume of flame harmlessly from the houses. And so they were preserved unhurt by his protection and, seeing that a miracle of God was plainly wrought among them, they gave thanks and blessed the Lord.

CHAPTER VIII. *How he healed a woman vexed by a devil*

There was a certain religious man, specially dear to the man of God, named Hildmer, whose wife was much vexed by a devil. She was greatly ravaged and afflicted to the point of death, grinding her teeth and uttering tearful groans. Now the above-mentioned man, not doubting that she would die a cruel death, set out for our monastery and called St Cuthbert to him (for at that time he was prior of our church) and explained to him that his wife was sick almost to death. He did not reveal that

26 nocebit HB.   27 procedens T.   28 orationem HB.
29–30 *om.* HB.   31 *ins.* ecce P.   32–33 *om.* HB.   34 *om.* P.
35 deprecanti T.   36 uentis O₁. *changed from* uentis A.   37 uenit HB.
38 flammae HB.   39 eo HTB.   40 *ins.* Dei T. *ins.* dum P.
41–42 *om.* HB.   43 *ins.* et T.   44 *add* que T.   45 Deum HTBP.
46 demone T.   47 reliosus T.   48–49 *om.* HB.   50 Hildmær A.
Hildimer TP.   51 lacrimabile O₁A.   52–53 huius HB.   54 nichil HTBP.
55 *om.* B.   56 Cuthbertum HBP.   Cudbertum T.   57 *capital letter*
in O₁. illo HB.   58 et T. *om.* P.   59 *om.* HB.   60 ecclesie TP.
ecclesiae B.   61 nostre TP.   62 pre... T.

infirmantem, non[1] quae[2] calamitas esset insaniae[3] reuelauit. [4]Iam enim[5] erubescebat illam olim religiosam,
tamen[6] a demonio uexatam indicare. Nesciebat etiam[7]
nec intellegens[8], quod[9] talis temptatio frequenter chris-
tianis[10] accidere[11] solet. Sed tantum presbiterum aliquem
secum[12] mittere[13], et[14] requiem sepulture[15] deposcebat[16].
Statim autem homo Dei preparare aliquem ad mittendum
cum illo exiit. Et primo recessu eius a spiritu Dei inbutus[17],
cito conuersus reuocans eum dixit, Hoc quippe[18] ministerium meum est, et non est alterius tecum pergere[19].
Tunc[20] uero preparauit se[21] homo Dei, et omnes [22]simul
portati sunt equis[23], et uidens socium suum flentem et
lacrimantem duobus[24] causis, hoc est pro moriente uxore
[25]sibi[27] deserto[28,26] et orbanis[29] relictis[30], et maxime[31] pro[32]
ignominiosa[33] insaniae[34], in qua horribiliter[35] redactam[36]
[37]et inpudenter[39] confractam[38] et saliua pollutam, olim
iam pudicam et castam, sciens[40] [41]homini Dei exspectanda[43]
erat[44,42], consolari[45] eum cepit[46] | mitissimis uerbis, et om-
nem infirmitatem quam ei[47] celauerat qualis esset reuelauit.
Et postremo addit[48], prophetico ore dicens[49], Iam enim[50]
quando ueniemus ad habitacula uestra, uxor tua quam
mortuam putas in[51] obuiam mihi[52] occurrens in accep-
tione habenarum[53] istius equi[54] quas[55] nunc[56] [57]in manibus[58] teneo per Dei adiutorium effugata[59] demone saluata
ministrabit nobis. Igitur[60] peruenerunt[61] sicut diximus[62],
homo Dei[63] ad uillam, et[64] mulier quasi de[65] somno
surgens uenit in obuiam, et primo tacto[66] freni plene[67]
pulsato[68] demone sanitati pristine[69] reddita, ut illa cum
gratiarum actione testata est[70] ministrauit illis.

Explicit liber II

1 nec HB. nam T.   2 que T.   3 insanie TBP.
4–5 namque P.   6 tunc HBP.   7 enim HBP.   8 intelligebat
HB. intelligens T. intellexit P.   9 quia HTBP.   10 ins. ob
negligentiam HB.   11 accedere T.   12 ins. rogat HB.
13 mitteret T. mitti P.   14 ob HB.   15 sepulturae B.
16 om. HB.   17 imb... HTBP.   18 om. HTB
19 ins. uolo T.   20 tum P.   21 se prep... HB.   22–23 sui T.
24 duabus de HB. duabus P.   25–26 om. HB.   27 se P.
28 desertum P.   29 orph... HTB. orphanos P.   30 relictos P.
31 maximae B.   32 om. HTBP.   33 ignominiose T.
34 insania HBP. insanie T.   35 orribiliter P.   36 redactum O₁.

she was afflicted with madness, for he was ashamed to declare that a woman once so religious was oppressed by a devil, neither knowing nor understanding that such a trial is wont to fall frequently upon Christians; but he only asked Cuthbert to send a priest with him and that she might find peace in the grave. Now forthwith, the man of God went out to prepare someone to send with him; but hardly had Hildmer departed, when being filled with the Spirit of God, he turned quickly, called him back and said: "It is my duty and not another's, to go with you." Then the man of God prepared himself and they all rode together on horseback; his companion was weeping and mourning for two reasons, because his wife was dying and he was bereaved and his children left desolate, and more especially because of the disgraceful insane condition in which he knew that she was about to be seen by the man of God, whereby she was horribly degraded and shamelessly destroyed and polluted with spittle, she who had once been so modest and chaste. Knowing this the man of God began to console him with kindly words and revealed fully the nature of her infirmity, which the husband had hidden from him, and finally added with prophetic words: "Now when we come to your house, your wife whom you believe to be dead will come to meet me and on receiving this horse's reins which I hold in my hand, will, through the help of God, be restored to full health and will minister to us, and the demon will be driven away." So they came to the homestead, as we have said, the man of God (and his friends); the woman, as if rising from sleep, came to meet them, and at the first touch of the reins, the demon was completely driven away, and, as she thankfully declared, she was restored to her former health and ministered to them.

End of Book II

37–38 *om.* T. 39 inprudenter H. imp... P. 40 *ins.* quia T. 41–42 sibi spectandam esse HB. 43 expectanda A. spectanda T. spectandam P. 44 esse P. 45 consolare T. 46 coepit H. 47 eum HBP. 48 addens HB. *ins.* et P. 49 dixit HB. dicit P. 50 *om.* HB. 51 *om.* HB. 52 michi TP. 53 freni HTB. frenorum P. 54 *om.* HB. 55 quem HTB. que P. 56 A *breaks off here.* 57–58 manu HB. 59 fugato HB. effugato TP. 60 *ins.* ut HB. 61 peruenit HB. 62 *om.* O₁. 63 *ins.* et sui T. (*Readings 61–63 are different attempts to remedy the faulty construction of the text.*) 64 *om.* HB. 65 e HB. 66 tactu HTBP. 67 *om.* HB. 68 pulso P. 69 pristinae H. 70 *om.* T.

Incipiunt[1] capitula libri III

I. De eo quod per scripturam uiuens, postremo solitariam uitam in insula ducebat, et ibi loci spatium de petra excidens.

II. De lapide quem iiii[or] fratres non mouerunt, ille uero solus in murum constituit.

III. De eo quod Dominus fontem de petra dedit ei.

IIII. De ligno quod mare seruiens ei detulit.

V. De auibus exterminandis iterumque cum munusculo reuersis ueniam dedit.

VI. De finiendo uite Ecfridi regis prophetia eius et herede et episcopatu eius.

VII. De conuersatione eius in solitaria uita.

I. [2]*De eo quod per scripturam uiuens, postremo solitariam uitam in insula ducebat, et ibi loci spatium de petra excidens*[3]

Bene igitur in supradicto cenobio[4] quod Mailros dicitur[5], praepositus[6] sanctus[7] Cuðberhtus[8] seruiens Domino et[9] plura[10] mirabilia [11] per eum[12] Dominus[13] faciens, quam[14] propter infirmorum infidelitate[15] conatus sum[16] scribere, postremo tamen secularem gloriam fugiens clam [17]et occulte[19] abscedens[20] enauigauit[21,18]. Deinde a uenerabili et sancto episcopo Eata[22] | inuitatus, et[23] coacte[24] ad hanc insulam nostram que dicitur Lindisfarnae[25] cum adiutorio Dei[26] [27]uoluntatis[29] aduenit[30,28] praesens[31] et absens demoniacos sanauit[32], et alios uarios languores curauit[33]. Viuens[34] quoque[35] ibi secundum sanctam scripturam[36], contemplatiuam uitam [37]in actuali agens[38], et nobis regularem uitam

f. 75b

---

1 HTBP *omit list of chapters.*   2–3 De eo quod religiose uiuens solitariam uitam duxit et ibi spacium loci sibi in petra excidit T. 4 coenobio H.   5 dicitur Mauros P.   6 pre... T. 7 sanctissimus T.   8 Cuthbertus HB. Cudbertus T.   9 *om.* HB. 10 *ins.* per eum HB.   11–12 *om.* HB.   13 Deus HTBP. 14 *capital letter in* O₁. quae P.   15 fidelitatem HB. fidem T. infidelitatem P.   16 sim HTBP.   17–18 nauigauit HB.   19 *ins.*

The chapters of Book III

CHAPTER I. *How, living according to the Scriptures, he finally took to a solitary life on an island and there cut himself a place out of the rock*

So St Cuthbert as prior served the Lord well in the aforesaid monastery which is called Melrose, and the Lord did more marvellous works by him than I have attempted to write down, because those that are weak in faith would hardly believe them; but finally he fled from worldly glory and sailed away privately and secretly. Then he was invited and constrained by the venerable and holy Bishop Eata and came, by God's help, to this island of ours which is called Lindisfarne, where, both present and absent, he healed those possessed of devils and cured various other infirmities. He dwelt there also according to Holy Scripture, following the contemplative amid the active life, and he arranged our rule of life which we composed then

---

secularia P.   20 adcides O₁. adcide T. abscidens P.   21 nauigauit TP.
22 beata O₁. euita HTBP.   23 *om.* HB.   24 coactus T.
25 Lindisfaronaeae H. Lindisfarne T. Lyndisfaronaeae B. Lindisfaronee P.
26 *ins.* et T.   27–28 peruenit HB.   29 uoluntate T.
30 peruenit TP.   31 pre... T.   32 sanans HB.   33 curans HB.
34 veniens P.   35 itaque HB.   36 script. sanct. HTBP.
37–38 elegit HB.

primum componentibus[1] constituit, quam usque hodie cum regula[2] Benedicti obseruamus. Post plures itaque annos ad[3] insulam quam Farne[4] nominant, undique in medio mari[5] fluctibus circumcinctam, solitariam uitam concupiscens conpetiuit[6]. Ubi prius pene nullus potuit solus[7] propter uarias demonum fantasias aliquod[8] spatium[9] manere, ille[10] quippe[11] intrepida mente fugauit eos, durissimam et[12] lapideam rupem deorsum ferme cubitum uiri in terram fodiens[13], [14]loci spatium[16] faciens[17,15]. Alterum uero cubitum mirabilem[18] desuper cum lapidibus incredibilis[19] magnitudinis nisi scientibus tantum[20] [21]Dei uirtutem [22]in eo esse[23], et terra commixtis[24] constructum aedificauit[25], faciens ibi[26] domunculas, de quibus nisi sursum coelum[27] uidere[28] nihil[29] potuit.

II. De lapide[30] quem iiii[or] fratres [31]non mouerunt[32] ille uero[33] solus in murum[34] constituit

Fuit namque lapis[35] in interiore[36] parte insule[37], quem uehere[38] in[39] uehiculo suo iiii[or40] fratribus uisitantibus eum in adiutorium edificii sui praecepit.[41] Illi[42] [43]sine mora[44] statim[45] obedientes, uenerunt ad lapidem quem in media uia, ne aut[46] uehiculum eius[47] confringerent, aut sibi[48] ipsis[49] lederent non perducentes reliquerunt[50]. Deinde ergo[51] fratres nauigantes, post non plures[52] dies iterum[53] uisitantes eum[54] uenerunt. Et uiderunt agnoscentes[55] lapidem suum[56] ab [57]illis[59] inmobilem[60,58] in structura[61] [62]serui Dei apte[63] compositum[64], [65]iam[67] laudantes[66] et glorificantes Dominum magnifice | in seruis[68] suis mira operantem, recordantes[69] psalmigrafi[70] dicentis[71], *Mirabilis Deus in sanctis [72]suis, et reliqua[73].*

f. 76
Psa. 67. 36

1 *om.* HB. profitentibus TP.   2 *ins.* sancti P.   3 *om.* HTB.
4 Farnea HTP. Farneam B.   5 mare T.   6 petiuit HB.
expetium T. comp... P.   7 *om.* HBP.   8 per aliquot HB.
aliquo T.   9 tempus HB. spacio T. spacium P.   10 *capital letter in* O₁. sed iste sanctus uir HB.   11 *om.* HB.   12 *om.* HB.
13 fod. in terr. B.   14–15 *om.* HB.   16 spacium P.
17 fodiens T.   18 *om.* HBP   19 incredibile O₁.
incredibili T.   20 tantam HTBP.   21–23 uir. Dei esse in eo HB.
22–23 esse in eo P.   24 comixtis O₁. commixtus P.

for the first time and which we observe even to this day along with the rule of St Benedict. And so, after some years, desiring a solitary life he went to the island called Farne, which is in the midst of the sea and surrounded on every side by water, a place where, before this, almost no one could remain alone for any length of time on account of the various illusions caused by devils. But he fearlessly put them to flight and, digging down almost a cubit of a man into the earth, through very hard and stony rock, he made a space to dwell in. He also built a marvellous wall another cubit above it by placing together and compacting with earth, stones of such great size as none would believe except those who knew that so much of the power of God was in him; therein he made some little dwelling-places from which he could see nothing except the heavens above.

CHAPTER II. *Concerning the stone which four brethren could not move and which he built into the wall alone*

Now there was a stone in the interior of the island which he commanded four brethren who were visiting him to carry in his cart for the use of his building. With prompt obedience they came at once to the stone, but they did not fetch it to him, for they left it behind half-way so as not to destroy his cart nor injure themselves. Afterwards the brethren sailed away. They came to visit him again not many days later and saw their stone, which they recognised as the one they had been unable to move, properly placed in the building of the servant of God; and they praised and glorified God who works great marvels in his servants, remembering the words of the psalmist: "God is wonderful in His saints", etc.

25 edif... HTB.   26 sibi P.   27 celum TBP.   28 uideri P.
29 nichil HTBP.   30 lapidibus O_1.   31–32 mouere non poterant T.
33 *om.* T.   34 edificium T.   35 *om.* HTBP.   36 exteriori HTBP.
37 insulae B. *ins.* lapis HTBP.   38 euehere HB.   39 *om.* P.
40 quatuor HTBP.   41 praefecit O_1. precepit T.   42 Ille O_1.
43–44 autem HTBP.   45 *om.* B. *ins.* sine mora TP.   46 ualent O_1.
47 *om.* HB.   48 se HTBP.   49 ipsos HTBP.   50 relinquerunt O_1.
51 *om.* HTBP.   52 multos HB.   53 et eum HB.   54 *om.* HB.
55 *om.* HB.   56 *om.* HB.   57–58 illo seruo Dei T.   59 ipsis HB.
60 imm... P.   61 structuram HTBP.   62–63 *om.* T.   64 conp... B.
65–66 *om.* HB.   67 *capital letter in* O_1.   68 sanctis HB.   69 recordati
sunt HBP.   70 psalmographi BP. *om.* O_1.   71 *om.* O_1.   72–3 *om.* P.

III. *De eo quod Dominus fontem de petra dedit ei*[1]

Iterum alia die uisitantes fratres uenerunt ad eum. Quibus ille secundum morem[2] eius primum uerbum Dei predicauit[3], deinde etiam post predicationem[4] cepit[5] dicere, O fratres carissimi[6], scitis quia locus iste pene ininhabitabilis[7] est[8], propter aquae[9] penuriam. Ideo oremus Domini auxilium, et fodite in medio pauimento domus meae[10] hanc saxosam terram, quia potens est Deus de [11]rupe petrina[13],[12]petenti[14] aquam suscitare. Ille enim olim Moysi percutienti uirga, de petra aquam sitienti[15] populo dedit. Samsonem quoque de maxillis[16] asini sitientem[17] potauit. Fratres uero secundum praeceptum[18] eius foderunt terram. Et[19] orante eo[20], statim fontem aquae[21] uiue[22], sursum in obuiam eius[23], de saxosa terra erumpere manantem inuenerunt[24]. Cuius nos magnam suauitatem dulcedinis usque hodie degustantes cum gratiarum actione[25] probauimus. Ille etiam seruus Dei anachorita professus est ut relatu fidelissimorum agnoui in ea aqua a Deo[26] donata omnis liquoris sibi[27] esse suauitas[28].

Exod.17,6
Judges 15,
19

IIII. *De ligno quod mare seruiens*[29] *ei detulit*

Miraculum quoque aliud quod Dominus[30] pro amore militis sui fecerat, silentio non praetereo[31]. Concupiscens enim a uenientibus fratribus et uisitantibus eum, lignum xii[32] pedum in longitudine[33] ad fundamentum alicuius domunculi[34] petiuit. Nam[35] [36]etenim[38] illic[37] scopulum[39] concauatum[40] fluctibus de mare[41],[42] erumpens, extremam partem loci illius contigit[43], supra[44] cuius autem[45] scopuli oram loco adherenti transuersum lignum xii[46] pedum ut diximus conponere[47] praedestinans[48], desuper[49] etiam aedi-

1 *om.* T.   2 mores P.   3 pred. uerb. Dei HTBP.
4 *ins.* eius HBP.   5 coepit H.   6 karissimi HTBP.
7 inhabitabilis HTBP.   8 *om.* P.   9 aque TP.   10 suae O₁.
mee TBP.   11-12 petra T.   13 petrinam HP.   14 petentibus T.
15 sicienti HTB.   16 maxilla HTBP.   17 sicientem HB.
18 pre... TB.   19 *om.* HTBP.   20 *ins.* et HTBP.
21 aque TBP.   22 uiuae H.   23 eis HTB.   24 uiderunt T.

CHAPTER III. *How the Lord gave him a well out of the rock*

Again on another day some brethren came to visit him. According to his custom, he first preached the word of God to them and then after his sermon he began to say: "Beloved brethren, you know that this place is almost uninhabitable owing to lack of water; so let us pray to God for help and do you dig this rocky ground in the middle of the floor of my dwelling, because God is able from the stony rock to bring forth water for him who asks; for he once gave water to the thirsty people from a rock when Moses struck it with a rod, and he also gave Samson drink, when he was thirsty, from the jaw-bones of an ass." So the brethren, according to his command, dug the earth and as he prayed, at once they discovered a fountain of living water which broke out of the rocky ground and poured forth before him. The great sweetness of its flavour we have proved and still thankfully prove by tasting it, even until the present day. And that servant of God and hermit declared, as I learned from the report of most trustworthy people, that he enjoyed in that God-given water the sweetness of every kind of drink.

CHAPTER IV. *How the sea served him by bringing him wood*

Another miracle also, which the Lord wrought out of love for His soldier, I will not pass over in silence. Now he asked the brethren who came and visited him for some wood twelve feet in length, which he desired as a foundation for a certain small building. For there was a rock hollowed by the waves, rising from the sea, near to the outermost part of his dwelling place; so he purposed to join the edge of this rock by a twelve-foot beam, as we have said, to the adjoining ground and on the beam

25 accione T. 26 *ins.* ibi HB. 27 *om.* HB. ibi TP.
28 suauitatem HTP. sanitatem B. 29 *om.* T. 30 Deus P.
31 pre... TB. 32 duodecim TP. 33 longitudinem O_1.
34 domuncule P. 35 *om.* H. 36–37 illic etenim HB. 38 *om.* TP.
39 scopulus HBP. 40 concauus HB. concauatus P. 41 de maris
fluctibus HB. 42 mari P. 43 contingit TP. 44 *capital letter in* O_1.
45 *om.* HTBP. 46 duodecim TP. 47 comp... TP. 48 pre... T.
49 *capital letter in* O_1.

ficium[1] domunculi construere[2] cogitauit. Quod uero[3]
a fratribus[4] deposcens non perpetrasset[5], et[6] hoc illis
Deus non inputet[7] in malum[8] nisi[9] a Domino[10] nostro
Iesu Christo facta oratione | adiutorium accepisset[11]. [12]Nam
cum[14,13] eadem nocte mare fluctibus undans[15] in honorem
serui Dei[16], stipitem xii[17] pedum detulens[18] [19]specialiter,
iam ad hostium[21] scopuli ubi ponendus erat in aedificium[22]
natantem deportauit[20]. Fratres itaque mane uigilantes[23],
uiderunt[24], gratias[25] agentes Domino, et[26] admirantes[27]
quod mare in[28] honorem Christi magis obediens anachorite[29] quam homines parauerunt[30], et adhuc usque
hodie nauigantibus domus super[31] lignum transuersum
aedificata[32] apparet.

f. 76b (margin)

V. De[33] auibus exterminandis[34] iterumque[35] cum munusculo reuersis ueniam dedit

Sicut ergo diximus[36] mare seruientem[37] homini Dei, ita
et[38] aues coeli[39] obedierunt ei. Nam cum[40] quadam die in
insula sua fodiens[41], sulcabat[42] terram[43], primum[44] enim
duobus[45] uel tribus annis de opere manuum suorum[46]
antequam clausus obstructis ianuis intus maneret, laborans
cotidianum[47] uictum acceperat, sciens dictum esse, Qui
non laborat *nec*[48] *manducet,* uidit duos coruos ante[49] illic
longo tempore[50] manentes tecta domus nauigantium in
portum[51] posite[52] dissipantes, nidumque sibi facientes.
Prohibuit autem eos leni[53] motu manus, ne hanc iniuriam
fratribus[54] nidificantes[55] facerent. Illis uero neglegentibus[56]
postremo[57] motato[58] spiritu, austere praecipiens[59] in
nomine[60] Iesu Christi de insula discedere[61] exterminauit[62].

2 Thess. (margin)
3. 10 (margin)

1 edif... HTB.   2 constituere HBP.   3 cum HBP.
4 fratre HB.   5 impetrasset HB. inpetrasset P.   6 *capital letter*
in O₁. *om.* T.   7 imp... HBP.   8 *ins.* a nullo HB.   9 *om.* T.
10 *ins.* quippe T.   11 accepit HTB.   12–13 *om.* P.
14 *om.* HTB.   15 inundans HB.   16 Christi T
17 duodecim TP.   18 detulit HB. *om.* T. detollens P.
19–20 *om.* HB.   21 ostium P.   22 ed... TP.
23 uililantes T.   24 supra HB.   25 *capital letter in* O₁ *add* que HTB.
26 *om.* HB.   27 mirabantur HB. ammirantes P.   28 ad HB.
29 anachoritae H.   30 paruisset HB paruissent P.

he thought to build a little chamber. He had asked the brethren for this beam but would not have obtained it—and may God not impute this to them for evil—had he not received aid from our Lord Jesus Christ in answer to his prayers; for that same night the sea, uplifting its waves in honour of the servant of God, landed a floating timber exactly twelve feet in length, just at the opening by the rock where it was to be placed for the building. And waking in the morning, the brethren saw it and gave thanks to God, marvelling that the sea in honour of Christ had accomplished more than men, in obedience to the hermit; and even until this day the house, built upon the cross-timbers, is still to be seen by mariners.

CHAPTER V. *Concerning the driving forth of the birds and again how he pardoned them when they returned with a little gift*

We have told how the sea served the man of God; so also the birds of the air obeyed him. For when on a certain day on his island, he was digging and trenching the land (for at first, for two or three years before he shut himself in behind closed doors, he laboured daily and gained his food by the work of his hands, knowing that it is said: "He that will not work, neither shall he eat"), he saw two ravens, who had been there a long time, tearing to pieces the roof of the shelter built near the landing-place for the use of those who came over the sea, and making themselves a nest. He bade them, with a slight motion of his hand, not to do this injury to the brethren, while building their nests. But when they disregarded him, at last his spirit was moved and sternly bidding them in the name of Jesus

31 supra HB.   32 *add* que HTBP. -di- *above* O₁. ed... HTBP.
33 quod T.   34 exterminatis T.   35 et T.   36 *om*. HB.
37 seruiuit HBP.   38 *om*. TP.   39 celi TP. *om*. HB.
40 dum TP.   41 *ins*. terram B.   42 sulcaret HTB.   43 *om*. B.
44 *capitai letter in* O₁. primo HB.   45 duob. enim T.   46 *changed from* suarum O₁. suarum HTBP.   47 cott... H.   48 non BP.
49 *om*. HTBP.   50 temp. long. HTBP.   51 *changed from* porte O₁.
portu HTBP.   52 posito HB.   53 leui HBP.   54 fratres HB.
55 ludificantes HB.   56 negligentibus HTP.   57 *om*. HB.   58 motus
HTBP.   59 pre... T.   60 *ins*. domini T.   61 *ins*. eos HB.   62 iussit T.

Illis igitur [1]nec[3] requies, nec[2] mora[4] patriam secundum
preceptum eius deserentibus, post[5] triduum alter e duobus
reuertens ante pedes hominis Dei fodienti[6] [7]iam ei[9,8]
terram supra sulcum expansis alis, et inclinato capite,
[10]sedens et[11] merens[12] humili uoce ueniam indulgentie[13]
deposcens, crocitare cepit[14]. Seruus autem Christi intellegens[15] penitentiam[16] eorum, [17]ueniam reuertendi[18] dedit[19].
Illi[20] uero[21] corui[22] in eadem hora[23] perpetrata[24] pace[25],
cum quodam munusculo ad insulam ambo reuersi sunt,
habens[26] enim[27] in ore[28] suo[29] quasi[30] dimidiam[31] suis[32] |
adipem[33] ante pedes eius deposuit. Illis iam[34] indulgens
hoc peccatum, usque adhuc illic manent. Haec[35] mihi[36]
testes fidelissimi uisitantes eum, et de adipe per totum[37]
anni spatium[38] calciamenta[39] sua liniantes[40] cum glori-
ficatione Dei indicauerunt.

f. 77

VI. [41]*De finiendo uite Ecfridi regis prophetia*
eius et herede et episcopatu eius[42]

Preterea[43] sanctimonialis uirgo et regalis Aelfleda[44] abbatissa sanctum anachoritam[45] Dei humiliter in nomine
Domini in[46] obuiam sibi nauigare ad[47] Cocpædesæ[48]
petiuit. Cui ancilla Dei flectens genua, multa interrogare cepit[49]. Postremo[50] autem per nomen [51]Domini
nostri[53,52] Iesu Christi et per nouem ordines angelorum,
et omnium sanctorum personas, fiducialiter[54] adiurauit[55],
interrogans de longitudine uitae[56] fratris sui regis[57] Egfridi.
Ipse autem homo Dei grauiter adiuratus, timens Dominum,
cepit[58] dicere de breuitate uite[59] hominis[60] circuitu[61] uerborum, et adiunxit[62] dicens[63], O ancilla Dei, numquid[64]

1–2 sine T.   3 *om.* HB.   4 *ins.* erat HBP. *ins.* nidum et T.
5 *capital letter in* O₁.   6 -i- *above* O₁. fodientem T.
7–8 *om.* HB. ei iam P.   9 *om.* T.   10–11 *om.* HB.
12 *ins.* resedit HB.   13 indulgentiae HB.   14 coep... H.
15 intelligens HTBP.   16 O₂ *begins again here.*   17–18 reu.
uen. O₂.   19 *ins.* eis HTBP.   20 ille O₁.   21 *om.* TP.
22 *om.* HB.   23 *ins.* sancti uiri T.   24 percepta T.
25 uoce HTBP.   26 *capital letter in* O₁.   27 alter HB. *ins.*
alter TP.   28 hore O₁.   29 *ins.* unus ex illis O₂.
30 *ins.* partem B.   31 *ins.* porci T.   32 partem HP. *om.* BT.

Christ to depart from the island, he banished them. Without any pause or delay, they deserted their homes according to his command, but after three days, one of the two returned to the feet of the man of God as he was digging the ground, and settling above the furrow with outspread wings and drooping head, began to croak loudly, with humble cries asking his pardon and indulgence. And the servant of Christ recognising their penitence gave them pardon and permission to return. And those ravens at the same hour having won peace, both returned to the island with a little gift. For each held in its beak about half of a piece of swine's lard which it placed before his feet. He pardoned their sin and they remain there until to-day. Most trustworthy witnesses who visited him, and for the space of a whole year greased their boots with the lard, told me of these things, glorifying God.

CHAPTER VI. *How he prophesied the end of King Ecgfrith's life and about his heir and about his own bishopric*

Furthermore there was a certain nun, a virgin and royal abbess called Aelfflaed who humbly asked the hermit of God in the name of the Lord to cross the sea and meet her at Coquet Island. The handmaiden of God on bended knees began to ask him many things and finally she adjured him boldly by the name of our Lord Jesus Christ and by the nine orders of angels and the persons of all the saints, and asked him concerning the length of life of her brother King Ecgfrith. Now the man of God, being so solemnly adjured and fearing the Lord, began to speak in an indirect way about the brevity of man's life and added these words: "O handmaiden of the Lord, is it not but

33 adipis HBP. *ins.* quam et HB.   34 itaque HB.   35 hec TP.
36 michi O₂TP.   37 totam O₁.   38 spacium O₂H.   39 caltiamenta O₁.
40 linientes HTBP.   41-42 De prophetia eius de morte Ekfridi regis, et de
piscopatu ipsius T.   43 *om.* HB.   44 Elbfleda HBP. Elfleda T.
45 anachoretam T.   46 *om.* B.   47 in portum HB. *ins.* portum P.
48 Coeuedesce HB. Cocuedes T. Concuedesee P.   49 coepit O₂H.
50 postrremo T.   51-52 *om.* HB.   53 *om.* TP.   54 fidutialiter B.
55 adorauit O₂.   56 uite HTBP.   57 *changed from* reges O₁.
58 coep... O₂H.   59 uitae O₂HB. *om.* T.   60 *ins.* per T.
61 circuitum T.   62 -n- *above* O₁.   63 *om.* HTBP.   64 nunquid P.

non[1] paruum[2] est licet[3] aliquis uiuat xii[4] menses? Illa
uero statim arripiens mente[5] de rege esse dictum, amaro
fletu lacrimauit[6]. [7]Sicut ei [9]et multis aliis[10] post anni
spatium[11] casus regalium a maligna manu hostilis gladii
omnem amaritudinem renouauit[8]. Adhuc[12] adiunxit[13]
dicens, Per eandem [14]unitatem[16] et[17] trinitatem[18],[15] supradictam[19] adiuro te ut dicas[20] quem heredem habebit
Ipse etiam[21] paululum tacens dixit, Illum autem[22] non
minus tibi esse fratrem usurpaueris, quam alterum. Hoc
quippe et[23] incredibile uidebatur[24], diligentius tamen interrogauit, in quo loco esset. Ipse uero patienter[25] sustinens
eam ait, O[26] serua[27] Dei, quid miraris licet[28] sit in aliqua
insula super hoc mare? Illa iam cito rememorauit de
Aldfrido[29] qui nunc regnat pacifice fuisse dictum, qui
tunc erat in insula quam Ii[30] nominant, addens quoque

f. 77b   interrogationem[31] de eomet[32] ipso, quia sciebat regem
inuitare eum uoluisse ad episcopatum[33] si sic rei[34] effectu
euenisset, et quale spatium[35] esset in episcopatu[36]. Ipse
uero se non esse dignum excusans, tamen neque in mari
neque in terra, a tali honore[37] gradus occultari[38] potuisse[3]
dicebat[40]. Et[41] in breui spatio[42] annorum duorum requiem
laboris[43] inueniam. Et tu quoque audi quod ego[44] prae
cipio[45] tibi[46] in[47] nomine Domini nostri Iesu Christi, u
quamdiu uixero, nulli hoc indicaueris. Et post mult
uerba prophetica quae[48] omnia sine dubio acciderant[49]
ad locum suum nauigauit.

VII. *De conuersatione eius in solitaria uita*[50]

Ath. Vit.   Sic namque uiuens [51]per plures[52] annos, *solitarius perdura*
Ant. c. 13   bat, *ab hominum* a*spectibus segregatus,* equali quoque ad cunct
ferebatur examine[53]. Nam eodem uultu, eodem[54] anim

1 *om.* HB.   2 parum HBP.   3 si HB.   4 duodecim TI
5 *ins.* hoc HB.   6 lacrimata est O₂HB.   7-8 *om.* HI
9-10 *om.* P.   11 spacium O₂.   12 at illa O₂. et HI
13 adiungit O₁.   14-15 trin. et un. O₂.   16 unitantem 7
17 *om.* HB.   18 trinitatis HB.   19 *om.* HB.   20 *ins.* michi O
21 *ins.* post HB. *om.* T.   22 *om.* T.   23 ei HTB
24 uid. incred. HTBP.   25 pacienter H.   26 *om.*
27 homo HBP. ancilla T.   28 *ins.* ut P.   29 Alfrido HB

a short time though a man were to live twelve months?" She immediately realised that he spoke of the king, and wept bitter tears; and the fall of the members of the royal house by a cruel hand and a hostile sword a year afterwards renewed all the bitterness for her and for many others. She then added: "By this same Unity and Trinity, I adjure you to tell me whom he will have as his heir." He was silent for a short time and then said: "You will find him to be a brother no less than the other one." This indeed seemed incredible; but she asked him more carefully in what place he was. He bore with her patiently, saying: "O handmaiden of God, why should you wonder though he be on some island beyond this sea?" She quickly realised that he had spoken of Aldfrith who now reigns peacefully and who was then on the island which is called Iona. She added also a question about himself, and knowing that the king had wished to offer him a bishopric, she asked if the matter would be settled thus, and how long he would be in the bishopric. He, pleading that he was not worthy and yet that neither on sea or land could he hide himself from so honourable a rank, said: "And after the brief space of two years, I shall find a rest from my labours. And you too hearken! I bid you in the name of our Lord Jesus Christ, tell this to no one while I live." And after many prophetic words, all of which came to pass without fail, he sailed to his own place.

CHAPTER VII. *Concerning his manner of life in solitude*

And so for several years he continued to live a solitary life cut off from the sight of men; and also in all conditions he bore himself with unshaken balance, for he kept throughout

30 Hii HTP. Hy B.   31 interrogare HTBP.   32 eo HB. semet P.
33 epyscopatum B.   34 regi O₁.   35 spacium O₂H. *ins.* ei P.
36 *ins.* habiturus T.   37 onere T.   38 *ins.* se HTB. occultare T.
39 potuisset O₁O₂.   40 *ins.* tunc dixit HBP.   41 *om.* HBP.
42 spacio O₂HP.   43 *om.* HB.   44 tibi HB.   45 pre... T.
46 *om.* HB.   47 *bis* O₂.   48 que T.   49 acciderunt TBP.
50 T *omits chapter heading.*   51-52 *om.* HB.   53 exanime O₁O₂.
examinae H.   54 *add* que HTB.

Ath. Vit.
Ant. c. 13

Rom.
8. 32

perseuerabat. Omni hora hilaris[1] et letus[2], nec *recorda-tione peccati tristia[3] ora[4] contraxit, [5]nec[7] magnis[8] stupentum[9] de conuersatione[10] eius elatus laudibus[6]. Sermo uerc eius[11], sale conditus[12], consolabatur[13] mestos[14], docebat inscios concordabat iratos, omnibus[15] suadens, nihil[16] amori[17] Christi[1] esse praeponendum. Preponebatque[19] ante oculos omnium magnitudinem bonorum futurorum[20], et Dei clementiam[21] e. beneficia retexebat indulta.* Quia[22] *proprio filio suo nor pepercit Deus[23], sed pro nostra[24] omnium salute[25] tradidi illum[26].*

Explicit liber III

1 hylaris O₂BP.   2 laetus O₂H.   3 tristicia TB
4 hora O₁. -h- *erased in* O₂. uota HB.   5-6 *om.* HB
7 *ins.* quod P.   8 magis P.   9 stupendum TP
10 conuersacione O₁.   11 mestus O₁ (in *above*).   12 *ins*
erat O₂. *ins.* mestos P.   13 solabatur HBP.   14 maesta
O₂. *om.* P.   15 *capital letter in* O₁.   16 nichil O₂TP. *om.* HB

the same countenance, the same spirit. At all hours he was happy and joyful, neither wearing a sad expression at the remembrance of a sin nor being elated by the loud praises of those who marvelled at his manner of life. His conversation, seasoned with salt, consoled the sad, instructed the ignorant, appeased the angry, for he persuaded them all to put nothing before the love of Christ. And he placed before the eyes of all the greatness of future benefits and the mercy of God, and revealed the favours already bestowed; namely that God spared not His own Son but delivered him up for the salvation of us all.

End of Book III

17 amore T.
18 *ins.* nil HB.
19 prae... O_2.
20 futuram HTBP.
21 *om.* et Dei clementiam $O_1 O_2$.
22 qui T.
23 *om.* HTBP.
24 nostrum HBP.
25 *ins.* eum HB.
26 *om.* HB.

[1]Capitula libri IIII

I. De eo quod ad episcopatum a synodo coactus est.

II. De eo quod in episcopatu quomodo uiueret.

III. De eo quod mulierem comitis de disperabili[2] languore sanauit.

IIII. De sancta moniale uirgine sanata.

V. De sanato puero paralitico[3].

VI. De infante mulieris curato [4]in mortale[5] et prophetia eius de tota familia.|

VII. De cuiusdam comitis seruo sanato.

VIII. De die et tempore horaque occisionis Egfridi regis.

VIIII. De anachorita qui eadem hora obiit qua sanctus episcopus [6]secundum prophetiam eius[7].

X. De eo quod uidit fratris de ligno cadentis ad coelum[8] animam eleuari.

XI. De eo quod de episcopatu sponte ad pristinam uitam reuersus est.

XII. De fratre qui desynterio[9] infirmitate liberatus est.

XIII. De eo quod sine labore migrauit ad Dominum et in basilica nostra honorifice sepultus est[10].

XIIII. De eo quod post xi annos corpus eius integrum inuenerunt.

XV. De eo quod cuiusdam patris familiae solus[11] a demonio[12] uexatus ad reliquias eius sanatus est[13].

XVI. De fratre infirmante qui pro honore martyris liberatus est.

XVII. De puero qui toto corpore solutus illic liberatus est.

XVIII. De uariis miraculis pretermissis[14].

1 *ins.* Incipiunt O₂. *No list of chapters in* HTBP.   2 desperabili O₂.
3 paralytico O₂.   4–5 *om.* O₂.   6–7 praedixit O₂.
8 caelum O₂.   9 desin... O₂.   10 sit O₂.   11 filius O₂.
12 daem... O₂.   13 sit O₂.   14 praeter... O₂.
ins. Expliciunt capitula. Incipit liber quartus O₂.

78

The Chapters of Book IV

I. *De eo quod ad episcopatum* [1] *a synodo* [2] *coactus est*

Postquam igitur ab Egfrido[3] rege et episcopis[4] Saxorum[5]
omnique senatu deposcenti[6], ad episcopatum nostrae[7]
aecclesiae[8] Lindisfarnensium[9] electus est. Tunc enim[10] su-
pradicto rege et episcopo[11] sanctae[12] memoriae[13] Tumma,
[14]et de familia nostra[16,15] electissimis uiris uenientibus[17]
ad eum, intus clausum[18] cum consilio senatus, prouolutis[19]
genibus[20] adiurantibusque eum per Dominum nostrum[21]
Iesum Christum[22], inuitus et coactus[23] lacrimans et flens,
abstractus est expectante[24] etiam [25]adhuc senatu[27], cum[28,26]

Sulp. Seu.
Vita
Martini,
c. 10

archiepiscopo Theodoro[29]. [30]*Iam uero* post spatium[32]
sumpto episcopatu[33,31] *qualem se quantumque praestitisset*[34],
non est nostrae[35] *facultatis*[36] *euoluere.* Sed tamen melius est[37]
partem aliquam exponere, quam totum[38] omittere. *Idem
enim constantissime perseuerabat*[39], *qui prius fuerat, eadem*[40] *in
corde humilitas, eadem in uestitu eius*[41] *uilitas erat*[42], *atque*[43] *ita
plenus auctoritatis et gratiae*[44], *implebat episcopi*[45] *dignitatem*[46],

f. 78*b*

non[47] *tamen ut*[48] *propositum monachi,* | *et anachoritae*[49] *uir-
tutem*[50] *desereret*[51]. In omnibus iam[52] obseruans Pauli apostoli doctrinam, ad Titum[53] [54]dicentem recordatus est[55],

Titus
1. 7–9
and 1 Tim.
3. 3

Oportet[56] *episcopum sine crimine esse*[57], *ut*[58] *Dei dispensatorem,
non*[59] *superbum, non iracundum, non uinolentum, non percus-
sorem, non litigiosum, non turpe*[60] *lucrum* sectantem, *sed
hospitalem, benignum, sobrium, iustum, sanctum, continentem,
amplectentem*[61] *eum qui secundum doctrinam est, fidelem sermonem, ut potens sit exortare*[62] [63]*ad doctrinam*[64], *et contradic-
entibus*[65] reuincere. Ideo namque [66]*purus*[68] fuit eius *sermo*[67],
et *apertus*[69] *plenus grauitatis et honestatis, plenus suauitatis*

1–2 *om.* T.   3 Ecfrido HT. Efrido P.   4 episcopatu T.
5 Saxanorum TP. Saxonum B.   6 deposcente HTBP.
7 nostre TP.   8 ecclesie T.   9 Lindisfaronensium HTP.
Lyndisfaronensium B.   10 *om.* O₂HB.   11 episcopis HTBP.
12 sanctissimis HTBP *ins.* Bosa scilicet HTBP.   13 et HTBP.
14–15 nostris HTBP.   16 nostrae O₁.   17 uen. uir. TB.
18 clauso O₁O₂T.   19 prouolutus P.   20 *ins.* eius O₂.
21 *om.* HB.   22 *ins.* egredi HB.   23 coacte O₁.
24 exspectante O₂.   25–26 et accersito HBP.   27 *ins.* accersito T.
28 et accersito P.   29 Theothoro T.   30–31 Postquam uero
ordinatus est episcopus HB.   32 spacium O₂T.   33 episcopo T.

Chapter I. *How he was compelled by the council to accept the bishopric*

So afterwards he was elected to the bishopric of our church at Lindisfarne at the request of King Ecgfrith and the bishops of the Saxons and all the council; for at that time the above-mentioned king and Bishop Tumma of holy memory and chosen men of our community came to him while he was within his cell, bearing the decision of the council, and on bended knees adjured him by our Lord Jesus Christ. So he was led away unwillingly and under compulsion, weeping and wailing, while the council together with Archbishop Theodore still awaited him. However after a time he accepted the bishopric, and though it is not in our power to narrate how he distinguished himself, yet it is nevertheless better to describe some part than to omit the whole. For he continued with the utmost constancy to be what he had been before; he showed the same humility of heart, the same poverty of dress, and, being full of authority and grace, he maintained the dignity of a bishop without abandoning the ideal of the monk or the virtue of the hermit. In all these things he observed the teaching of the apostle Paul to Titus, remembering that he said: "A bishop must be blameless as the steward of God, not selfwilled, not soon angry, not given to wine, no striker, not quarrelsome, not given to filthy lucre, but a lover of hospitality, a lover of good, sober, just, holy, temperate; holding fast the faithful word as he hath been taught, that he may be able by sound doctrine both to exhort and to convince the gainsayers." For his discourse was pure and frank, full of gravity and probity, full of

34 pre... TP.   35 nostre TP.   36 fragilitatis O_2.   37 *om.* T.
38 totam T.   39 perseuerat O_1O_2.   40 eodem O_1.
41 *om.* O_1O_2.   42 fuit HTBP.   43 adque O_1.
44 grauitate T.   45 episcopii O_1O_2. episcopatus HTBP.   46 *ins.* ut T.
47 ut HB.   48 *om.* HTBP.   49 anachorite HTBP.   50 non HB.
51 *ins.* uirtutem HB. deserens sed P.   52 *om.* HB.   53 Tytum BP.
54–55 sic dicentis HB.   56 *ins.* ergo HBP. *ins.* esse T.   57 *om.* T.
58 sicut O_2.   59 *capital letter in* O_1.   60 turpi O_1O_2.
61 amplectantem T.   62 exhortare O_2. exortari H. exhortari BP.
63–64 in doctrina HTB. in doctrinam P.   65 contradicentem HTBP.
66–67 serm. eius fuit pur. HTBP.   68 purum O_1.   69 perfectus P.

et gratiae[1], tractans[2] de ministerio[3] legis, de doctrina fidei, de uirtute continentiae[4], de disciplina iustitiae[5]. Unumquemque diuersa ammonens exhortatione[6] secundum morum[7] qualitatem, uidelicet ut praenosceret quid cui quando uel quomodo proferret[8]. Cui[9] prae[10] ceteris[11] speciale officium erat, ut ieiuniis et orationibus et uigiliis[12] incumberet[13] scripturas legens. Memoriam enim[14] pro libris habuit, percurrens canones, exempla sanctorum imitatus[15], cum fratribus pacem implens, tenens[16] quoque [17]humilitatem, et illam[18] supereminentem omnibus donis[19] caritatem sine qua omnis uirtus nihil[20] est. Curam pauperum gerens, esurientes pascens, nudos uestiens, peregrinos suscipiens, captiuos redimens, uiduas[21] et[22] pupillos tuens, ut mercedem uitae aeternae[23] inter[24] choros[25] angelorum cum Domino nostro Iesu Christo accipere mereatur[26].

II. [27]De eo quod in episcopatu quomodo uiueret[28]

In episcopatu igitur sanctus[29] Cudbertus[30], pollens uirtutibus[31], dignitatem gradus et auctoritatem Dominus per eum in signis et prodigiis perfecte pleneque augebat.

Matth.
18. 18
Quia[32] namque quod[33] de apostolis[34] legimus, quaecumque[35] solueritis [36]super terram[37], [38] et reliqua. Et quodcumque[40] alligaueritis[41] super terram, et reliqua[39], spiritaliter[42] et carnaliter in eo inplebatur[43]. Sicut presbiteri[44] et diaconi[45] eius qui praesentes[46] erant, indicauerunt nobis. Erant[47] enim ut in[48] actibus apostolorum dictum est[49], signa et prodigia multa in plebe. |

Acts 5, 12

1 gratia O₂. gracie T.   2 tranctans P.   3 mysterio HTB. misterio P.   4 continentie TB.   5 iusticiae H. iusticie TBP. 6 exhortacione H. exortatione T.   7 morem HTP. 8 proferet O₁.   9 cuius HT.   10 pre T.   11 caet... O₂H. 12 uig. et orat. P.   13 ins. et HTBP.   14 om. HTBP. 15 A begins again here.   16 capital letter in O₁.   17–18 om. P. 19 bonis HB.   20 nichil O₂HTBP.   21 capital letter in O₁. 22 ac TP.   23 eterne TP.   24 in HTBP.   25 choro HTBP. 26 mereretur O₂. meretur T.   27–28 Quomodo in episcopatu

sweetness and grace, dealing with the ministry of the law, the teaching of the faith, the virtue of temperance, and the practice of righteousness. To each one he gave varied advice with exhortation suitable to his character; that is to say he always knew beforehand what advice to give to any man and when and how it should be given. Before everything it was his special care to take part in fastings, prayers, vigils and reading of the Scriptures. His memory served him instead of books when he rehearsed the Old and New Testaments; he followed the example of the saints, fulfilling the duty of peace among his brethren; he held fast humility also and that most excellent gift of charity without which every other virtue is nothing worth. He cared for the poor, fed the hungry, clothed the naked, took in strangers, redeemed captives, and protected widows and orphans, that he might merit the reward of eternal life amid the choirs of angels in the presence of our Lord Jesus Christ.

CHAPTER II. *How he conducted himself in the bishopric*

Therefore as Saint Cuthbert excelled in virtues in his bishopric, the Lord completely and fully increased the dignity and authority of that office through him by signs and wonders; for what we read concerning the Apostles, "Whatsoever ye shall loose on earth", etc. and "Whatsoever ye shall bind on earth", etc. was fulfilled in him with respect to men's souls and bodies; as his priests and deacons who were with him have told us. For "many signs and wonders", as it says in the Acts of the Apostles, "were wrought among the people".

uixerit T.   29 *om.* H.   30 Cuðberhtus O₂. Cuthberhtus
AP. multis HB.   31 uirtutus T.   32 quae HB. que P.
33 *om.* HBP. que T.   34 apostolo T.   35 quemcumque O₁.
36–37 *om.* HTBP.   38–39 erunt soluta et in caelis et quaecumque ligaueritis
super terram (terras A) erunt ligata et in caelis O₂A.   40 quemcumque P.
quaecumque HTB.   41 alligaueris A.   42 spiritalis A. spiritualiter H.
43 imp... O₂A. implebantur HTBP.   44 presbiter HTBP.
45 diaconus HTP. dyaconus B.   46 pre... O₂T.   47 erat HTBP.
48 *om.* O₁.   49 *ins.* faciens HTBP.

f. 79   III. [1]*De eo quod mulierem comitis de disperabili*
                    languore sanauit[2]

Ex quibus est[3] quod cuiusdam comitis Aldfridi[4] [5]regis
nomine Hemma[7] in regione quae[8] dicitur Kintis[9]
habitans[10,6], uxor eius[11] pene usque ad mortem infirmitatis
languore detinebatur. Pergens uero sanctus[12] episcopus
noster praedicans[13] uerbum Dei [14]in populo[15], peruenit
ad supradicti comitis uicum. Ille autem statim in obuiam
exiens episcopo, et gratias agens Domino pro aduentu
eius[16], [17]suscipiens[19] benigne[18] ministrauit eis, lauatis[20]
manibus et pedibus[21], rem ut erat miserabilis et lacrimabilis
omni familiae[22], hoc est uxoris uelut[23] mortuae[24] disperabilem[25] uitam episcopo sancto[26] reuelauit. Benedictionem[27] aquae[28] ab eo petiuit[29], credens[30] si obitu[31]
addicta esset, facilius moriretur[32], aut si uita reddita[33],
citius[34] sanaretur[35]. [36]Ille sanctus episcopus[37] sedens, coram
omnibus benedixit aquam[38] deditque[39] presbitero suo Beta
nomine[40] [41]adhuc uiuens[43,42]. Ipse[44] uero suscipiens, por-
tauit ad cubiculum ubi illa[45] uelut[46] mortua ultimum
spiritum trahens[47] iacebat. Aspergensque[48] super[49] eam
et lectum eius [50]osque aperiens[51], partem aque[52] degus-
tauit. [53]Ipsa itaque[55] arripiens[54] statim[56] sensum[57] intellec-
tus[58], gratias agens benedixit Deum, qui tales hospites ad
reddendam[59] sanitatem emiserat[60] ei. Iamiamque[61] sur-
Matth.   gens[62], sicut socrus Petri sanata[63], ministrauit eis. [64]Illa
8. 15   enim primum[66] totius[67] familiae[68] episcopo[65] poculum
letitie[69] dedit, qui sibi[70] exspiranti[71] calicem mortis
auferebat.

1-2 Quomodo uxorem cuiusdam comitis a magno languore curauerit T.   3 *ins.* non minimum HB.   4 Aldefridi HB.
Alfridi T.   5-6 *om.* HB.   7 Hemini TP.   8 que T.
9 Kyntis O₂. Hintis TP.   10 habitantis P.   11 *om.* HB.
12 *om.* HB.   13 predicando HB. pre... T.   14-15 *om.* H.
16 ipsius B.   17-18 benigneque suscipiens HB.   19 *add* que TP.
20 *add* que HB.   21 *ins.* eorum HB.   22 familie TP.
23 uelud P.   24 mortue TP.   25 desp... O₂HTBP.
26 *om.* HB.   27 *add* que HB.   28 aque ATBP.
29 *ins.* cum qua eam spargeret HB.   30 *ins.* ut HB. *ins.* aut TP.
31 obitui HB.   32 moreretur O₂HTBP.   33 reddenda

CHAPTER III. *How he healed the wife of a gesith of a desperate illness*

Among these miracles there is the case of Hemma a certain gesith of Aldfrith, dwelling in a district called *Kintis*, whose wife was almost at the point of death through her infirmity. As our holy bishop was preaching the word of God to the people, he came to the village of the above-mentioned gesith, who immediately went out to meet the bishop, and, thanking the Lord for his coming, received him and his company with kindness and ministered to them; after washing their hands and feet, he revealed to the holy bishop the sorrow and grief of all his family, namely that his wife's life was despaired of even as if she were already dead. He prayed him to bless some water, believing that by means of it, if she had been appointed to die, she would die more easily, or if life were given back she would be healed more quickly. The holy bishop sat down and blessed the water in front of them all and gave it to his priest named Beta who still lives. He took it and carried it to her chamber where, like a dead woman, she lay breathing her last. He sprinkled it over her and her bed and, opening her mouth, she tasted some of the water. She at once recovered her senses and blessed God who had sent her such guests to restore her to health. And forthwith, rising up healed, like Peter's wife's mother, she ministered to them. For she was the first of the whole household to give the chalice of joy to the bishop who had taken from her, as she lay dying, the cup of death.

uitae HTBP.   34 cicius HTB.   35 *ins.* cum aqua benedicta
aspergeret eam P.   36–37 qui HB.   38 aq. ben. O₂.   39 dedit T.
40 nomine Beda HTBP.   41–42 qui adhuc uiuit HBP.   43 *om.* T.
44 ille HB.   45 *om.* HB.   46 uelud P.   47 trahens spiritum HB.
48 aspersitque HB.   49 *om.* H.   50–51 aperiensque os HB.
52 aquae O₂.   53–54 quia gustata H. qua gustata B.   55 utique P.
56 stat. arr. O₂.   57 *ins.* et O₂HBP.   58 intellectum O₂HBP.
ins. et H. *ins.* recepit et B.   59 reddam O₁.   60 miserat T.
61 *om.* HB.   62 *add* que HB.   63 sana HB.   64–65 et sibi prima HB.
66 prima TP.   67 tocius TP.   68 familie ATP.   69 leticie O₁TBP.
laetitiae O₂. letitiae A. laeticiae H.   70 ei HB.   71 expiranti P.

IIII. *De sancta moniale uirgine sanata*

Presbiter[1] Aedeluuald[2] qui nunc est praepositus[3] cenobii[4] quod dicitur Mailros[5] sibi[6] praesente[7] alteram[8] infirmitatis languorem[9] sanare[10] [11]relatu eius[13] agnoui[14,12]. Nam etenim[15] dixit[16], Quadam die cum episcopo sancto[17] uenimus ad[18] uicum[19] [20]ubi[22] Bedesfeld[23] dicitur. Ibi autem[21] quaedam[24] puella cognata mea [25]et propinqua[26] infirmabatur. Iam enim dolorem capitis et totius[27] alterius lateris pene per totum anni spatium[28] patiebatur[29], quod[30] nullus medicus malagma[31] corporali potuit sanare. Noster itaque[32] episcopus | audiens [33]infirmitatem qua premebatur puella[34], rogantibus nobis misertus [35]est ei[36], unguens[37] eam crisma[38] benedictione sua consecrata[39], quae[40] ab illa hora cito[41] uirtute proficiens[42], dolorem de die in diem deserens, sanitati pristinae[43] reddita est.

f. 79b

V. [44]*De sanato puero paralitico*[45]

Simile quoque huic aliud[46] miraculum[47] ostensione multorum probabilium[48] uirorum qui praesentes[49] fuerant[50], ex[51] quibus [52]est Penna[53] sine dubio didici dicentis[54]. Quodam tempore episcopus sanctus proficiscens ab Hagustaldesae[55], tendebat ad ciuitatem quae[56] Luel[57] dicitur. [58]Mansio tamen[60] in media uia facta est[61], in regione ubi[62] dicitur Ahse[63,59]. Namque[64] congregato populo de montanis, manum ponens super capita singulorum, liniens unctione consecrata benedixerat[65] uerbum Dei predicans[66], manserat ibi duos dies. Interea itaque uenerunt mulieres

---

1 prespiteri H. presbiteri P.   2 Aeðeluuald A. Edilualdi HB.
Ediluald T. Ediliuualdi P.   3 pre... A.   4 coen... A.
5 *ins.* relatu agnoui HB.   6 se HBP.   7 pre... O₂B. presenti T.   8 *ins.* feminam ab eo ab HB. alterum T. *ins.* feminam P.
9 languore HBP.   10 sanatam HB. sanasse P.   11–12 *om.* HB.
13 *om.* P.   14 annoui O₂.   15 sic HB.   16 dicit P.
17 sanct. epis. HB.   18 *ins.* quendam HB.   19 locum P.
20–21 in qua HB.   22 qui P.   23 Bedesfled T. Bedesfied P.
24 quedam O₂HTBP.   25–26 *om.* HB.   27 tocius TP.
28 spacium O₂HT.   29 paciebatur H.   30 quam P. quem HB.
31 medicina HBP.   32 autem HB.   33–34 infirmantem eam HB.

CHAPTER IV. *How a nun was healed*

I learned from the personal account of the priest Aethilwald who is now prior of the monastery which is called Melrose, how another infirmity and sickness was healed when he himself was present. For he said: "On a certain day we came with the holy bishop to a village which is called *Bedesfeld*. Now there a certain maiden, a relation and kinswoman of mine, was ill; for she had suffered great pain in her head and in the whole of one side for the space of nearly a year, and no doctor could heal her with any poulticing of the body. And so our bishop, hearing of the illness with which the maiden was afflicted, on our request took pity on her, anointing her with chrism consecrated by his blessing, and she quickly recovered strength from that hour; the pain left her gradually from day to day, and she was restored to her former health."

CHAPTER V. *How a paralytic boy was healed*

There is also another similar miracle which I have plainly learned about from the account of many reliable men who were present, one of whom is Penna, who said: "At a certain time the holy bishop was making his way from Hexham to the city which is called Carlisle. Nevertheless a halt was made in the middle of the journey in a district which is called *Ahse*. For when the people had gathered together from the mountains, he placed his hand on the head of each of them, and anointing them with consecrated oil he blessed them, and remained there two days preaching the word of God. Meanwhile there came

35–36 eius HTB. ei P.   37 ungens TP. unxit HB.   38 crismate HBP.
39 consecrato HBP.   40 que TP.   41 cita HBP. scita T.
42 proficiscens T.   43 pristine TBP.   44–45 De puero paralitico
sanato T.   46 *ins.* est P.   47 *ins.* Dominus per eum operatus est HB.
48 probatium O_1.   49 pre... T.   50 *ins.* probatum HB.
51 a HB.   52–53 ego HBP.   54 dicentes T. haec H.
hec BP.   55 Hagustaldese O_2. Hagustaldesæ A. Hagustaldense HTBP.
56 que B.   57 Uel O_1O_2.   58–59 *om.* HB.   60 tantum TP.
61 *ins.* ei TP.   62 que P.   63 Æhse A. Echse TP.
64 nam HB. nam quia TP.   65 *ins.* et HB.   66 prae... O_1.
add que T.

portantes quendam iuuenem, in grabato[1] iacentem. De-
portaueruntque[2] eum in silua, haud[3] procul a tentoriis[4]
nostris ubi erat sanctus episcopus, et rogauerunt eum per
nuntium adiurantes[5] in nomine Domini nostri Iesu
Christi, ut cum[6] reliquiis[7] suis sanctis [8]benedicens [9]eum
et[10] orationem funderet pro eo ad Dominum, ueniam[11]
peccatorum suorum a Deo peteret pro quibus ligatus
uindictam sustinebat. Ille [12]igitur episcopus[13]indubitantem
uidens fidem illarum expellens nos [14]ab eo[15] orauit ad
Dominum, benedicens puerum, morbum depellens, sanitatem adiungens. Glorificauit Dominum[16] Iesum Christum,
adiuuantem seruum suum in se sperantem[17]. Surrexit
enim[18] puer in illa hora manducans, et[19] cum mulieribus
pergens[20], gratias agens magnificauit Dominum in seruis
suis mira[21] facientem.

VI. De infante[22] mulieris curato et[23] prophetia
eius[24] [25]de tota familia[26]

Presbiter[27] Tydi[28] [29]a me[31],[30] memoratus, [32]mihi[34] indicauit[33] dicens[35], Sanctus episcopus noster in quodam uico
[36]qui dicitur Medilpong[38],[37] in mortalitate[39] illa, quae[40]

f. 80

plures | depopulauit regiones, praedicans[41] uerbum Dei
[42]reliquis hominum[43], conuersus[44] ad me mitissime[45] dixit,
Estne aliquis in uilla hac adhuc pestilentia ista[46] languens,
ut exeam ad eum [47]praedicans[49] et benedicens[48] ei[50]? Ego
iam[51] ostendens[52] signaui[53] ei[54] mulierem, stantem haud[55]
procul a nobis, lacrimantem et plorantem propter filium
suum nuper mortuum[56], alterumque toto corpore tumes-
centem et in ultimo spiritu[57] anhelantem[58], inter[59] ulnas
semimortuum tenentem. Ille uero sine mora surgens,

---

1 grabbato P. 2 deposueruntque HTBP. 3 aut O₁A.
haut HT. hanc B. 4 O₂ damaged and cut. 5 om. HB.
6 eum P. 7 reliquis B. 8–10 om. T. 9–10 deum HBP.
11 add que HB. 12–13 autem HB. 14–15 foras HB.
16 O₂ legible again. 17 sper. in se HB. 18 ergo HB.
19 om. HTBP. 20 ins. et HB. 21 mirabilia HTBP.
22 ins. cuiusdam T. 23 ins. de T. 24 ipsius T. 25–26 om. T.
27 prespiter H. 28 Tydius HB. Tidi O₁O₂T. 29–30 ante sepe HB.

some women bearing a certain youth who lay on a litter; they carried him to the wood not far from our tents where the holy bishop was, and sent a messenger asking and adjuring him in the name of our Lord Jesus Christ that he would bless him with his holy relics and would utter a prayer for him to the Lord, beseeching God's pardon for the sins by which he was bound and on account of which he endured punishment. So the bishop, seeing their unwavering faith, put us forth from him and prayed to the Lord, and, blessing the boy, he drove away the disease and restored him to health. He glorified the Lord Jesus Christ who helped His servant who trusted in Him. For the boy arose that very hour and took food, and departed with the women, thanking and magnifying the Lord who had wrought wonderful things in His servants."

CHAPTER VI. *How the infant child of a woman was healed and of his prophecy concerning the whole family*

Tydi, the priest whom I have mentioned, told me the following: "Our holy bishop, during the plague which depopulated many places, was preaching the word of God to the people who survived in a certain village called *Medilwong*, when he turned to me and said gently: 'Is there anyone in the village still suffering from that pestilence so that I may go forth and preach to him and bless him?' I pointed out to him a woman who was standing not far from us, weeping and wailing on account of her son who was lately dead, and holding another one in her arms, with his whole body swollen, half-dead and breathing his last. He straightway rose and approached her,

31 *ins.* sepe TP.   32–33 ind. mihi HTB.   34 michi O₂.   35 *ins.* michi P.
36–37 *om.* HB.   38 Medinluong T. Mediluong P.   39 immortalitate B.
40 *ins.* aput B. que TP.   41 predicauit HTBP.   42–43 *om.* HB.
hominibus P.   44 *add* que HB.   45 *om.* B.   46 illa HB.
47–48 et benedicam HB.   49 pre... AT. *ins.* uerbum Domini P.
50 eum T.   51 uero HB. *om.* T.   52 ostendi HB.   53 *om.* HB.
54 ad P.   55 aut O₁A. haut HT.   56 mortuo A.
57 *om.* O₁O₂.   58 *ins.* et HB.   59 uitam H.

accessit ad eam, benedicens[1] osculatus est infantem[2], dixit[3] ei[4], O mulier noli flere. Filius tuus iste[5] saluus erit, et nullus de [6]uiuentibus adhuc totius[8] familiae tuae[9,7] pestilentia peribit. Cuius[10] rei [11]sic factum esse[12], mulier et filius[13] adhuc [14]uitam comitem ducentes[15] testes sunt.

VII. *De cuiusdam comitis seruo sanato*

Nec silentio praetereundum[16] existimo, quod quidam[17] presbiter noster adhuc uiuens, iam tunc laicus cuiusdam comitis minister, praesente[18] eo opus misericordiae[19] factum recordauit[20] dicens[21], Eo[22] autem[23] tempore quo sanctus episcopus[24] inter populares uerbum Dei praedicans, cepit[25] pergere[26] a domino meo[27] nomine Sibba[28] Ecgfridi[29] regis[30] comite[31], [32]iuxta fluuium etiam quod[34] dicitur Tpide[35] habitante[36], inuitatus ad uicum eius cum psalmis et ymnis[37] cantantibus[38] religiose[39] peruenit[33]. Suscepto[40] ergo[41] benigne dominus meus[42] cuiusdam serui eius[43] disperabilem[44] et miserabilem uitam in[45] infirmitate iam[46] depressum, quin immo in ultimo adhuc spiritum anhelantem et morièntem indicauit.[47] Misertus[48] est autem sanctus episcopus[49], benedicens[50] ei aquam ministranti[51], etenim[52] mihi[53] praecipiens[54] dixit, Da seruo domini tui[55] infirmanti aquam[56] [57]Deo adiuuante, secundum fidem[59] nostram salutiferam[58], ut Dominus ei indulgens delicta peccatorum suorum pro quibus afflictus est[60], aut in praesenti[61] uita uicturo[62] aut in futuro saeculo[63] obituro requiem laboris donaberit[64]. Ego iamiamque[65] praecepto[66] obediens[67], [68] per ter[69] depotaui[72] eum[70], quem[71] sine mora

1 *add* que HB.   2 *ins.* et O₂HBP.   3 *add* que T.   4 *om.* HB.
5 *om.* HB.   6-7 tota familia tua hac HB.   8 *om.* O₂.
tocius TP.   9 *ins.* hac TP.   10 Cui O₂T. Huius HB.
11-12 *om.* HB.   13 *ins.* eius O₂.   14-15 uiuentes HTB.
16 pret... AT. praet. sil. HB. praetereundo sil. P.   17 Baldhelm
HTP. Baldelin B.   18 pre... O₂TP.   19 misericordie T.
20 recordatus est O₂. recordatus HBP.   21 dicit HP.   22 eodem T.
23 *om.* HTB.   24 *ins.* noster Luel HB.   25 coepit O₂H.   26-27 ad
dominum meum HBP.   28 Sibcam HP. Sibca T. Sybcam B.
29 Egfridi O₁O₂. Ecfridi HTBP.   30 *om.* B.   31 comitem HBP.
32-33 *om.* HB.   34 qui P.   35 Tuuide dicitur TP.   36 *om.* P.

and blessing the infant, kissed it, saying to the mother: 'Woman, do not weep; your son will be saved and no one of all your household, who is still alive, will perish by the plague.' And the mother and son who are still alive are witnesses of the truth of this."

CHAPTER VII. *How the servant of a certain gesith was healed*

I consider that I ought not to pass over in silence a work of mercy which a priest of our monastery described as happening in his presence; he is still alive, but he was then a layman and the servant of a certain gesith. He says: "Now at that time when the holy bishop set out to preach the word of God among the common people, he was invited by my master Sibba, a gesith of King Ecgfrith, who lived near the river called the Tweed, and came to his village with a company of people piously singing psalms and hymns. My master received him kindly and told him of a servant of his who was wretchedly afflicted with infirmity and whose life was despaired of and who was even now dying and breathing his last. The holy bishop had pity on him and blessing some water bade me administer it to him, saying: 'Give the water to your lord's sick servant, with the help of God, according to our faith which brings salvation, and may the Lord pardon him for the sins for which he is afflicted; and either in this present world, if he is to live, or in the world to come, if he is to die, may he grant him rest from his labour.' I forthwith obeyed his command and thrice I gave him to drink and without delay (for the Holy Spirit knows

37 hymnis O₂A.   38 et canticis T. et cantibus P.   39 reliose T.
40 suscepit P.   41 *ins.* eo HTB. *ins.* eum P.   42 O₂ *damaged and cut and only partly legible here. ins.* et P.   43 sui HB.   44 desperabilem O₂HTBP. diss...O₁.   45 *om.* P.   46 *om.* HB.   47 indicantem O₁.
48–49 autem eius HB.   50 benedixit HTBP.   51 ministrante T. *add* que HB.   52 *om.* HB.   53 michi O₂TP.   54 pre... TB.
55 *ins.* hanc HB.   56 aq. inf. P.   57–58 *om.* HB.   59 fide O₁A.
60 *ins.* ut P.   61 pre... TB.   62 uixuro O₁AH.   63 sec... T.
64 O₂ *legible again.* concedat O₂. donet HTBP.   65 namque HB.
autem T. *ins.* sancti T.   66 pre... TB.   67 oboediens O₂.
68–69 preteritum P.   68–70 cum aqua benedicta ipsum adii T.
68–71 *om.* HB.   72 deputaui P.

f. 80b
Ambrosii
Exp.
euang.
sec.Lucam
II. 19 (c. I,
v. 39)

spiritu Dei auxiliante, | [1]ut *spiritus sanctus nescit tarda moli-*
mina[2], uiuificatum atque[3] antiquae[4] sanitati[5] redditum
aspexi. Et[6] adhuc uiuens [7]Domino[9] gratias[8] [10]agebat[12]
benedicens[13] episcopo[14], sine intermissione orauit[15] pro
eo[11].

VIII. De die et [16]tempore horaque[17] occisionis Ecgfridi[18] regis

Eo[19] tempore quo Ecgfridus[20] rex Pictorum[21] regionem[22]
depopulans, postremo[23] tamen secundum praedestinatum[24]
iudicium Dei[25] superandus[26] et occidendus uastabat[27],
sanctus episcopus noster [28]ad ciuitatem Luel[30],[29] pergens,
uisitauit[31] reginam illic rei effectum exspectantem[32].
Sabbato[33] ergo die, sicut presbiteri et diaconi[34] ex quibus
multi adhuc supersunt adfirmauerunt[35], hora nona con-
siderantibus illis[36] murum ciuitatis, et fontem in ea a
Romanis mire olim constructum, secundum id[37] quod
paga[38] ciuitatis praepositus[39] ducens eos reuelauit[40]. Stans
episcopus iuxta[41] baculum sustentationis[42], inclinato capite
ad terram deorsum[43], et iterum eleuatis oculis ad celum[44]
suspirans[45] ait, O O O, existimo enim[46] perpetratum esse
bellum, iudicatumque est[47] iudicium[48] de populis nostris
bellantibus aduersum[49]. Tunc iam[50] diligenter sciscitan-
tibus[51] illis quid factum esset, [52]scire uolentibus[53] occultans
respondit, O filioli[54] mei considerate, quam admirabilis[55]
sit aer, et recolite quam inscrutabilia sunt iudicia Dei[56],
[57]et reliqua[58]. Itaque post paucos dies miserabile[59] et
lacrimabile bellum in eadem [60]hora et eadem die[61] qua
illi ostensum est longe lateque nuntiatum esse audierunt.

1-2 *om.* HTBP. 3 adque T. 4 *om.* HB. 5 sanitate T.
6 qui HB. 7-8 grat. Dom. TP. 9 *om.* HB. 10-11 Domino
agit HB. 12 egit T. agit P. 13 *add* que P. 14 *ins.* et T.
15 orans T. orabat P. 16-17 hora T. 18 Egfridi O₁. Ekfridi T.
19 eodem T. 20 Egfridus O₁O₂. Ecfridus HBP. 21 Pyctorum B.
22 regem O₂. 23 *capital letter in* O₁. 24 pre... T.
25 Dei iuditium H. Dei iudicium TBP. 26 *altered from* super-
andum O₂. 27 astabat O₂. 28-29 Luel ciuitatem HBP.
ad Luel ciuitatem T. 30 Lues O₁O₂. 31 uisitabat O₂.
32 expectantem AHTBP. 33 sabbati HB. sabato T.

nothing of tardy endeavours), I beheld him brought back to life and restored to his former health by the help of the Spirit of God. He is still alive and giving thanks to the Lord and blessing the bishop, for whom he has never ceased to pray."

CHAPTER VIII. *Concerning the day and the hour of the slaying of King Ecgfrith*

At the time when King Ecgfrith was ravaging and laying waste the kingdom of the Picts, though finally in accordance with the predestined judgment of God he was to be overcome and slain, our holy bishop went to the city of Carlisle to visit the queen who was awaiting there the issue of events. On the Saturday, as the priests and deacons declare of whom many still survive, at the ninth hour they were looking at the city wall and the well formerly built in a wonderful manner by the Romans, as Waga the reeve of the city, who was conducting them, explained. The bishop meanwhile stood leaning on his supporting staff, with his head inclined towards the ground and then he lifted up his eyes heavenwards again with a sigh and said: "Oh! oh! oh! I think that the war is over and that judgment has been given against our people in the battle." Then when they urgently asked him what had happened and desired to know, he said evasively: "Oh, my sons, look at the sky, consider how wonderful it is, and think how inscrutable are the judgments of God" and so forth. And so after a few days they learned that it had been announced far and wide that a wretched and mournful battle had taken place at the very day and hour in which it had been revealed to him.

34 dyaconi B.   35 affi... O₂HBP.   36 *ins.* ad HTBP.
37 *om.* HB.   38 Uacha HTBP.   39 *om.* O₂. pre... T.
40 *ins.* illis P.   41 super B.   42 sustentacionis H.   43 *om.* HB.
44 caelum O₂. coelum AH.   45 susurrans HBP.   46 *om.* HB.
47 *om.* HTBP.   48 iuditium H.   49 inter se O₂. *ins.* hostem HTBP.
50 *om.* HB.   51 scisscitantibus P.   52–53 *om.* HB.   54 filii TP.
55 ammi... O₂BP.   56 Dei iudicia HB.   57–58 *om.* O₂P.
59 mirabile O₁O₂.   60–61 die et eadem hora HTBP.

VIIII. *De anachorita qui eadem hora obiit qua sanctus*
episcopus [1]prophetauit discessum suum[2]

Ad eandem supradictam ciuitatem Luel[3] quidam anachorita probabilis[4] nomine[5] Hereberht[6], ab insulis[7]
occidentalis maris ante[8] ad eum[9] assidue pergens[10], [11]ad[13]
episcopi[14] nunc[15,12] conloquium[16] [17]tetendit. Secundum
consuetudinem suam, conloquium[19,18] spiritale[20] querens[21],
orationem[22] [23]inter eos[24] frequentatam[25] renouauit[26]. Igitur
episcopus sanctus post multa[27] [28]uerba spiritalia[29] quibus in-
struebat eum, ait ei[30] prophetice[31], | hoc enim multis dixerat,
O frater carissime[32] loquere[33], interroga necessaria tibi.
Iam[34] enim[35] [36]ab hac hora numquam[38] iterum[39] in hoc
saeculo[40,37] sicut Paulus Effesis[41] promiserat, nos[42] inuicem
[43]erimus uisuri[44]. Tunc uero[45] anachorita [46]uolutis genibus,
ante pedes eius[47], flens et lacrimans ait, Adiuro te per Iesum[48]
Christum filium Dei, ut roges sanctam trinitatem ut[49]
ne me in praesenti[50] saeculo[51] orbatum a te[52] post obitum
tuum derelinquat, sed[53] in gaudium aeterni[54] regni tecum
me recipiat. Cui[55] [56]autem ille[58,57] statim orans[59,60], respondit[61] adhuc iacenti[62], Surge, [63]et gaude[64]. [65]Hoc enim
a Domino Iesu Christo [67]secundum uerbum tuum [69]per-
petratum[68] et indubitatum[71] recipies[70,66]. Ergo[72] quid
magis moror[73] longe[74] ambitu uerborum[75]? Uno tempore
unaque[76] nocte et eadem hora noctis episcopus et anachorita[77] uterque obiit, secundum promissionem episcopi,
regnantes simul cum Christo in[78] secula seculorum.

f. 81

Acts
18. 21

1-2 secundum prophetiam eius A. per prophetiam predixit T.
3 Lues O₁O₂.   4 *ins.* et fidelis HTBP.   5 cui nomen T.
6 Heribertus HB. Herebret T. Herebertus P.   7 insula HTBP.
8 *om.* HTBP.   9 ipsum T.   10 perrexit HB.
11-12 ab eo HB.   13 *om.* T.   14 episcopum O₂T.   15 *om.* HB.
16 coll... HTBP.   17-18 *om.* HB.   19 coll... O₂TP.
20 spirituale P.   21 *om.* O₁O₂. quaerens H.
22 orationumque HB.   23-24 *om.* HB.   25 frequentiam HB.
26 renouari T. renouans HB.   27 O₂ *cut and damaged and only partly*
legible.   28-29 spiritualia uerba P. spir. uerb. HTB.   30 *om.* O₁O₂.
31 prophaetice A. propheticae B.   32 karissime O₂TP. care HB.
33 *ins.* et HTBP.   34 *om.* HBP.   35 *ins.* permitto iam P.

CHAPTER IX. *Concerning the hermit who died in that hour which the holy bishop had prophesied for his own decease*

At the above-mentioned city of Carlisle there was a certain worthy anchorite named Hereberht from the islands of a western lake. He had constantly on previous occasions made his way to the bishop and now again sought to have converse with him. According to his custom, he sought spiritual converse and renewed their frequent prayers together. And the holy bishop, after many spiritual words whereby he gave him instruction, said prophetically to him, as he had told many: "O beloved brother, speak and ask what things are necessary for you, for from this hour, as St Paul declared to the Ephesians, we shall never again see each other in this world". Then the anchorite, falling on his knees at his feet, with lamentation and tears said: "I adjure you by Jesus Christ, the Son of God, that you ask the Holy Trinity not to leave me in this present world bereaved of you after your death, but that He may receive me with you into the joy of the eternal kingdom." Cuthbert immediately prayed to Him and then answered him as he lay there: "Rise and rejoice, for your request has been obtained for you by the Lord Jesus Christ according to your words and you will undoubtedly receive it." Why should I delay by making a long story of this? At the same time, in the same night, and at the same hour of the night, the bishop and the anchorite both died according to the bishop's promise, and they reign together with Christ for ever and ever.

36–37 permitto HB.   38 nunq... P.   39 *om.* TP.   40 sec... T.
41 Effesiis HT. Ephesiis BP.   42 *ins.* ab hac hora numquam in hoc seculo HB.   43–44 uisuros HB.   45 *om.* HB.   46–47 prostratus pedibus eius HB.   48 Ihesum P.   49 *om.* HBP.   50 pre... T.
51–52 *om.* HB.   53 O₂ *legible again.*   54 eter... TBP.   55 cum O₂.
56–57 *om.* T.   56–60 episcopus HB.   58 *om.* P.   59 orasset O₂.
61–62 *om.* HB.   63–64 gaudens HB.   65–66 quem (quod B) quae petisti a Domino obtinuisti HB.   67–68 impetraui O₂.   69–70 donatum et indultum est T.   71 indultum P.   72 *om.* T.   73 moret H.
74 longo HTBP. *ins.* licet T.   75 *om.* HBP. ab inuicem T.
76 *om.* que P.   77 anachoreta T.   78 per immortalia HP.

X. *De eo quod uidit[1] fratris [2] de ligno cadentis[3]*
ad coelum[4] animam[5] eleuari

Fidelissima abbatissa Aelfleda[6] de sancto episcopo aliud
scientie[7] spiritalis miraculum mihi[8] reuelauit. Nam cum
quadam[9] die in parrochia[10] eius, [11] quae dicitur Osingadun[13]
simul[12] in[14] conuiuio sedentes[15], uidit hominem Dei mire[16]
stupore in excessu mentis occupatum, cultrumque quod
habebat in manu, super mensam deserens[17] cecidit. At
illa aliis non audientibus, humiliter[18] interrogauit, quid
esset quod ostensum [19]ei erat[21],[20]. Ipse uero respondit, Vidi
animam serui Dei ex familia tua[22] inter manus angelorum
ad celum[23] efferri, et in choro angelorum[24] sanctorum
martyrum[25] collocatam[26]. Interroganti autem[27] ei quo
nomine uocaretur, respondit, Tu [28]enim[30] [31]mihi[33] cras[32],[29]
celebranti[34] missam nominabis eum. Itaque, in illa hora
abbatissa[35] mittebat nuntium ad cenobium[36] suum, interrogare quis ex fratribus nuper esset defunctus. Ille autem
omnes uiuentes illic inuenerat. Postremo tamen[37] diligenter inquirentes[38], unum ex fratribus eorum in pastorali-
f. 81b   bus[39] | habitaculis de summo[40] cacumine ligni deorsum
cadentem[41] fracto[42] corpore exanimem audierunt[43]. Nuntius autem crastina die reuersus[44] [45]ad abbatissam[46], res ut
erat[47] gesta[48] referebat. Illa[49] uero[50] statim ad episcopum
sanctum[51] cucurrit. Dedicanti namque eo[52] die ibi aecclesiam[53] et missam cantantibus[54], tunc[55] in[56] eo loco[57] ubi
dicitur, *Memento Domine famulorum[58]*, anhelans in basi-
licam peruenit, nomenque fratris [59]qui dicebatur Had-
puald[61],[60] indicauit, intellegens[62] in eo non solum [63]in hoc[64]
prophetiae[65] spiritum[66], sed et in omnibus apostolicam[67]

1 *ins.* animam T.   2-3 *om.* T.   4 celum T.   5 *om.* T.
6 Ælflaeda A. Elbflaeda HTBP.   7 scientiae O₂AHB.
8 michi O₂TP.   9 quodam HTBP.   10 parroechia O₂.
11-12 *om.* HB.   13 Osingadum TP.   14 cum P.
15 sederet HB.   16 miro HTBP.   17 *om.* HB.   18 *om.* B.
19-20 erat ei O₂. fuerat ei HBP.   21 fuerat T.   22 sua HB.
23 caelum O₂A. coelum AH.   24 *ins.* ac O₂. *om.* HTBP.
25 martirum P.   26 collocatum O₁A. collocari HB.
27 quoque HB. *om.* TP.   28-29 cras michi HB.   30 *om.* T.
31-32 cras michi P.   33 michi O₂T.   34 cael... O₂.

CHAPTER X. *How he saw the soul of a brother, who*
fell from a tree, being carried to Heaven

The most faithful abbess Aelfflaed related to me another miracle
of spiritual knowledge concerning the holy bishop. For when
on a certain day, she was sitting feasting with him at a place
in his diocese called Ovington she saw the man of God in
a trance and seized with ecstasy; and the knife which he had
in his hand dropped and fell on to the table. Then unheard by
the others, she humbly asked him what it was that had been
revealed to him. He answered: "I saw the soul of a servant of
God from your household being carried to heaven in the hands
of angels and being set amid the choir of angels, saints, and
martyrs. When she asked his name he replied: "You will
name him to me to-morrow when I am celebrating mass!"
And that same hour the abbess sent a messenger to her monastery
to ask which of the brethren had lately died, but he found them
all alive there. Finally, after diligent enquiries, they heard that
one of the brethren in the shepherds' huts had fallen down
from the top of a tree and was dead, all his bones being broken.
Now the messenger on the next day returned to the abbess and
told her what had happened. She immediately ran in to
the holy bishop, who was dedicating a church there on that
day and, as they were singing mass, at the place where it says,
"Remember, Lord, thy servants", she came breathless into the
church and declared the name of the brother, who was called
Hadwald, realising not only that in this matter there was in
him a spirit of prophecy, but also perceiving in all things his

35 abbas HBP.   36 coen... O₂.   37 autem B.   38 inquirens HB.
39 pastoribus HB.   40 summa HB.   41 *changed from* cadens O₂.
cadens O₁AT.   42 *ins.* toto HTBP.   43 audiuit HB.
44 reuertens B.   45–46 abbatisse T. abbatissae HB. abbati P.
47 erant HB.   48 gestae H. geste B.   49 ille P.   50 autem HB.
51 *om.* T.   52 eodem P.   53 ecclesiam TBP.   54 *changed to* cantanti
O₂. cantanti HTBP.   55 *om.* HB.   56 O₂ *damaged and cut and only*
partly legible.   57 ea loca O₁. eodem loco P.   58 *ins.* et reliqua HTBP.
59–60 *om.* HB.   61 Haduuuald TP.   62 intelligens O₂HTBP.
63–64 *om.* HB.   65 prophetie T.   66 *ins.* inesse T.
67 aposcolicam T.

prouidentiam agnoscebat[1], quae[2] et mortem eius multis
modis euidenter[3] praedixit.

XI. De eo quod de episcopatu sponte[4] ad pristinam uitam reuersus est[5]

Igitur post duos annos episcopatus[6] sui secularem honorem
sponte deserens, prophetali[7] spiritu Dei imbutus, uite[8]
obitum prouidens[9], pristinae[10] solitariae[11] conuersationis
[12]amore inlectus,[14,13] ad insulam unde olim coacte[15]
abstractus est, iterum reuertebatur. Conloquio[16] et ministerio[17] angelorum contentus, fungens[18] [19]spem fidem-
que[20] ad Deum plene ponens[21] [22]languente iam corpore
quadam infirmitate depresso[24] solus manebat[23].

XII. De eo[25] qui disenterio[26] infirmitate[27] liberatus est

In ultimo itaque tempore[28] infirmitatis suae[29], fratrem
quendam fidelem[30] et probatum qui [31]adhuc [33]uiuens
palhstod[35] dicitur[34,32], desyntirie[36] languore infirmantem,
specialiter[37] ad se uenire, et ministrare intus[38] clausus[39]
praecepit. Ille uero gratanter accedens, primo tactu eius,
sicut [40]memorans frequenter[41] cum lacrimis indicare solet,
plene[42] omnem grauitatem languoris[43] deseruisse eum[44],
[45]qui prius depressus quasi morti addictus[46], sanitati[47] [48]se
uite[50,49] redditum esse[51], sentiens, cum gratiarum actione[52]
fratribus indicauit.

---

1 esse HB. 2 quia HBP. 3 *om.* T. 4 suo T. 5 sit T.
6 episcopii HBP. 7 O₂ *legible again here. changed from*
prophetalis A. 8 uitae O₂. 9 prae... O₂. 10 pristine TP.
11 solitarie TP. 12–13 locum desiderans T. 14 illectus HBP.
15 coactus HTBP. 16 coll... HBP. 17 mynisterio A.
18 fingens HB. figens T. 19–20 spe fideque P. 21 potens
HBP. *om.* T. 22–23 quamuis corporis infirmitate languens HB.
24 depressus T. 25 fratre AT. 26 de sinterio A. et sinteria TP.

apostolic foresight whereby he also clearly foretold his own death in many ways.

CHAPTER XI. *How, of his own accord, he returned from his bishopric to his former mode of life*

So after two years he resigned of his own will the worldly honours of his bishopric, for being filled with the prophetic spirit of God, he foresaw his death and, being attracted by the love of his former solitary way of life, he returned to the island from which he had formerly been withdrawn by compulsion. So he remained alone, satisfied with the converse and ministry of angels, full of hope and putting his trust wholly in God, though his body was now infirm and afflicted with a certain sickness.

CHAPTER XII. *Concerning the one who was healed of dysentery*

And so during the last period of his illness, he ordered a certain faithful well-tried brother, still surviving and called Walhstod, who at that time suffered from dysentery, to come specially to minister to him in his cell. He gladly consented and at the saint's first touch, as he frequently narrated, recalling the story with tears, the grievous sickness entirely deserted him, and though afflicted before and, as it were, given up to death, he felt himself to be restored to life and health, and thankfully informed the brethren.

27 *om.* AT.   28 *om.* HB.   29 sue TP. *ins.* tempore HB.   30 *om.* P. 31–32 *om.* H.   33–34 uiuit HB.   35 Ualhstod TP.   36 syntirie *changed from* syntiru O₁ *and* synterie A. sinteriae O₂. de sentinae HB. desinterie T. dissenterie P.   37 *om.* HB.   38 sibi HB.   39 clauso HB.   40–41 ipse HB. 42 *capital letter in* O₁.   43 languorem T.   44 eum deseruisse HB. 45–46 *om.* HB.   47 *add* que HB. sanitate TP.   48–49 uite se P. 50 uitae O₂. *om.* HB.   51 *om.* HB.   52 accione T.

XIII. De eo quod sine labore[1] migrauit ad Dominum et in basilica [2] nostra honorifice[3] sepultus est

Postquam ergo sanctae[4] memoriae[5] Cudberhtus[6] episcopus peracta communione eleuatis oculis et manibus ad
coelum[7], | commendans[8] Domino[9] animam suam, [10]emit-
tens[12] spiritum[11], sedensque[13] sine gemitu obiit[14] in uiam[15]
patrum, a nauigantibus ad insulam nostram[16] delatus, toto
corpore lauato, capite[17] sudario circumdato, oblata[18] super
sanctum pectus[19] posita, uestimento[20] sacerdotali indutus,
in obuiam Christi calciamentis suis praeparatus[21], in sindone[22] cerata curatus[23], animam habens cum Christo
gaudentem[24], corpus incorruptibile[25] requiescens[26], et[27]
quasi dormiens in sepulchro[28] lapideo, honorabiliter [29]in
basilica[31] deposuerunt[30].

f. 82

XIIII. De eo quod post xi annos corpus eius integrum inuenerunt

[32]Nam etenim[33] post annos[34] xi[35] spiritu sancto suadente
[36]et docente[37] consilio a decanibus[38] facto, et a[39] sancto
episcopo Eadberhto[40] [41]licentia data[42], reliquias ossium
sancti Cudberhti[43] episcopi totius[44] familiae[45] probatissimi
uiri de sepulchro[46] proposuerunt eleuare. Inuenerunt
itaque in prima apertione sepulchri[47], quod dictu mirum
est totum corpus tam[48] integrum, [49]quam[51] ante annos xi[52]
deposuerunt[50]. Non enim[53] marcescente[54] [55]et senescente
cute et arescentibus[56] neruis [57]strennue[59] corpus erectum
et rigidum est[58], sed[60] membra[61] [62]plena uiuaciter[64,63] in

1 dolorè T.   2–3 om. T.   4 sancte TBP.   5 memorie TBP.
6 Cudbertus O₁. Cuðberhtus A. Cuthbertus HBP.   7 caelum
O₂. celum A. Deum HTBP.   8 commendasset HB.
9 dominum O₁. ei HTBP. O₂ cut and damaged and only partly legible.
10–11 om. HB.   12 add que P.   13 sedens HB.   14 ab... P.
15 add que HB.   16 ins. est HB.   17 caput P.   18 oblato O₁O₂A.
19 pect. sanct. HTBP.   20 uestimenta O₁O₂A.
21 praeparatiss O₁. preparatis O₂A.   22 syndone B.
23 gloss above uel uolutus O₁AT. uolutus O₂. inuolutus HBP.
24 gaudentium O₁A.   25 incorruptibilem O₁A.   26 om.

CHAPTER XIII. *How he departed to be with the Lord without a struggle and was honourably buried in our church*

But after Bishop Cuthbert of holy memory had taken communion and lifted up his eyes and hands to heaven, he commended his soul to the Lord, and, sitting there, he breathed his last, and without a sigh went in the way of his fathers. He was carried by ship to our island; but first his whole body was washed, his head wrapped in a head cloth and an obley placed upon his holy breast. He was robed in his priestly garments, wearing his shoes in readiness to meet Christ and provided with a waxed shroud. His soul rejoicing in Christ, his body remained incorrupt, resting as though asleep in his stone coffin; and so they placed him with honour in the church.

CHAPTER XIV. *How after eleven years they found his body incorrupt*

After eleven years, through the prompting and instruction of the Holy Spirit, after a council had been held by the elders and licence had been given by the holy Bishop Eadberht, the most faithful men of the whole congregation decided to raise the relics of the bones of the holy Bishop Cuthbert from his sepulchre. And, on first opening the sepulchre, they found a thing marvellous to relate, namely that the whole body was as undecayed as when they had buried it eleven years before. The skin had not decayed nor grown old, nor the sinews become dry, making the body tautly stretched and stiff; but the limbs lay at rest with all the appearance of life and were

HB. *add* que P.   27 O₂ *legible again.*   28 sepulcro T.
29–30 depos. in bas. P.   31 basisilica B.   32–33 *om.* HB.
34 *ins.* autem HB.   35 undecim TP.   36–37 *om.* HB.
38 decanis P.   39 *om.* O₁O₂.   40 Eadberto O₂. Eodberto HTBP.
41–42 *om.* B.   43 Cudberti O₁. Cuðberhti A. Gudberti T. Cuthberti HBP.   44 tocius P.   45 familie TBP.   46 sepulcro B.
47 sepulcri B.   48 *om.* HB.   49–50 *om.* HB.   51 sicut T.
52 undecim TP.   53 *om.* HB.   54 marcescentibus HB.
55–56 *om.* HB.   57–58 *om.* HB.   59 strenue O₂TP.   60 set T.
61 memba A. menbra BP.   62–63 quasi uiuentia HB.   64 uiuacitate O₂.

articulis motabilia requiescebant. Collum [1]enim capitis[2] et genua crurum sicut uiuentis hominis. Eleuantes[3] eum[4] de sepulchro[5], ut uoluerunt flectere[6] potuerunt. Omnia autem[7] uestimenta et calciamenta[8] quae[9] pelli corporis eius adherebant, attrita non erant. Nam sudarium reuoluentes [10]quo capud[12] eius cingebatur, pristine[13] candiditatis[14] pulchritudinem[15] custodiens, et ficones[16] noui quibus calciatus[17] est[18,11] in basilica nostra [19]contra[21] reliquiis[22] pro testimonio[23,20] usque hodie habentur.

XV. De eo quod.[24] cuiusdam patris familie solus a demonio uexatus, ad reliquias eius sanatus est[25]

Dominus itaque [26]pro honore[27] [28]sancti[30] martyris[31,29] sui post obitum eius plurimorum hominum sanitates secundum fidem eorum donauerat. Nam quidam pater familias [32]filium suum[33] a demonio[34] fatigatum uociferantem[35] et lacrimantem[36], lacerantemque[37] | corpus suum in plaustro ad insulam nostram uehebat, et[38] ad reliquias sanctorum apostolorum et martyrum Dei, [39]ita[41] ut occulte erat edoctus[42] a presbitero[43] sepe memorato nomine Tydi qui sanare filium eius, et fugare demonium[44] non ualebat[40]. Igitur[45] sicut diximus clamante[46] et uociferante[47] demonioso[48], plurimorum[49] aures horror inuasit. Multis[50] namque[51] disperantibus[52] aliquod[53] sanitatis remedium miserabili puero posse contulere[54], quidam tamen[55] bone[56] et integre[57] fidei ad Deum spem ponens et deposcens sancti Cudberhti[58] adiutorium, misericordia commotus, aquam benedixit, et partem humi de illa fossa[59] in qua[60] lauacrum[61] corporis [62]sancti episcopi nostri[63] post obitum

f. 82b

1–2 uero HB.   3 eleuatis O[1]. eleuatus O[2]. eleuantis A. ins. autem HB.   4 enim O[2].   5 sepulcro T.   6 ins. non HB. 7 etiam HB.   8 calcimenta O[1].   9 que TB.   10–11 pro reliquiis HB.   12 caput O[2]TP.   13 pristini O[2].   14 candoris O[2]. 15 pulcr... T.   16 uicones T.   17 caltiatus O[1].   18 om. P. 19–20 om. HB.   21 cum T.   22 reliquias O[2].   23 testimonia O[1]A.   24–25 quidam demoniacus ad reliquias eius sanatus sit T.   26–27 ad honorem HB.   28–29 dilecti T.   30 om. HBP. 31 ins. Cudberti T.   32–33 om. HB. 34 daem... O[2]. ins. filium HB.   35 om. HB.   36 om. HB.

still moveable at the joints. For his neck and knees were like those of a living man; and when they lifted him from the tomb, they could bend him as they wished. None of his vestments and footwear which touched the flesh of his body was worn away. They unwound the headcloth in which his head was wrapped and found that it kept all the beauty of its first whiteness; and the new shoes, with which he was shod, are preserved in our church over against the relics, for a testimony, up to this present day.

CHAPTER XV. *How the only son of a certain father, being vexed by a devil, was healed at his remains*

And so our Lord, in honour of His holy martyr, after his death granted health to many men, according to their faith. For a certain father brought his son who was afflicted with a demon, and was shouting and weeping and tearing his body, in a wagon to our island, to the relics of the holy apostles and martyrs of God; for so he had been secretly instructed to do by a priest named Tydi, often before mentioned, who had been unable himself to heal the man's son and drive out the demon. So, as we have said, the demoniac cried and shouted and very many heard it with dread. And many despaired of finding any health-giving remedy for the wretched boy. Nevertheless a certain man of good and sound faith placed his trust in God and prayed for the help of St Cuthbert; moved to pity, he blessed some water and took and sprinkled in it some of the earth from the trench in which that water had been poured, wherein the body of our holy bishop had been washed after his death. As soon as

37 laceratumque O₂. *om.* que HB.   38 *om.* HB.   39–40 sed per eos omnipotens eum curare nolebat (cur. eum omn. B) HB.   41 *capital letter* in O₁. itaque T. *om.* P.   42 edoc. er. TP.   43 populo O₁O₂.
44 daem... O₂.   45 *om.* T.   46 clamantem O₁A.
47 uociferantem O₁A.   48 daem... O₂.   49 plurimum O₂.
50 *ins.* his A. *add* que T.   51 autem HB. *om.* T.   52 desp... O₂HTBP.
53 aliquot B.   54 conferri O₂. contingere HBP. prouenire T.
55 *om.* HTB.   56 bonae O₂.   57 integrae O₂H.
58 Cudberti O₁. Cuðberhti A. Cuthberti HBP.   59 fossa illa HB.
60 quam HB.   61 lavachrum HBP.   62–63 eius HB.

eius effusus[1] est capiens[2] aspersit in eam[3]. Puer uero[4]
degustata[5] aqua benedicta[6], a garrula uoce nocte illa[7]
desinit[8]. Crastinoque[9] die [10]cum patre suo gratias agens
Domino, ad reliquias[11] sanctorum pro quorum amore
sanatus[12] se a Deo credidit, in conspectu familiae[13] nostrae[14]

Psa. 67. 36 orauit, glorificans Dominum[16,15] [17]*in sanctis suis*[19] ad
domum[18] unde uenerat sanatus[20] reuersus est.

XVI. *De fratre infirmante qui* [21]*pro honore martiris*[23] *liberatus*[22] *est*

In honore[24] quoque sancti[25] confessoris [26]Dei et[27] incorruptibilis corporis uolente Domino[28] [29]in eo[30] complere
quod de Iohanne euangelista[31] [32]Christus Iesus proficis-

John
21. 22 cens[34,33] promisit[35], ait[36], *Volo* [37]*eum sic*[38] *manere,* [39]*donec
ueniam*[40], multa[41] mirabilia[42] cotidie[43] in praesentia[44]
nostra [45]Domino prestante[47,46] aguntur, ex quibus est quod
nuper factum recolimus. Quidam namque frater[48] de
familia Uuilbrordi[49] episcopi [50]trans mare[51] ueniens [52]usque
ad nos [54]in hospitalem[55] susceptus[56] est[53], [57]quem[59] manen-
tem in hospitio[60] grauis infirmitas arripuit. Fatigatus enim
longo tempore et[61] postremo pene consumptus est[62], de
uita praesenti[63] dubitans disperauit[64,58]. Ministro autem
cenobii[65] nostri dominica[66] die dixit[67], Deduc me [68]hodie
post celebratam[70] missam[69] si aliquo modo potueris [71]ad
locum[72] ubi corpus[73] confessoris Dei requiescit[74]. Credo
enim sperans[75] in Deum pura fide[76], [77]mente fideli, ut aut[78] |

1 effusum HTBP.   2 tollens HB.   3 eum O₂. *ins.* potumque
dedit pacienti HB.   4 autem O₂.   5 gustata HB.   6 *om.* HB.
7 il. noct. O₂.   8 desiit O₂T. desiuit HB.   9 crastina
quoque O₂. crastinaque HTBP.   10–15 Deum benedicens
mirabilia HB.   11 requias O₂.   12 sanatum O₁O₂P.
13 familie T.   14 nostre O₂. *om.* T.   16 Deum P.   17–18 per
sanctos suos operantem HB.   19 *ins.* et T.   20 sanus O₂.
incolomis HB.   21–22 ad sepulchrum sancti episcopi curatus T.
23 martyris A.   24 honorem HTBP.   25 eiusdem HB.
26–27 *om.* HB.   28 Deo HB.   29–30 *om.* H.   31 euu... O₂.
32–33 *om.* HB. Dominus Iesus Christus perficiens P.   34 proficiens T.   35 *ins.* et P.   36 dicens HB. *ins.* sic eum HB.

the boy had tasted the holy water, he ceased from his ravings that very night. On the following day, together with his father he gave thanks to God at the relics of the saints, for the love of whom he believed that God had healed him. He prayed in the presence of our congregation, and, glorifying the Lord in his saints, returned healed to the home whence he had come.

CHAPTER XVI. *Concerning a brother who was freed from his infirmity in honour of the martyr*

In honour also of the holy confessor of God and of his incorruptible body, since the Lord wished to fulfil in him what Christ Jesus promised, when He went away, concerning the evangelist John, saying: "I will that he remain thus until I come", many miracles are wrought daily in our midst by the power of the Lord; we recall one of these which happened lately. A certain brother of the household of Bishop Willibrord came across the sea to us and was hospitably received, but while living in the guest-house he was seized with a grave illness. He was afflicted for a long time and at last was almost worn out and in despair, and had no hope of the present life. On the Sunday he said to a servant of our monastery: "Take me to-day after the celebration of mass, if you are able by any means, to the place where the body of the confessor of God rests. For I believe and hope in God with pure faith and a faithful

37–38 *om.* HB. sic eum TP.   39–40 *om.* HB. et multa reliqua TP.
41 *om.* TP.   42 mirabili T.   43 cotidiae A.   44 pres... ATP.
45–46 *om.* HB.   47 praes... O₂.   48 *om.* P.   49 Uuillebrordi O₂.
Willibrordi H. Willebrordi B. Uuillibordi P.   50–51 trasmare T.
52–53 apud nos hospitatus est HB.   54–55 hospitalitate TP.
56 receptus P.   57–58 grauique ex longitudine itineris languore
depressus HB.   59 *capital letter in* O₁.   60 hospiti O₁A. hospicio O₂T.
61 *om.* T.   62 *ins.* et T.   63 pre... T.   64 desp... O₂TP.
65 coen... O₂.   66 dominico HTBP.   67 dixit die B.
68–69 queso HB.   70 cael... O₂.   71–72 post celebratam missam HB.
73 *ins.* sancti P.   74 req. Dei B.   75 *om.* HB.   76 *ins.* et T.
77–78 quod HB.

f. 83

pro honore serui sui [1]de incorruptibili[3] et pleno corpore membris[4] meis languore[5] marcescentibus[6],[2] plenitudinem[7] sanitatis augeat[8], aut celestis[9] glorie[10] quam anima eius possidet[11], mihi[12] de uinculis[13] liberato angustie[14] partem aliquam tribuat[15]. Quid magis moror[16] uerbis? Difficulter[17] a ministro deductus, prosternens se [18]in faciem[19] ante reliquias orauit. [20]Iamiamque facta[21] oratione, gratias agens Domino sanatus[22] surrexit. [23]Deambulansque sibi[25],[24] sine ductu alterius, ad[26] diuersorium rediit, et[27] post paucos[28] dies [29]in uoluntate Dei[30] sospes[31] proficiscebat[32].

XVII. *De puero qui toto corpore solutus* [33]*illic liberatus est*[34]

Miraculum aliud simile huic silentio non praetereo[35], quod in praesenti[36] anno factum est. Fuit namque quidam adolescens paraliticus[37] de alio monasterio in plaustro deductus[38] ad[39] medicos edoctos[40] [41]cenobii[43] nostri[42]. Illi enim[44] omni cura eum qui pene cunctis membris[45] mortifactis dissolutus iacebat, [46]medere ceperunt[48],[47], nihilque[49] proficientes, [50]post longum laborem[51] omnino deseruerunt, disperantes[52] curare[53] eum. Puer itaque[54] desertum se[55] a medicis carnalibus ut[56] uidit, plorans et lacrimans ministro suo dixit, Primum utique[57] mihi[58] hoc malum desolutionis[59] [60]et mortificationis[61] inchoans a pedibus per omnia[62] membra[63] deseminauit[64]. Ideo namque[65] deposco [66]ab[68] abbate[67] calciamenta[69] [70]que[72] circumdederunt pe-

f. 83 b

des[71] | sancti martyris[73] Dei[74] incorruptibilis[75], [76]et secundum consilium eius ficones[78] detulit[77], pedibus suis[79]

1–2 *om.* HB.   3 *changed to* incorruptibilis A.   4 menbris P.
5 *changed to* languores A.   6 marcesscentibus A. marcentibus P.
7 *ins.* mihi HB.   8 conferat HB.   9 coel... O₂AH.
10 gloriae O₂AHB.   11 possedit HT.   12 michi O₂TP.   13 uinculo HTBP.   14 angustiae O₂AHB. requiei T.   15 tribuit O₁O₂A.
16 morer O₂.   17 *om.* T.   18–19 *om.* HB.   20–21 completa HB.
22 sanus O₂. satus T. *ins.* facile HTBP.   23–24 et HB.   25 *ins.*
ipsi P. *om.* T.   26 a O₁A.   27 *om.* HB.   28 *add* que HB.
29–30 *om.* HB.   31 sospis O₁A.   32 proficiscebatur
TP. profectus est HB.   33–34 sanatus sit T.   35 pret... AT.

heart that in honour of his servant, He will either supply from the whole and incorruptible body fullness of health to my limbs now wasting with disease; or else He will grant some share of the heavenly glory which his soul possesses, when I have been set free from the bonds of distress." To be brief, he was taken thither with difficulty by the servant, and, stretching himself on his face, he prayed before the relics, and, when he had prayed, he rose up cured and gave thanks to God. Then walking away without the assistance of anyone, he returned to the guest-house and a few days afterwards, by the will of God, went away whole.

CHAPTER XVII. *Concerning a boy who, being paralysed in every limb, was healed there*

I will not pass over in silence a miracle similar to this last which happened only this year. There was a certain youth, a paralytic, who was brought in a wagon from another monastery to the skilled physicians of our monastery. They began to try every cure on him as he lay with almost all his limbs mortified and powerless. After toiling long, they had no success and gave him up altogether, despairing of curing him. When the boy saw himself deserted by human doctors, he said to his servant with lamentations and tears: "This powerlessness and mortification first began from my feet and so spread through all my members. So I ask the abbot for the shoes which were on the feet of the holy and incorruptible martyr of God." According to his counsel, the servant brought the shoes and

36 pre... T.   37 paralyticus O₂. *om.* HB.   38 *om.* O₂.
39 *om.* T.   40 *om.* HB.   41–42 nost. cen. HTBP.   43 coen... O₂.
44 autem HB.   45 menbris BP.   46–47 ceperunt mederi HBP.
48 coep... O₂A.   49 nichil O₂. nichilque HTBP.   50–51 tantum HB.
52 desp... O₂HTBP.   53 curari P.   54 autem ut HBP. *ins.* ut se T.
55 *om.* T.   56 *om.* HTBP.   57 itaque O₂A.   58 michi O₂TP.
59 diss... HTBP.   60–61 *om.* HB.   62 *ins.* mea HB.   63 mebra A.
menbra P.   64 deseminatum est T. disseminatum est HBP.
65 itaque HB.   66–67 *om.* HB.   68 a O₁.   69 caltiamenta O₁.
70–71 *om.* HB.   72 quae O₂A.   73 martyres O₁. confessoris HB.
om. T.   74 adhuc HB.   75 incorruptibilia HB. incorruptibiles T.
76–77 mihi dari. quibus acceptis HB.   78 uicones T.   79 *om.* TP.

[1]nocte illa[3,2] circumdedit, et[4] requieuit. Surgens[5] in matutinis quod dictu mirum est[6], [7]Domino [9]laudem stans[10,8] cantauit[11], qui prius pene absque lingua nullum membrum[12] mouere potuit. Crastina autem[13] die circuibat[14] loca sanctorum martyrum, gratias agens Domino[15], quod meritis[16] sancti episcopi secundum fidem eius[17] pristine[18] sanitati redditus est.

XVIII. *De uariis miraculis praetermissis*[19]

Igitur fratres mei pauca dictaui, multa et innumerabilia omittens, ne[20] crapulatus aliquis et grauatus, omnia simul respueret. Nam[21] [22]etenim de[24,23] hoc sileo quomodo [25]in multis locis[26] infirmantes demoniaci[27] professi sunt, pro[28] eo [29]tantum[31] futuro deseruisse demones[32], et numquam iterum possessuros[30], uel iterum[33] quomodo praesens[34] uerbo tantum[35] alios sanauit[36]. [37]De fratribus quoque taceo[39] qui in corde suo proposuerunt, nullo alio scienti[40] sibi necessaria[41] deposcere[42]. Ille uero prophetali spiritu praecuenit[43] eos, praeparans[44] eis secundum desideria cordis eorum[38], antequam aliquis [45]ex eis[46] peteret eum[47]. De quo spiritu Paulus dixit[48], *Nobis autem reuelauit per spiritum suum.* Necnon[49] de pane benedicto[50] in duobus locis, qualia et quanta mirabilia facta sunt dico[51], [52]uel [54]de aquae[55,53] potu benedicto. [56]Et post eum alio bibenti omnis[58] suauitas liquoris apparuit[57], uel quomodo diaconus[59] [60]sancti episcopi pynfridi[62,61] a reliquiis[63] [64]supradicti[66] confessoris Dei[65] per duas uices de infirmitate sanatus sit. [67]Finit hoc opus, uale in Christo semper[68].

1 Cor.
2. 10

1-2 *om.* HB.   3 uia T.   4 *ins.* in eis HB.   5 *ins.* autem HB.
6 *om.* P.   7-8 stans Dom. laud. HB.   9-10 stans laud. P.
11 cecinit HB. cantare cepit TP.   12 mebrum A. menbrum HBP.
13 *om.* HB.   14 circumibat P.   15 *om.* HTBP.   16 merita
O₁. per merita T. pro meritis P.   17 suam HB.
18 pristinae O₂AB.   19 pre... T. *add* et iterum additis aliorum
assertionibus fidelissimorum T.   20 nec O₁O₂A.
21 *om.* HB.   22-23 *om.* P.   24 *om.* HTB.   25-26 *om.* HB.
27 daem... O₂.   28 *om.* HB.   29-30 adueniente se liberatos HB.
31 *ins.* in P.   32 daem... O₂.   33 *om.* HB.   34 pre... O₂TBP.

he put them on his feet that night and rested. He arose in the morning and, marvellous to relate, he stood up and sang praise to the Lord, he who before could hardly move any of his members except his tongue. On the next day he went round the places of the sacred martyrs, giving thanks to the Lord because he had been restored to his former health, according to his faith, through the merits of the holy bishop.

CHAPTER XVIII. *Of various miracles omitted*

So, my brethren, I have related a few things and have left out innumerable others, lest anyone should be surfeited and over-burdened and should reject them all. For I have said nothing of how, in many places, people afflicted with demons have declared that the demons deserted them for his sake and would never possess them again, and further how, when he was present, he healed others with a mere word. I say nothing either of the brethren who decided in their own hearts and without the knowledge of others, to ask him for what they required; and he, by his prophetic spirit, forestalled them, providing for them according to the desires of their heart before any of them asked for anything. Of this spirit Paul said: "He revealed it to us by His Spirit." Nor do I tell what great miracles were wrought in two places by bread he had blessed; nor of the draught of water blessed by him, and how it appeared to another who drank after him to have all the sweetness of wine; nor how a deacon of the holy bishop Winfrith was healed of his infirmity on two occasions by the relics of the above-mentioned confessor of God. This work is ended. Fare well ever in Christ.

35 tamen P.   36 *om.* HB.   37–38 uel quomodo desideria fratrum preueniens HB.   39 sileo O₂.   40 *changed from* sciente A. sciente TP. 41 necessario O₁O₂A.   42 deposscere P.   43 pre... T. 44 pre... AT.   45–46 eum HB. *om.* P.   47 indulserit HB. 48 dicit HB.   49 nec HB. nec nunc P.   50 benedicta O₁. 51 *om.* O₂.   52–53 et de HB.   54–55 ea que T. de aque A. de aqua que P. 56 *om.* P.   56–57 *om.* HB.   58 *ins.* suaui O₁.   59 dyaconus B. 60–61 quidam HB.   62 Uinfridi T. Uuinfridi P.   63 reliquis O₁O₂A. 64–65 eius HB.   66 *ins.* con P.   67–68 *om.* O₂HTBP. *ins.* Explicit liber quartus in uita sancti Cudberhti episcopi et confessoris O₂.

VITA SANCTI CUTHBERTI
AUCTORE BEDA

BEDE'S LIFE OF
ST CUTHBERT

VITA SANCTI CUTHBERTI
AUCTORE BEDA

Prologus beati Bedae[1] presbiteri in uitam Sancti Cuthberti[2].

DOMINO sancto ac beatissimo patri Eadfrido episcopo[3], sed[4] et omni congregationi[5] fratrum qui in Lindisfarnensi[6] insula Christo deseruiunt[7], Beda[8] fidelis uester conseruus salutem. Quia iussistis dilectissimi ut[9] libro quem de uita beatae[10] memoriae patris nostri Cuthberti[11] uestro rogatu composui[12], praefationem aliquam [13]in fronte iuxta morem[14] praefigerem[15], per quam[16] legentibus uniuersis et uestrae uoluntatis desiderium[17], et oboeditionis nostrae pariter assensio[18] fraterna claresceret, placuit in capite praefationis[19] et uobis qui nostis ad memoriam reuocare, et eis[20] qui ignorant haec forte legentibus notum facere, quia nec sine certissima exquisitione[21] rerum gestarum aliquid de tanto uiro[22] scribere, nec tandem ea | quae scripseram sine subtili[23] examinatione testium indubiorum passim transcribenda[24] quibusdam dare praesumpsi[25], quin potius primo diligenter exordium, progressum, et terminum gloriosissimae conuersationis ac uitae illius ab his[26] qui nouerant inuestigans[27]. Quorum etiam nomina in ipso libro aliquotiens[28] ob[29] certum cognitae ueritatis inditium[30] apponenda[31] iudicaui, et[32]

1 *Capitals are preserved as in* O9 *but are added in the case of proper names and titles of God. The punctuation represents that of* O9.
2 Incipit prefatio Bede presbiteri de uita sancti Cuthberti Lindisfarnensis episcopi ad Eadfridum episcopum C1VHO4. Incipit prologus in uita sancti Cuthberti episcopi P1. Incipit prologus in librum uitae beati patris Cuthberti Lindisfarnensis episcopi C3. Incipit prefatio in librum uitae beati patris Cuthberti Lindisfarnensis episcopi O8O3M.
3 *om.* O9.   4 set O3.   5 congregacioni O3. *and throughout* O3 t *is written as* c *before* i.   6 Lindisfarnensis P1. Lindispfarnensi C3. Lyndisfarnensi O3.   7 deserunt, ui *above* V.
8 Baeda VH.   9 *ins. in* C1VHP1O4.   10 ae *is represented in* O9 *by* ę, *also occasionally* œ. *It is everywhere* e *in* O3. beati C1.

THE LIFE OF ST CUTHBERT
BY BEDE

❀

The prologue of the blessed priest Bede to the life of St Cuthbert.

To the holy and most blessed father, Bishop Eadfrith, and also to the whole congregation of brethren who serve Christ on the island of Lindisfarne, Bede, your faithful fellow-servant, sends greeting.

Since, beloved friends, you have bidden me put, as is customary, some kind of preface to the book which I have composed, at your request, concerning the life of our father Cuthbert of blessed memory, that thereby all readers might see your will and pleasure as well as my brotherly assent and obedience thereto, I decided in the prefatory chapter to remind you who know, and to inform those readers who perchance do not know, that I have not presumed to write down anything concerning so great a man without the most rigorous investigation of the facts nor, at the end, to hand on what I had written to be copied for general use, without the scrupulous examination of credible witnesses. Nay rather, it was only after first diligently investigating the beginning, the progress, and the end of his most glorious life and activity, with the help of those who knew him, that I began at last to set about making notes: and I have decided occasionally to place the names of these my

11 Cudberhti C_1. Cuthberchti V. Cuthberhti H. Cutberti O_4.   12 conp... C_1VH.   13–14 iux. mor. in fron. C_1VHP$_1O_4$.   15 pre... O_8.   16 *gloss above* scilicet praefationem VH.   17 des. uol. C_1VHP$_1O_4$.   18 adsentio C_1VH.   19 pre... C_3O_8.   20 *om.* O_4.   21 adquisitione, uel ex *above* V. exquisicione O_3.   22 *ins.* potui C_1O_9 (*above*). 23 ...issima C_1VHP$_1O_4$.   24 transs... C_1P_1.   25 praesumsisse O_9. praesumsi P_1. praesumpsisse C_3M. presumpsisse O_8O_3.   26 hiis O_3. 27 inuestigasse $O_9C_3O_8O_3$M. vi *above* C_1. inuestigaui P_1.   28 aliquoties $C_1P_1O_4$. aliquociens O_3.   29 *ins.* indicium C_1VHP$_1$. *ins.* inditium O_4. 30 *om.* C_1VHP$_1O_4$. indicium O_3.   31 adp... C_1V.   32 *om.* C_1VHP$_1O_4$.

sic[1] demum ad scedulas manum mittere incipio. At digesto opusculo sed adhuc in scedulis retento[2], frequenter et reuerentissimo fratri nostro Herefrido presbitero huc aduentanti, et aliis qui diutius cum uiro Dei conuersati uitam illius optime[3] nouerant, quae scripsi legenda atque ex tempore praestiti retractanda[4], ac nonnulla ad arbitrium eorum prout uidebantur sedulus emendaui, sicque [5]ablatis omnibus[7] scrupulorum ambagibus ad purum[6], certam ueritatis indaginem simplicibus explicitam sermonibus commendare menbranulis[8], atque ad[9] uestrae quoque fraternitatis praesentiam asportare curaui, quatinus uestrae auctoritatis[10] iudicio uel emendarentur falsa[11], uel probarentur uera esse, quae scripta sunt. Quod cum Domino adiuuante[12] patrarem, et coram senioribus ac doctoribus uestrae congregationis libellus biduo | legeretur, ac sollertissime per singula ad uestrum pensaretur examen, nullus omnimodis inuentus est sermo qui mutari debuisset, sed cuncta quae scripta erant communi consilio decernebantur[13] absque ulla ambiguitate[14] legenda, et his[15] qui religionis studio uellent ad transcribendum[16] esse tradenda. Sed et alia multa nec minora his[17] quae[18] scripsimus praesentibus[19] nobis ad inuicem conferentes, de uita et uirtutibus beati uiri superintulistis, quae prorsus memoria[20] digna uidebantur, si non deliberato ac perfecto operi noua interserere, uel supradicere minus congruum atque indecorum esse constaret. Dehinc ammonendum[21] uestrae almitatis coronam ratus sum, ut sicut ipse munus oboedientiae[22] meae quod iubere estis dignati promptus soluere non distuli, ita uos quoque ad reddendum[23] mihi[24] uestrae intercessionis praemium pigri non sitis, sed[25] cum eundem librum[26] relegentes, pia sanctissimi patris memoria uestros animos

1 *add* que P$_1$.   2 ret. in sced. C$_1$VHP$_1$O$_4$.   3 optimae C$_1$.
4 retr. praes. C$_1$VHP$_1$O$_4$.   5–6 scrup. amb. ad pur. abl. C$_1$VHP$_1$O$_4$.
7 *om.* C$_1$P$_1$. *above* VHO$_4$.   8 memb… C$_1$VHO$_8$O$_3$M.   9 *above*
C$_1$V.   10 autoritatis P$_1$.   11 *om.* C$_1$VHP$_1$O$_4$.   12 iuuante C$_1$
VHP$_1$O$_4$.   13 *gloss above* id est iudicabantur VH.   14 dubietate

authorities in the book itself, to show clearly how my knowledge of the truth has been gained. Further, when my little work was arranged, though still kept in the form of notes, I often showed what I had written both to our most reverend brother, the priest Herefrith, when he came hither, and to others who had lived some considerable time with the man of God and were fully conversant with his life, so that they might read and revise it at their leisure; and I diligently amended some things in accordance with their judgment, as seemed good to them. And thus I made it my business to put down on parchment the results of my rigorous investigation of the truth, expressed in simple language quite free from all obscurities and subtleties, and to bring what was written into the presence of your brotherhood, in order that it might be corrected if false, or, if true, approved by the authority of your judgment. And when I had done this with the help of the Lord, and my little work had been read for two days before the elders and teachers of your congregation and carefully weighed in every detail under your examination, no word of any sort was found which had to be changed, but everything that was written was pronounced by common consent to be, without any question, worthy of being read, and of being delivered to those whose pious zeal moved them to copy it. But, consulting together in our presence, you brought forward many other facts concerning the life and virtues of the blessed man no less important than those which we have written down, which well deserved to be mentioned if it had not seemed scarcely fitting and proper to insert new matter or add to a work which was planned and complete.

Furthermore I have thought you should be reminded of that which will crown your kindness, so that, just as I myself did not delay to fulfil with promptitude the task which you thought fit to lay upon my obedience, so you also may not be slow to grant me the reward of your intercession: but reading the same book, and by the pious memory of the holy father

ad desideria regni coelestis ardentius attollitis[1], pro mea
quoque paruitate memineritis diuinam exorare clementiam, quatinus et nunc pura mente desiderare, et in futuro
perfecta beatitudine merear *uidere bona Domini in terra
uiuentium*, sed et me[2] defuncto pro redemtione[3] | animae[4]
meae quasi pro[5] familiaris et uernaculi uestri orare et
missas facere, et nomen meum inter uestra scribere dig-
nemini. Nam et tu sanctissime antistes[6] hoc te mihi[7]
promisisse iam retines. In cuius etiam testimonium futurae
conscriptionis religioso fratri nostro Gudfrido[8] mansio-
nario praecepisti, ut in albo[9] uestrae sanctae congregationis
meum nunc[10] quoque nomen apponeret[11]. Sciat autem
sanctitas uestra quia uitam eiusdem Deo dilecti patris
nostri quam uobis prosa editam dedi, aliquanto quidem
breuius, sed eodem tamen ordine rogantibus[12] quibusdam
e nostris fratribus heroicis[13] dudum uersibus edidi. Quos
si uos habere delectat, a nobis exemplar accipere potestis.
In cuius operis praefatione[14] promisi me alias de uita
et miraculis eius latius esse scripturum. Quam uidelicet
promissionem in praesenti[15] opusculo, prout Dominus[16]
dederit[17] adimplere satago[18]. Orante[19] pro nobis[20] beatitudinem[21] uestram[22] Dominus omnipotens custodire[23]
dignetur incolumem[24], dilectissimi fratres et domini mei.
Amen[25,26]. |

Psa. 26. 13
p. 4

p. 5   I. [27]Quomodo puer Dei Cuthbertus[29] per infantem sit
predicto episcopatu ammonitus[30,28].

II. Quomodo genu dolente claudus effectus sit[31], et angelo
medicante[32] sanatus.

---

1 adt... C_1VHP$_1$.   2 *om.* O$_9$.   3 redemp...
C_1VHP$_1$C$_3$O$_8$O$_4$M. redempcionem O$_3$.   4 anime C_1HP$_1$O$_3$.
5 *om.* C_1VHP$_1$O$_8$O$_4$.   6 antestis VH.   7 michi O$_4$M.
8 Guthfrido C_1VHC$_3$O$_4$. Cuthfrido P$_1$.   9 halbo P$_1$.   10 tunc O$_4$.
11 adp... C_1V.   12 *changed in later hand from* regnantibus C_1.
13 eroicis P$_1$.   14 pre... O$_8$.   15 pre... O$_8$.   16 Deus O$_8$O$_3$M.
17 dedit O$_4$.   18 sategi O$_4$.   19 orantem O$_9$C$_3$O$_8$O$_3$M.
ins. ergo C_1VHC$_3$O$_4$. *ins.* me VH. P$_1$ *illegible to end of Prologue.*
20 uobis VH.   21 *changed to* beatitudine C_1. beatitudine O$_4$.
22 *changed to* uestra C_1. uestra O$_4$.   23 *ins.* uos C_1O$_4$.

uplifting your hearts to a more eager desire for the heavenly kingdom, you may remember also to intercede with the divine clemency on behalf of one so insignificant, that I may be worthy, now, with a pure heart to long for, and hereafter, in perfect bliss, "to see the goodness of the Lord in the land of the living". Moreover when I am dead, deign to pray for the redemption of my soul, and to celebrate masses as though I belonged to your family and household, and to inscribe my name among your own. For, most holy bishop, you remember that you have already promised me this, and, in witness to my future enrolment, you gave orders to our pious brother Guthfrith the sacrist that he should even now place my name in the register of your holy congregation. You should also know, holy father, that the life of this same father of ours, the beloved of God, which I have given you in a prose version, I also formerly produced, at the request of some of our brethren, in heroic verse, somewhat shorter indeed, but similarly arranged: if it would please you to have it, you can obtain a copy from us. In the preface of that work, I promised that I would write more fully on another occasion about his life and miracles, and in the present work I am striving to fulfil that same promise, so far as the Lord permits. So I pray on our behalf, my beloved brethren and masters, that the almighty Lord may vouchsafe to keep you in perfect blessedness. Amen.

I. How Cuthbert, the child of God, was warned by an infant and his bishopric foretold.

II. How he became lame as the result of a diseased knee and was cured by the ministration of an angel.

24 incolumes C_1O_4.   25 om. VH. *There are no separate lists of chapters in* HM.   26 *ins.* Explicit prologus libri sequentis Deo gratias, fiat. Incipiunt capitulae libri sequentis C_1. Explicit praefatio Bedae presbiteri de uita sancti Cuhtberhti Lindisfarnensis episcopi H. Explicit prologus. Liber de uita et miraculis necnon et de transitu beati patris Cuthberti Lindispharnensis episcopi C_3. Incipiunt capitula libri de uita et miraculis sancti Cuthberti O_8. Explicit prologus. Incipiunt capitula libri sequentis O_4.   27–28 Quomodo ipse octennis puer per trinum infantem de constancia animi et episcopatu sit premonitus O_3.   29 Cuthberhtus V.   30 adm...C_1VO_4.   31 sit. eff. P_1O_3.   32 *ins.* sine mora O_3.

III. Quomodo uentis oratione mutatis rates oceano[1] delapsas [2]reuocauerit[4] ad litus[3].

IIII. Quomodo cum pastoribus positus animam sancti Aidani [5]episcopi ad coelum [7]ab angelis ferri[8] aspexerit[9,6].

V. Quomodo iter faciens cibos[10] Domino procurante perceperit.

VI. Quale[11] [12]ei testimonium[13] [14]uenienti ad monasterium[15] Boisilus[16] uir sanctus[17] perhibuerit[18].

VII. Quomodo angelum hospitio[19] suscipiens dum panem querit ministrare[20] terrenum, coelesti[21] ab eodem[22] remunerari meruerit[23].

VIII. Quod[24] sanato[25] a languore Cuthberto[26] Boisilus[27] moriturus, quae illi[28] essent[29] uentura praedixerit.

IX. Quam sedulus erga ministerium uerbi[30] Cuthbertus[31] extiterit.

X. Quomodo animalia maris in quo pernox orauerat[32] illi egresso[33] praebuerint[34] obsequium, et frater qui haec uidebat prae timore languescens eius[35] sit[36] oratione recreatus.

XI. Quomodo nautis tempestate praeclusis[37] serenum mare[38] ad certum diem[39] praedixerit et orando cibos[40] impetrauerit.

XII. Quomodo iter[41] faciens[42] aquila ministra uiaticum et percepturum se esse praedixerit, [43]et perceperit[44].

XIII. Quomodo praedicans populis fantasticum[45] subito ignem diaboli et praeuiderit[46] uenturum, et uenientem extinxerit[47].

XIIII. Quomodo flammas domus cuiusdam [48]uero [50]igne[52,49] ardentis[51] orando[53] restrinxerit[54].

XV. Qualiter demonium[55] ab uxore[56] prefecti necdum adueniens eiecerit.

1 in oceanum O3.   2–3 ad lit. reuoc. O3.   4 reuocarit C1C3O4. reuocauit V.   5–6 in celum ferri uidit O3.   7–8 ferri ab ang. C1VP1O4.   9 uidit P1.   10 cybos P1.   11 quod C1VO4. quomodo P1.   12–13 test. illi O3.   14–15 ad mon. ueni. O3. 16 Boisil C1VP1O4. Boysilus O3.   17 ins. in spiritu C1VP1C3O8O3O4.   18 prophetauerit C1VP1. ins. utque ipse ibidem susceptus conuersatus sit O3.   19 ospitio P1. hospicio O8O3O4. 20 ministare O9.   21 cel... O8O3.   22 eo O3. 23 meruit O9.   24 quomodo O3.   25 saluato C1VP1C3O8O4.

III. How he changed the winds by prayer and brought the rafts, which had been carried out to sea, safe to land.

IV. How, being in the company of some shepherds, he saw the soul of the holy Bishop Aidan carried to heaven by angels.

V. How, while he was on a journey, he received food through God's care.

VI. What manner of testimony the holy man Boisil gave to him as he came to the monastery.

VII. How he entertained an angel, and whilst seeking to minister to him earthly bread, was thought worthy to be rewarded by him with heavenly bread.

VIII. How Cuthbert was healed of sickness and how Boisil, when about to die, prophesied things which were to come to him.

IX. How Cuthbert was diligent in the ministry of the word.

X. How the animals of the sea, in which he had passed the night in prayer, ministered to him when he came out, and how a brother who saw it, being ill through fear, was restored by his prayers.

XI. How he promised the sailors who were cut off by the storm that the sea would be calm by a certain day, and how his prayer for food was answered.

XII. How, while making a journey, he prophesied that he would receive provisions on the way by the ministration of an eagle, and how it came to pass.

XIII. How, when he was preaching to the people, he suddenly foresaw that a phantom fire would come from the devil, and how he extinguished it when it came.

XIV. How by his prayers he checked the flames of a certain house which was really on fire.

XV. How he drove out a demon from the wife of a reeve, even before his arrival.

26 Cudberhto C_1. Cuthberhto V.   27 Boisil $C_1VP_1O_4$. Boysilus O_3.
28 eum C_1. ei $VP_1O_3O_4$.   29 erant O_3.   30 *ins.* Dei O_3.
31 Cudberhtus C_1V.   32 orauerit C_1P_1.   33 regresso $C_1VP_1O_4$.
34 prohibuerint C_3. preb... VO_8.   35 illius O_3.   36 *ins.* iterum O_3.
37 pre... VO_8.   38 *om.* O_3.   39 *om.* $O_9C_3O_8O_3$.
40 cybos P_1.   41 *ins.* ad predicandum O_3.   42 *ins.* ab *above* V.
43–44 *om.* C_3O_8.   45 phantasticum O_3.   46 pre... VO_8.
47 ext. uen. O_4.   48–49 *om.* O_3.   50–51 ard. ig. V.   52 igni O_4.
53 oratione $C_1VP_1O_3O_4$.   54 restinxerit $C_1VP_1C_3O_8$. extinxerit O_3.
55 daem... O_4.   56 *ins.* cuius O_3.

XVI. Qualiter[1] in Lindisfarnensi[2] [3]monasterio uixerit uel docuerit[4].

XVII. Qualiter[5] sibi[6] in insula Farne pulsis demonibus[7,8] habitationem fecerit. |

XVIII. Quomodo[9] precibus aquam de arida produxerit, [10]uel qualiter ipse in anachoresi uixerit[12,11].

XIX. Qualiter a messe quam sua manu seruerat[13] uerbo uolucres abegerit[14].

XX. Quomodo corui iniuriam[15] quam uiro[16] Dei intulerant precibus et munere purgauerint[17].

XXI. Qualiter eius necessitatibus etiam mare seruierit.

XXII. Quomodo multis ad se uenientibus monita dans salutis fragiles exposuerit[18] antiqui hostis insidias.

XXIII. Quomodo Elfled[19] abbatissa uel [20]puella eius[21] per zonam ipsius sint ab infirmitate[22] sanatae.

XXIIII. Quid sciscitanti eidem Elfledae[23] de uita Ecgfridi[24] regis et episcopatu suo praedixerit.

XXV. [25]Quod[27] electus ad episcopatum seruum comitis languentem aqua[28] benedicta curauerit[26].

XXVI. Qualiter in episcopatu uixerit.

XXVII. Quomodo interitum Ecgfridi[29] regis et militiae ipsius[30] quem praedixerat futurum, [31]absens corpore in spiritu uiderit factum[32].

XXVIII. Quomodo Hereberto[33] anachoritae[34] obitum suum praedixerit, comitatumque illius a Domino precibus obtinuerit[35].

XXIX. Quomodo uxorem comitis per presbiterum suum aqua benedicta sanauerit.

XXX. Quomodo puellam oleo perunctam a dolore capitis laterisque curauerit.

1 *ins.* anachoresim meditatus O₃.   2 apud Lindisfarnenses O₃.
3-4 monachos uixerit O₃.   5 qualem C₁VP₁O₃.   6 *om.* O₃.
7 dem. puls. O₃.   8 daem... O₄.   9 qualiter O₃.
10-11 quam quondam in uinum conuerterat O₃.   12 profecerit
C₁VP₁O₄.   13 seruierat C₁. seruerat O₄.   14 abiecerit C₃O₈.
15 noxam O₃.   16 seruo P₁.   17 purgarint C₁VO₄.
praedixerit C₃O₈.   18 posuerit O₈.   19 Aelflaed C₁VP₁. Aelfled O₄.

XVI. How he lived and taught in the monastery at Lindisfarne.

XVII. How he drove out the demons and made himself a dwelling-place on the island of Farne.

XVIII. How he produced water from dry land by his prayers and how he lived as a hermit.

XIX. How, with a word, he drove away the birds from the crops which he had sown with his own hand.

XX. How the ravens atoned for the injury which they had done to the man of God by their prayers and by a gift.

XXI. How even the sea ministered to his necessities.

XXII. How he gave instruction in the way of salvation to many who came to him and showed the weakness of the snares of the ancient foe.

XXIII. How the abbess Aelfflaed and one of her nuns were healed of their infirmity by means of his girdle.

XXIV. How in answer to the same Aelfflaed, he made predictions about the life of King Ecgfrith and about his own bishopric.

XXV. How, when he was elected to the bishopric, he cured the ailing servant of a gesith with holy water.

XXVI. Of his manner of life in his bishopric.

XXVII. How, though absent in the body, he saw in spirit the destruction of King Ecgfrith and of his army, in accordance with his own prediction.

XXVIII. How he predicted his own death to Hereberht the hermit and obtained this man's company from the Lord by his prayers.

XXIX. How through his priest he cured the wife of a gesith with holy water.

XXX. How he cured a girl of pains in the head and the side by anointing her with oil.

20–21 eius filia P_1.   22 infirmitatae O_9.   23 Aelflaede C_1P_1. Aelflede V. Elflede O_8. Aelfledae O_4.   24 Ec... O_9. Eg... $P_1O_4O_8O_3$. 25–26 Quomodo uiro Dei comes Ecgfridi regis in uia occurrit et quomodo per gustum aquae quam benedixit infirmus sanatus est V.   27 Quomodo O_3.   28 *ins.* per se O_3.   29 Eg... $O_9P_1O_8O_3O_4$.   30 *om.* O_3. 31–32 in spiritu uiderit absenti (absens O_4) $C_1VP_1O_4$. absens uiderit in spiritu O_3.   33 Hereberhto C_1VP_1.   34 anachorite O_8.   35 opt... O_3. *ins.* sine mora O_3.

XXXI. Quomodo [1]per panem[2] ab eo benedictum[3] sit infirmus[4] sanatus[5].

XXXII. Qualiter oblatum sibi in itinere iuuenem moriturum orando reuocauerit[6] ad [7]sospitatem uitae[9,8].

XXXIII. Quomodo tempore mortalitatis morientem puerum matri[10] sanum restituerit.

XXXIIII. Quomodo[11] animam cuiusdam qui de arbore cadendo mortuus est, ad coelum[12] ferri conspexerit. |

p. 7   XXXV. Quomodo aquam gustando[13] in uini saporem conuerterit.[14]

XXXVI. Quomodo inoboedientes[15] ei quosdam fratres tempestas maris obsederit.

XXXVII. Quanta egrotus[16] temptamenta[17] pertulerit quidue de sepultura sua[18] mandauerit migraturus[19].

XXXVIII. Quomodo ministrum suum a profluuio uentris[20] [21]ipse egrotus sanauerit[22].

XXXIX. Quae ultima fratribus[23] mandata[24] dederit, et ut[25] percepto uiatico inter uerba orationis spiritum reddiderit.

XL. Quomodo iuxta prophetiam psalmi quem eo moriente cantauerant[26] Lindisfarnenses sint[27] impugnati[28], sed Domino iuuante protecti.

XLI. Quomodo puer demoniacus sit humo cui lauacrum[29] corporis[30] infusum est in aquam[31] missa[32] sanatus.

XLII. Quomodo corpus ipsius post undecim[33] annos sine corruptione sit[34] repertum.

XLIII. Quomodo corpus Eadberti[35] in tumulo uiri sancti[36] ponentes, sarcophagum[37] illius desuper posuerunt[38].

XLIIII. Qualiter aegrotus[39] ad tumbam eius[40] orando sit[41] curatus[42].

XLV. Quomodo paraliticus sit[43] per eius calciamenta[44] sanatus.

1–2 pane O8.   3 benedicto O8.   4 inf. sit O4.
5 curatus O3.   6 reuocaret C1VO4.   7–8 uitam C1VP1O4.
9 uite O8.   10 om. O3.   11 qualiter C1VP1.   12 cel... O8O3.
13 bibendo P1.   14 conuerteret O8.   15 inobed... O8.
16 aegrotans O4.   17 temtamenta P1.   18 sua sep. C1VP1O4.

XXXI. How a sick man was healed with bread which he had blessed.

XXXII. How, by his prayers, he recalled to life a dying youth who was brought to him when he was on a journey.

XXXIII. How, during the time of plague, he restored a dying boy in sound health to his mother.

XXXIV. How he beheld the soul of a certain man, who was killed by falling from a tree, being carried to heaven.

XXXV. How, by tasting water, he gave it the flavour of wine.

XXXVI. How a storm at sea detained certain brethren who were disobedient to him.

XXXVII. What trials he endured while sick and what he commanded concerning his burial, when about to depart this life.

XXXVIII. How, though sick himself, he healed his attendant of diarrhoea.

XXXIX. Of his last commands to his brethren and how, when he had received the viaticum, he yielded up his spirit in prayer.

XL. How, in accordance with the prophecy of the psalm which they had been singing when he died, the Lindisfarne brethren were attacked but, with the help of the Lord, were protected.

XLI. How a demoniac boy was healed by an infusion of some of that soil on which was poured the water wherein his body had been bathed.

XLII. How his body was found incorrupt eleven years afterwards.

XLIII. How the body of Eadberht was placed in the tomb of the holy man, and the sarcophagus of the saint placed upon it.

XLIV. How a sick man was cured by praying at his tomb.

XLV. How a paralytic was healed by his shoes.

19 om. $C_1VP_1O_4$.   20 ins. uir beatus O_3.   21–22 sanauerit egrotus $C_1VP_1O_3O_4$.   23 om. O_8.   24 uerba O_4. 25 ut et O_8.   26 cantauerunt O_8.   27 sunt C_3.   28 inp... C_1VP_1. 29 lauacram O_4.   30 ins. eius $C_1VP_1O_4$.   31 aqua C_1VP_1. 32 misso $C_1VP_1O_4$.   33 ins. sit $C_1VP_1O_4$. xi C_3O_8.   34 om. $C_1VP_1O_4$. 35 Eadberhti C_1V. Edberti O_8. ins. episcopi $C_1VP_1O_3O_4$.   36 Dei $C_1VP_1O_4$.   37 sarcof... $C_1VP_1O_3$. sarchophagum O_8.   38 ...erint C_1.   39 eg... $C_1VP_1C_3O_8O_3$.   40 illius P_1.   41 sit or. $C_1VP_1O_4$. 42 sanatus O_3.   43 om. O_3.   44 ins. sit O_3.

XLVI. Qualiter anachorita Felgildus[1] operimento parietis eius[2] a uultus tumore est[3] mundatus[4]. |

I. [5]*Quomodo puer Dei Cuthbertus*[7] *per infantem sit predicto episcopatu ammonitus*[8],[6]

Principium nobis scribendi de uita [9]et miraculis[10] beati patris[11] Cuthberti[12] Ieremias[13] propheta consecrat, qui anachoreticae perfectionis statum glorificans ait, *Bonum*

est uiro cum portauerit iugum ab adolescentia sua[14], *sedebit*[15] *solitarius et tacebit*[16], *quia*[17] *leuabit*[18] *se super se.* Huius nanque[19] boni dulcedine accensus uir Domini Cuthbertus[20], ab ineunte adolescentia iugo monachicae institutionis collum subdidit, et ubi oportunitas[21] iuuit, arrepta etiam conuersatione anachoretica[22], non pauco tempore soli-

tarius sedere[23], atque ob sua|uitatem diuinae contem-plationis ab humanis tacere delectabatur alloquiis. Sed[24] ut haec in maiori[25] aetate posset[26], superna illum gratia ad uiam ueritatis paulatim a primis iam puericiae[27] inci-tauerat annis. Siquidem usque ad octauum aetatis annum, qui post infantiam puericiae[27] primus est, solis paruulorum[28] ludis et lasciuiae mentem dare nouerat, ita ut illud beati Samuelis[29] tunc de ipso posset testimonium dici. *Porro*

Cuthbertus[30] *necdum sciebat Dominum, neque reuelatus fuerat ei sermo Domini.* Quod in praeconium laudis dictum est puericiae[31] illius, qui aetate[32] maior perfecte iam cogni-turus erat[33] Dominum, ac sermonem Domini reuelata cordis aure percepturus. Oblectabatur ergo ut diximus

---

1 Felgeldus C₁VP₁. Felgendus P₁.   2 *ins.* sit C₁VP₁O₄.
3 *om.* C₁VP₁O₄. sit O₈O₃.   4 *On p. 8 in* O₉ *are the chapter headings of nine miracles, two from the Ecclesiastical History, the other seven being post-Bedan. ins.* Incipit liber de uita et miraculis sancti Cuthberti Lindisfarnensis episcopi C₁O₄. *There are no separate chapter headings in* C₁Pr. Incipit liber de uita sancti Cuthberhti episcopi Lindisphar-nensis aecclesiae H. Liber de uita et miraculis necnon et de transitu beati patris Cuthberti Lindispharnensis episcopi (Lindisfarnensis M) C₃M.   5–6 Quomodo ipse octennis puer per trimum infantem de con-stantia animi et episcopatu sit premonitus C₃M. Quomodo ipse puer a puero pro instabilitate corripiebatur O₄. *omit chapter heading* O₈O₃.
7 Cuthberhtus V. Cuhtbertus H.   8 episcopatui adm... VH.

XLVI. How the hermit Felgild was cured of a swelling in the face by the covering of his wall.

CHAPTER I. *How Cuthbert, the child of God, was warned by an infant and his bishopric foretold*

The prophet Jeremiah consecrates for us the beginning of our account of the life and miracles of the blessed father Cuthbert when, praising the hermit's state of perfection, he says: "It is good for a man to have borne the yoke in his youth; he shall sit in solitude and be silent because he will raise himself above himself." For being stirred up by the sweetness of this blessing, Cuthbert the man of God submitted his neck from early youth to the yoke of monastic discipline; and at a favourable opportunity, he also took to the hermit's way of life, rejoicing to sit in solitude for no short time, and, for the sake of the sweetness of divine contemplation, to be silent and to hear no human speech. But in order that he might be able to do these things in his later years, the heavenly grace had urged him little by little into the way of truth, from the earliest years of his boyhood. For up to the eighth year of his age, which is the end of infancy and the beginning of boyhood, he could devote his mind to nothing but the games and wantonness of children, so that it could be testified of him as of the blessed Samuel: "Now" Cuthbert "did not yet know the Lord, neither was the word of the Lord yet revealed unto him." This was spoken as a prelude to the praise of his boyhood, for, when he became older, he was to know the Lord perfectly and to receive the word of the Lord, when once the ears of his heart had been

9–10 *om.* $C_1VHP_1C_3O_8O_3O_4M$. 11 *om.* $C_1VHP_1C_3O_8O_3O_4M$.
12 Cudberhti C_1. Cuthberchti V. Cuthberhti H. Cudberti O_4.
13 Hieremias $C_1VHC_3O_8O_4$. Iheremias M. 14 *ins.* si *above* C_1.
15 sederit (*uel* -bit *above*) P_1. 16 tacuerit (*uel* -cebit *above*) P_1. 17 *ins.*
non (*above* C_1) P_1. 18 leuauit C_1VHM. 19 namque C_1VHP_1.
20 Cudberhtus C_1. Cuthberhtus VH. Cudbertus O_4. 21 opp... C_3O_3.
22 annachoretica (na *above*) V. 23 *om.* O_9. 24 set O_3.
25 *ins.* implere *above* V. maiore O_8. 26 posset aetate O_4. 27 pueritiae
$C_1VHP_1C_3O_8O_4M$. 28 puerorum P_1. 29 Samuhelis M.
30 Cudberhtus C_1. Cuthberhtus VH. Cudbertus P_1. 31 pueritiae
$C_1VHP_1C_3O_8O_4M$. 32 etate O_3. 33 er. cog. P_1.

iocis[1] [2]et uagitibus[3], [4]et iuxta[5] quod aetatis[6] ordo
poscebat, paruulorum conuenticulis interesse cupiebat,
ludentibus colludere[7] desiderabat, et quia agilis natura
atque acutus erat ingenio, contendentibus ludo sepius
preualere[8] consueuerat, adeo ut fessis nonnunquam[9]
caeteris[10] ille indefessus adhuc si quis[11] ultra secum uellet[12]
certare, quasi uictor laetabundus[13] inquireret. Siue enim
saltu, siue cursu, siue luctatu, seu quolibet alio membrorum[14] sinuamine se exercerent[15], ille omnes aequeuos[16],

p. 11   et nonnullos | etiam maiores a se gloriabatur esse superatos.
1 Cor.   *Cum* enim *esset paruulus*, [17]*ut paruulus sapiebat, ut paruulus*
13. 11   *cogitabat*[18], qui postmodum *factus uir*, plenissime ea *quae*
paruuli erant deposuit. Et quidem diuina dispensatio[19]
primitus elationem animi puerilis digno se[20] pedagogo[21]
compescere dignata est. Nam sicut beatae memoriae
Trumwine[22] episcopus ab ipso Cuthberto[23] sibi dictum
perhibebat, dum quadam die solito luctamini[24] in campo
quodam non modica puerorum turba[25] insisteret, in-
teresset et ipse, et sicut ludentium leuitas[26] solet contra
congruum naturae statum uariis flexibus membra[27] plerique
sinuarent, repente unus de paruulis triennis ferme ut
uidebatur accurrit[28] ad eum, et quasi senili constantia
coepit[29] hortari[30] ne iocis et otio indulgeret, sed stabilitati
potius mentem simul et menbra[31] subiugaret. Quo[32]
monita spernente, luget ille[33] corruens in terram, et faciem
lacrimis rigans. Accurrunt[34] consolaturi caeteri[35], sed[36]
ille[37] perstat in fletibus. Interrogant quid haberet repen-
tinum, unde tantis afficeretur lamentis. At ille tandem
exclamans, consolanti se Cuthberto[38], Quid inquit[39] sanctissime antistes[40] et presbiter Cuthberte[41] haec[42] et naturae

---

1 *ins.* et iuxta C_1M.   2–3 uagtiri V. uagari H.   4–5 *om.*
$C_1VHP_1C_3O_4M$.   6 et... $C_1C_3O_3$.   7 conl... C_1VP_1.
8 prae... VHO_8.   9 nonnumquam C_1VHP_1.   10 cet... VC_3O_3.
11 qui (s *above*) C_1. qui VH.   12 uellent VH.   13 let... C_3O_3M.
14 menb... P_1O_4.   15 id est si *above* V.   16 co- *above* C_1. equ...
C_3O_3. et aequaeuos O_4.   17–18 sap. ut paru., cog. ut paru. VH.
19 disp. diu. P_1.   20 *om.* VH.   21 *gloss above* id est magistro VH.
22 Trumuuine $C_1VHP_1O_4$. Trumwyne O_3.   23 Cudberhto C_1.
Cuthberhto (*first* h *above* V) H. Cudberto P_1.   24 luctamine V.

opened. Therefore, as we have said, he amused himself with noisy games, and further, as was natural at his age, he loved to be in the company of children and delighted to join in their play. And because he was agile by nature and quick-witted, he very often used to prevail over his rivals in play, so that sometimes, when the rest were tired, he, being still untired, would triumphantly look round to see whether any of them were willing to contend with him again. Whether they were jumping or running or wrestling or exercising their limbs in any other way, he used to boast that he had beaten all who were his equals in age and even some who were older. For when he was a child he understood as a child, he thought as a child; but after he became a man, he put away childish things entirely. And indeed the divine providence at first deigned to check the exuberance of his childish mind by means of a fitting teacher. For Bishop Trumwine of blessed memory used to relate what had been told him by Cuthbert himself, how on a certain day, a large crowd of boys in a field were engaged in the usual contests and he himself was present: in accordance with the usual thoughtlessness of children at play, most of them were twisting their limbs into various unnatural contortions, when suddenly one of the little ones, apparently hardly three years old, runs up to him and begins to exhort him with the gravity of an old man not to indulge in idle games but rather stead-fastly to control both mind and limbs. When Cuthbert scorns his warnings, he throws himself on the ground, wailing and bedewing his face with tears. The rest run up to him to console him, but he persists in his weeping. They ask him what is the reason why he is suddenly overcome with such grief. But when Cuthbert begins to console him he exclaims at length: "Why, O Cuthbert, most holy bishop and priest, do you do these

changed from luctamine H. 25 turb. puer. C_3. 26 laeu... VH.
27 menbra P_1O_4. 28 adcucurrit C_1V. accucurrit H. 29 cepit C_3O_3.
30 ortari P_1. 31 mem... C_1VHO$_8$O$_3$. 32 *gloss above* scilicet
Cuthberhto VH. 33 *gloss above* scilicet infans VH. ipse P_1. 34 oc...
C_1VHP$_1$O$_4$. 35 cet... O_3M. 36 et O_4. 37 *gloss above*
scilicet infans VH. 38 Cudberhto C_1. Cuthberhto VH. Cudberto P_1.
39 inquid $P_1C_3O_8O_3$. *ins.* haec C_1VHP$_1$O$_4$. *gloss above* praedixit VH.
40 antestes V. *changed from* antestis H. anthistes O_3. 41 Cudberhte C_1.
Cuthberhte VH. Cudberte P_1. 42 *om.* C_1VHP$_1$O$_4$. hec O_3.

p. 12   et gradui tuo contraria geris? | Ludere te inter paruulos
non decet, quem Dominus etiam maioribus natu magi-
strum uirtutis consecrauit. Audiens haec[1] bonae[2] indolis
puer[3], fixa intentione suscepit, mestumque infantem piis
demulcens blanditiis, relicta continuo ludendi uanitate
domum rediit, ac stabilior iam ex illo tempore animoque
adolescentior[4] existere coepit[5], illo nimirum spiritu in-
terius eius praecordia[6] docente, qui per os infantis
extrinsecus[7] eius auribus insonuit. Nec[8] mirandum[9] cuiquam paruuli lasciuiam per paruulum potuisse Domino
2 Pet.   agente[10] cohiberi[11], qui ad *prohibendam[12] prophetae in-*
2. 16   *sipientiam[13],* ore *subiugalis muti* rationabilia uerba cum
uoluit edidit, in cuius[14] laude ueraciter dictum est, quia[15]
Psa. 8. 3   *ex ore infantium et lactantium[16] perfecisti laudem.* |

p. 13   II.   [17]*Quomodo genu dolente claudus sit effectus[19],*
et angelo medicante [20]sine mora[21] sanatus[18]

Matth.   Verum quia[22] *omni habenti dabitur et abundabit[23],* id est
25. 29   habenti propositum amoremque uirtutum harum copia
superno munere donabitur. Quoniam puer Domini Cuthbertus[24], quae per hominem accepit hortamenta[25] sedulo
corde retinebat, etiam angelico uisu et affatu confortari
promeruit. Nam subito dolore genu correptum illius,
acri coepit[26] tumore grossescere, ita ut neruis in poplite
contractis, pedem primo a terra suspensum claudicans
portaret, dehinc ingrauescente[27] molestia, omni poene[28]
priuaretur incessu. Qui die quadam deportatus foras a
ministris atque sub diuo recumbens, uidit repente uenientem [29]de longe[31] equitem[30] albis indutum uestimentis et

1 hec O₃.   2 bone O₃.   3 *gloss above* scilicet Cuthberhtus VH.
4 *gloss above* id est mitior uel mansuetior VH.   5 cepit O₃M.
6 pre... VO₈.   7 exterius O₄.   8 *gloss above* scilicet est V.
9 mirum O₄.   10 *om.* P₁.   11 chohiberi C₃.   12 prohibendum
VH.   13 *ins.* in C₁VHP₁O₄.   14 *gloss above* scilicet Domini VH.

things so contrary to your nature and your rank? It is not fitting for you to play among children when the Lord has consecrated you to be a teacher of virtue even to your elders." The boy, being of a good disposition, listened to these words with fixed attention, and soothing the sorrowful infant with kindly caresses, he forthwith gave up the idle games and, returning home, he began from that time to be steadier and more mature in mind. That Spirit assuredly instructed his heart from within, which had sounded in his ears from without through the mouth of an infant. Nor need anyone wonder that the wantonness of a child should be checked through a child by the Lord who, when He wished, placed rational words in the mouth of a dumb beast of burden to check the madness of a prophet: and it has truly been said in praise of Him that "out of the mouth of babes and sucklings thou hast perfected praise".

CHAPTER II. *How he became lame as the result of a diseased knee and was promptly cured by the ministration of an angel*

Truly "to everyone that hath shall be given, and he shall have abundance"; that is, to him who hath the desire and love for virtues, an abundance of them shall be granted by the heavenly gift. For since Cuthbert, the child of the Lord, held fast with diligent heart what he received by exhortations through man, he also earned the privilege of being comforted by seeing and speaking with an angel. For his knee was afflicted by a sudden torment and began to swell into a painful tumour, so that the sinews contracted in the knee; at first he carried his foot hanging lamely off the ground, and then, when the trouble grew worse, he was hardly able to walk at all. On a certain day he had been carried outside by servants and was lying in the open air, when he suddenly saw a horseman coming from

15 *om.* O$_4$.   16 lactentium P$_1$C$_3$O$_8$O$_3$M.   17–18 Quomodo per angelum curabatur O$_4$.   19 effectus sit VH.   20–21 *om.* VH.   22 *om.* P$_1$. 23 hab... C$_1$VHP$_1$C$_3$O$_3$M.   24 Cudberhtus C$_1$. Cuthberhtus VH. Cudbertus P$_1$.   25 ortamenta P$_1$.   26 cepit O$_3$.   27 ingrauascente O$_9$C$_3$O$_8$.   28 *om.* VH. pene C$_3$O$_3$O$_4$M.   29–30 eq. de longe P$_1$. 31 de long. uen. C$_3$.

honorabilem uultu, sed et equum cui[1] sedebat[2] incomparandi decoris. Qui cum adueniens mansueto illum salutaret alloquio, addidit quasi per iocum inquirere, si aliquod tali hospiti praebere[3] uellet obsequium. At ille, Iam inquid[4] promptissime tuis cuperem[5] astare[6] deuotus[7] obsequiis, sinon exigentibus culpis huius compede lan-

p. 14   guoris[8] retinerer. Diu nanque[9] est quod molestia | genu tumentis oppressus, nulla cuiuslibet medicorum industria possum sanari. Qui desiliens equo ac genu languidum diligentius considerans, Coque inquit[10] triticeam in lacte farinam, et hac confectione calida tumorem superungue, et sanaberis. Et his[11] dictis, ascendens equum abiit. Ille iussis obtemperans, post dies paucos[12] sanatus est, agnouitque angelum fuisse qui haec sibi[13] monita dedisset,

Tob. c. 11   mittente illo qui quondam Raphaelem[14] archangelum ad sanandos[15] Tobiae[16] uisus destinare dignatus est. Quod si cui uidetur incredibile angelum in equo apparuisse[17],

2 Mach.   legat historiam[18] Machabeorum, in qua angeli in equis,
11. 8   et ad Iudae Machabei, et ad ipsius templi defensionem aduenisse memorantur. |

p. 15   III.   [19]Quomodo uentis oratione mutatis rates[21]
delapsas [22]reuocauerit[24] ad litus[23,20]

Ab hoc autem tempore deuotus Domino puer sicut ipse postea familiaribus suis attestari[25] solebat, sepe in angustiis se uallantibus orans[26] Dominum, angelica meruit opitulatione defendi. Nec[27] non etiam pro aliis in[28] periculo constitutis quia benigna pietate supplicabat, exaudiebatur

Psa. 33. 18   ab illo, qui clamantem pauperem[29] exaudire, et ex omnibus tribulationibus eius consueuit eripere. Est denique monasterium non longe ab hostio[30] Tini fluminis[31] ad meridiem situm, tunc quidem uirorum, nunc autem mutato ut

---

1 quo P₁.   2 insidebat O₄.   3 pre... O₈O₄M.   4 inquid P₁O₃.
5 cup. tu. C₁VHP₁.   6 adstare C₁V. changed from adstare H. asstare
P₁O₄.   7 changed from deuotis C₁.   8 lang. comp. C₁VHP₁O₄.
9 namque C₁VHO₃.   10 inquid O₃.   11 hiis O₃.   12 pauc. dies O₄.
13 sibi hec O₃.   14 Raphahel V.   15 ...das C₁. ...dum P₁.
16 Tobie O₃.   17 apar... P₁.   18 hystoriam O₈.

afar, dressed in white robes and honourable of countenance, and the horse, too, on which he sat was of incomparable grace. He approached and saluted Cuthbert with gentle words and then enquired, as if in jest, whether he was willing to minister to such a stranger. But Cuthbert said: "Most readily would I rise and offer you devoted service, if I were not restrained by the fetter of this weakness, the penalty for my sins. I have long been afflicted by this trouble of a swelling in the knee and no doctor with all his care can heal me." The stranger jumped from his horse and examined the afflicted knee very carefully. Then he said: "Boil some wheaten flour in milk, spread this poultice while hot upon the swelling, and you will be healed." With these words he mounted his horse and departed. Cuthbert followed his commands and in a few days was healed. He recognised that he who had given him this advice was an angel, sent by One who once deigned to send the archangel Raphael to cure the eyes of Tobias. And if it should seem incredible to anyone that an angel appeared on horseback, let him read the history of the Maccabees in which angels on horseback are said to have appeared to defend Judas Maccabaeus and the temple itself.

CHAPTER III. *How he changed the winds by prayer and brought the rafts, which had been carried away, safe to land*

From this time the boy was wholly given to the Lord, and, as he was afterwards wont to testify to his friends, often prayed to the Lord when surrounded by difficulties and was counted worthy to be defended by angelic assistance; and moreover, because he prayed with kindly piety for others who were placed in danger, he was heard by Him who is wont to hear the cry of the poor and to "deliver him out of all his troubles". Now there is a monastery not far from the mouth of the Tyne, on the south side, filled with a noble company, in those days

19–20 Quomodo orando rates a tempestate liberauit O_4.   21 *ins.* oceano VH. *ins.* in oceanum C_3O_8. in occeanum O_3M.   22–23 ad lit. reuoc. $C_3O_8O_3M$.   24 reuocauit VH.   25 adt... V.   26 *ins.* ad $C_1VHP_1O_4$.   27 *gloss above* id est similiter VH.   28 im C_1. 29 peccatorem O_4.   30 ostio P_1O_4M.   31 flum. Tini C_3O_2.

solet[1] per tempora rerum statu, uirginum Christo ser-
uientium nobili examine pollens. Qui uidelicet famuli
Christi dum ligna monasterii usibus apta per memorati
alueum fluminis de longe ratibus ueherent, iamque e
regione eiusdem monasterii uehendo deuenirent, ac rates
ad terram educere[2] conarentur, ecce [3]uentus[5] subito[4] ab
occasu[6] tempestiuus[7] assurgens[8], abripuit rates, atque
[9]ad hostium [11],[10] fluminis trahere coepit. Quod uidentes e
monasterio fratres, emissis in[12] fluuio[13] nauiculis, eos qui |
in ratibus laborabant adiuuare nitebantur, sed ui fluminis
ac uentorum uiolentia superati nequaquam ualebant. Unde
facta desperatione humani adiutorii, confugerunt[14] ad
diuinum. Egressi nanque[15] de monasterio, et labentibus
in oceanum[16] ratibus collecti in proxima obice[17] flectebant
genua, supplicantes Domino[18] pro his[19] quos in tantum
mortis discrimen iamiamque[20] irruere[21] cernebant. Sed[22]
prouisione diuina, quamuis[23] diu precantium uota sunt
dilata, ut uidelicet quanta esset in Cuthberto[24] uirtus
precandi patesceret. Stabat enim in altera amnis[25] ripa
uulgaris turba non modica, in qua stabat et ipse[26]. Quae
cum aspectantibus cum tristitia[27] monachis raptas porro
per mare cerneret rates, adeo ut quasi quinque aues
paruulae, quinque enim erant[28] rates, undis insidentes ap-
parerent[29], coepit[30] irridere[31] uitam conuersationis eorum,
quasi merito talia paterentur, qui communia mortalium
iura spernentes, noua et ignota darent statuta uiuendi.
Prohibuit[32] probra deridentium Cuthbertus[33], Quid agitis
inquiens fratres, maledicentes his[34] quos in loetum[35] iam
trahi uidetis? Nonne melius esset et humanius Dominum |
pro eorum deprecari salute[36], quam de illorum gaudere

p. 16

p. 17

---

1 adsolet *changed in later hand to* assolet C₁. assolet P₁O₄.   2 ed.
ad ter. P₁.   3-4 sub. uent. C₁VHP₁.   5 *om.* O₄.
6 *ins.* uentus O₄.   7 *gloss above* uel -uosus O₄.   8 ads... C₁V.
9-10 *changed to* ab hostio VH.   11 ostium P₁M.   12 *om.* VHP₁.
13 fluuium C₃O₈O₃M.   14 fugerunt C₁VHP₁O₄.   15 namque
C₁VHP₁C₃O₃.   16 occeanum O₃M.   17 *gloss above* id est
litore VH.   18 Dominum P₁.   19 hiis O₃.   20 iam C₁P₁O₄.
21 *changed in later hand from* inruere C₁V.   22 set O₃.
23 *gloss above* scilicet precantur V.   24 Cudberhto C₁. Cuthberhto

of men but now, changed like all else by time, of virgins who serve Christ. Now once these same servants of Christ were bringing from afar in rafts, along the bosom of the river, wood suitable for the use of the monastery. They had already in their course reached a point opposite the same monastery, and were attempting to bring their rafts to land, when lo! a sudden storm of wind, arising from the west, dragged their rafts away and began to carry them off towards the mouth of the river. When the brethren in the monastery saw this, they launched some boats on the river and attempted to help those who were toiling on the rafts, but they were overcome by the force of the river and the violence of the winds and could do nothing. So, despairing of human help, they fled to the divine. Therefore, while the rafts were drifting out to sea, they left the monastery and, gathering on the nearest rock, they knelt down interceding with God on behalf of those whom they perceived to be even now in imminent risk of death. But though the answer to their prayers was long delayed, it was by divine providence, in order that it might be made plain how much virtue there was in Cuthbert's prayers. For on the other bank of the river stood no small crowd of the common people, and he was standing among them. These were watching the rafts on which the monks were sadly gazing, being carried so far out to sea that they looked like five tiny birds riding on the waves, for there were five rafts. Thereupon they began to jeer at the monks' manner of life, as if they were deservedly suffering, seeing that they despised the common laws of mortals and put forth new and unknown rules of life. Cuthbert stopped the insults of the blasphemers, saying: "Brethren, what are you doing, cursing those whom you see being carried away even now to destruction? Would it not be better and more kindly to pray to the Lord for their safety rather than to rejoice over their

VH. Cudberto P₁.   25 *changed from* annis C₁. ampnis O₃.
26 *gloss above* scilicet Cuthberchtus V. *gloss above* scilicet Cuthberhtus H.
27 tristicia P₁C₃O₈M.   28 *om.* VH.   29 apar... P₁.
30 cepit O₃. caep... C₁VP₁. *gloss in margin* scilicet turba uulgaris VH.
31 *changed in later hand from* inridere C₁. inridere V.   32 *ins.* Cuthberhtus
VO₄. *ins.* Cuthbertus H.   33 Cudberhtus C₁. *om.* VHO₄. Cudbertus P₁.
34 hiis O₃.   35 laet... P₁. let... O₈.   36 sal. precari C₁VHP₁Q₄.

periculis? At illi rustico et animo et ore stomachantes
aduersus eum, Nullus inquiunt hominum pro eis roget[1],
nullius eorum misereatur Deus, qui et ueteres culturas
hominibus tulere, et nouas[2] qualiter obseruare[3] debeant
nemo nouit[4]. Quo accepto responso, ipse oraturus
Dominum genua flexit, caput[5] in terram declinauit,
statimque retorta uis uentorum, rates cum his[6] qui duce-
bant gaudentibus integras ad terram eiecit, et iuxta ipsum
monasterium in loco oportuno[7] deposuit. Videntes autem
rustici erubuerunt de sua infidelitate, fidem uero uenerabilis Cuthberti[8] et tunc laude digna predicabant, et
deinceps predicare[9] nullatenus cessabant, adeo ut frater[10]
quidam nostri monasterii probatissimus [11]cuius ipse[13,12]
haec [14]relatione didici, sese haec[16,15] ab uno ipsorum[17]
rusticae simplicitatis uiro, et simulandi prorsus ignaro,
coram multis sepe[18] assidentibus[19] audisse narrauerit.

IV. *Quomodo cum pastoribus positus animam sancti Aidani*[20]
episcopi [21]*ad coelum*[22] *ab angelis ferri*[23] *aspexerit*[24] |

p. 18

At ubi gubernatrix uitae[25] fidelium gratia Christi uoluit
famulum suum artioris[26] propositi subire[27] uirtutem,
altioris praemii gloriam promereri[28], contigit eum remotis
in montibus[29] commissorum sibi pecorum agere custo-
diam. Qui dum nocte quadam dormientibus sociis ipse
iuxta morem[30] peruigil in oratione duraret, uidit subito
fusum de coelo[31] lumen medias longae[32] noctis interrupisse
tenebras in quo[33] coelestium[34] choros agminum terras[35]
petisse, nec[36] mora rapta[37] secum anima claritatis eximiae[38],

1 oret O₄.   2 nouae VH.   3 obseruari VHO₄.   4 *Note in
margin in sixteenth-century hand:* "Eadem uox papistarum nostri
temporis" C₁.   5 capud C₁P₁.   6 hiis O₃.   7 opp... C₃O₃.
8 Cudberhti C₁P₁. Cuthberhti VH.   9 prae... O₈.
10 *in margin* Nomen fratris Baella C₃O₃.   11–12 *om.* P₁.
13 se ipsum *in later hand above* C₁.   14–15 *om.* C₁P₁. *ins. above* V.
16 hec O₃.   17 illorum C₃.   18 saepe C₁VH.
19 ads... C₁V. *ins.* se P₁.   20 *ins.* Lindisfarnensis C₃O₃M.

dangers?" But they fumed against him with boorish minds and boorish words and said: "Let no man pray for them, and may God have no mercy on any one of them, for they have robbed men of their old ways of worship, and how the new worship is to be conducted, nobody knows." When Cuthbert heard this reply, he knelt down to pray to God, bending his head to the ground, and immediately the violent wind turned about and bore the rafts safe and sound to land, amid the rejoicings of those who were guiding them, and left them in a convenient place near the monastery itself. When the countryfolk saw this, they were ashamed of their own unbelief, but forthwith they duly praised the faith of the venerable Cuthbert, and thereafter never ceased to praise it. In fact a very worthy brother of our monastery, from whose lips I heard the story, declared that he himself had often heard these things related in the presence of many by one of these same people, a man of rustic simplicity and absolutely incapable of inventing an untruth.

CHAPTER IV. *How, being in the company of some shepherds, he saw the soul of the holy Bishop Aidan carried to heaven by angels*

Now when Christ, whose grace is the guide of the life of the faithful, wished his servant to subject himself to the power of a more rigorous dispensation, and to earn the glory of a greater reward, it happened that he was keeping the flocks committed to his care on some distant mountains. On a certain night while his companions were sleeping, he himself was keeping watch and praying according to his custom, when he suddenly saw a stream of light from the sky breaking in upon the darkness of the long night. In the midst of this, the choir of the heavenly host descended to the earth, and taking with them, without

21–22 *om.* O$_4$.   23 ferri ab ang. VHC$_3$O$_8$O$_3$M.   24 uidit O$_4$.
25 *om.* P$_1$.   26 arctioris (c *above* V) HC$_3$. arcioris O$_4$.   27 adire P$_1$.
28 *gloss above* scilicet et VH.   29 *in margin* Juxta flumen Ledir C$_3$O$_3$.
30 *changed from* montem P$_1$.   31 celo O$_3$.   32 longe O$_3$M.
33 *gloss above* scilicet uidit V.   34 cel... O$_3$M.   35 terram C$_1$VHP$_1$O$_4$.
36 naec V. *gloss above* id est sine VH.   37 sumpta C$_1$VHP$_1$O$_4$.
38 eximie C$_3$O$_3$.

supernam[1] redisse[2] ad[3] patriam. Compunctus[4] est mul-

p. 19

tum | hoc uisu Deo[5] dilectus adolescens, ad subeundum[6] gratiam [7]spiritualis exercitii[8], ac promerendae[9] inter magnificos uiros uitae [10]felicitatisque perennis[12,11], confestimque[13] Deo laudes gratiarumque referens actiones, sed[14] et socios ad laudandum Deum fraterna exhortatione[15] prouocans, Heu miseri inquit[16] qui somno[17] et inertiae[18] dediti, non meremur semper uigilantium ministrorum Christi cernere lucem. En ipse cum modico noctis tempore peruigil orarem, tanta Dei magnalia conspexi. Aperta est ianua coeli[19], et inductus[20] illuc[21] angelico comitatu spiritus[22] cuiusdam sancti, qui nunc nobis in infima caligine uersantibus, supernae mansionis gloriam ac regem illius Christum perpetuo beatus intuetur. Et quidem hunc uel episcopum quemlibet sanctum, uel eximium de fidelium numero uirum fuisse existimo, quem tantae splendore lucis, tot[23] ducentium choris angelorum coelos[24] allatum[25] uidi. Haec dicens uir Domini[26] Cuthbertus[27], non parum corda pastorum ad reuerentiam diuinae laudationis accendit, agnouitque mane facto antistitem Lindisfarnensis aecclesiae[28] Aidanum[29] magnae[30] [31]utique uirtutis[32] uirum, per id[33] temporis quo uiderat raptum de corpore, coelestia[34] regna petisse, ac statim commendans suis pecora[35] |

p. 20

quae pascebat[36] dominis, monasterium petere decreuit.

1 coelestem C_1VHP_1.   2 *gloss above* scilicet et VH. repedasse P_1. 3 *om.* C_1. *ins. above* V.   4 conp... C_1VHO_3.   5 *om.* P_1. 6 ...dam C_1VHP_1.   7–8 exerc. spiritalis C_1VH. exerc. spiritualis P_1O_4.   9 ...dam P_1. ...de O_3.   10–11 perhennis felicitatem P_1. 12 perhennis O_3.   13 que *erased* V. *om.* que H.   14 set O_3. 15 exort... C_1VH.   16 inquid O_3.   17 sompno O_3. 18 inertie O_3.   19 celi O_3.   20 *gloss above* scilicet est VH. 21 *changed from* illic V. illic C_1P_1.   22 anima P_1.   23 *gloss above*

delay, a soul of exceeding brightness, returned to their heavenly
home. The youth beloved of God was strongly moved by this
vision to subject himself to the grace of spiritual discipline and
of earning everlasting life and happiness amid God's mighty
men, and immediately he gave praise and thanks to God and
also called upon his companions with brotherly exhortation
to praise the Lord. "Alas," said he, "wretches that we are,
who are given up to sleep and sloth and are not worthy to
behold the glory of those servants of Christ who are ever
watchful. For I myself, though I was watching in prayer for
but a short part of the night, have nevertheless seen the wonders
of God. The gate of heaven was opened and the spirit of a
certain saint was conducted thither with an angelic retinue;
and while we dwell in utter darkness, he now, blessed for ever,
beholds the glory of the heavenly abode and Christ its King.
And indeed I think that it was either some holy bishop or some
specially distinguished man from among the number of the
faithful, whom I saw carried to heaven amid the splendour of
so great a light and accompanied by so many bands of angels."
With these words Cuthbert, the man of the Lord, kindled the
hearts of the shepherds in no little measure to the worship and
praise of God. And in the morning, learning that Aidan,
bishop of the church at Lindisfarne, a man of specially great
virtue, had entered the Kingdom of Heaven at the very time
when he had seen him taken from the body, Cuthbert forthwith delivered to their owners the sheep which he was tending
and decided to seek a monastery.

scilicet et VH.   24 *changed to* coelis V. coelis H. celos O_3.   25 *changed
in later hand from* adlatum C_1. adlatum V. illatum P_1.   26 Dom. uir O_4.
27 Cudberhtus C_1. Cuthberhtus VH. Cudbertus P_1. Cutbertus O_4.
28 ecclesie O_3.   29 *changed from* Aedanum C_1. Aydanum O_3. Aedanum V.
30 magne O_3.   31-32 *om.* O_4.   33 *gloss in margin* id est spatium V.
gloss above scilicet spatium H.   34 cel... C_3O_3.   35 *om.* O_4.
36 *ins.* pecora O_4.

V. *Quomodo iter faciens cibos Domino procurante perceperit*[1]

Cunque[2] nouum uitae[3] continentioris ingressum sedulo iam corde meditaretur, affuit[4] gratia superna, quae animum eius artius[5] in proposito firmaret, ac manifestis
Matth.
6. 33 edoceret indiciis[6] quia *quaerentibus*[7] *regnum Dei et iustitiam*[8] *eius*[9], ea quae ad uictum corporis [10]pertinent beneficio[12] diuinae[11] prouisionis *adiciuntur*. Quadam nanque[13] die dum[14] iter solus ageret, diuertit hora tertia[15] in uillam quam eminus positam forte repperit, intrauitque
p. 21 domum cuiusdam | religiosae matris familias, paululum ibidem quiescere desiderans, et iumento potius cui[16] sedebat quam sibi alimentum poscere curans. Erat enim[17] tempus incipientis brumae[18]. Suscepit ergo eum mulier benigne rogauitque sollicite ut prandium parare atque illum reficere liceret. Negauit uir Domini, Non possum inquiens adhuc manducare, quia dies ieiunii[19] est. Erat nanque[20] sexta sabbati, qua plerique fidelium ob reuerentiam dominicae passionis usque ad horam nonam[21] solent protelare ieiunium. Perstitit in rogando mulier hospitalitatis studio deuota, Ecce inquiens[22] itinere quo uadis nullum uiculum nulla hominum habitacula repperies[23]. Et quidem longum restat iter, neque ante solis occubitum ualet consummari. Unde precor[24] antequam egrediaris accipias cibos[25], ne tota die ieiunium sustinere uel etiam procrastinare cogaris. At ille quamuis[26] multum rogante femina rogantis instantiam religionis amore deuincens[27] ieiunus [28]uiam repetiit, ieiunus diem duxit ad uesperam. Cunque[30] instante iam uespera cerneret se iter quod proposuerat eodem die non posse finire[32], neque ulla[33] in proximo[34] hominum hospicia

---

1 percepit VHO₄.   2 cum... C₁VHP₁C₃O₈O₃M.   3 uite O
4 *changed from* adfuit C₁. adfuit V.   5 arctius C₃. *ins.* suo VP
6 inditiis P₁O₈M.   7 quer... P₁C₃M.   8 iusticiam P₁C₃O₈M
9 *ins.* et VH.   10–11 *ins. above* C₁. *in margin* V.   12 munere P
13 namque C₁VHP₁O₃.   14 cum M.   15 tercia P₁C₃O₈O₄N
16 quo (*changed from* cui C₁) P₁.   17 autem P₁.   18 brume O

CHAPTER V. *How, while he was on a journey, he received food through God's care*

While, with diligent heart, he was now meditating entrance into a stricter course of life, the heavenly grace was present to confirm his spirit more resolutely in his decision and to show, by manifest signs, that to those who seek the Kingdom of God and His righteousness, those things which appertain to the nourishment of the body are added by the favour of divine providence. For on a certain day, while he was travelling alone, he turned at the third hour into a village some distance away which he happened upon by chance. And he entered the house of a certain religious housewife, wishing to rest there for a little and purposing to ask for food for the horse on which he was riding, rather than for himself; for it was the beginning of the winter season. The woman received him kindly and earnestly begged him to allow her to prepare him a morning meal to refresh him. The man of God refused saying, "I cannot eat yet because it is a fast day." For it was Friday, a day on which most of the faithful are accustomed to protract their fast until the ninth hour out of reverence for the passion of the Lord. The woman, being given to hospitality, persisted in her entreaties. "Look", she said, "you will find no village and no human habitation on the road you are taking; and you have a long journey before you, which you cannot finish before sunset. So I pray you to accept food before you set out, so that you may not be compelled to fast the whole day or even wait until to-morrow." But though the woman urged him greatly, his love of religion overcame the urgency of her entreaty, and he set out once more fasting, and fasted the whole day until evening. And when, with evening at hand, he discovered that he could not finish the journey he had undertaken on the same day, and that there were no

19 *ins.* dies C_3. 20 namque $C_1VHP_1O_3$. 21 non. hor. $C_1VHP_1O_8O_3O_4$. 22 inquit C_1VHP_1. *ins.* in (*above* V) H. 23 rep... O_9. repperiens O_3. 24 prae... H. 25 cybos HP_1. 26 quan... P_1. 27 restitit $C_1P_1O_4$. *altered from* restitit VH. *ins.* et P_1. 28–29 *om.* C_1VHP_1. 30 cumque $C_1VHP_1C_3M$. 31 uespere $C_1P_1O_4$. 32 fin. non posse... P_1. 33 *om.* P_1. 34 proxima C_1. 35 hospitia $C_1VHP_1C_3O_4M$.

ubi manere posset adesse, ecce subito | iter faciens, uidit iuxta pastorum tuguria[1], quae aestate[2] infirmiter posita, tunc iam deserta patebant[3]. Huc propter manendum ingrediens[4], equum in quo uenerat alligauit ad parietem, collectumque foeni[5] fasciculum quem tecto uentus abstulerat, edendum illi apposuit[6], ipse orando horam ducere coepit[7]. At subito inter psallendum[8] uidit equum[9] elato sursum capite, tecta casae[10] carpentem ore iusumque[11] trahentem atque inter cadentia foena[12] tecti inuolutum pariter decidere linteum[13]. Volensque dinoscere certius quid esset, finita oratione accessit, et inuenit inuolutum linteo[14] dimidium[15] panis calidi et carnem, quae ad unam sibi refectionem[16] sufficere possent. Laudemque decantans beneficiis coelestibus[17], Deo inquit gratias[18] qui et mihi[19] pro eius amore[20] ieiunanti et meo comiti coenam[21] prouidere[22] dignatus est. Diuisit ergo fragmen panis quod inuenit, partemque eius dimidiam equo[23] dedit, reliquum suo esui[24] reseruauit, atque ex illo iam die promptior factus est ad ieiunandum, quia nimirum intellexit eius dono sibi refectionem procuratam in soli-
tudine, qui quondam Heliam[25] solitarium, quia nullus hominum aderat qui ministraret, eiusdem modi cibo[26] per
uolucres | non pauco tempore pauit. Cuius *oculi super*
timentes eum, sperantes autem in *misericordia eius, ut eripiat a morte animas eorum, et alat eos in fame.* Haec[27] mihi[28] religiosus[29] nostri monasterii quod est ad hostium[30] Wiri[31] fluminis presbiter nomine Inguuald[32], qui nunc longe gratia senectutis magis corde mundo[33] · coelestia[34] quam terrena carnalibus contemplatur aspectibus, ab ipso Cuthberto[35] iam tunc episcopo se audisse[36] perhibuit.

---

1 tug. past. M.   2 est... $P_1C_3O_3$.   3 *in margin*: Loedra locus uocatur in quo uidua manebat ad quem sanctus Cuthbertus itinerans ueniebat. Aloent uero locus dicitur ubi equus tecti fasciculum carpebat et mappulam cum pane calido candente et carne extraxerat O_3. 4 *changed from* ingressu P_1.   5 faeni VP_1. feni O_8O_3.   6 adp... C_1V. *ins.* et P_1.   7 caepit VP_1. cepit O_3.   8 ...andum C_1. psalmodiam VH.   9 aequum O_9.   10 case O_3.   11 *changed from* iosumque C_1. iosumque VH. *gloss above* vel u H.   12 faena VP_1. fena O_3M.   13 lintheum $C_1VHC_3O_3$.   14 lintheo $O_9VHC_3O_3$. h *above* V.   15 dimidio P_1.   16 ref. sibi M.   17 cael... C_1VHP_1. cel... C_3O_3.   18 *ins.* ago VH.   19 michi O_4.

lodgings in the neighbourhood where he could stay, he suddenly saw, as he made his way along, some shepherds' huts close by, which had been roughly built during the summer time and were then lying open and deserted. He entered one in order to shelter there, and fastening to the wall the horse he had been riding, he collected a bundle of straw which the wind had removed from the roof, and gave it to the horse to eat. He himself began to spend the time in prayer, when suddenly in the midst of his psalm-singing, he saw the horse lift up its head, seize the thatching of the house with its mouth and drag it down. Amid the straw falling from the roof, he saw a folded cloth fall as well; wishing to discover more certainly what it was, he drew near, when his prayer was finished, and found, wrapped in the cloth, half a loaf still warm, and some meat, sufficient for one meal for himself. Then he uttered praises for the heavenly favours. "Thanks be to God", he said, "who has deigned to provide a supper for me who am fasting out of love for Him, and also for my comrade." So he divided the piece of bread which he found and gave half of it to the horse and the rest he kept for his own food: and from that day he became readier than ever to fast, because indeed he understood clearly that this food had been provided for him in a solitary place, by the gift of Him who once for many days fed Elijah in solitude, with food of the same kind, through the ministrations of birds, there being no man there to minister to him. "His eyes are upon them that fear Him and that hope in His mercy, in order that He may snatch their soul from death and feed them in a time of famine". These things a priest named Ingwald, a monk of our monastery at Wearmouth, related that he had heard from Cuthbert himself, who was then a bishop. This Ingwald now, thanks to a lengthy old age, no longer with carnal eyes gazes on things earthly, but rather, with a pure heart, contemplates things heavenly.

20 amore eius H.   21 caenam C_1VHP$_1$. cenam O_3.   22 preuidere VH.
23 aequo O_9.   24 usui O_8.   25 *om.* P$_1$.   26 cybo P$_1$.   27 Hec O_3.
28 michi O_4.   29 *ins.* et C_1P$_1$.   30 ostium VHP$_1$.   31 Uiri *changed to*
Uuiri C_1. Uuiri H. Uiri O_3.   32 Inguald *changed to* Inguuald C_1. Ingwald
$C_3O_8O_3$M.   33 mun. cord. M.   34 cel... C_3O_3.   35 Cuthberhto
VH. Cudberhto C_1. Cudberto P$_1$. Cuhtberto C_3.   36 *ins.* se P$_1$.

VI. *Quale*[1] *testimonium illi*[2] [3]*ad monasterium uenienti*[4] *Boisilus*[5] [6]*uir sanctus in spiritu prohibuerit*[8,7], [9]*utque ipse ibidem* [11]*susceptus uel conuersatus sit*[12,10]

Interea uenerabilis Domini seruus relictis seculi rebus mo-
nasterialem properat subire disci|plinam, utpote coelesti[13]
uisione ad appetenda perpetuae gaudia beatitudinis[14] incitatus, ad tolerandam pro Domino esuriem sitimque
temporalem, epulis inuitatus[15] coelestibus[16]. Et quidem
Lindisfarnensem aecclesiam[17] multos habere sanctos uiros,
quorum doctrina et exemplis instrui posset nouerat, sed
fama preuentus[18] Boisili sullimium[19] uirtutum monachi
et sacerdotis Mailros petere maluit. Casuque contigit, ut
cum illo perueniens equo desilisset[20], ingressurusque ad
orandum[21] aecclesiam[22], ipsum pariter equum[23] et hastam[24]
quam tenuerat manu ministro dedisset[25], necdum enim
habitum deposuerat saecularem, Boisilus ipse prae foribus
monasterii consistens prior illum uideret[26]. Preuidensque[27]
in spiritu quantus conuersatione esset futurus quem cerne-
bat, hoc unum dixit astantibus[28], Ecce seruus Dei, imitatus
illum qui uenientem ad se Nathanael[29] intuitus, *Ecce*
inquit[30] *uere*[31] *Israelita*[32] *in quo dolus non est*, sicut religiosus
ac ueteranus Dei famulus[33] et presbiter[34] Sigfridus solet
attestari[35], qui eidem Boisilo haec[36] dicenti inter alios
asstabat[37], tunc in ipso monasterio[38] adolescens primis adhuc
monachicae[39] uitae[40] rudimentis institutus, nunc in nostro
id est[41] Gyruensi[42] monasterio perfectum in Christo | agens
uirum et [43]inter [46]egra[45,44] spiritus extremi[47] suspiria
laetum[48] uitae alterius sitiens[49] introitum. Nec plura
loquens Boisilus peruenientem mox[50] ad se[51] Cuthbertum[52]

p. 24

John 1. 47

p. 25

---

1 quod ei VH.   2 *om*. VH. sibi O₄.   3–4 uen. ad mon. VH. ad
conuersationem uenienti O₄.   5 Boisil VH. Boysilus C₃.   6–7 dedit
O₄.   8 prophetauerit VH.   9–10 *om*. VHO₄.   11–12 uixerit M.
13 cel... O₃.   14 *om*. P₁.   15 incitatus P₁.   16 cel... O₃.
17 aecl... V. ecc... O₃.   18 prae... H.   19 subl... C₁VHO₄.
20 desiluisset VH.   21 adorandum HP₁.   22 aecl... V.   23 *om*.
C₁P₁O₄.   24 *changed to* astam V.   25 *gloss above* scilicet cum VH.
26 uidit P₁.   27 prae... H.   28 ads... C₁V. ass... P₁O₄.
29 Nathanahel VH. Nathanaelem P₁.   30 inquid O₃.   31 uir VH.
32 Israhel... C₁VHP₁M.   33 seruus O₄.   34 presbsbiter P₁.

CHAPTER VI. *What manner of testimony the holy man Boisil gave to him in the spirit, as he came to the monastery, and how he was received and lived there*

Meanwhile the reverend servant of the Lord, having forsaken the things of the world, hastens to submit to monastic discipline, since he had been urged by the heavenly vision to seek the joys of eternal bliss and to endure temporal hunger and thirst for the Lord's sake as one who had been invited to the heavenly feasts. And though he knew that the church at Lindisfarne contained many holy men by whose learning and example he might be instructed, yet learning beforehand of the fame of the sublime virtues of the monk and priest Boisil, he preferred to seek Melrose. And by chance it happened that, having jumped down from his horse on reaching the monastery, and being about to enter the church to pray, he gave both his horse and the spear he was holding to a servant, for he had not yet put off his secular habit. Now Boisil himself, who was standing at the gates of the monastery, saw him first; and foreseeing in spirit how great the man whom he saw was going to be in his manner of life, he uttered this one sentence to those standing by: "Behold the servant of the Lord!" thereby imitating Him who, looking upon Nathanael as he came towards Him, said: "Behold an Israelite indeed in whom there is no guile." Thus is wont to testify that pious and veteran servant and priest of God, Sigfrith, who was standing with others near Boisil himself when he said these words. Sigfrith was then a young man in that monastery, having learned as yet only the first rudiments of monastic life; now he is in our monastery, namely Jarrow, living the life of a perfect man in Christ and, amid the feeble sighs of his latest breath, thirsting for a joyful entry into another life. Without saying more, Boisil forthwith kindly received Cuthbert on his arrival, and when the latter had explained the

35 adt... C₁V. at... P₁.   36 hec O₃.   37 astabat C₃O₈O₃M.
ads... C₁VH.   38 mon. ipso O₄.   39 monachice O₃.   40 uite O₃.
41 *ins.* in O₄.   42 Gyruuensi C₁. Giruuensi O₄. Giruensi P₁O₃.
Girwensi C₃.   43–44 integra V.   45 aegra HP₁O₈M.   46–47 ext.
spir. aeg. O₄.   48 letum O₃.   49 siciens O₉O₃.   50 *om.* O₄.
51 *ins.* mox O₄.   52 Cudberhtum C₁V. Cuthberhtum H. Cudbertum P₁.

benigne suscepit, causamque[1] itineris exponentem, quia
uidelicet monasterium saeculo praetulerit benignius[2] secum
retinuit. Erat enim praepositus eiusdem monasterii. Et
post dies paucos adueniente uiro beatae[3] recordationis
Eata[4] tunc presbitero et abbate monasterii ipsius, postea
Lindisfarnensis[5] aecclesiae[6] simul et eiusdem loci antistite,
indicauit ei de Cuthberto[7], et quia boni propositi animum
gereret[8] exposuit, obtinuitque[9] apud eum, ut accepta
tonsura, fratrum iungeretur consortio[10]. Quod ingressus
monasterium, confestim aequalem[11] caeteris[12] fratribus
uitae[13] regularis obseruantiam tenere, uel etiam artioris[14]
disciplinae studiis supergredi curabat, legendi uidelicet,
operandi, uigilandi, atque orandi sollertior. Sed et iuxta
exemplum[15] Samsonis[16] fortissimi quondam Nazarei *ab
omni quod inebriare*[17] *potest* sedulus[18] abstinebat. Non
autem[19] tantam escarum ualebat subire continentiam, ne[20]
necessariis minus idoneus[21] efficeretur operibus. Erat enim
robustus corpore, et integer uiribus[22], atque[23] ad quae-
cunque[24] uolebat aptus[25] exercitia laboris. |

Judges c.
13
Num. 6. 3

p. 26

VII. [26]*Quomodo angelum hospicio*[28] *suscipiens, dum panem
querit*[29] *ministrare terrenum, coelesti*[30] *ab eo*[31] *remunerari
meruit*[32],[27]

Cunque[33] post aliquot annos regi Alchfrido[34] placeret,
pro redemptione[35] animae[36] suae[37] locum quendam regni
sui qui uocatur in Ripum[38] ad construendum[39] [40] ibidem[42]
monasterium[41] Eatan[43] abbati donare[44], tollens idem
abbas quosdam e[45] fratribus secum, in quibus et Cuthbertum[46], condidit[47] ibi[48] quod petebatur[49] monasterium[50],

---

1 *ins.* sui $C_1VHP_1O_4$.   2 benignus $C_1VP_1O_4$.   3 beate O_3.
4 Heata P_1. Eatha O_3.   5 Lyndisfarnensis O_3.   6 eccl... C_1O_3.
aecl... V.   7 Cudberhto C_1V. Cuthberhto H. Cudberto P_1.
8 *changed in later hand from* generet C_1.   9 opt... VH.·   10 cons.
iung. $C_1VHP_1O_4$.   11 equ... O_3.   12 cet... VC_3O_3.
13 uite O_3.   14 arctioris (c *above* V)HC_3. altioris O_8.   15 exempla M.   16 Sampsonis O_3.   17 inebriari C_1.   18 *om.* P_1.
19 *ins. above* C_1.   20 *om.* C_1P_1. *ins.* ut (*above* C_1) P_1.   21 *from
here to end of chapter in different hand* V. ydoneus O_3.   22 *ins.* et
above V.   23 *om.* C_1VP_1. et H.   24 quaecumque $C_1VHP_1C_3O_3$.

reason of his journey, namely that he preferred the monastery to the world, Boisil still more kindly kept him. For he was the prior of that same monastery. And after a few days, when Eata of blessed memory arrived, who was then a priest and the abbot of the monastery and afterwards both abbot and bishop of the church at Lindisfarne, Boisil told him about Cuthbert, declaring that his mind was well disposed, and obtained permission from him for Cuthbert to receive the tonsure and to join the fellowship of the brethren. And entering this monastery, he sought at once to observe the rules of the regular life equally with the other brethren, or even to excel them in zeal for a stricter discipline, being more diligent in fact in reading and working, in watching and praying. Moreover in accordance with the example of Samson the strong, who was once a Nazarite, he sedulously abstained from all intoxicants; but he could not submit to such abstinence in food, lest he should become unfitted for necessary labour. For he was robust of body and sound in strength and fit for whatever labour he cared to undertake.

CHAPTER VII. *How he entertained an angel and whilst seeking to minister to him earthly bread, was thought worthy to be rewarded by him with heavenly bread*

Some years after, it pleased King Alhfrith for the redemption of his soul to give Abbot Eata a certain place in his kingdom which is called Ripon in which to build a monastery. This same abbot took with him certain of the brethren, amongst whom was Cuthbert, and founded there the desired monastery, instituting

25 *changed from* aptas C_1.   26–27 Quomodo angelum hospitio susceperit O_4.
28 hospitio VHM.   29 quaer... H.   30 cael... VH. cel... O_3.
31 eodem VH.   32 meruerit $VHC_3O_8O_3M$.   33 cumque
$C_1VHP_1C_3O_3O_4M$.   34 Alhfrido C_1VH. Alhcfrido O_4.
35 redemtione P_1C_3.   36 anime O_3.   37 sue O_3.   38 Hrypum
C_1VH. Hripum $P_1C_3O_8M$. Rypum O_4.   39 edibus M.   40–41 *ins.*
above V.   42 *om.* M.   43 Eatano O_8O_3M. Eata O_4.   44 *changed to*
donabat C_1.   45 ex P_1.   46 Cudberhtum C_1. Cuthberhtum (*first*
h *above* V) H. Cudbertum P_1. *gloss above* scilicet tulit VH.   47 *changed
from* condi C_1.   48 *ins.* monasterium O_4.   49 paet... V.   50 *om.* O_4.

atque eisdem quibus antea[1] Mailros institutis disciplinae
regularis imbuit. Ubi famulus Domini Cuthbertus[2] suscipiendorum officio praepositus hospitum probandae[3]
suae[4] gratia deuotionis, angelum Domini suo suscepisse
fertur hospitio[5]. Exiens enim[6] primo mane de interioribus
monasterii aedibus ad hospitum[7] cellulam[8], inuenit inibi[9] |
p. 27   quendam sedentem iuuenem, quem hominem estimans[10]
solito mox humanitatis more suscepit. Nam lauandis
manibus aquam dedit, pedes ipse abluit, linteo[11] extersit,
fouendos humiliter manibus suo in sinu composuit[12],
atque ut horam diei tertiam[13] etiam cibo[14] reficiendus
expectaret rogauit, ne si ieiunus iret, fame pariter et
frigore lassaretur hiberno. Putabat nanque[15] hominem
nocturno itinere simul et flatibus defessum[16] niueis, illo
requiescendi gratia diluculo diuertisse[17]. Negauit ille, et se
cito iturum quia longius esset mansio ad quam properaret,
respondit. At Cuthbertus[18] diu multumque[19] rogans,
tandem adiuratione addita diuini nominis, ad manendum
coegit. Statimque ut expletis horae[20] tertiae[21] precibus[22],
uescendi tempus aderat, apposuit[23] mensam, sumendas
obtulit[24] escas, Et obsecro te inquit frater reficias, dum
rediens panem calidum affero[25]. Spero enim quia iam
cocti sint[26]. At ubi rediit, non inuenit hospitem quem
edentem reliquerat. Explorat uestigia qua[27] iret, sed nulla
uspiam inuenit[28]. Recens[29] autem nix[30] terram texerat[31],
quae facillime uiantis iter proderet[32], et quo declinaret
monstraret[33]. Stupefactus ergo uir Dei[34], et secum querens[35] de facto, reposuit mensam in conclaui. Quod in-
p. 28   gressus, conti|nuo obuiam habuit *miri odoris fragrantiam*[36].
Greg.
Dial.iv.16

1 *gloss above* scilicet imbuit VH.   2 Cudberhtus C_1P_1. Cuthberhtus
(*first* h *above* V) H.   3 probande O_3.   4 sue O_3.   5 hospicio
C_3O_8.   6 etenim C_1VHO_4.   7 ospitum P_1.   8 cellam P_1.
9 ibi O_3.   10 aest... VHM.   11 lintheo HO_3.   12 conp...
C_1VH.   13 terciam $C_3O_8O_4M$.   14 cybo HP_1.   15 namque
$C_1VHP_1O_3$.   16 defessus $O_9C_1P_1C_3O_8$.   17 devert... H.
changed from aduenisse P_1.   18 Cudberhtus C_1. Cuthberhtus (*first* h
above V) H. Cudbertus P_1.   19 *om.* que $C_1VHP_1O_4$.   20 hore O_3.

therein the same rules of discipline as were observed at Melrose. Cuthbert, the servant of the Lord, was appointed guestmaster and is said to have entertained in his guesthouse an angel of the Lord who was sent to test his devotion. Going out in the early morning from the inner buildings of the monastery to the guests' chamber, he found a certain youth sitting within, and, thinking that he was of the race of men, he speedily welcomed him with his accustomed kindness. He gave him water to wash his hands; he washed his feet and wiped them with a towel and placed them in his bosom so as to chafe them humbly with his hands; and asked him to wait until the third hour of the day and be refreshed with food, lest, if he went away fasting, he might faint from hunger as well as from the wintry cold. For he thought that the man had been tired both by a night journey and by the snow-laden winds, and that he had turned aside thither at dawn to rest. The youth refused, answering that he would go quickly because the dwelling to which he was hastening was very far away. But Cuthbert, after he had asked him many times, at length compelled him to remain by adjuring him with the divine name; and as soon as the prayers were finished at the third hour and the time for food had come, he placed a table before him and offered him food to eat, saying: "I pray you, brother, refresh yourself while I go and bring you a warm loaf, for I expect that they are now baked." But when he returned, he did not find the guest whom he had left eating; he searched for his footsteps to see whither he had gone, but he found none at all, though fresh snow had covered the earth which would very easily betray the steps of a person walking over it and would show whither he had turned. The man of God was amazed and wondering within himself concerning this event, he replaced the table in the store-house. And as he entered, he immediately encountered a wonderfully fragrant odour. Looking round

21 terciae $C_3O_8O_4$.   22 praec... H.   23 adp... C_1V.   24 optulit C_3.
25 *changed in later hand from* adfero/C_1. adfero V.   26 sunt modo C_1VH.
sunt P_1O_4.   27 quo VH.   28 cernit C_1VHP_1. *gloss above* uel cernit O_4.
29 recentes C_1O_4.   30 niues C_1O_4. niuis H.   31 texerant C_1O_4.
32 proderent C_1O_4.   33 monstrarent C_1O_4.   34 Domini C_1VHP_1.
35 quaer... HO_8.   36 flagrantiam $C_1P_1O_3$. fraglantiam $VHC_2O_8O_4M$.

Circumspiciens autem unde esset orta *tanta* nidoris[1] *suauitas*,
uidit iuxta positos tres panes calidos insoliti candoris et
gratiae, pauensque talia secum loquitur, Cerno quod
angelus Dei [2]erat quem suscepi[4], pascere non pasci
ueniens. En[3] panes attulit[5], quales terra gignere nequit.
Nam et lilia candore, et rosas odore, et mella praecellunt
sapore. Unde constat quia non de nostra tellure orti, sed
de paradiso[6] uoluptatis sunt allati[7]. Nec mirum quod
epulas in terris sumere respuerit humanas, qui aeterno[8]
uitae[9] pane fruitur in coelis[10]. Itaque uir Domini de
ostensa miraculi uirtute conpunctus[11], maiorem ex eo
uirtutum operibus curam impendebat[12]. Crescentibus
autem uirtutibus, creuit et gratia coelestis[13]. Denique
sepius[14] ex eo tempore angelos uidere et alloqui[15], sed et
esuriens cibis[16] speciali[17] sibi munere[18] a Domino prae-
paratis meruit refici. Nam quia affabilis et iocundus erat
moribus[19], plerunque[20] dum ad[21] exemplum uiuendi praesentibus[22] patrum praecedentium[23] gesta referret, etiam
quid sibi doni spiritualis[24] superna pietas contulerit, humiliter interserere solebat. Et aliquando [25,27]quidem palam,

p. 29 aliquando[26] autem uelate[28], quasi sub persona | alterius id
facere curabat. Quod tamen qui audiere, quia de se ipso
dixerit intelligebant[29], iuxta exemplum magistri[30] gentium,
qui modo aperte suas uirtutes replicat, modo sub praetextu

2 Cor. alterius personae loquitur dicens[31], *Scio hominem in Christo*
12. 2 *ante annos quattuordecim*[32] *raptum usque ad tertium*[33] *coelum*[34],
[35]*et caetera illius loci*[36].

1 odoris VH.	2–3 *om.* P₁.	4 suscaepi V.
5 adt... C₁.	6 paradyso HM.	7 adlati sunt C₁V. allati
sunt HP₁O₄.	8 aeternae P₁. eterno O₃.	9 uite O₃.
10 cel... C₃O₃.	11 comp... O₈O₄M.	12 inp... C₁VH.
13 cel... O₃.	14 saepius VH.	15 *changed from* adloqui C₁.
adloqui V.	16 cybis HP₁.	17 specialibus C₁VHP₁.
18 *om.* C₁VHP₁.	19 mor. erat C₁VHP₁O₄.	20 plerumque

to see whence so sweet an odour had arisen, he saw near by three warm loaves of unusual whiteness and excellence. And trembling, he said to himself: "I see that it was an angel of God whom I received and that he came to feed and not to be fed. Behold, he has brought loaves such as the earth cannot produce; for they excel the lily in whiteness, the rose in fragrance, and honey in taste. Hence it follows that they have not come from this earth of ours but they have been brought from the paradise of joy. Nor is it wonderful that he should refuse to partake of our human feasts on earth, when he enjoys the eternal bread of life in heaven." And so the man of God, being moved by the manifest virtue of this miracle, gave the greater heed for this reason to works of virtue; and as his virtues grew so also grew the heavenly grace. For from that time he was very often held worthy to see and talk with angels, and when hungry, to be refreshed by food prepared for him by the Lord as a special gift. He was affable and pleasant in his manners, and while for the most part he would relate the deeds of the fathers who had departed as an example of godly living to those still alive, yet he was also wont to add in all humility something about any spiritual gift which the heavenly grace had bestowed on himself; sometimes he would do so openly, but sometimes he would also be at pains to do this in a veiled manner, as though it had happened to another person. Nevertheless those who heard understood that he was speaking of himself after the example of the teacher of the Gentiles, who now recounts openly his own virtues, and now speaks under the guise of another person, saying: "I knew a man in Christ above fourteen years ago, such an one caught up even to the third heaven", and so on.

C_1VHP$_1$C$_3$O$_8$O$_3$O$_4$. 21 *om.* C_1. 22 *pre...* VO$_8$. 23 *pre...* VM.
24 *changed from* spiritalis C_1. spiritalis VH. 25-26 *om.* C_1VH.
27-28 *om.* P$_1$. 29 *changed from* intellegebant C_1. intellegebant VH.
ins. Hoc igitur P$_1$. 30 *gloss above* scilicet Pauli VH. 31 *om.*

C_1VHP$_1$O$_4$. *gloss above* scilicet dicens VH. 32 IIII decim P$_1$.

XIIII VO$_4$. quatuordecim C_3M. 33 III V. tercium P$_1$C$_3$O$_8$O$_4$M.
34 cael... C_1V. cel... C_3O$_3$. 35-36 *om.* C_1VHP$_1$O$_4$.

VIII.   [1] Quod[3] sanato[4] a languore Cuthberto[5], Boisilus[6]
moriturus[7], quae illi[8] [9]essent[10] uentura[11] praedixerit[12,2]

Interea quia fragilis est et more freti uolubilis omnis
saeculi[13] status, instante subito turbine, praefatus abbas
Eata[14] cum Cuthberto[15] et caeteris[16] quos secum adduxerat
fratribus domum repulsus est, et locus monasterii quod
condiderat aliis ad incolendum monachis datus[17]. Nec
memoratus athleta[18] Christi mutatione[19] loci[20] | mutauit
mentem ab arrepto[21] semel proposito militiae[22] coelestis[23],
uerum diligentissime iuxta quod et ante facere consueuerat,
beati Boisili dictis pariter auscultabat et actis[24]. Quo
tempore sicut Herefridus familiaris eius presbiter et abbas
quondam monasterii Lindisfarnensis[25] ipsum referre soli-
tum testatur, morbo pestilentiae[26] quo tunc plurimi per
Brittanniam[27] longe lateque deficiebant, correptus est. At
fratres monasterii illius totam pro eius uita et salute pre-
cantes[28] duxere noctem[29] peruigilem. Omnes enim quasi
hominis sancti[30] necessariam sibi eius adhuc in carne
praesentiam rebantur[31]. Quod dum ipsi mane quidam
de illis indicaret[32], nam nescio[33] eo fecerant, respondens
statim, Et quid iaceo inquit[34]. Neque enim[35] dubitandum[36]
est, quia tot taliumque uirorum preces[37] Deus non[38]
despexerit. Date baculum et caligas. Statimque[39] exurgens[40], coepit[41] temptare[42] incessum baculo innitens, et
crescente per dies uirtute sanitatem quidem recepit[43], sed
quia tumor qui in femore[44] parebat, paulatim a superficie
detumescens corporis, ad uiscerum interiora perlapsus est,
toto pene[45] uitae[46] suae[47] tempore aliquantulum interan-

---

1–2 Quomodo Boisilus moriturus Cuthberto quae ei uentura erant
praedixit O_4.   3 quomodo $C_3O_8O_3M$.   4 saluato VH.
5 Cuthberchto V. Cuthberhto H.   6 Boisil VH. Boysilus C_3.
7 *ins.* omnia $C_3O_8O_3M$.   8 *om.* VH. ei $C_3O_8O_3M$.   9–11 uentura
erant M.   10 erant $C_3O_8O_3$.   12 pre... O_8. praedixit M.
13 sec... O_3.   14 Eatha O_3. Eta M.   15 Cudberhto C_1V.
Cuthberhto H. Cutberto P_1.   16 cet... C_1VO_3.   17 datur
VHP_1.   18 adhleta $C_1P_1C_3$. *changed from* adthleta VH.
19 mutacione O_4.   20 locorum $C_1VHP_1O_4$.   21 arrecto P_1.
22 miliciae C_3O_8. militie O_3. 23 cael... C_1. cel... O_3. 24 uel -bus
above C_1. actibus P_1.   25 Lyndisfarnensis O_3. 26 pestilencie O_3.

CHAPTER VIII. *How Cuthbert was healed of· sickness and how Boisil, when he was about to die, prophesied things which were to come to him*

Meanwhile because the whole state of the world is frail and unstable as the sea when a sudden tempest arises, the aforesaid Abbot Eata with Cuthbert and other brethren whom he had brought with him was driven home, and the site of the monastery, which he had founded, was given to other monks to dwell in. Yet this same champion of Christ did not change his mind as a result of this change of place, nor abandon his determination once taken to wage the heavenly warfare; but most diligently he paid heed both to the words and the deeds of the blessed Boisil as he had been accustomed to do before. At that time (as Herefrith, a priest who belonged to his community and who was once abbot of the monastery of Lindisfarne, testifies that Cuthbert was wont to relate), he was stricken down with the plague which at that time carried off very many throughout the length and breadth of Britain. Now the brethren of that monastery spent the whole night in watching and praying for his life and safety; for they all thought that inasmuch as he was a holy man, his continued presence in the flesh was necessary to them. When one of them told him about this in the morning—for they had done it without his knowledge—he replied forthwith: "And why do I lie here? for doubtless God has not despised the prayers of so many good men. Give me my staff and shoes." And immediately he arose and began to try to walk, leaning upon his staff; and as his strength grew from day to day, he recovered his health; but as the swelling which appeared in his thigh gradually left the surface of his body, it sank into the inward parts and, throughout almost the whole of his life, he continued to feel some inward

27 Brittaniam C_1. Britanniam VO_3M.   28 praec... H.   29 noct. dux. $C_1VHP_1O_4$.   30 Dei P_1.   31 *changed to* reuerebantur O_9 *in later hand.*   32 indicarent O_9.   33 nesciente C_1VHP_1.   34 inquid O_3. 35 inquid O_8O_3.   36 putandum $C_1VHP_1O_4$.   37 praeces O_8. 38 *om.* $C_1VHP_1O_4$.   39 confestimque C_1VHP_1.   40 exsurgens C_1VHP_1. 41 caep... VP_1. cep... O_3M.   42 temtare P_1O_4.   43 recaep... V. 44 *ins.* eius $C_1VHP_1O_4$.   45 paene C_3.   46 uite O_3.   47 sue O_3.

p. 31
2 Cor.
12. 9

Gal. 5. 6

p. 32

eorum non cessabat[1] sentire dolorem, uidelicet ut iu|xta apostolum *uirtus in infirmitate perficeretur*. Quem cum famulus Domini Boisilus[2] a ualitudine sanatum cerneret[3], ait, Vides frater quia liberatus es a molestia qua laborabas, et dico tibi quod ea iam ultra tangendus non es, neque hoc moriturus in tempore. Simulque moneo ut quia me mors uicina praestolatur[4], discere[5] a me aliquid quamdiu docere[6] ualeam non omittas. Non enim plus quam septem dies sunt, quibus mihi[7] ad docendum sanitas corporis et linguae suppetat[8] uirtus. Respondit Cuthbertus[9] nichil[10] hesitans de ueritate dictorum[11] illius, Et quid rogo optimum mihi[12] est legere, quod tamen una[13] ualeam consummare septimana[14]? At ille, Iohannem inquit[15] euangelistam[16]. Est autem mihi[17] codex habens quaterniones septem, quas singulis diebus singulas possumus Domino adiuuante legendo, et quantum opus est inter nos conferendo percurrere. Factumque[18] est ut dixerat. Quam ideo lectionem tam citissime complere ualebant, quia solam in ea *fidei quae per dilectionem operatur* simplicitatem, non autem questionum profunda tractabant. Completa ergo post dies septem[19] lectione, memorato morbo arreptus[20] uir Domini Boisilus[21] diem peruenit ad ultimum, et hoc magna cum[22] exultatione transcenso[23] ad[24] | gaudium[25] perpetuae lucis intrauit. Ferunt illum his[26] septem[27] diebus omnia Cuthberto[28] quae ei futura restabant, exposuisse. Propheticus nanque[29] ut dixi, et mirae sanctitatis erat homo. Denique [30] praefatae[32] acerbitatem[31] pestilentiae triennio priusquam ueniret, Eatano[33] abbati suo praedixit[34] [35]fuisse[37] futuram[36], nec se illa tollendum [38]celauit, ipsum uero abbatem suum non ea[39] moriturum sed illo potius morbo quem dissenteriam[40] medici appellant, ueridico ut

---

1 cessauit (uel -bat *above*) C₃.   2 Boisil VH. Boysilus C₃.
3 cern... san... C₃.   4 *gloss in margin* id est expectat uel praesens
est V. *same gloss above* H. pre... O₄M.   5 docere M.   6 dicere M.
7 michi O₄.   8 subp... C₁VHP₁.   9 Cudberhtus C₁V.
Cuthberhtus H. Cudbertus P₁.   10 nihil C₁VHP₁.
11 *changed from* doctorum C₁.   12 michi O₈O₄M.   13 *ins.*
septimana O₄.   14 *om.* O₄.   15 inquid O₃.   16 aeuang...
O₉. euuang... C₁P₁.   17 michi O₄. *om.* M.   18 *om.* que

pains, so that, in the words of the apostle, "strength was made perfect in weakness".

When the servant of the Lord, Boisil, saw that he had been healed of his sickness, he said: "You see, brother, that you have been freed from the affliction by which you were beset, and I declare to you that you will not be stricken again nor will you die now: and at the same time, since death is upon me, I admonish you to lose no opportunity of learning from me so long as I am able to teach you. For not more than seven days remain in which I shall have sufficient health of body and strength of tongue to teach you." Cuthbert, never doubting the truth of his words, answered: "And what, I ask you, is it best for me to read, which I can yet finish in one week?" He replied: "The evangelist John. I have a book consisting of seven gatherings of which we can get through one every day, with the Lord's help, reading it and discussing it between ourselves so far as is necessary." They did as he said. They were able to finish the reading so quickly because they dealt only with the simple things of the "faith which worketh by love" and not deep matters of dispute. So when the reading had been completed in seven days, Boisil the man of the Lord, having been attacked by this said disease, reached his last day and, having spent it in great gladness, he entered into the joy of perpetual light. It is said that he declared all Cuthbert's future to him during these seven days: for, as I have said, he was a prophet and a man of marvellous sanctity. And in fact he had predicted this virulent pestilence to his abbot Eata three years before it appeared, and did not hide the fact that he himself would be carried off by it; but he declared that the abbot himself would not die of this but rather of a disease which the doctors call dysentery, and, as events proved, his prophecy was true. But

$C_1VHP_1O_4$.   19 sept. di. $C_1VHP_1O_4$. VII V.   20 arr. morb. $C_1VHP_1O_4$.   21 Boisil VH.   22 *om.* $C_1VHP_1O_4$.   23 transcurso O_4. 24 *om.* VHO_4.   25 gaudia VHO_4.   26 hiis O_3.   27 VII V. 28 Cudberhto C_1V. Cuthberhto H. Cudberto P_1.   29 namque C_1VHP_1. 30–31 acerb. praef. O_4.   32 prefate O_3.   33 Eatan (n *above* V) HP_1. Eata O_4.   34 pre... M.   35–36 fut. fuisse O_4.   37 *om.* P_1. 38–39 nec C_1VHP_1.   40 dyssinterian C_1. dyssinteriam VH. dissenteria P_1. dissinterian O_4.

rerum exitus docuit sermone praemonuit. Sed et Cuthberto[1] inter alia, quia episcopus esset ordinandus insinuauit.
Unde idem Cuthbertus[2] postmodum in secessu ana-
choreseos positus, dicere quidem nulli uolebat quia episcopum eum praedixerat[3] futurum, sed tamen uisitantibus
se [4]aliquotiens[6] fratribus[5], solebat multo cum dolore
protestari [7]quia Etiam [9]si fieri possit[10] ut in caute per-
modicam[11,8] domunculam[12] habens deliteam[13], ubi cir-
cumferentes[14] me undique fluctus oceani tumescentis[15]
a cunctorum mortalium uisu[16] pariter et cognitione
secludant[17], nec[18] sic quidem liberum me[19] ab insidiis
mundi fallentis estimo[20], sed ibi quoque quia qualibet
ex causa filargiria[21] me temptans abripere possit uereor.

p. 33

IX. *Quam sedulus erga | ministerium uerbi*
Cuthbertus[22] extiterit[23]

Post obitum uero[24] dilecti Deo[25] sacerdotis Boisili memora-
tum praepositi officium Cuthbertus[26] suscepit, et per
aliquot annos spirituali[27] ut sanctum decebat exercens
industria, non solum ipsi monasterio regularis uitae[28]
monita, simul et exemplum[29] praeferebat[30], sed et uulgus
circumpositum longe lateque a uita stultae[31] consuetudinis,
ad coelestium[32] gaudiorum[33] conuertere curabat amorem.
Nam et multi fidem quam habebant, iniquis profanabant[34]
operibus, et aliqui etiam tempore mortalitatis neglecto
fidei quo imbuti erant sacramento, ad erratica idolatriae[35]
medicamina concurrebant, | quasi missam a Deo conditore

p. 34

plagam per incantationes uel alligaturas, uel alia quaelibet[36]
demoniacae[37] artis archana cohibere ualerent[38]. Ad utro-
rumque ergo corrigendum errorem crebro ipse de monas-

---

1 Cudberhto C₁V. Cuthberhto H. Cudberto P₁.   2 Cudberhtus
C₁V. Cuthberhtus H. Cudbertus P₁.   3 praedixerit C₁VHP₁O₄.
pre... O₈.   4–5 frat. aliq. P₁.   6 ...ties C₁VHP₁.   7–8 *in
different hand* V.   9–10 *om.* C₁P₁.   11 ...ica C₁P₁C₃O₈O₃.
12 ...ula C₁P₁.   13 delitheam O₃.   14 circumferente P₁.
circumfrementes C₃.   15 *changed from* tumescentes C₁.
tumescentes P₁.   16 *changed from* uisa C₁.   17 recludant VH.
claudant P₁.   18 *changed from* nes C₁. ne VHO₄.   19 me lib. C₁P₁.
20 aest... C₁VH.   21 filargyria VO₈. philargiria O₄.

amongst other things, he suggested to Cuthbert that he would be made a bishop. So, in after days, when he was living a hermit's life, Cuthbert would not tell anyone that Boisil had predicted to him that he should be a bishop: but nevertheless, to the brethren who sometimes visited him, he used to declare with much sorrow: "Even if I could possibly hide myself in a tiny dwelling on a rock, where the waves of the swelling ocean surrounded me on all sides, and shut me in equally from the sight and knowledge of men, not even thus should I consider myself to be free from the snares of a deceptive world: but even there I should fear lest the love of wealth should tempt me and somehow or other should snatch me away."

CHAPTER IX. *How Cuthbert was diligent in the ministry of the word*

So after the death of Boisil the priest beloved of God, Cuthbert undertook the office of prior which we have mentioned before, and, for a number of years, he was busy with spiritual works, as befitted a holy man; and not only did he give the monastery itself counsels concerning life under the rule and an example of it, but he sought moreover to convert the neighbouring people far and wide from a life of foolish habits to a love of heavenly joys. For many of them profaned the faith they held by wicked deeds, and some of them also at the time of the plague, forgetting the sacred mystery of the faith into which they had been initiated, took to the delusive cures of idolatry, as though by incantations or amulets or any other mysteries of devilish art, they could ward off a blow sent by God the creator. So he frequently went forth from the monastery to correct the errors of both kinds of sinners, sometimes riding on a horse

22 Cuthberhtus VH. *om.* O_4.   23 exstiterit O_3.   24 ergo $C_1VHP_1O_4$.
25 Deo dil. C_3.   26 Cudberhtus C_1V. Cuthberhtus H. Cudbertus P_1.
27 spiritali C_1VH.   28 uite O_3.   29 exempla VHO_4.
30 pre... O_8.   31 stulte O_3.   32 cael... C_1. cel... M. celeste O_3.
33 *ins. in margin* H.   34 prophanabant $P_1C_3O_3$.   35 ydolatrie O_3.
36 que... O_3.   37 demonice C_1. *altered from* demonice V. demoniace O_3.
38 possent O_4.

terio egressus aliquotiens[1] equo[2] sedens, sed sepius pedes[3]
incedens, circumpositas ueniebat ad uillas[4], et uiam ueri-
tatis praedicabat errantibus, quod ipsum[5] etiam Boisilus[6]
suo tempore facere consueuerat. Erat quippe moris eo
tempore populis Anglorum, ut ueniente in[7] uillam clerico
uel presbitero cuncti ad eius imperium uerbum audituri
confluerent, [8]libenter ea quae[10] dicerentur audirent[11,9],
libentiusque[12] quae audire et intelligere[13] poterant ope-
rando sequerentur. Porro Cuthberto[14] tanta erat[15] docendi
peritia[16], tantus[17] amor persuadendi quae coeperat[18], tale
uultus angelici lumen, ut nullus praesentium[19] latebras
ei sui cordis celare[20] praesumeret, omnes palam quae
gesserant confitendo proferrent[21], quia nimirum haec[22]
eadem illum latere nullomodo[23] putabant, et confessa

Luke 3. 8 dignis ut imperabat poenitentiae[24] fructibus abstergerent[25].
Solebat autem ea maxime loca peragrare[26], illis predicare[27]
in uiculis, qui in arduis asperisque montibus procul positi
p. 35 aliis hor|rori erant ad uisendum, et paupertate pariter ac
rusticitate sua doctorum prohibebant accessum. Quos
tamen ille pio libenter mancipatus labori[28], tanta doctri-
nae[29] excolebat industria, ut de monasterio egrediens,
sepe[30] ebdomada[31] integra, aliquando duabus uel tribus,
nonnunquam[32] etiam mense pleno domum non rediret,
sed demoratus in montanis[33] plebem rusticam uerbo predi-
cationis simul et exemplo uirtutis ad coelestia[34] uocaret.

1 n above V. aliquoties O[4].   2 aequo O[9].   3 pedibus VH.
4 uillulas P[1].   5 ipse O[9].   6 Boysilus C[3].   7 om. C[1]VH.
ad P[1].   8-9 om. P[1].   10 que O[3].   11 gloss above scilicet
ut VH.   12 om. que O[4].   13 intellegere C[1]V. changed from
intellegere H.   14 Cudberhto C[1]V. Cuthberhto H. Cudberto P[1].
15 om. O[4].   16 pericia C[3].   17 ins. erat O[4].   18 cep...

but more often going on foot, and came to the neighbouring villages and preached the way of truth to these wanderers, just as Boisil had been accustomed to do in his time.

Now it was the custom at that time amongst the English people, when a clerk or a priest came to a village, for all to gather together at his command to hear the word, gladly listening to what was said, and still more gladly following up by their deeds what they could hear and understand. So great was Cuthbert's skill in teaching, so great his love of driving home what he had begun to teach, so bright the light of his angelic countenance, that none of those present would presume to hide from him the secrets of his heart, but they all made open confession of what they had done, because they thought that these things could certainly never be hidden from him; and they cleansed themselves from the sins they had confessed by "fruits worthy of repentance," as he commanded. Now he was wont to penetrate those parts especially and to preach in those villages that were far away on steep and rugged mountains, which others dreaded to visit and whose poverty as well as ignorance prevented teachers from approaching them. And giving himself up gladly to this pious labour, he attended to their instruction with such industry, that, leaving the monastery, he would often not return home for a whole week, sometimes even for two or three weeks, and even occasionally for a full month; but he would tarry in the mountains, summoning the rustics to heavenly things by the words of his preaching as well as by the example of his virtue.

$P_1C_3O_8O_3$. 19 pre... VO_8O_4. 20 caelare O_4.
21 *gloss above* scilicet ut V. pro. conf. O_4. 22 hec O_3.
23 null. lat. O_4. 24 pen... P_1O_8. 25 *gloss above* scilicet ut VH.
extergerent O_4. 26 *gloss above* et VH. 27 prae... O_8.
28 labore VH. 29 *om.* O_4. 30 saepe VH.
31 ebdomade C_1P_1. 32 nonnumquam C_1VHO_4. 33 *gloss above*
scilicet locis VH. 34 cael... C_1. cel... C_3O_8.

X. *Quomodo animalia maris* [1] *in quo pernox orauerat*[3], *illi egresso*[4] *praebuerint*[5] *obsequium, et*[6] *frater qui haec*[7] *uiderat*[8] *prae*[9] *timore languescens eius*[10] *sit oratione recreatus*[2]

p. 36
Cum uero[11] sanctus uir in eodem monasterio uirtutibus signisque succresceret, famaque | operum[12] eius circunquaque[13] crebresceret, erat sanctimonialis femina et mater ancillarum Christi nomine Ebbae[14], regens monasterium quod situm est in loco quem Coludi urbem nuncupant, religione pariter et nobilitate cunctis honorabilis. Nanque[15] erat soror uterina regis Oswiu[16]. Haec[17] ad uirum Dei mittens, rogauit ut se suumque monasterium gratia exhortationis[18] inuisere dignaretur. Nec negare potuit, quod ab eo caritas ex ancillae[19] Dei corde poposcit[20]. Venit igitur ad locum, diesque aliquot ibi permanens, uiam iusticiae[21] quam precabatur[22] omnibus actu pariter et sermone pandebat. Qui cum more sibi solito quiescentibus noctu caeteris[23] ad orationem solus exiret, et post longas intempestae[24] noctis uigilias tandem instante hora communis sinaxeos[25] domum rediret, quadam nocte unus e fratribus eiusdem monasterii cum egredientem illum silentio cerneret, clanculo[26] secutus eius uestigia, quo iret[27], quidue agere[28] uellet dinoscere querebat[29]. At ille egressus[30] monasterio sequente exploratore[31] descendit ad mare, cuius ripae[32] monasterium idem[33] superpositum erat. Ingressusque[34] altitudinem maris, donec ad col|lum

p. 37
usque et[35] brachia unda tumens assurgeret[36], peruigiles undisonis[37] in laudibus tenebras noctis exegit. Appropinquante[38] autem diluculo, ascendens in[39] terram denuo coepit[40] in litore[41] flexis[42] genibus orare. Quod dum[43] ageret[44], uenere continuo duo de profundo maris qua-

1–2 illi inde egresso obsequium praebuerint O₄.   3 orauerit VH.
4 regresso VH.   5 pre… HO₈.   6 *ins.* ut C₃O₈O₃.   7 hec O₃.
8 uidebat VHC₃O₈O₃M.   9 pre O₈.   10 uel illius *above* C₃.
11 ergo O₄.   12 *changed from* uirtutum P₁.   13 circumquaque C₁VHP₁M.   14 Aebbe C₁VHP₁. Ebbe C₃O₈O₃M. Aebbae O₄.
15 namque C₁VHP₁O₃.   16 Osuuii C₁P₁. Oswyu O₃. Osuiu VO₄. *changed from* Osuiu *to* Osuii H.   17 hec O₃.   18 exortationis VHC₃.   19 ancille C₃O₃M.   20 poposcerat C₁P₁O₄.
21 iusticiae C₁VH.   22 predicabat (di *above* V) P₁. praedicabat H.

CHAPTER X. *How the animals of the sea, in which he had passed the night in prayer, ministered to him when he came out, and how a brother who saw it, being ill through fear, was restored by his prayers*

Now while the holy man was going from strength to strength in that monastery by his signs and miracles, and the fame of his works had spread everywhere, there was a nun, a mother of the handmaidens of Christ, called Aebbe, who ruled over the monastery situated in a place called Coldingham, a woman honoured among all as well for her piety as for her noble birth, for she was own sister of King Oswiu. She sent to the man of God asking that he would deign to visit her and her monastery for the sake of exhorting them. Nor could he deny the loving request of the handmaiden of God. So he came to the place and remained there some days and opened up to them all the path of righteousness about which he preached, as much by his deeds as by his words. Now, according to his custom, while the others were resting at night, he would go out alone to pray, and after watching long throughout the dead of night, he would return home just at the hour of common worship; and on a certain night one of the brethren of the same monastery, seeing him go silently out, followed in his footsteps secretly, seeking to discover whither he meant to go and what he intended to do. Cuthbert left the monastery with the spy following him and went down to the sea, above whose shores the monastery was built; going into the deep water until the swelling waves rose as far as his neck and arms, he spent the dark hours of the night watching and singing praises to the sound of the waves. When daybreak was at hand, he went up on to the land and began to pray once more, kneeling on the shore. While he was doing this, there came forth from the depths of the sea

23 cet... VO_3M. 24 intempeste O_3. 25 syn... $C_1VHO_8O_3O_4$.
26 *gloss above* uel e uestigio, id est celeriter, uelociter, festinanter, cito, ocius, propere V. 27 ire $VHC_3O_8O_3O_4M$. 28 *changed from* ageret P_1.
29 quaer... $VHP_1C_3O_8O_4$. *from* exploratione C_1. 30 *ins.* e P_1. 31 *changed in later hand* 32 ripe $P_1O_8O_3$. 33 id. monast. O_4.
34 ingrediensque $C_1VHP_1O_4$. 35 ac VH. *ins.* ad P_1O_8. 36 ads...
C_1V. 37 undissonis O_3. 38 adp... C_1VP_1. 39 ad O_3O_4.
40 caep... C_1VP_1. cep... O_3. 41 litt... $C_3O_3O_4M$. 42 fexis P_1.
43 cum P_1. 44 faceret P_1.

drupedia quae uulgo lutraeae[1] uocantur. Haec[2] ante illum
strata in arena[3], anhelitu suo pedes eius fouere coeperunt[4],
[5]ac uillo satagebant extergere[6]. Completoque[7] ministerio, percepta ab eo benedictione patrias sunt relapsa sub
undas. Ipse [8]quoque mox[9] domum reuersus, canonicos[10]
cum fratribus ymnos[11] hora competente[12] compleuit[13].
At frater qui eum de speculis[14] prestolabatur, perculsus
pauore ingenti, uix prae angustia[15] premente domum
nutante gressu peruenit. Primoque mane accedens ad
eum sese in terram strauit, ueniam de reatu stulti ausus
cum lacrimis flagitauit[16], nil dubitans illum nosse quid
ipse [17]noctu egerit, quidue[18] pateretur. Cui ille, Quid
inquit[19] habes frater? Quid fecisti? Num nostrum iter
nocturnum lustrando explorare temptasti? Sed[20] ea solum
conditione[21] tibi hoc indulgeo[22] commissum, si promiseris
te quae uidisti nulli ante meum obitum esse dicturum.

p. 38   In quo nimirum | praecepto[23] eius secutus est exemplum,
qui discipulis in monte gloriam suae[24] maiestatis ostendens
Matth.   ait, *Nemini dixeritis uisionem, donec filius hominis a mortuis*
17. 9   *resurgat.* Promittentem[25] ergo quae iusserat fratrem benedixit, pariterque culpam et molestiam quam temerarius
incurrerat[26] abstersit[27]. Qui uirtutem quam uiderat ipso
uiuente silentio tegens, post obitum eius plurimis indicare
curabat[28].

1 lutreae C₁P₁O₈O₄M. lutrae VH. lutree O₃.   2 Hec O₃.
3 harena C₁VHC₃O₄.   4 ceperunt (*above*) V. cep... P₁O₈M. *om.* O₄.
5-6 *om.* C₁VHP₁.   7 conp... VH.   8-9 *om.* C₁VHO₄. uero P₁.
10 *changed from* canonicas C₁. canonicas P₁.   11 hymnos C₁VH.
ympnos O₃.   12 conp... C₁V. competenti HP₁.   13 conp... VH.
14 *gloss above* ofperd stoʃum V.   15 *ins.* se P₁O₄.   16 *gloss above*
uel postulauit O₃.   17-18 *om.* C₁VHP₁O₄.   19 inquid O₈O₃.

two four-footed creatures which are commonly called otters. These, prostrate before him on the sand, began to warm his feet with their breath and sought to dry him with their fur, and when they had finished their ministrations they received his blessing and slipped away into their native waters. He forthwith returned home and sang the canonical hymns with the brethren at the appointed hour. Meantime the monk who stood watching him from the cliffs was stricken with such deadly fear and weighed down with such distress, that he could scarcely reach home with faltering footsteps; and in the early morning he approached Cuthbert and, stretching himself on the ground, tearfully entreated his pardon for the guilt of his foolish daring, not doubting that Cuthbert knew what he had done that night and why he was suffering. Cuthbert said to him: "What is the matter, brother? What have you done? Have you attempted to view and spy upon my nightly journey? But I will grant you pardon for this fault only on one condition, that you promise you will not tell anyone about what you have seen before my death." In this command he followed the example of Him who, when He showed the glory of His majesty to the disciples on the mount, said: "Tell the vision to no man until the Son of Man be risen again from the dead." So the promise being given, he blessed the brother, and freed him both from the fault and from the affliction which he had so rashly incurred; and the brother kept silence about the miracle he had seen so long as Cuthbert was alive, but after the saint's death he took care to tell it to many.

20 *ins.* et M.   21 condicione C_1VH.   22 ind. tib. hoc P_1.
23 pre... VM.   24 su. glor. $C_1VHP_1O_4$.   25 promittente P_1.
26 incurrebat VHP_1.   27 *changed from* abstergit C_1.   28 curauit
$C_1VHP_1O_4$.

XI. *Quomodo nautis* [1]*tempestate praeclusis*[3] *serenum mare*[4]
    ad certum[5] *praedixerit et orando cibos impetrauerit*[2]

Greg.
Dial.
   II. 11

p. 39

Coepit[6] *inter ista*[7] *uir Dei etiam prophetiae spiritu pollere,*
uentura praedicere, praesentibus absentia nuntiare[8]. Quodam
etenim tempore pergens de suo monasterio pro necessitate[9]
causae[10] accidentis[11] | ad terram Pictorum qui[12] Niduari[13]
uocantur[14], nauigando peruenit, comitantibus eum[15] duobus e[16] fratribus, quorum unus postea presbiterii[17] functus
officio, uirtutem miraculi quam ibidem uir Domini
monstrauit, multorum noticiae[18] patefecit. Uenerunt autem
illo post natalis[19] dominici diem, sperantes se quia undarum
simul et aurarum arridebat[20] temperies, citius esse redituros,
ideoque nec cibaria[21] secum tulere, tanquam[22] otius[23]
reuersuri. Sed longe aliter quam putabant euenit. Nam
mox ut terram tetigere tempestas fera[24] suborta est, quae
iter eis omne remeandi praecluderet[25]. Cunque[26] per dies
aliquot ibidem inter famis et frigoris pericula taberent[27],
quo tamen tempore [28]uir Dei[29] non marcida luxu[30] otia[31]
gerere, nec somnis[32] uacare uolebat inertibus[33], sed[34]
pernox in oratione[35] perstare satagebat, aderat sacratissima
dominicae apparitionis[36] dies. Tum ille socios blando ut
iocundus atque affabilis erat sermone alloquitur, Quid rogo
tanta ignauia torpemus, et non quacunque[37] iter salutis
inquirimus? En tellus niuibus, nebulis coelum[38] horrescit,
aer flatibus, aduersis[39] furit fluctibus equor[40], ipsi inopia
deficimus, nec adest homo qui reficiat. Pulsemus ergo
Dominum precibus[41], qui suo quondam populo maris
rubri uiam aperuit, eumque in deserto mirabiliter pauit, |

1–2 serenitatem praedixerit O₄.   3 pre... HO₈.   4 *om.* C₃.
5 *ins.* diem VH.   6 caep... C₁V. cep... O₉.   7 interea
O₉C₃O₈O₃O₄M.   8 nunciare O₄.   9 necessitatis VH.   10 causa
VH.   11 *changed from* accedentes C₁.   12 quae VH.   13 Niduuari
C₁P₁.   14 uocatur VH.   15 secum C₁VHP₁O₄.   16 *om.*
P₁.   17 *in margin:* Nomen presbyteri (presbiteri O₄) Tydi C₃O₃.
18 notitiae C₁VH.   19 nathalis O₃.   20 adr... C₁V.

CHAPTER XI. *How he promised the sailors who were cut off by the storm that the sea would be calm by a certain day, and how his prayer for food was answered*

Meanwhile the man of God began to grow strong in the spirit of prophecy also, to foretell the future and to describe to those with him events that were happening elsewhere. Now at a certain time, having left the monastery on account of some necessity which arose, he came by boat to the land of the Picts who are called Niduari, accompanied by two brethren, one of whom afterwards became a priest. It was he who made known to many the miracle which the man of God worked at that place. Now they came thither after Christmas day, expecting that they would return quickly because the state both of the winds and waves was favourable. For this reason, that is in view of their early return, they did not take provisions with them. But things turned out very differently from what they expected. For as soon as they reached land a fierce tempest arose, which entirely prevented their return. And so they languished for some days amid the dangers of hunger and of cold, but the man of God refused to spend this time of leisure in sluggish sloth or give himself up to idle slumber, choosing rather to spend the night in prayer. Now when the most sacred day of the Epiphany was at hand, he spoke to his companions with persuasive words, for he was of a pleasant and kindly disposition: "Why, I ask, do we remain inactive and slothful and not seek some way of safety in every direction? Lo! the land is grim with snow and the sky with clouds; the heavens rage with adverse winds and the sea with waves. We ourselves are in want and there is no man to refresh us. So let us importune the Lord with prayers, that as He once opened up a path in the Red Sea for His people and fed them in a wondrous manner

---

21 cybaria H.   22 tamquam C_1VH.   23 ocius VH.   24 *om.* P_1.
25 pre... O_8.   26 cumque C_1VHP$_1$M.   27 *gloss in margin* panhaledan
V. *gloss above* id est debilitarent H.   28–29 *om.* O_4.   30 luxus VH.
31 ocia P_1.   32 somno P_1.   33 inerti P_1.   34 set O_3.
35 orationibus P_1.   36 aparitionis P_1.   37 quacumque C_1VHP$_1$.
ins. parte (*in margin* V) H.   38 cael... C_1V. cel... C_3O_3.   39 ...sus
C_1VH.   40 aeq... VHO$_4$M.   41 praec... VH.

p. 40

orantes ut nostri quoque misereatur in periculis. Credo si non nostra fides titubat non uult nos hodierna die ieiunos permanere[1], quam[2] ipse per tot ac tanta suae miracula maiestatis illustrare[3] curauit. Precorque eamus alicubi quaerentes[4], quid nobis epularum in gaudium suae festiuitatis prestare dignetur. Haec[5] dicens, eduxit eos sub ripam[6] quo ipse noctu peruigil orare consueuerat. Ubi aduenientes inuenerunt tria frusta[7] delphininae[8] carnis, quasi humano ministerio secta, et preparata ad cocturam, flexisque genibus gratias egerunt Domino[9]. Dixit autem Cuthbertus[10], Videtis dilectissimi quae sit gratia confidendi[11] et sperandi[12] in Domino? Ecce et cibaria[13] famulis suis preparauit[14], et ternario quoque numero[15] quot diebus hic residendum sit nobis[16] ostendit. Sumite ergo munera quae misit nobis[17] Christus et abeuntes[18] reficiamus nos maneamusque intrepidi, certissima enim nobis post triduum serenitas coeli[19] et maris adueniet. Factum est ut dixerat. Manente triduo tempestate perualida, quarto demum die tranquillitas promissa secuta est, quae illos secundis[20] flatibus patriam referret.

XII.   [21] *Quomodo iter faciens[23] aquila ministra uiaticum et[24] percepturum se esse praedixerit[25] et perceperit[26],[22]*

p. 41

Quadam quoque die cum predicaturus iuxta consuetudinem suam populis, de monasterio exiret uno comite puero, iamque diu gradiendo fatigatis[27] non parum adhuc restaret itineris, quousque ad uicum quo tendebant peruenirent, ait ad puerum temptans eum, Dic age sodalis ubi hodie refici disponas, an habeas aliquem in uia ad quem diuertere ualeas hospitem? At ille respondens, Et haec[28] ipsa

1 in *erased* C$_1$.   2 *gloss above* scilicet diem VH.   3 inl... C$_1$VH.
4 quer... C$_1$VP$_1$C$_3$O$_3$O$_4$M.   5 hec C$_3$O$_3$.   6 ripa C$_1$P$_1$.
7 *changed from* frustra O$_9$. frustra C$_3$. fusta O$_3$.   8 delfininae
P$_1$C$_3$. delphinine O$_3$.   9 Deo C$_1$VHP$_1$.   10 Cudberhtus C$_1$V.
Cuthberhtus H. Cudbertus P$_1$.   11 fidendi C$_1$P$_1$. fidenti VH.
confitendi C$_3$. *ins.* Dei C$_1$VHP$_1$.   12 speranti VH.   13 cybaria H.

in the desert, so He may also have mercy on us in our danger. I believe that, if our faith does not waver, He will not allow us to remain fasting to-day, a day which He has illuminated with so many wondrous tokens of His majesty. Let us go somewhere, I beg you, and find out what banquet He will deign to bestow upon us, so that we may keep His festival with joy." With these words he led them to the shore on which he was accustomed to spend the night in prayer. And when they came there, they found three pieces of dolphin's flesh looking as though some human hand had cut and prepared them for cooking; and kneeling down they gave thanks to God. Then Cuthbert said: "You see, beloved, what divine favour comes from trusting and hoping in the Lord. Look how He has prepared food for His servants, and has also showed us by the fact that there are three pieces, how many days we must remain here. So take these gifts which Christ has sent us and let us go and refresh ourselves and remain here undaunted, for most certainly after three days we shall get a calm sea and sky." It happened as he had said; a very fierce tempest lasted for three days and, on the fourth day, the promised calm arrived to bring them to their own country with favourable breezes.

CHAPTER XII. *How, while making a journey, he prophesied that he would receive provisions on the way by the ministration of an eagle, and how it came to pass*

Now on a certain day he had left the monastery to preach according to his wont, attended by a youth only; they were already tired with the long journey and no little distance still remained before they would reach the village for which they were making. He said to the boy to test him: "Come, tell me, comrade, where do you intend to refresh yourself to-day? or have you any host on the way to whom you can turn in?" But the boy answered: "I have long been silently pondering

---

14 prae... O₈O₄.   15 num. quoq. O₉.   16 nobis sit P₁.
17 nobis misit O₄.   18 hab... O₃.   19 caeli C₁V. celi O₃.   20 *gloss in margin* id est serenis VH.   21–22 Quomodo sibi aquila cibum ministrauerit O₄.   23 *ins.* ab VH.   24 *om.* VH.   25 pre... O₈.
26 percoeperit O₉.   27 *changed from* fatigaris C₁.   28 hec O₂.

inquit mecum[1] tacito in corde tractaui, quia nec[2] uiaticum ituri[3] tulimus nobiscum, neque aliquem in[4] itinere notum | habemus, qui nos suo[5] recipere uelit hospitio[6], et non parum adhuc itineris superest quod ieiuni sine molestia complere nequimus. Cui uir Domini[7], Disce inquit[8] filiole fidem semper et spem habere in Domino[9], quia nunquam[10] fame perit, qui Deo fideliter seruit. Et sursum aspectans[11] uidensque aquilam in alto uolantem, Cernis[12] inquit[13] aquilam [14]illam porro uolantem[15]? Etiam per huius ministerium possibile est Domino nos hodie reficere. Talia confabulantes, agebant iter iuxta fluuium[16] quendam, et ecce subito uident aquilam in ripa[17] residentem[18], dixitque uir Dei, Uides ubi nostra quam praedixi ministra residet[19]? Curre rogo, et quid nobis epularum[20] Domino mittente attulerit[21] inspice, et citius affer[22]. Qui accurrens[23] attulit[24] piscem non modicum, quem illa nuper de fluuio prendiderat[25]. At uir Dei[26], Quid inquit[27] fecisti fili? Quare ministrae suam partem non dedisti? Seca citius[28] medium, et illi partem quam nobis ministrando meretur remitte. Fecit ut iusserat, tultaque[29] secum parte[30] reliqua[31] ubi tempus reficiendi[32] aderat diuerterunt ad proximum uicum, et dato ad assandum pisciculo, se pariter et eos ad quos intrabant gratissimo refecere[33] conuiuio, predicante Cuthberto[34] | uerbum Dei atque eius beneficia collaudante[35], et quia *beatus uir cuius est nomen Domini*[36] *spes eius et non respexit in uanitates et in*[37] *insanias falsas.* Ac sic resumpto itinere, ad docendum eos, quos proposuere[38] profecti sunt.

1 mecum inquit M. 2 *om.* P₁. 3 *ins.* non P₁. 4 in *above* C₁.
5 suos C₁. 6 hospicio C₃. 7 Dei C₁VHP₁O₄.
8 inquid O₈O₃. 9 in Dom. hab. M. 10 numquam C₁VHP₁.
11 asp. surs. C₁VHP₁O₄. 12 uides P₁. 13 *ins.* hanc P₁.
inquid O₃. 14–15 *om.* P₁. 16 *in margin* Nomen fluuii
Iccabicide C₃. 17 *in margin* Nomen fluminis Tabiade V.
18 consedisse O₄. 19 resedit C₁P₁O₄. 20 *changed from*

this matter in my heart; for we have brought with us no provision for the journey, nor have we anyone we know on the way who will receive us hospitably, and no little part of the journey remains which we cannot complete, fasting, without suffering." Then the man of God replied: "Learn, my dear son, always to have faith and trust in the Lord; for he who serves God faithfully never perishes of hunger." And, looking up, he saw an eagle flying aloft. "Do you see that eagle," he said, "flying afar off? It is possible for God to refresh us to-day even by the ministration of that eagle." With such words they went on their way along a certain river when, lo, suddenly they see an eagle settling on the bank; and the man of God said: "Do you see where our handmaid, as I foretold, is settling? Run, I pray you, and see what food she has brought us from the Lord, and bring it quickly here." He ran up and brought a large fish which the eagle had just taken from the river. But the man of God said: "What have you done, my son? Why have you not given our handmaiden her share? Cut it quickly in half and take her the share which she deserves for ministering to us." He did as he was bidden and carried the rest with him. When the time for refreshment arrived, they turned into the next village and, giving the portion of fish to be broiled, they refreshed themselves and those too into whose house they had entered, with a most acceptable repast, while Cuthbert preached the word of God to them and praised Him for his benefits; for "blessed is the man whose hope is in the name of the Lord and who has not looked after vanity nor idle folly". And so having resumed their journey, they set out to reach those whom they purposed to teach.

epularem C_1.   21 adt... C_1.   22 adf... C_1V.   23 adc... C_1V.
24 adt... C_1.   25 *changed to* prenderat C_1.   26 Domini P_1.
27 inquid O_8O_3.   28 cito O_4.   29 allataque *above* C_1. tulitque VH.
uel allata *above* P_1. lataque O_8.   30 partem VH.   31 reliquam VH.
32 refitiendi P_1.   33 reficiebant VH.   34 Cudberhto C_1V.
Cuthberhto H. Cudberto P_1.   35 conl... C_1V.   36 *om.* P_1.
37 *om.* $P_1O_8O_3O_4$M.   38 proposuerat P_1.

XIII.   [1]*Quomodo predicans populis fantasticum subito ignem diaboli et praeuiderit[3] uenturum, et uenientem extinxerit[2]*

Eodem tempore dum congregatis in quadam uillula perplurimis uerbum uitae[4] predicaret[5], preuidit[6] subito in spiritu antiquum hostem ad retardandum opus salutis adesse. Moxque eius insidias quas futuras intellexit, docendo preoccupare[7] curauit. Nanque[8] inter ea quae disputauerat, repente huius modi monita inse|ruit, Oportet karissimi[9] ut quotiens[10] uobis mysteria[11] regni coelestis[12] predicantur[13], intento haec[14] corde et sensu semper uigilantissimo audiatis, ne forte *diabolus* qui *mille nocendi* habet *artes*, superuacuis uos curis ab aeternae[15] salutis auditione prepediat[16]. Et haec[17] dicens, denuo sermonis quem intermiserat ordinem repetiit. Statimque hostis ille nequissimus fantasticum deferens ignem, domum iuxta positam incendit, ita ut uiderentur faces ignium totam uolitare[18] per uillam[19], ac iuuante[20] uento fragor aera concutere. Tum exiliens quasi ad extinguendum[21] ignem turba pene[22] tota quam docebat, nam paucos ipse manu missa retinuit, certatim aquas[23] iactabat. Nec tamen unda uera[24] falsas potuit restinguere flammas[25], donec orante uiro Dei Cuthberto[26] fugatus[27] auctor fallaciarum[28] ficta[29] secum incendia *uacuas* reportaret in *auras*. Quod uidens turba multum salubriter erubuit, rursusque ad uirum Dei ingressa, flexis genibus instabilis animi ueniam precabatur, confitens se intellexisse quia diabolus ab impedienda[30] salute humana ne ad horam uacaret. At ipse confirmans inconstantiam fragilium, rursus quae[31] coeperat[32] uitae monita exequitur[33].

p. 44

Sulpicii
Seueri
Vita S.
Martini
c. 22

Vergil.
Aen.
XII. 592

1–2 Quomodo fantasticum ignem diaboli extinxerit O₄.   3 pre...
HO₈.   4 uite O₃.   5 prae... VHO₈.   6 prae... VHO₈.
7 preocupare P₁. prae... VHO₈.   8 namque C₁VHP₁O₈.
9 car... C₁VH.   10 quoties C₁VHP₁O₄. *gloss above* uel n H.
11 misteria P₁C₃O₈O₃M.   12 cael... C₁V. cel... O₃.   13 prae...
HO₈.   14 hec C₃O₃.   15 eterne C₃O₃.   16 prae... HO₈.

CHAPTER XIII. *How, when he was preaching to the people,
he suddenly foresaw that a phantom fire would come from the devil,
and how he extinguished it when it came*

At the same time, when he was preaching the word of life to
a crowd of people in a certain little village, he suddenly foresaw
in the spirit that the ancient enemy would be present to hinder
the work of salvation, and forthwith he set out to forestall, by
his teaching, the snares which he knew would come. For he
suddenly broke into the discourse he was giving with warnings
of this kind: "Beloved, it is necessary, as often as the mysteries
of the Kingdom of Heaven are preached to you, that you should
listen with attentive mind and most watchful ear, lest haply
the devil, who has a thousand wiles for injuring you, should
with vain cares hinder you from hearing about your eternal
salvation." And with these words he once more took up
the thread of the discourse which he had interrupted, and at
once that most evil foe, producing a phantom fire, set light
to a house near by, so that firebrands seemed to be flying all
through the village and, fanned by the wind, their crackling
rent the air. Then almost the whole crowd that he was teaching
leapt up intending to extinguish the fire, though he himself
kept back a few with outstretched hand: the rest eagerly threw
on water, but with all their real water they could not extinguish
the false flames, until at the prayers of Cuthbert the man of
God, the author of lies was put to flight, carrying with him his
phantom fires into the empty air. Seeing this, the crowd,
filled with wholesome shame, approaching the man of God
again, prayed on bended knees to be forgiven for their
fickleness of mind, confessing that they realised that the devil
never ceased, even for an hour, from hindering the work of
man's salvation. And he, confirming the weak and inconstant,
continued his interrupted discourse on the way of life.

17 hec C_3O_3. 18 uolare C_1VHP_1. 19 uillulam $C_1VHP_1O_4$.
20 *gloss above* scilicet uideretur VH. 21 extinguere C_1P_1. 22 paene P_1O_8.
23 *first a above* C_1. 24 *changed from* fera C_1. 25 ignes C_1V. 26 Cudberhto
C_1V. Cuthberhto H. Cudberto P_1. 27 *changed from* fugatos C_1.
28 fallat... C_3. 29 cuncta VH. *gloss above* uel ficta VH. 30 inp...
C_1V. 31 rursusque O_9. 32 caep... V. cep... P_1C_3. 33 exsequitur C_1.

XIV. | *Quomodo flammas domus* [1] *cuiusdam uero igne* [2] *ardentis orando restrinxerit* [3]

Nec tantum ignem fantasticum, sed [4] etiam uerum quem multi frigidis fontium undis minime ualebant extinguere, ipse solus feruentibus lacrimarum riuulis compressit [5]. Si quidem dum more apostolorum gratia salutiferae instructionis uniuersa pertransiret, deuenit die quadam in domum cuiusdam [6]deuotae [8] Deo [7] feminae [9], quam crebrius inuisere curabat, quia et bonis operibus [10] intentam nouerat [11], et ipsa eum primis pueritiae nutriebat [12] ab annis, unde et mater ab eo cognominari solebat. Habebat autem domum in occidentali parte uiculi [13]. Quam [14] cum uir Domini Cuthbertus [15] uerbum seminaturus intraret, repente in orientali | plaga [16] eiusdem uici *per culpam incuriae* domus *incensa uehementer* [17] coepit [18] *ardere.* Nam et uentus ab eodem climate [19]assurgens non modicus [20], abripiebat ignitos [21] fenei [22] tecti fasciculos [23], et totam late iactabat [24] per uillam. Iactantes aquam qui aderant [25] fortior flamma reppulit [26], longiusque fugauit. Tum praefata Dei famula [27] cucurrit concita ad domum in qua uirum Dei receperat, obsecrans ut orando succurreret, priusquam domus ipsius et tota simul uilla periret. At ille, Ne timeas inquit [28] mater, animaequior [29] esto, non enim tibi tuisue [30] haec [31] quamlibet [32] ferox [33] flamma nocebit. Statimque egressus, ante hostium [34] sternitur [35] in terram. Quo adhuc orante mutatur flatus uentorum, spiransque ab occasu totum tanti [36] incendii periculum ab inuasione uillulae [37], quam uir Domini intrauerat reiecit. Sicque in duobus miraculis duorum

---

1–2 *om.* O$_4$.   3 restinxerit C$_3$O$_8$M. extinxerit O$_4$.   4 set O$_3$.
5 *gloss above* id est domauit VH.   6–7 Deo deu. P$_1$.
8 deuote O$_3$.   9 femine O$_3$. *gloss at top of page* Nomen feminae
Quenspið V. *in margin* Nomen feminae Quoinsuid C$_3$. Nomen
femine Quonsuid O$_3$.   10 actibus C$_1$VHP$_1$O$_4$.   11 *gloss above*
scilicet eam VH.   12 *gloss above* uel r H. nutrierat P$_1$.   13 *gloss
at top of page* Nomen uiculi Hruningaham V. *in margin* Nomen uiculi
Hruningaham C$_3$. Nomen uiculi Runingaham O$_3$.   14 *gloss above*
scilicet domum VH.   15 Cudberhtus C$_1$V. Cuthberhtus H.
Cudbertus P$_1$.   16 parte P$_1$.   17 uehementissime C$_1$VHP$_1$.

CHAPTER XIV. *How by his prayers he checked the flames of a certain house which was really on fire*

And not only phantom fires but even real fires, which many people could not extinguish with cold water from the wells, he put out unaided with his warm streams of tears. For when, after the manner of the Apostles, he was going through all parts in order to teach the way of salvation, one day he entered the house of a certain faithful handmaid of God, whom he was careful to visit very frequently, because he knew she was given to good deeds, and also because she had brought him up from his boyhood's earliest years and was therefore called mother by him. Now she had a house in the west part of the village, and no sooner had Cuthbert the man of God entered it to sow the seed of the word than a house in the eastern quarter of the same village caught fire owing to carelessness and began to burn very fiercely. Moreover a great wind arose from the same quarter, which tore away the blazing thatch of the straw roof and carried it far and wide throughout the whole village. The fierce flame kept off those who were engaged in throwing water, and even drove them farther back. Then the said handmaiden of God ran excitedly to the house in which she had received the man of God, entreating him to help by his prayers before her house and the whole village perished together. But he said: "Do not be afraid, mother, be calmer; for this fire, however fierce, will not harm you and yours." Immediately he went out and cast himself upon the ground in front of the door; and while he was still praying, the winds changed and, blowing from the west, removed all danger of the fire attacking the house which the man of God had entered. Thus in two miracles he imitated

18 caep... VP₁. cep... O₃M.   19-20 non mod. ads... C₁VH. non mod. ass. P₁O₄. exurgens non mod. M.   21 ignitas P₁. *changed from* ignitas C₁.   22 foeni C₁. faenei VP₁C₃O₈. foenei HO₄.   23 *changed from* fasciculas C₁. fasciculas P₁.   24 iac. lat. C₁VHP₁O₄.   25 qui ad. aq. O₄.   26 repulit O₄.   27 fam. Dei praef. O₄.   28 inquid P₁O₃. 29 o *above the* m C₁. animo aequior P₁. animequior O₃.   30 *changed from* tuisse C₁.   31 hec O₃.   32 *gloss above* scilicet sit VH. 33 forax C₁. uorax, *gloss above* uel ferox VH. uorax P₁.   34 ostium VHP₁M.   35 prosternitur VH.   36 *om.* P₁.   37 uillule O₃.

patrum est uirtutes imitatus. In fantasticis[1] quidem prae-
uisis[2] et euacuatis incendiis, uirtutem reuerentissimi et
sanctissimi patris Benedicti, qui simulatum ab antiquo
hoste quasi ardentis coquinae[3] incendium ab oculis dis-
cipulorum orando pepulit. In ueris[4] uero aeque[5] uictis
ac *retortis*[6] ignium globis[7], uirtutem *uiri*[8] *uenerabilis*
Marcellini | *Anchonitani antistitis*[9], qui ardente *eadem ciuita*te
ipse *contra ignem positus* orando *flammas* compescuit[10], quas
tanta ciuium manus *aquam proiciendo*[11] nequiuerat[12]. Nec[13]
mirandum perfectos et fideliter Deo seruientes uiros
tantam contra *uim flamma*rum accipere potestatem[14], qui
cotidiana uirtutum industria et incentiua[15] suae carnis
edomare[16], et *omnia tela nequissimi*[17] *ignea* [18]norunt[20]
extinguere[19]. Quibus aptissime congruit illud propheticum,
Cum transieris [21]*per ignem*[22] *non combureris*[23], *et flamma non*
ardebit in te. At ego et mei similes propriae fragilitatis
et inertiae[24] conscii, certi quidem sumus quia contra
ignem materialem nil tale audemus[25], incerti[26] autem an
ignem illum inextinguibilem[27] futurae[28] castigationis im-
munes[29] euadere queamus. Sed potens est et larga pietas
saluatoris nostri, quae[30] indignis nobis et nunc ad extin-
guenda uiciorum[31] incendia, et ad euadendas in futuro
poenarum[32] flammas, gratiam suae[33] protectionis impen-
dat[34].

p. 47
Greg.
Dial. I. 6

Eph. 6. 16

Isa. 43. 2

p. 48

XV. | [35]*Qualiter demonium ab uxore*[37] *praefecti*
necdum adueniens eiecerit[36]

Verum quia[38] paulo superius quantum idem uenerabilis
Cuthbertus[39] aduersum[40] simulaticias diaboli fraudes ualu-
erit exposuimus, nunc etiam quid aduersus uerum apertum-

1 *gloss above* scilicet imitatus est VH.   2 pre... O8M.   3 coq.
ard. C₁VHP₁O₄.   4 *gloss above* scilicet imitatus est VH.
5 aequae O₉. equae O8M. eque O₃.   6 *gloss above* id est reflexis
VH.   7 *gloss above* id est radiis VH.   8 *om.* M.   9 antestitis V.
changed from antestitis H. episcopi O₄.   10 conposuit C₁O₄. *gloss*
above id est mitigauit VH.   11 proitiendo P₁.   12 *gloss above*
scilicet compescere VH.   13 *gloss above* scilicet est VH.
14 potentiam C₁VHP₁O₄.   15 *gloss above* id est uoluptates VH.
16 *gloss above* id est refrenare VH.   17 *gloss above* scilicet hostes VH.
18–19 exting. nor. O₄.   20 *gloss above* id est cognouerunt VH.

the miracles of two of the fathers: in foreseeing and getting rid of phantom fires he imitated the miracle of the most reverend and holy father Benedict who, by his prayers, drove away from the sight of his disciples a fire kindled by the ancient foe to simulate a kitchen burning; and equally in overcoming and changing the direction of volumes of real flame, he imitated a miracle of the venerable Bishop Marcellinus of Ancona who, when that city was burning, took up his position over against the fire and prayed, thus subduing the flames which a very great crowd of citizens could not subdue by throwing water on them. Nor is it to be wondered at that such perfect men who served God faithfully, received great power against the strength of flames, when, by daily practice of virtue, they learned both to overcome the lusts of the flesh and "to quench all the fiery darts of the wicked one". Them indeed this prophecy most aptly fits: "When thou walkest through the fire thou shalt not be burned neither shall the flame kindle upon thee." But I and those like me, conscious of our weakness and helplessness, are certain that we dare take no such measures against material fire; we are also uncertain whether we can escape unharmed from that inextinguishable fire of future punishment. But the loving-kindness of our Saviour is mighty and abundant; and He will use the grace of His protection even now to extinguish the flames of vices in us, unworthy though we be, and to enable us to escape the flames of punishment in the time to come.

CHAPTER XV. *How he drove out a demon from the wife of a reeve, even before his arrival*

Seeing that we have shown above how the same venerable Cuthbert had power against the illusory deceits of the devil, now we will also show what power he had also against his

---

21–22 in igne C₁VHO₄. 23 conb... C₁. 24 inertie O₃.
25 haud C₁. *om*. P₁. 26 *gloss above* scilicet sumus VH. 27 *ins*. et C₁P₁.
28 future O₃. 29 inm... C₁VP₁. *gloss above* id est indempnes VH.
30 *om*. P₁. 31 uitiorum. *changed from* uitiarum C₁. uitiorum VHP₁C₃O₄.
32 pen... C₃O₃M. 33 sue O₃. 34 inpendere C₁P₁. inpendat VH.
35–36 Qualiter ab uxore praefecti demonium eiecerit O₄. 37 *ins*.
cuiusdam C₃ (*above* O₃). 38 *om*. C₁P₁. 39 Cudberhtus C₁V.
Cuthberhtus H. Cudbertus P₁. Cutbertus O₄. 40 aduersus VH.

que eius furorem ualeat explicemus. Erat praefectus Egfridi[1] regis Hildmer[2] nomine, uir religiosis[3] cum omni domo[4] sua deditus operibus, ideoque a beato Cuthberto[5] specialiter[6] dilectus, et cum itineris propinquitas congrueret, crebro ab eo uisitatus. Cuius uxor[7] cum elemosinis et caeteris[8] uirtutum fructibus esset intenta, subito correpta a demone[9] acerrime coepit[10] uexari, ita ut stridendo dentibus, [11]uoces miserabiles[12] emittendo[13], brachia uel caetera[14] sui corporis membra[15] in diuersa raptando, non minimum cunctis intuentibus uel audientibus incuteret horrorem. Cunque[16] iaceret explosa, et iamiamque uideretur esse[17] moritura, ascendit uir eius equum[18] et concitus uenit ad hominem Dei, precatusque[19] est eum dicens, Obsecro quia uxor mea male habet, et uidetur iam proxima morti, ut mittas presbiterum qui illam priusquam moriatur uisitet, eique dominici[20] corporis et sanguinis[21] sacramenta ministret, sed[22] et corpus illius[23] hic in lo|cis sanctis sepeliri permittas. Erubescebat enim eam confiteri[24] insanam quam uir Domini sobriam semper uidere consueuerat. Qui cum parumper ab eo diuerteret uisurus quem mitteret presbiterum cum illo, cognouit repente in spiritu quia non communi infirmitate sed[25] demonis[26] infestatione premeretur coniux[27], pro qua supplicabat. Reuersusque ad eum, Non inquit[28] alium mittere, sed ipse ad uisitandam eam tecum pergere debeo. Cunque[29] agerent iter[30] coepit[31] flere homo, et dolorem cordis profluentibus in maxillam prodere lacrimis[32]. Timebat enim ne cum eam demoniosam[33] inueniret, arbitrari inciperet, quia non integra Domino, sed ficta fide[34] seruisset. Quem uir Domini blande consolatus, Noli inquit[35] plorare quasi inuenturus sim coniugem tuam qualem non uelim. Scio enim ipse quamuis te dicere pudeat, quia[36] demonio[37] uexatur, scio[38]

p. 49

1 Ecgfridi C₁VP₁. Egcfridi H. Ecfridi O₄.   2 Hildmaer C₁VH. Hildemaer P₁.   3 religiosus V. *changed from* religiosus H. 4 *changed to* domu V. domu H.   5 Cudberhto C₁V. Cuthberhto H. Cudberto P₁.   6 spetialiter P₁.   7 *in margin* Nomen uxoris Eadsuid VC₃O₃.   8 cet... O₃.   9 daem... HC₃O₈. daemonio O₄.   10 caep... C₁V. cep... O₃.   11–12 uociferando mirabiliter P₁.   13 comedendo C₁P₁. committendo VH.   14 cet... O₃.   15 menbra O₄M.   16 cumque C₁VHP₁M.   17 *om.* O₄.

undisguised and open fury. There was a reeve of King Ecgfrith called Hildmer, a man devoted to religious works together with all his household, and therefore specially beloved by the blessed Cuthbert, who, when he happened to be travelling that way, frequently visited him. His wife, though given to works of charity and other fruits of virtue, was suddenly seized upon by a demon and most cruelly afflicted, so that she gnashed her teeth and uttered piteous cries, flinging her arms and limbs about in agitation, and so inspiring no little horror in all who saw or heard her. And when she lay cast out and apparently at the point of death, her husband got on his horse and came in haste to the man of God, and entreated him, saying: "My wife is ill and seems already at the point of death; I beg you that you will send a priest to visit her before she dies and minister to her the sacrament of the body and blood of the Lord; and also that you will permit her body to be buried here in holy ground." For he was ashamed to confess that she was insane because the man of God had always been accustomed to see her in her right mind. When Cuthbert had turned away from him for a short time to see what priest he should send with him, he suddenly realised in his spirit that the wife for whom the man was pray-ing was afflicted by no ordinary infirmity but by the attack of a demon. And turning to him he said: "I must not send another but I myself must go with you to visit her." And when they were on the way, the man began to weep and to reveal the grief of his heart by the tears that flowed down his cheeks; for he feared that when Cuthbert found her possessed of a devil, he would begin to think that she had served the Lord with a feigned and not a real faith. But the man of God consoled him with gentle words. "Do not weep", he said, "as though I were about to find your wife in such a condition as I should not wish. For I know myself, though you are ashamed to say it, that she is afflicted by a demon; but I also know that before

18 aequum O_9.   19 prae... O_8.   20 *om.* $C_1VHP_1O_4$.   21 *ins.* dominici $C_1VHP_1O_4$.   22 set O_3.   23 ipsius C_1VHP_1.   24 profiteri P_1. 25 set O_3.   26 daem... O_8O_4.   27 coniunx VHC_3O_8M. *ins.* sua P_1. 28 inquid P_1O_3.   29 cumque C_1VHM.   30 it. ag. C_3.   31 caep... C_1VP_1. cep... O_3M.   32 lac. prod. $C_1VHP_1C_3O_4$.   33 daem... C_3O_4. 34 fid. fict. C_3.   35 inquid HO_3.   36 *ins.* a C_3.   37 daem... O_4. 38 *ins.* enim P_1.

etiam quia priusquam illo peruenerimus, fugato demonio[1] liberabitur, ac nobis aduenientibus cum gaudio occurrens, has ipsa[2] habenas sanissima mente excipiet, nosque intrare citius obsecrans, ministerium quod consueuerat[3] nobis[4] sedula impendet[5]. Neque enim tali[6] tormento soli subiciuntur mali, sed occulto Dei iudicio[7] aliquotiens[8] etiam

p. 50

innocentes in hoc saeculo[9] non tan|tum corpore sed et[10] mente captiuantur a[11] diabolo. Dumque haec[12] et[13] huius modi uerba in consolationem et eruditionem illius perorante Cuthberto[14] appropinquarent[15] domui, fugit repente spiritus[16] nequam, aduentum spiritus sancti, quo plenus erat uir Dei ferre non ualens. Cuius soluta uinculis mulier,

Gen.
45. 26

quasi graui[17] experrecta[18] *de somno*[19] surrexit continuo, ac uiro Dei gratulabunda occurrens, iumentum quo sedebat per frenum tenuit. Moxque ad integrum recepto uigore mentis et corporis eum cito descendere atque ad benedicendam domum suam precabatur[20] ingredi, deuotumque illi ministerium praebens[21], testabatur palam quomodo ad primum freni eius[22] tactum omni se molestia priscae uexationis absolutam sensisset.

XVI. *Qualiter in Lindisfarnensi monasterio uixerit* [23] *uel docuerit*[25,24] |

p. 51

Cum ergo uenerabilis Domini famulus multos in Mailrosensi monasterio degens annos, multis uirtutum spiritualium[26] claresceret signis, transtulit eum reuerentissimus abbas ipsius Eata[27] in monasterium quod in Lindisfarnensium[28] insula situm est, ut ibi quoque regulam monachicae perfectionis et praepositi auctoritate doceret, et exemplo[29] uirtutis ostenderet. Nam et ipsum locum tunc idem reuerentissimus pater abbatis iure regebat. Neque aliquis miretur quod in eadem insula Lindisfarnea,

1 daem... O8O4.   2 ipsas P1.   3 consuaeu... V.
4 *om.* O4.   5 inp... C1.   6 hoc P1.   7 iuditio P1C3.
8 ...ies C1VP1. n *above* H.   9 sec... O3.   10 etiam O4.
11 *om.* C1. *ins. later* V.   12 *om.* C1P1. hec O3.   13 *om.* P1.
14 Cudberhto C1V. Cuthberhto H. Cudberto P1.   15 adp...

we arrive, the demon will be driven away and she will be freed and will come to meet us joyfully, as sound in mind as ever; and she will herself take these reins, and, bidding us enter quickly, will diligently perform her accustomed services for us; for it is not only the wicked who are subjected to such torments, but sometimes also in this world, by the inscrutable judgment of God, the innocent are taken captive by the devil, not only in body but also in mind." And when Cuthbert had spoken these and like words for his consolation and instruction, they approached his home, and the evil spirit suddenly fled, not being able to endure the coming of the Holy Spirit which filled the man of God. And the woman, being loosed from the demon's chains, thereupon rose as if wakened from a deep sleep and, running to greet the man of God, she took the horse on which he was seated by the bridle: and having wholly recovered her strength both of mind and body, she prayed him to dismount quickly and to enter and bless her home; and offering him devoted service, she openly testified how, as soon as she touched his bridle, she felt herself to be freed from all the trouble of her old affliction.

CHAPTER XVI. *How he lived and taught in the monastery at Lindisfarne*

So when the venerable servant of God had passed many years in the monastery at Melrose and had distinguished himself by the many signs of his spiritual powers, his most reverend abbot Eata transferred him to the monastery which is situated in the island of Lindisfarne, in order that there also he might both teach the rule of monastic perfection by his authority as prior and illustrate it by the example of his virtue; for the same most reverend father ruled this place also as abbot at that time. And let no one be surprised that, though we have said above that in this island of Lindisfarne, small as it is, there is found the

C_1VH.   16 spir. rep. O_8.   17 *om*. P_1.   18 *changed to*
expergefacta V. expergefacta $HC_3O_8O_3$.   19 sompno P_1O_3.
20 prae... HO_8.   21 prebens O_8.   22 *om*. $C_1VHP_1O_4$.
23-24 *om*. O_4.   25 do O_9.   26 spiritalium C_1VH.   27 Eatha O_3.
28 Lindisfarnensi C_3. Lyndisfarnensium O_3.   29 exempla C_3.

cum permodica sit et supra episcopi et nunc abbatis et[1] monachorum esse, locum dixerimus, re uera enim ita est. Nanque[2] una eademque seruorum Dei habitatio, utrosque[3] simul tenet, immo omnes monachos tenet. Aidanus[4] quippe qui primus eiusdem loci episcopus fuit[5] monachus erat[6], et monachicam cum suis omnibus uitam semper agere solebat. Unde ab illo omnes loci ipsius antistites[7] usque hodie sic episcopale exercent officium[8], ut regente monasterium abbate, quem ipsi cum consilio fratrum elegerint, omnes presbiteri, diacones[9], cantores, lectores, caeterique[10] gradus aecclesiastici[11], monachicam per omnia cum ipso episcopo regulam seruent. Quam uiuendi normam multum se diligere probauit[12] beatus papa |

p. 52

Gregorius, cum sciscitanti[13] per litteras[14] Augustino[15] quem primum genti Anglorum episcopum miserat, qualiter episcopi cum suis clericis conuersari debeant, respondit

Cf. H.E.
I. 27

inter alia, *Sed[16] quia tua fraternitas monasterii regulis erudita seorsum fieri [17]non debet a [19]clericis suis[20,18], in aecclesia[21] Anglorum quae Deo auctore[22] nuper adhuc[23] ad fidem perducta est, hanc debet[24] conuersationem instituere quae in[25] inicio[26] nascentis[27] aecclesiae[28] fuit patribus nostris, in quibus nullus eorum ex his[29] quae possidebant[30] aliquid suum[31] esse dicebat, sed erant illis[32] omnia communia.* Igitur ad Lindisfarnensem[33] aecclesiam[34] siue monasterium uir Domini adueniens, mox instituta monachica fratribus uiuendo pariter et docendo tradebat, sed et circunquaque[35] morantem uulgi multitudinem more suo crebra uisitatione ad coelestia[36] querenda[37] ac promerenda succendebat. Nec non etiam signis clarior effectus, plurimos uariis languoribus et tormentis comprehensos[38] orationum instantia priscae[39] sanitati restituit, nonnullos ab[40] immundorum[41] spirituum uexatione non solum praesens orando, tangendo[42], imperando,

---

1 ac C₁VHP₁.　　　　2 namque C₁VHP₁.　　　　3 uirosque C₁.
4 Aidan C₁VHP₁O₄.　　　　5 fu. ep. P₁.　　　　6 fuit O₄.
7 antestites V. *changed from* antestites H.　　　　8 offitium P₁.
9 *gloss above* uel i V. diaconi H.　　　10 cet... O₃.　　　11 eccl...
C₁O₃.　　　12 *gloss above* id est manifestauit VH.　　　13 sciscitante
C₁VHO₄.　　　14 litterulas C₁VHP₁.　　　15 Agustino C₁VH.
16 set O₃.　　　17–18 a cler. su. non deb. P₁.　　　19–20 su. cler. O₄.

seat of a bishop, now we say also that it is the home of an abbot and monks; for it is actually so. For one and the same dwelling-place of the servants of God holds both; and indeed all are monks. Aidan, who was the first bishop of this place, was a monk and always lived according to monastic rule together with all his followers. Hence all the bishops of that place up to the present time exercise their episcopal functions in such a way that the abbot, whom they themselves have chosen by the advice of the brethren, rules the monastery; and all the priests, deacons, singers and readers, and the other ecclesiastical grades, together with the bishop himself, keep the monastic rule in all things. The blessed Pope Gregory showed that he greatly approved of this mode of life, when Augustine, the first bishop he had sent to the English, asked him in his letters how bishops ought to live with their clergy; for he answered amongst other things: "You, my brother, having been brought up under monastic rules, ought not to live apart from your clergy in the church of the English which, by God's help, has lately been brought to the faith; but you ought to introduce that way of living which, at the beginning of the life of the church, was found among our fathers, none of whom said that anything that he possessed was his own, but they had all things in common." So the man of the Lord came to the church or monastery of Lindisfarne, and soon equally by his life and by his doctrine taught the monastic rule to the brethren. Moreover in accordance with his custom he also by frequent visits aroused the common people round about to seek and earn heavenly rewards. He also became very famous for his miracles; for by the importunity of his prayers he restored to their former health very many who had been seized with various kinds of diseases and afflictions; and some he cured that were vexed by unclean spirits, not only when present by praying, touching, commanding and exorcizing,

21 eccl... C_1O_3.   22 auct. Deo $C_1VHP_1O_4$.   23 *om.* P_1.
24 debes VH.   25 *om.* VH.   26 initio $C_1VHP_1C_3$.   27 *om.* P_1C_3.
28 eccl... $C_1O_3O_8$.   29 hiis O_3.   30 possidebat P_1.   31 suum ali. P_1.
32 eis C_1VHP_1.   33 Lyndisfarnensem O_3.   34 eccl... $C_1O_3O_8$.
35 circum... C_1VH.   36 cael... C_1V. cel... C_3O_3.   37 quaer...
$C_1VHP_1O_8O_4$.   38 conp... C_1V.   39 prisce O_3.   40 *om.* P_1.
41 inm... C_1VH.   42 tang. or. $C_1VHP_1O_4$.

exorcizando, sed et absens uel tantum orando, uel certe
eorum sanationem praedicendo curauit, in quibus erat et
p. 53 illa praefecti | uxor de qua supra retulimus. Erant autem
quidam in monasterio fratres, qui priscae[1] suae[2] con-
suetudini quam regulari mallent obtemperare custodiae[3].
Quos tamen ille modesta patientiae[4] suae uirtute superabat,
et cotidiano exercitio paulatim ad melioris propositi statum
conuertebat. Denique sepius in cetu[5] fratrum de regula
disputans cum acerrimis contradicentium fatigaretur iniu-
riis, exurgebat[6] repente, et placido uultu atque animo
egrediens dimittebat conuentum, ac sequente[7] nichilo-
minus[8] die quasi nil obiectionis[9] pridie sustinuisset, eadem
quae prius[10] monita eisdem dabat auditoribus, donec illos
paulatim ut diximus ad ea quae uellet conuerteret. Erat
nanque[11] uir patientiae[12] uirtute praecipuus, atque[13] ad[14]
perferenda fortiter omnia[15] quae uel animo uel corpori
aduersa ingerebantur inuictissimus, nec minus inter tristia
quae contigissent faciem praetendens[16] hilarem[17], ita ut
palam daretur intelligi[18] quia interna[19] spiritus sancti
consolatione pressuras contempneret[20] extrinsecas[21]. Sed
et uigiliarum atque orationis ita[22] studiosus existebat, ut
aliquotiens[23] tres siue quattuor[24] noctes continuas peruigil
transegisse[25] credatur, cum per tantum temporis nec[26] ad
p. 54 lectum proprium ueniret[27], neque[28] extra dormitorium |
fratrum locum aliquem in quo pausare posset haberet. Siue
enim locis secretioribus solus orationi uacabat, siue inter
psallendum operabatur[29] manibus torporemque dormien-
di[30] laborando propellebat, seu certe circuibat[31] insulam,
quomodo se singula quaeque haberent pius explorator
inquirens, pariter et longitudinem sibi psalmodiae[32] ac
uigiliarum incedendo alleuians[33]. Denique arguere solebat
pusillanimitatem fratrum, qui grauiter ferrent[34], si qui se

---

1 prisce C_1O_3.   2 sue C_1O_3.   3 custodie C_1O_3.
4 pac ... O_9O_8.   5 coetu $C_1VHP_1C_3O_8O_4$.   6 exsur...
C_1VH.   7 sequenti VH.   8 nihil... C_1VHP_1.   9 abiect...
C_1VHP_1.   10 *gloss above* scilicet dabat VH.   11 namque C_1VHP_1.
12 pacientiae O_8. paciencie O_3. patienciae M.   13 adque C_1.
14 *om.* C_1. *added later* V.   15 omn. fort. O_4.   16 pre... O_8.
17 ilarem P_1. hylarem M.   18 intellegi C_1V. *changed from*

but also when absent either by prayer alone or even indeed by predicting their cure; among these was the wife of the reeve of whom we spoke above. Now there were certain brethren in the monastery who preferred to conform to their older usage rather than to the monastic rule. Nevertheless he overcame these by his modest virtue and his patience, and by daily effort he gradually converted them to a better state of mind. In fact very often during debates in the chapter of the brethren concerning the rule, when he was assailed by the bitter insults of his opponents, he would rise up suddenly and with calm mind and countenance would go out, thus dissolving the chapter, but none the less on the following day, as if he had suffered no repulse the day before, he would give the same instruction as before to the same audience until, as we have said, he gradually converted them to the things that he desired. For he was a man remarkable for the strength of his patience and unsurpassed in bravely bearing every burden whether of mind or body. At the same time he kept a cheerful countenance though sorrows overtook him, so that it was made clear to all that, by the inward consolation of the Holy Spirit, he was enabled to despise outward vexations. Moreover he was so zealous in watchings and prayer that he is believed many times to have spent three or four nights on end in watching; since during that length of time he did not go to his own bed, nor had he any place outside the dormitory of the brethren to rest in. Meanwhile he either devoted himself to private prayer in some retired spot, or else while he sang his psalms, he worked with his hands, and so by toil he drove away the heaviness of sleep, or else indeed he went round the island finding out in his pious search how everything was getting on, and at the same time relieving the tediousness of his psalm-singing and his watching by walking about. Moreover he used to blame the faintheartedness of brethren who were vexed if

intellegi H.   19 internas C_1.   20 contemn... C_1.   21 extrinsecus C_1VHP_1.   22 adeo C_1VHP_1O_4.   23 ...ties C_1VP_1O_4. n *above* H.

24 iiii P_1. quatuor VC_3O_4.   25 exegisse. *gloss above* uel trans. O_4.
26 neque C_1VHO_4.   27 *om.* $O_9P_1C_3O_8O_3$M.   28 nec C_3O_8.   29 *ins.* aliquid C_1VHO_4. *ins.* aliquit P_1.   30 dormitandi C_1VHP_1O_4.   31 circumibat O_8M.   32 psalmodie O_3.   33 adl... C_1V.   34 ferebant O_4.

nocturnae[1] uel meridianae[2] quietis tempore importuna[3] forte inquietudine suscitarent, Nemo inquiens mihi[4] molestiam facit me excitando de sompno[5], sed potius laetificat[6] me qui excitat[7]. Facit enim me discusso[8] torpore[9] sompni[10] utilitatis aliquid[11] agere uel cogitare. Tantum autem conpunctioni[12] erat deditus, tantum coelestibus[13] ardebat desideriis, ut missarum sollennia[14] celebrans[15], nequaquam sine profusione lacrimarum implere posset officium. Sed congruo satis ordine dum passionis dominicae[16] misteria[17] caelebraret[18], [19]imitaretur ipse quod ageret[20], se ipsum uidelicet Deo in cordis contritione[21] mactando, sed et astantes[22] populos sursum[23] corda habere, et gratias agere Domino Deo nostro magis ipse cor[24] quam

p. 55 uocem exaltando, potius gemendo quam canendo | ammoneret[25]. Erat[26] zelo iusticiae[27] feruidus ad arguendum peccantes, erat spiritu mansuetudinis modestus ad ignoscendum poenitentibus[28], ita ut nonnunquam[29] confitentibus sibi peccata sua his[30] qui[31] deliquerant, prior ipse miserans[32] infirmos lacrimas[33] funderet, et quid peccatori agendum esset ipse iustus suo praemonstraret exemplo. Uestimentis utebatur communibus, ita temperanter agens, ut horum neque mundiciis[34] neque sordibus esset notabilis. Unde usque hodie in eodem monasterio exemplo eius obseruatur, ne quis uarii aut preciosi[35] coloris habeat indumentum, sed ea maxime uestium specie[36] sint contenti, quam naturalis ouium lana ministrat. His[37] et huiusmodi spiritualibus[38] exercitiis[39] uir uenerabilis et bonorum quorunque[40] ad [41]se imitandum[42] prouocabat affectum, et improbos quosque[43] ac rebelles uitae[44] regularis[45] a pertinatia[46] sui reuocabat erroris.

---

1 nocturne C_3O_3.   2 meridiane C_3O_3.   3 inportuno C_1V. *changed from* inportuno *to* inportuna H.   4 michi O_4.   5 somno $C_1P_1C_3O_8O_4M$. p *above* V.   6 let... O_3M.   7 exscitat V. exsuscitat H.   8 *ins.* somnii O_4.   9 tepore O_4.   10 somni $C_1VHP_1C_3M$. *om.* O_4.   11 aliquit P_1.   12 comp... P_1M.   13 cael... C_1V. cel... C_3O_3. sollemnia VM. solemnia C_3. solennia O_4.   14 sollempnia $C_1HO_8O_3$.   15 cael... C_1VH.   16 dominice O_3.   17 mysteria $C_1VHO_8O_4$.   18 cel... C_3O_4.   19-20 *om.* C_1P_1. *added in margin* V.   21 contricione O_8.

anyone aroused them during the period of their nightly or midday rest by some untimely restlessness. He used to say: "No
one annoys me by arousing me from sleep, but rather he who
awakens me gladdens me; for, by driving away the heaviness
of sleep, he makes me do or think of something useful." He
was so full of penitence, so aflame with heavenly yearnings,
that when celebrating Mass he could never finish the service
without shedding tears. But, as was indeed fitting while he
celebrated the mysteries of the Lord's passion, he would himself
imitate the rite he was performing, that is to say, he would
sacrifice himself to God in contrition of heart. Moreover he
would urge the people who stood by to lift up their hearts and
to give thanks to our Lord God, himself lifting up the heart
rather than the voice, sighing rather than singing. In his zeal for
righteousness he was fervid to reprove sinners, yet he was
kindhearted and forbearing in pardoning the penitent, so that
sometimes when wrongdoers were confessing their sins to
him, in his pity for their weakness he would be the first to
burst into tears and thus, though himself righteous, by his own
example would show the sinner what he ought to do. He wore
ordinary garments and, keeping the middle path, he was not
noteworthy either for their elegance or for their slovenliness.
Hence his example is followed in the same monastery even to
this day, so that no one has a garment of varied or costly colour-
ing, but they are fully satisfied with that kind of garment which
the natural wool of the sheep provides. The venerable man,
by these and other spiritual exercises of the same kind, aroused
in all good men the desire to imitate him and recalled the
wicked and those who rebelled against the rule from the
obstinacy of their error.

22 stantes, *with* ad *above* C_1. adstantes V. ass... P_1O_4.   23 rursum C_1.
24 corde C_1P_1. *changed from* corde V.   25 adm...$C_1VP_1C_3O_8O_3M$.
26 *ins.* enim P_1.   27 iustitiae C_1VH. iusticie O_3O_8.   28 pen... C_1VO_3.
29 nonnumquam C_1VH.   30 hiis O_3.   31 quae C_1P_1.
32 misertus O_4.   33 lacrimos C_1VH.   34 munditiis $C_1VHO_8O_4M$.
munditia P_1.   35 pretiosi C_1VP_1. praet... H.   36 speciae C_1C_3.
37 hiis O_3.   38 spiritalibus C_1VH.   39 exerciis O_9O_3.
40 quorumque C_1VHP_1.   41–42 semitandum C_1.   43 quoque C_1VH.
44 uite O_3.   45 regulari $P_1C_3O_8$.   46 pertinacia $C_1VHO_8O_3M$.

XVII. [1]Qualiter[3] sibi in insula Farne[4] pulsis demonibus[5] habitationem fecerit[2] |

p. 56 At[6] postquam in eodem monasterio multa annorum curri-
cula expleuit, tandem diu concupita, quaesita[7], ac petita
solitudinis secreta, comitante praefati abbatis sui simul et
fratrum gratia multum laetabundus adiit. Gaudebat namque[8] quia[9] de longa[10] perfectione[11] conuersationis actiuae,
ad otium diuinae speculationis iam mereretur[12] ascendere.
Laetabatur[13] ad[14] eorum sortem se[15] pertingere[16] de quibus
Psa. 83. 8 canitur in psalmo, *Ambulabunt*[17] *de uirtute in uirtutem,*
uidebitur Deus deorum in Syon[18]. Et quidem in primis
uitae solitariae rudimentis, secessit ad locum quendam
qui in exterioribus eius cellae partibus secretior apparet[19].
At cum ibidem aliquandiu[20] solitarius cum hoste inuisibili
orando ac ieiunando certaret, tandem maiora praesumens,
longinquiorem ac remotiorem ab hominibus locum certaminis petiit. Farne dicitur insula medio in mari posita,
quae non sicut Lindisfarnensium incolarum regio, bis[21]
Vegetius cotidie accedente *aestu*[22] oceani[23], quem *reuma*[24] *uocant*
Epitoma Greci, fit insula, bis renudatis abeunte reumate litoribus[25]
rei mili- contigua terrae redditur, sed aliquot milibus passuum[26]
taris IV. 42 ab hac semiinsula[27] [28]ad eurum[30] secreta[31,29], et[32] hinc
p. 57 altissimo, et inde infinito clauditur | oceano[33]. Nullus hanc
facile ante famulum Domini Cuthbertum[34] solus ualebat
inhabitare colonus, propter uidelicet demorantium[35] ibi
phantasias[36] demonum[37]. Verum intrante eam milite
Eph. 6. Christi, armato *galea salutis, scuto fidei, et gladio spiritus*
16, 17 *quod est uerbum Dei, omnia tela nequissimi*[38] *ignea extin*cta[39]
et ipse nequissimus cum omni satellitum suorum turba
porro fugatus est hostis[40]. Qui uidelicet miles Christi ut

1–2 Qualem in Farne habitationem sibi fecit O$_4$.   3 qualem VH.
4 Farnae H.   5 daem... O$_8$.   6 ad C$_1$. ac VH.   7 ques... M.
8 nanque P$_1$O$_4$M.   9 *om.* P$_1$.   10 longe V.   11 per *inserted*
above C$_1$.   12 meretur C$_1$. *om.* P$_1$.   13 let... O$_3$.   14 *ins.* hanc
C$_1$VHP$_1$.   15 se sort. C$_1$VHP$_1$O$_4$.   16 pertinere P$_1$.   17 *ins.* sancti
C$_1$VHP$_1$O$_4$.   18 Sion C$_1$VHC$_3$.   19 aparet C$_1$.   20 aliquam-
diu O$_3$.   21 biss C$_1$.   22 estu P$_1$O$_8$O$_3$.   23 occeani O$_3$M.
24 *gloss above* id est eruptio uel fluor H.   25 littoribus O$_9$.
26 *gloss above* id est stadiorum H.   27 *ins.* distans C$_1$VH. *ins.*

CHAPTER XVII. *How he drove out the demons and made himself a dwelling place in the island of Farne*

Now after he had completed many years in that same monastery, he joyfully entered into the remote solitudes which he had long desired, sought, and prayed for, with the good will of that same abbot and also of the brethren. For he rejoiced because, after a long and blameless active life, he was now held worthy to rise to the repose of divine contemplation. He rejoiced to attain to the lot of those concerning whom the Psalmist sings: "The saints shall go from strength to strength; the God of Gods shall be seen in Zion." Now indeed at the first beginning of his solitary life, he retired to a certain place in the outer precincts of the monastery which seemed to be more secluded. But when he had fought there in solitude for some time with the invisible enemy, by prayer and fasting, he sought a place of combat farther and more remote from mankind, aiming at greater things. There is an island called Farne in the middle of the sea which is not like the Lindisfarne region—for that owing to the flow of the ocean tide, called in Greek "rheuma", twice a day becomes an island and twice a day, when the tide ebbs from the uncovered shores, becomes again contiguous to the land; but it is some miles away to the south-east of this half-island, and is shut in on the landward side by very deep water and on the seaward side by the boundless ocean. No one had been able to dwell alone undisturbed upon this island before Cuthbert the servant of the Lord, on account of the phantoms of demons who dwelt there; but when the soldier of Christ entered, armed with the "helmet of salvation, the shield of faith, and the sword of the spirit which is the word of God, all the fiery darts of the wicked one" were quenched, and the wicked foe himself was driven far away together with the whole crowd of his satellites. This soldier of Christ, as

distat P$_1$.   28–29 *om*. H.   30 eius C$_1$VP$_1$.
31 *ins*. proficiscens C$_1$V. *ins*. proficiscitur P$_1$.   32 quae C$_1$VP$_1$.
33 occeano O$_3$.   34 Cudberhtum C$_1$V. Cuthberhtum H. Cuthbertum P$_1$.   35 demorantes C$_1$P$_1$.   36 fantasias C$_1$VHM.
37 daem... C$_3$O$_8$O$_4$.   38 nequissima C$_1$.   39 *gloss above* scilicet
sunt VH.   40 *fresh paragraph begins in* O$_9$.

deuicta tyrannorum[1] acie monarcha[2] terrae quam adierat factus est, condidit ciuitatem suo aptam imperio, et domos in hac aeque[3] ciuitati congruas erexit. Est autem aedificium[4] situ pene[5] rotundum, a muro usque ad murum mensura quattuor[6] ferme siue quinque[7] perticarum distentum, murus ipse[8] de foris altior longitudine stantis hominis. Nam intrinsecus uiuam[9] cedendo[10] rupem, multo illum[11] fecit altiorem, quatinus[12] ad cohibendam[13] oculorum siue[14] cogitationum[15] lasciuiam, ad erigendam in superna desideria totam mentis intentionem, pius incola nil de sua mansione praeter[16] coelum[17] posset intueri. Quem uidelicet murum non de[18] secto[19] lapide uel latere et cemento[20], sed[21] impolitis[22] prorsus lapidibus et cespite

p. 58 quem de medio loci fodiendo tulerat[23] composuit[24]. | E quibus quidam tantae[25] erant granditatis, ut uix a quattuor[26] uiris uiderentur potuisse leuari, quos tamen ipse[27] angelico adiutus auxilio illuc attulisse[28] aliunde et muro imposuisse[29] repertus est. Duas in mansione habebat domos, oratorium scilicet et aliud[30] ad communes usus aptum[31] habitaculum. Quorum parietes quidem de naturali terra multum intus forisque circumfodiendo[32] siue cedendo[33] confecit. Culmina uero de lignis informibus et foeno[34] superposuit. Porro ad portum insulae[35] maior erat domus, in qua uisitantes eum fratres suscipi et quiescere possent, nec[36] longe ab ea fons eorundem usibus accommodus.

XVIII. *Quomodo precibus aquam de arida produxerit,* [37]*uel qualiter ipse in anachoresi*[39] *uixerit*[40, 38] |

p. 59 At uero ipsa eius mansio aquae[41] erat indiga, utpote in durissima et prope saxea rupe condita. Accitis[42] ergo uir Domini fratribus, necdum enim se ab aduenientium

1 tirannorum C₃.   2 monarchus C₁VHP₁.   3 eque O₃.
4 edi... C₁P₁O₃.   5 penae C₁.   6 quatuor VO₄. iiii P₁.
7 v P₁.   8 *gloss above* scilicet est VH.   9 i mam V. imam H.
gloss above uel imam C₃O₈.   10 caed... O₄.   11 eum O₄.
12 quatenus C₁.   13 choibendam C₃. coibendam P₁.   14 simul
et C₁VHP₁O₄.   15 cogitatuum C₁VHP₁.   16 preter O₈O₄M.
17 cael... C₁V. cel... O₃.   18 *om.* C₁VHP₁O₄.   19 secta C₁P₁.
20 cimento C₁H. *gloss above* uel e H.   21 set O₁.   22 *gloss above*

soon as he had become monarch of the land he had entered
and had overcome the army of the usurpers, built a city
fitted for his rule, and in it houses equally suited to the city.
It is a structure almost round in plan, measuring about
four or five poles from wall to wall; the wall itself on the
outside is higher than a man standing upright; but inside he
made it much higher by cutting away the living rock, so that
the pious inhabitant could see nothing except the sky from his
dwelling, thus restraining both the lust of the eyes and of the
thoughts and lifting the whole bent of his mind to higher things.
He made this same wall, not of cut stone nor of bricks and
mortar, but just of unworked stone and of turf which he had
removed from the excavation in the middle of his dwelling.
Some of these stones were so great that it would seem to have
been scarcely possible for four men to have lifted them, but
nevertheless he was found to have brought them thither from
elsewhere with angelic aid, and to have placed them in the
wall. He had two buildings in his dwelling-place, namely an
oratory and another habitation suitable for common uses. He
finished the walls by digging and cutting away the natural
soil both inside and outside, and he placed on them roofs of
rough-hewn timber and straw. But away at the landing-place
in the island there was a larger house in which the brethren
who visited him could be received and rest, and not far away
was a well for their use.

CHAPTER XVIII. *How he produced water from dry land
by his prayers and how he lived as a hermit*

Now his dwelling-place was lacking in water inasmuch as it
was built on very hard and almost stony rock. So the man of
God summoned the brethren, for he had not yet secluded
himself from the sight of visitors. "You see", he said, "that

id est incesis H. inp... C_1VHC_3.   23 tul. fod. O_4.   24 conp... C_1VH.
25 tante O_3.   26 iiii P_1. quatuor VO_3.   27 ille O_4.   28 adt... C_1VH.
29 inp...$C_1VHP_1C_3$.   30 alium C_1. *changed from* alium V.   31 *om.* O_4.
32 circun... P_1.   33 caed... C_1VHO_4.   34 faeno V. feno C_3O_3M.
35 insule O_3.   36 *gloss above* scilicet erat VH.   37–38 *om.* O_4.
39 anchoresi, *with* n *above* VH. achoresi O_9M.   40 proficerit VH.
41 aque O_3.   42 accitus O_9.

secluserat[1] aspectibus, Cernitis, inquit quia fontis inops[2]
sit mansio quam adii, sed rogemus obsecro illum *qui*
conuertit solidam *petram in stagn*um[3] *aquae et rupes in*
fontes aquarum, ut *non nobis sed nomini* suo *dans gloriam*
de hac quoque rupe[4] saxosa nobis uenam fontis aperire
dignetur. [5]Fodiamus in medio tuguriunculi mei, credo
torrente uoluptatis[6] su*ae potabit* nos[7]. Fecerunt ergo foueam,
quam in crastinum emanante ab internis unda repletam
inuenerunt. Unde dubium non erat hanc orationibus uiri
Dei de aridissima [8]ac durissima[9] prius terra elicitam
fuisse aquam. Quae[10] uidelicet aqua mirum in modum
primis contenta ripis, nec foras[11] ebulliendo pauimentum
inuadere[12], nec hauriendo nouit deficere, ita moderata[13]
gratia largitoris, ut nec necessitati[14] accipientis super-
flueret, nec sustentandae necessitati copia deesset. Facta
ergo iuuantibus se fratribus mansione ac domibus prae-
fatis[15], incipit[16] habitare solus uir Domini Cuthbertus[17],
et[18] primo quidem uenientibus ad se fratribus de sua cel|la[19]
egredi[20] eisque[21] ministrare solebat. Quorum dum pedes[22]
aqua calida deuotus lauaret[23], coactus est aliquotiens[24]
ab eis etiam se discalciare[25], suosque pedes illis ad abluen-
dum praebere[26]. Nanque[27] in tantum a cultu sui corporis
animum sustulerat, atque ad animae solius cultum contu-
lerat, ut semel calciatus [28]tibracis[30] quas pellicias habere
solebat[31], sic menses perduraret integros. Aliquando etiam
calciatus[29] in pascha[32] non nisi post annum redeunte
paschae[33] tempore, propter lauationem pedum quae in
coena[34] Domini fieri solet, se discalciasse[35] dicatur. Unde
ob crebras[36] preces[37] incuruationesque genuum quas calciatus exercebat, callum oblongum nec exilem in confinio
pedum[38] et tibiarum habuisse deprehensus est. Deinde

1 recl... C₁VHP₁.   2 inobs VH.   3 stangnum C₃.   4 *om.* P₁.
5–7 *om.* M.   6 uoluntatis O₄.   8–9 *om.* C₁VHP₁O₄.   10 que O₃.
11 foris P₁.   12 eu... O₉.   13 moderante VH.
14 necessitatis C₁.   15 pre... M.   16 incaepit O₄. incepit P₁.
17 Cudberhtus C₁V. Cuthberhtus H.   18 ex C₁.   19 cellula
C₁VHP₁O₄.   20 egrediens P₁.   21 *om.* que P₁.

the dwelling-place I have chosen lacks a well; but let us, I beseech you, pray Him 'who turns the solid rock into a standing water and the flint into fountains of waters', that, giving 'glory not unto us but unto His name', He may vouchsafe to open to us also a spring of water from the stony rock. Let us dig in the midst of my little dwelling and I believe that He will 'make us drink from the river of His pleasures'." So they made a pit and on the next day they found it full of water which came from within. Hence there was no doubt that this water had been drawn from ground which before had been exceedingly dry and hard, through the prayers of the man of God. And this water was in a wonderful way kept within its first limits so that it never bubbled over and covered the floor, nor failed through exhaustion of its supply; but the grace of the Giver so controlled it that it did not exceed the necessities of the receiver, nor was the supply for those necessities ever lacking. Now when this same dwelling-place and these chambers had been built with the help of his brethren, Cuthbert the man of God began to dwell alone. At first, indeed, he used to go forth from his cell to meet the brethren who came to him, and to minister to them. And when he had devoutly washed their feet in warm water, he was sometimes compelled by them to take off his shoes and to allow them to wash his feet. For he had so far withdrawn his mind from the care of his body and fixed it on the care of his soul alone that, having once been shod with the boots of skin that he was accustomed to use, he would wear them for whole months together. And let it be said that once he had put on his boots at Easter, he did not take them off until Easter came round again a year later, and then only for the washing of the feet which takes place on Maundy Thursday. So, on account of the frequent genuflexions at prayer which he made while wearing his boots, he was found to have a long and thickish callus at the junction of his feet and his shins. Then, when his zeal for perfection grew,

22 pedes dum O$_4$.   23 lau. deu. O$_4$.   24 ...ties C$_1$VHO$_4$.   25 discaltiare P$_1$.   26 preb... HM.   27 namque C$_1$VHO$_3$.   28–29 *om.* C$_1$VHP$_1$.
30 tribracis O$_9$.   31 consueuerat O$_4$.   32 pasca V.   33 pasche O$_3$.
34 caena C$_1$VH. cena P$_1$O$_3$O$_4$.   35 ...are C$_1$VHO$_4$. discaltiare P$_1$.
36 sacras P$_1$.   37 praeces HO$_8$.   38 *changed from* pedem C$_1$.

increscente[1] studio perfectionis includitur in suo monasterio, atque ab hominum remotus aspectibus, solitariam
in ieiuniis orationibus et uigiliis discit agere uitam, rarum[2]
cum aduenientibus de intus habens colloquium[3], et hoc
per fenestram. Qua primitus aperta et uideri a fratribus,
et fratres quos alloquebatur[4] ipse uidere gaudebat, exin[5]
praecedente[6] tempore et ipsam obclusit, nec nisi[7] dandae
benedictionis uel alterius cuiuslibet certae[8] necessitatis
gratia[9] reserabat[10].

XIX. *Qualiter a messe quam* [11] *sua manu*[12] *seruerat*[13],
[14] *uerbo uolucres abegerit*[15] |

p. 61　Et primum quidem permodicum ab eis panem[16] quo
uesceretur accipiebat[17], ac[18] suo bibebat e fonte. Post
modum uero proprio manuum labore iuxta exempla
patrum uiuere magis aptum ducebat. Rogauit ergo
[19]afferri[21] sibi instrumenta[20] quibus terram exerceret, et
triticum quod sereret. Sed[22] seminata uerno tempore
terra, nullos usque ad medium aestatis[23] reddidit fructus.
Unde uisitantibus se iuxta morem fratribus aiebat uir Dei,
Forsitan aut[24] telluris huiusce[25] natura, aut uoluntas Dei
non est ut hoc in loco mihi[26] triticum nascatur. Afferte[27]
rogo ordeum, si forte uel illud fructum facere possit.
Quod si nec illi Deus incrementum dare uoluerit, satius[28]
p. 62　est me ad cenobium[29] reuerti, quam alieno hic la|bore
sustentari. Allatumque[30] ordeum dum ultra omne tempus
serendi, ultra omnem spem fructificandi terrae[31] commendaret, mox abundanter[32] exortum[33] fecit fructum
copiosum. Qui[34] dum maturescere coepisset[35], uenere
uolucres, et huic depascendo certatim insistebant. Ad
quos piissimus Christi seruus appropinquans[36] sicut post
ipse[37] referebat, solebat enim sepe[38] quia laeti[39] uultus et

1 crescente P₁.　　　2 raro C₁VHP₁.　　　3 conl... VH.
4 alloquaeb... V.　　5 sed P₁.　　6 pro... O₄M.　　7 *ins.* uel
C₁VHP₁O₄.　　　8 certe O₃.　　　9 *ins.* poscente C₁VHP₁O₄.
10 reserebat C₁. *changed from* reserebat V.　　11–12 ipse O₄.
13 seuerat VH.　　　14–15 aues uerbo abegit O₄.　　　16 *ins.* accipiens O₄.　　17 *om.* O₄.　　18 *om.* O₄.　　19–20 inst. sibi aff. O₄.

he shut himself up in his hermitage, and, remote from the gaze
of men, he learned to live a solitary life of fasting, prayers and
vigils, rarely having conversation from within his cell with
visitors and that only through the window. At first he opened
this and rejoiced to see and be seen by the brethren with whom
he spoke; but, as time went on, he shut even that, and opened
it only for the sake of giving his blessing or for some other
definite necessity.

CHAPTER XIX. *How, with a word, he drove away the birds
from the crops which he had sown with his own hand*

Now at first he received a little bread to eat from his visitors
and drank from his own well; but afterwards, in accordance
with the example of the fathers, he considered it more fitting
to live by the labour of his own hands. So he asked for tools
to be brought to him with which to work the land, and also
some wheat to sow; but though the land was sown in spring-
time, it had produced no fruit up to midsummer. So, when
the brethren were visiting him after their custom, the man of
God said: "Perchance it is not in accordance either with the
nature of this land or with the will of God that wheat should
grow for me in this place; bring me, I beg you, some barley,
to see if perchance that may produce a crop. And if God does
not grant me any increase from that, I would rather return to
the monastery than be kept here by the labours of others."
The barley was brought long after the proper time for sowing
it, and when there seemed no hope of any harvest, yet when he
put it in the ground, it soon sprang up and brought forth a very
abundant crop. And when it had begun to ripen, some birds
came and eagerly set about consuming it. The most pious
servant of God approached them and, as he afterwards related—
for, being of a happy disposition and very friendly, he was often

21 adf... C_1VH.   22 set O_3. *ins.* et H.   23 estatis P_1O_8.   24 aud
$C_1C_3O_4$.   25 huius P_1. huiuscae H.   26 michi O_3.   27 adf... C_1VH.
28 sacius O_8O_3M.   29 coen... C_1VP_1.   30 allatum nanque P_1.
31 terre O_3.   32 hab... $C_1VHP_1C_3O_3$.   33 exhortum C_1.
34 quod P_1.   35 caep... VP_1. cep... O_3C_3.   36 adpropians C_1VH.
appropians $P_1C_3O_3M$.   37 *om.* M.   38 saepe C_1VH.   39 leti O_3.

affabilis erat ad confirmandam fidem audientium, aliqua
etiam de eis quae ipse credendo optinuerit[1] in medium
proferre[2], Quid tangitis inquit[3] sata quae non seruistis?
An forte uos plus me his[4] opus habetis? Si tamen a
Deo licentiam accepistis, facite quod ipse[5] permisit[6]. Sin
autem, recedite neque ulterius aliena ledatis. Dixerat[7],
et ad primam[8] iubentis uocem[9] uniuersa uolucrum multi-
tudo recessit, seque per omnia deinceps ab eiusdem[10]
messis inuasione continuit. Et hic quoque uenerabilis
Christi famulus in duobus miraculis duorum patrum est
facta secutus. In aqua uidelicet elicita de rupe, factum[11]
beati patris Benedicti qui idem pene[12] et eodem modo
legitur fecisse miraculum, sed iccirco[13] uberius quia plures
p. 63   erant qui aquae[14] inopia laborarent[15]. Porro in arces|sitis
a messe uolatilibus reuerentissimi et sanctissimi patris
Antonii sequebatur exemplum, qui a lesione hortuli quem
ipse plantauerat uno onagros sermone compescuit[16].

XX.   [17]*Quomodo corui iniuriam[19] quam uiro Dei intulerant,
precibus et munere purgauerint[20], [18]*

Libet etiam quoddam beati Cuthberti[21] in exemplum
praefati patris Benedicti factum narrare miraculum, in quo
auium oboedientia[22] et humilitate palam contumatia[23] et
superbia condempnatur[24] humana. Erant siquidem corui
multo ex[25] tempore eiusdem insulae[26] sedibus assueti[27].
Quos cum die quadam [28]uir Dei[29] nidificantes hospitiolum[30]
fratrum de quo praefatus sum rostro lacerare, ablatosque
culmos quibus tectum fuerat ad fabricam nidi ore ferre[31]
conspiceret, coercuit[32] eos leui protensione[33] dexterae,|
p. 64   atque a lesura fratrum iam cessare praecepit[34]. [35]Sed illis
imperium spernentibus[36], In nomine inquit[37] Iesu Christi

1 obt... C₁VHP₁O₈O₄M.   2 profferre O₄.   3 inquid C₁O₃.
4 hiis O₃.   5 uobis O₈.   6 permiserit O₈.   7 *gloss above*
scilicet haec VH.   8 *ins.* eius O₄.   9 uocem iubentis O₄.
10 eisdem C₁. u *above* V.   11 *om.* O₄.   12 paene C₁.
13 idcirco C₁VH.   14 aque O₃.   15 laborabant P₁O₄.
16 conp... C₁VH.   17–18 Quomodo coruis noxam quam fecerunt
indulsit O₄.   19 iniur. coru. M.   20 purgarint VH.
21 Cudberhti C₁V. Cuthberhti H.   22 obaed... VP₁. obed... O₃.

in the habit of disclosing some of the blessings which he had
gained by his own faith, in order to confirm the faith of his
listeners—"Why", said he, "do you touch the crops that you
did not sow? Or is it, perchance, that you have greater need of
them than I? If, however, you have received permission from
God, do what He has allowed you; but if not, depart and do
not injure any more the possessions of another." Thus he spoke
and, at the first sound of his commands, the whole multitude
of birds departed and thenceforward refrained altogether from
attacking his crops. And on this occasion also, the venerable
servant of Christ followed in these two miracles the deeds of
two of the fathers; namely, in obtaining water from the rock,
a deed of the blessed father Benedict, who is said to have wrought
an almost identical miracle in the same way, but more copiously
because there were more who were suffering from lack of
water. Further, in driving away the birds from the crops,
he followed the example of the most reverend and holy father
Antony, who with one exhortation restrained the wild asses
from injuring the little garden that he himself had planted.

CHAPTER XX. *How the ravens atoned for the injury which they
had done to the man of God by their prayers and by a gift*

Let us also tell of a miracle wrought by the blessed Cuthbert
after the example of the above-mentioned father Benedict, in
which human pride and contumacy are openly condemned by
the obedience and humility of birds. There were some ravens
that had long been accustomed to dwell on that island, and
one day, as they were building their nests, the man of God saw
them tear with their beaks the little guest-house of the brethren
of which I have spoken before, and carry off in their bills the
straw with which it was thatched, as material for their nests.
He checked them with a slight motion of his right hand, and
bade them cease from injuring the brethren. When they ig-
nored his command, he said: "In the name of Jesus Christ,

23 contumacia C₁VHO₃O₄M.   24 condemn... C₁C₃.   25 *om.* P₁.
26 insule O₃.   27 ads... C₁. *altered from* ads... V. *altered from* assueta O₃.
28–29 *om.* O₄.   30 hospiciolum O₈O₄.   31 *ins.* uir dei O₄.
32 coher... C₁P₁O₄.   33 protentione C₁.   34 pre... M. praecaepit C₁V.   35–36 spernentibusque imperium C₁VHP₁O₄.   37 inquid O₃.

abite quantotius[1], neque in loco quem leditis[2] ultra
manere praesumatis. Uix uerba compleuerat[3], et confestim tristes abiere. Peracto autem triduo unus e duobus
rediit, et fodientem reperiens[4] famulum Christi, sparsis
lamentabiliter pennis, et summisso[5] ad pedes eius capite,
atque humiliata uoce quibus ualebat indiciis ueniam precabatur[6]. Quod intelligens[7] uenerabilis pater, dedit facultatem remeandi. At ille impetrata redeundi licentia[8], mox
sodalem adducturus abiit. Nec mora redeunt ambo, et[9]
secum[10] digna munera ferunt[11], dimidiam uidelicet axun-
giam porcinam. Quam uir Domini aduentantibus postea
fratribus sepius[12] ostendere atque ad unguendas caligas
praebere[13] solebat, contestans eis[14] quanta hominibus
oboedientiae[15], quanta sit cura humilitatis[16] habenda, cum
auis superbissima iniuriam quam [17]uiro Dei[18] intulerat[19],
precibus[20], lamentis, et muneribus festinauit[21] abluere.
Denique ad dandum hominibus exemplum correctionis,
multos deinceps annos in ipsa insula manebant et nidifica-
bant, neque aliquid[22] molestiae cuiquam irrogare[23] aude-
bant. Nulli autem uideatur ab|surdum a uolatilibus
formam discere uirtutis, cum Salomon dicat, *Vade ad
formicam o piger, et considera uias eius et disce sapientiam.*

p. 65
Prov. 6. 6

XXI.   [24]*Qualiter eius necessitatibus etiam mare seruierit*[25]

Non sola[26] autem aeris sed[27] et maris animalia, immo et
ipsum mare sicut et aer et ignis iuxta quod in superioribus
exposuimus, uiro uenerabili praebuere[28] obsequium. Qui
enim auctori omnium creaturarum fideliter et integro
corde famulatur, non est mirandum si eius imperiis ac
uotis omnis creatura deseruiat[29]. At nos plerunque[30]
iccirco[31] subiectae nobis creaturae dominium perdimus,
quia Domino et creatori omnium ipsi seruire negligimus[32].

1 quantocius VHO₃O₄M.   2 laed... O₈. ledetis H.   3 conp... H.
4 repp... C₁VHP₁C₃O₃O₄.   5 subm... C₁VH.   6 praec...
HO₈. *ins.* admissi C₁VHP₁O₄.   7 intellegens C₁VH.   8 lic.
red. C₃.   9 at C₁. ad VH.   10 se C₁VH.   11 ferentes C₁.
ferent *changed to* ferunt V.   12 saepius C₁. *om.* O₄.   13 prebere M.
14 eos C₁P₁O₄. *om.* C₃.   15 obaed... VP₁. obed... O₃.

go away forthwith, and do not presume to remain any longer in the place that you are damaging." Scarcely had he finished these words when they forthwith flew dismally away. Now when three days had passed, one of a pair returned and found the servant of Christ digging. With its feathers sadly ruffled and its head drooping to its feet, and with humble cries it prayed for pardon, using such signs as it could; and the venerable father, understanding what it meant, gave it permission to return. And having got leave to come back, it soon went off in order to bring back its mate. Without delay they both returned bringing a worthy gift, namely a portion of hog's lard; and this the man of God used often afterwards to show to the brethren when they visited him, and to offer it to grease their shoes; declaring how carefully men should seek after obedience and humility, seeing that even a proud bird hastened to atone for the wrong that it had done to a man of God, by means of prayers, lamentations and gifts. And in order to give mankind an example of reformation, they remained for many years in that island and built their nests, not daring to inflict any injury on anyone. Let it not seem absurd to anyone to learn a lesson of virtue from birds, since Solomon says: "Go to the ant, thou sluggard, consider her ways and be wise."

CHAPTER XXI. *How even the sea ministered to his necessities*

Moreover not only the creatures of the air but also of the sea, yes, and even the sea itself, as well as air and fire as we have shown above, did honour to the venerable man. For if a man faithfully and wholeheartedly serves the maker of all created things, it is no wonder though all creation should minister to his commands and wishes. But for the most part we lose dominion over the creation which was made subject to us, because we ourselves neglect to serve the Lord and Creator of all things.

16 humilibus O_9.　　17–18 homini C_1VHO_4.　　19 intulisset C_1VH.
20 praec... O_8.　　21 festinaret C_1VHP_1. festinarit O_4.　　22 aliud O_8O_3M.　　23 inr... C_1VH.　　24–25 Quod etiam mare suis necessitatibus seruierit O_4.　　26 solum VH.　　27 set O_3.
28 preb... O_9.　　29 deseruit P_1.　　30 plerumque $C_1VHP_1O_3$.
31 idc... C_1VH.　　32 neglegimus C_1VH.

Et ipsum inquam mare promptum famulo Christi ubi opus habuit, impendebat[1] officium. Disponebat nanque[2]

p. 66 paruulam sibi in suo | monasterio sed[3] cotidianis necessitatibus aptam[4] condere casulam, cui a parte maris qua alluuione[5] frequentium gurgitum excauata rupis altissimum nec breuem fecerat hiatum[6], basis supponenda[7] erat, et haec[8] iuxta[9] latitudinem hiatus[10] duodecim[11] pedes[12] longa. Rogauit ergo fratres qui se uisitaturi aduenerant, ut cum redire uellent, lignum sibi longitudinis duodecim[13] pedum ad faciendam domunculae[14] basim deferrent. Qui promiserunt se libentissime facturos quod petiit, sed[15] accepta ab eo benedictione ubi[16] domum sunt reuersi[17], fugit mentem petitio[18] patris, reuersique die debito ad eum non attulere[19] quod rogabantur[20]. Quibus ille benignissime receptis, et oratione solita Deo commendatis, [21]Ubi est inquit[23] lignum[22] quod uos afferre[24] rogabam? Tum illi reminiscentes petitionem[25] eius, suamque confitentes obliuionem, ueniam de admisso precabantur[26]. At uir mitissimus[27] blando illos sermone consolatus, usque ad mane in[28] insula manere et quiescere[29] praecepit[30] dicens, Credo quia Deus non obliuiscatur meae[31] uoluntatis et necessitatis. Fecerunt ut dixerat, et exurgentes[32] mane uiderunt quia nocturnus oceani[33] estus[34]

p. 67 lignum memoratae[35] | longitudinis attulit[36], et in[37] ipso insuper loco deposuit, ubi in aedificium[38] desuper erat imponendum[39]. Uidentes autem, mox et uiri uenerabilis sanctitatem mirabantur, cui etiam elementa seruirent, et suae mentis tarditatem debito cum pudore culpabant, quos etiam insensibile elementum[40] quam sit sanctis obtemperandum doceret.

---

1 inp... C_1VHC_3. 2 namque C_1VHO_3. 3 *ins.* et H.
4 apt. necess. O_4. 5 aluuione C_1. 6 hyatum O_3.
7 subp... C_1VH. super... P_1. 8 hec O_3. 9 *gloss above* scilicet
debuit esse VH. 10 hyatus O_3. 11 xii P_1. 12 pedum VHP_1.
13 xii V. xii P_1. 14 domuncule O_8. 15 *ins.* ubi C_1V
HP_1O_4. 16 *om.* $C_1VHP_1O_4$. 17 reu. sunt $C_1VHP_1O_4$.
18 peticio C_3O_8. 19 adt... C_1VH. 20 rogabatur P_1.

The very sea, I say, was ready to do service to the servant of
Christ when he needed it. For he was intending to build a hut
in his monastery, very small but suited for his daily needs;
it was to be on the seaward side where the hollowing out of
a rock by the washings of continual tides had made a very deep
and wide gap; a flooring had to be placed under the hut, and
this had to be twelve feet long so as to fit the width of the gap.
So he asked the brethren who had come to visit him, that
when they were returning, they would bring with them some
timber twelve feet long, to make a flooring for his little house.
They promised gladly to do what he asked. But after they
had received his blessing and returned home, the father's request
escaped their mind; and when they returned to him on the
appointed day, they did not bring what they had been asked
for. When he had received them most kindly and had commended them to God with his accustomed prayer, he said:
"Where is the timber that I asked you to bring?" Then they
remembered his petition and, confessing their forgetfulness, they
craved pardon for their trespass. But the kindly man consoled
them with gentle words and bade them remain on the island
until morning and rest, for he said: "I believe that God will
not forget my desire and my needs." They did as he had said
and rising up in the morning, they saw that the night tide had
carried up some timber of the required length, and had placed
it over the very spot whereon it was to be set for the building.
As soon as they saw this, they marvelled at the holiness of the
venerable man for whom even the elements did service; and
with fitting shame they blamed their slothful minds, for even
the insensible elements taught them what obedience ought to
be shown to saints.

21-22 ubi... lignum *bis* M.   23 inquid O_3.   24 adf... C_1VH.
25 peticionem C_3O_8.   26 *changed from* precabatur C_1. praec... O_8.
27 mitt... C_1.   28 *om.* O_3.   29 requiescere C_1VH.   30 pre... M.
31 mee O_3.   32 exsurg... C_1VH.   33 occeani O_3.
34 aestus C_1VHP$_1O_4$.   35 memorate O_3M.   36 adt... C_1V.
37 *om.* O_3.   38 edif... C_1O_3.   39 inp... C_1VHC$_3$.
40 elementa C_1.

XXII. [1] *Quomodo multis ad se uenientibus monita dans salutis fragiles exposuerit antiqui hostis insidias*[2]

Ueniebant[3] autem multi ad uirum Dei non solum de proximis Lindisfarnensium finibus, sed etiam de remotioribus Brittanniae[4] partibus fama nimirum uirtutum eius acciti[5], qui uel sua quae commisissent[6] errata, uel demonum[7] quae[8] paterentur temptamenta profitentes, uel certe communia mortalium quibus affligerentur aduersa|

p. 68   patefacientes, a tantae[9] sanctitatis uiro se consolandos sperabant. Nec eos fefellit spes. Nanque[10] nullus ab eo sine gaudio consolationis abibat, nullum dolor animi quem illo attulerat[11] redeuntem comitatus est. Nouerat quippe mestos pia exhortatione[12] refouere, sciebat angustiatis[13] gaudia uitae[14] coelestis[15] ad memoriam reuocare, fragilia saeculi[16] huius et prospera simul et aduersa monstrare[17], didicerat temptatis multifarias antiqui hostis pandere uersutias, quibus facile caperetur animus, qui uel fraterno uel diuino[18] amore nudatus existeret[19], at qui integra fide roboratus incederet, insidias aduersarii Domino auxiliante quasi casses[20] transiret araneae. Quociens[21] inquit[22] me ipsum de alta rupe[23] per praeceps[25,24] misere, quociens[26] quasi ad interficiendum me lapides iactabant, sed et aliis aliisque fantasiarum temptamentis[27] me appetentes[28] deterrere, ac[29] de loco huius certaminis conabantur eliminare. Nec tamen ullatenus uel corpus meum lesura aliqua, uel mentem timore contaminare ualebant. Hoc quoque fratribus solebat crebrius intimare, ne conuersationem eius quasi singulariter celsam[30] mirarentur, quia contemptis

p. 69   saecularibus[31] curis secretus uiuere mal|let. Sed iure inquit[32] est coenobitarum[33] uita miranda, qui abbatis per omnia

---

1-2 Quod fragiles diaboli exposuerit omnibus insidias O₄.   3 venerunt P₁.   4 Britannie O₃. Britanniae P₁M.   5 acti O₄. 6 commiserant O₄.   7 daem... O₄.   8 que O₃.   9 tanto C₁VH. tante O₃.   10 namque C₁VHO₃.   11 adt... C₁. 12 exortatione VHC₃O₃.   13 angustias O₃.   14 uite O₃. 15 cael... C₁V. cel... O₃.   16 sec... O₃O₄.   17 *gloss in margin* scilicet sciebat V. *gloss above* scilicet sciebat H.   18 diu. uel frat. O₄.   19 esset O₄.   20 cassas O₈.   21 quoties C₁VHO₄.

CHAPTER XXII. *How he gave instruction in the way of salvation to many who came to him and showed the weakness of the snares of the ancient foe*

Now many came to the man of God, not only from the neighbourhood of Lindisfarne but also from the remoter parts of Britain, having been attracted by the report of his miracles; such people declared to him either the sins they had committed or the temptations of devils to which they were exposed, or else revealed the common troubles of mankind by which they were afflicted, hoping that they would get consolation from a m. n of such sanctity. Nor did their hope deceive them. For no c e went away from him without enjoying his consolation, and no one returned accompanied by that sorrow of mind which he had brought thither. He knew, in fact, how to refresh the sad by his pious exhortation; he could recall to the memory of the afflicted the joys of the heavenly life, and show them how fleeting were both the pleasures and the sorrows of this world; he had learned how to lay bare before tempted men the manifold wiles of the ancient foe, by which the soul that is without brotherly or divine love may easily be entrapped: but he who goes strengthened by unwavering faith passes with the help of the Lord through the snares of the enemy as though they were spiders' webs. "How many times", he said, "have they cast me down headlong from a high rock; how many times have they hurled stones at me as if to kill me! But though they sought to frighten me away by one phantasmal temptation or another, and attempted to drive me from this place of combat, nevertheless they were unable in any way to mar my body by any injury, or my mind by fear!" He was also accustomed very frequently to bid the brethren not to wonder at his way of life, as though it were specially exalted, because he despised worldly things and preferred to live alone. "But", said he, "the life of monks ought rightly to be admired, for they

quotiens $P_1C_3O_8M$.   22 inquid O_3.   23-24 in praecipitium P_1.
25 pre... O_8O_4.   26 quoties C_1VHO_4. quotiens $P_1C_3O_8M$.
27-28 mea petentes C_1. me apetentes (*with second* p *above*) V.   29 atque O_4.   30 excelsam $C_1VHP_1O_4$.   31 secu... O_3M.
32 inquid O_3.   33 caen... V. cen... $P_1C_3O_3$.

subiciuntur[1] imperiis[2]. Ad eius arbitrium cuncta uigilandi, orandi, ieiunandi, atque operandi tempora mode-
rantur, quorum plurimos noui paruitatem meam[3] longe et
mundicia[4] mentis et culmine gratiae prophetalis[5] anteire.
E quibus est uenerabilis et cum omni honorificentia nomi-
nandus seruus Christi Boisilus[6], qui me in Mailrosensi
monasterio quondam senex adolescentem[7] nutriebat, et
inter enutriendum[8] cuncta quae[9] mihi[10] erant uentura[11]
prophetica ueritate praedixit. Et unum [12]tantummodo
restat ex omnibus[13] ab eo mihi[14] praedictis, quod utinam
nunquam[15] impleatur. Hoc autem dicebat quia praefatus
Christi famulus episcopatus[16] eum gradu[17] significabat
esse functurum, cuius perceptionem ipse [18]non parum[19]
desiderio uitae secretioris horrebat.

XXIII. *Quomodo Ælfled[20] abbatissa et[21] puella eius[22]*
per zonam [23]ipsius sint[25] sanatae[26, 24] |

p. 70 Neque uero sanitatum miracula per hominem Dei tametsi
longe ab hominibus positum fieri cessabant. Si quidem
uenerabilis ancilla Christi[27] Elfled[28], quae inter gaudia
uirginitatis non paucis[29] famularum Christi agminibus
maternae[30] pietatis[31] curam adhibebat, ac regalis[32] stemata[33]
nobilitatis potiori nobilitate summae[34] uirtutis accumula-
bat, multo uirum Dei semper excolebat[35] amore. Haec[36]
eo tempore sicut ipsa postea reuerentissimo Lindisfarnensis
aecclesiae[37] presbitero Herefrido et ille[38] mihi[39] referebat,
graui percussa languore ac diu uexata, pene[40] uisa est,
peruenisse ad mortem. Cui cum nil curationis possent[41]
adhibere medici, subito diuina intrinsecus gratia curante
paulatim morti subtracta est, nec tamen plene[42] sanata[43].
Nam dolor quidem interaneorum abscessit, membrorum[44]

1 subitiuntur P₁C₃.   2 *ins.* atque P₁O₄.   3 meam paru. C₁VH.
4 munditia C₁VHP₁C₃O₄M.   5 prophaet... V.   6 Boysilus C₃.
7 adul... C₁. aduliscentem V.   8 erudiendum C₁VHP₁.
9 que O₃.   10 michi O₄.   11 euent... O₄.   12–13 ex om.
tant. rest. O₄.   14 michi O₄.   15 numquam C₁VH.
16 episcopatu O₄.   17 *om.* O₄.   18–19 *om.* P₁.   20 Aelflaed
VH. Elfled C₃O₃M.   21 uel VH. *ins.* eius O₄.   22 *om.* O₄.
23–24 illius sanate sint O₄.   25 *ins.* ab infirmitate VH.
26 sanate O₃.   27 Chr. anc. O₄.   28 Aelflaed

are in all things subject to the commands of the abbot and govern all their times of watching, praying, fasting and working by his judgment; and I have known many of those who, both in purity of heart and in loftiness of prophetic grace, far exceed me in my weakness. Among these is the venerable servant of Christ, Boisil, a man to be named with all honour, who formerly in his old age, when I was but a youth, brought me up in the monastery of Melrose, and, amid his instructions, predicted with prophetic truth all the things which were to happen to me. And of all those things which he predicted to me, only one remains, which I would might never be fulfilled." He said this because that servant of Christ revealed that he would hold the office of a bishop, and he trembled at the thought of taking it, owing to his great longing for a more solitary life.

CHAPTER XXIII. *How the abbess Aelfflaed and one of her nuns were healed by means of his girdle*

Now the miracles of healing wrought by the man of God did not cease although he was far removed from mankind. For the venerable handmaiden of Christ, Aelfflaed, who to the joys of virginity added a maternal and pious care of no small company of the handmaidens of Christ, and increased the nobility of a royal pedigree by the much more potent nobility of the highest virtue, always had a great affection for the man of God. At that time (as she herself afterwards related to the most reverend priest Herefrith of the church of Lindisfarne, and he to me) she had been stricken by a grievous sickness and long afflicted, and seemed almost to have reached the point of death. But when the physicians could not cure her, she was suddenly cured by divine grace within, and gradually escaped the imminent danger of death, though she was not entirely healed. For the internal pain indeed departed and her strength

C₁VH. Aelfled O₄.   29 *gloss above* id est multis VH.   30 materne O₃.
31 piaet... V.   32 regali C₁. regularis P₁.   33 stemmate C₁VH.
stemmata P₁C₃O₈O₃O₄M.   34 summe O₃.   35 *gloss above* id est
uenerabatur VH.   36 hec P₁O₃.   37 ecclesie O₃.   38 *gloss above*
scilicet retulit VH. ipse O₄.   39 michi O₄.   40 paene C₁O₈.
41 ualuissent C₁VHP₁O₄.   42 plaene V.   43 *gloss above* scilicet est VH.
44 menb... O₄.

uigor rediit, sed facultas standi uel ambulandi prorsus defuit[1], quia nec ad standum erigi, nec nisi quadrupes ualebat ingredi[2]. Coepit[3] ergo tristis aeternam[4] timere debilitatem, nam et[5] de medicorum auxilio iam pridem[6] fuerat facta desperatio[7]. Cui cum die quadam inter angustias tristium cogitationum[8] ueniret in mentem beata

p. 71 et quieta[9] conuersatio reueren|tissimi patris Cuthberti[10], Utinam inquit[11] haberem aliquid de rebus Cuthberti[12] mei, scio certe et [13]credo et[14] confido in Domino, quia cito sanarer. Et[15] non multo post aduenit qui ei zonam lineam ab eo missam deferret. Quae multum gauisa de munere et desiderium suum uiro sancto iam coelitus[16] patefactum intelligens[17], succinxit se illa, et mane mox erecta ad standum, tercia[18] uero die plene[19] est reddita sanitati. Post dies autem paucos coepit[20] egrotare quaedam de uirginibus monasterii ipsius dolore capitis intolerabili. Quae cum ingrauascente[21] morbo per dies uideretur esse moritura, intrauit ad uisitandam eam uenerabilis[22] abbatissa. Cunque[23] eam grauiter afflictam conspiceret, tulit memoratam uiri Dei zonam, et hac illi[24] caput[25] circumligare curauit, quae eodem mox die abeunte dolore [26]curata[28] est[27], tollensque zonam, sua condidit[29] in capsa. Quam cum[30] post dies aliquot abbatissa[31] requireret, neque in capsa eadem neque[32] uspiam prorsus potuit inueniri. Quod diuina dispensatione factum intelligitur[33], uidelicet ut et[34] per duo sanitatis miracula Deo dilecti patris sanctitas

p. 72 appareret credentibus, et deinceps dubitandi de | sanctitate illius occasio tolleretur incredulis. Si enim eadem zona semper adesset, semper ad hanc concurrere uoluissent egroti[35], et dum forte[36] aliquis ex his[37] non mereretur[38] a sua infirmitate curari, derogaret impotentiae[39] non saluantis, cum ipse potius esset salutis indignus[40]. Unde

---

1 affuit C_1. abfuit VP_1O_4. afuit H.   2 *gloss above* id est ambulare VH.   3 caep... C_1V. cep... $P_1O_8O_3$.   4 eternam O_3. 5 *om.* P_1.   6 fides C_1. fidei VH.   7 disp... C_1.   8 cogitacionum C_3O_3.   9 quiacta V.   10 Cudberhti C_1V. Cuthberhti H. 11 inquid O_3.   12 Cudberhti C_1V. Cuthberhti H. Cudberti P_1. 13–14 *om.* $C_1VHP_1O_4$.   15 at C_1VH.   16 cael... C_1V. cel... O_3. 17 intellegens C_1VH.   18 tertia C_1VHP_1M.   19 plenae O_4. 20 caep... C_1V. cep... O_3.   21 ingrauescente $C_1VHP_1O_4$.   22 *ins.*

of limb returned, but her power of standing or of walking was wholly gone, for she could neither stand upright nor move about except on all fours. She therefore began sadly to fear that the weakness would last always, for she had long since despaired of any help from doctors. One day amid the afflictions of her sad thoughts, the blessed and quiet life of the most reverend father Cuthbert came into her mind and she said: "Would that I had something belonging to my Cuthbert! I know well and believingly trust in God that I should speedily be healed." Not long afterwards there came one who brought her a linen girdle which he had sent. She greatly rejoiced at the gift and, realizing that her desire had been made known to the holy man by heavenly means, she girded herself with it, and in the morning she was able forthwith to stand erect, and on the third day was entirely restored to health. A few days afterwards, one of the virgins of her monastery began to suffer from an intolerable pain in the head. Since the disease grew worse daily and she seemed about to die, the venerable abbess came in to visit her. Seeing her grievously afflicted, she brought this same girdle of the man of God and had it bound around her head: on that same day the pain departed and she was healed. The abbess, however, took away the girdle and placed it in her box. After a few days, when she sought it again, it could neither be found in the box nor anywhere else. It is clear that this was done by divine dispensation, so that the holiness of the father beloved of God might be made apparent to believers through these two miracles of healing, and that henceforth all occasion for doubting his sanctity might be removed from the incredulous. For if that girdle had always been there, sick people would always have wished to flock to it; and when perhaps one of them did not deserve to be healed of his infirmity, he would disparage its power, because it did not heal him, when really he was not worthy of being healed. Hence,

eius C_1VHP$_1$O$_4$.   23 cumque C_1VHO$_4$.   24 illius P$_1$.   25 capud C_1.
26–27 integram circumsecuta est sanitatem P$_1$.   28 sanata C_1VHO$_4$.
29 condit C_1VH. recondidit O$_4$.   30 om. O$_4$.   31 ins. above cum O$_4$.
32 om. P$_1$.   33 intellegitur VH.   34 om. O$_3$.   35 aeg... O$_4$.   36 om. C_1VHP$_1$O$_4$.   37 ins. forte C_1VHP$_1$O$_4$. hiis O$_3$.   38 meruisset C_1VHP$_1$O$_4$.
39 inp... C_1VHP$_1$. impotencie O$_3$.   40 indig. sal. C_3.

prouida ut dictum est dispensatione supernae[1] pietatis, postquam fides credentium confirmata est, mox inuidie[2] perfidorum materia detrahendi est prorsus ablata.

XXIV. [3]Quid[5] sciscitanti eidem Elfledae[6] de uita Egfridi[7] regis et episcopatu suo praedixerit[8,4]

Alio item[9] tempore misit eadem reuerentissima uirgo et mater uirginum Christi Elfled[10], rogauitque uirum Dei adiurans in nomine Domini ut eum uidere, et de necessariis mereretur alloqui[11]. Qui ascensa cum fratribus naui[12], uenit ad insulam[13] quae Coquedi[14] fluminis hostio[15] praeiacens,| ab eodem nomen[16] accepit[17], et ipsa[18] monachorum coetibus[19] insignis. Nam praefata[20] abbatissa illo eum sibi occurrere rogauerat[21]. Cuius potita colloquiis[22], cum multa ab eo quae sciscitabatur audiret, ecce repente in medio sermone aduoluta pedibus eius, adiurauit eum per nomen illud terribile ac uenerabile superni regis et angelorum eius, ut diceret illi quam longo tempore uicturus esset Egfridus[23] frater illius et regnum[24] gubernaturus Anglorum. Scio enim inquit quia prophetiae[25] spiritu quo[26] polles[27], etiam hoc dicere potes si uis. At ille expauens adiuramentum, nec tamen uolens aperte[28] quod petebatur reuelare secretum[29], Mirum inquit quare sapiens femina et in sanctis erudita scripturis, longa uocare uelis [30]humanae[32] tempora uitae[33,31], dicente psalmista quia anni nostri sicut aranea[34] meditabuntur, et [35]cum moneat[36] Salomon Si annis multis uixerit homo et in his[37] omnibus letus[38] fuerit, meminisse debet tenebrosi temporis[39] et dierum

p. 73 (left margin)

Psa. 89. 9 (left margin)
Eccl. 11. 8 (left margin)

1 superne O₃.   2 inuidiac VHO₈M.   3–4 Quomodo Egfridi regis mortem praedixit O₄.   5 quomodo VH.   6 Aelflaede C₁VH. 7 Ecfridi VHO₈. Ecgfridi C₃.   8 pred... C₃M.   9 om. C₁VHO₄.   10 Aelflaed C₁VH. Aelfled P₁O₄.   11 adl... C₁VH. 12 naui cum fratr. P₁.   13 in margin Nomen insule cocuedadedes eu C₃. in margin Nomen insule Cocuedeseu O₃.   14 cocuedi P₁O₄. 15 ostio C₁VHP₁O₄.   16 om. C₁VH. cognomen P₁O₄.   17 ins. cognomen C₁VH.   18 gloss above scilicet erat VH.   19 caetibus VP₁. cet... O₃M.   20 pre... M.   21 rogabat C₁VHP₁O₄.

as has been said, by the providential dispensation of heavenly
grace, after the faith of believers had been strengthened, forthwith the opportunity for the envious and unbelievers to disparage was entirely taken away.

CHAPTER XXIV. *How, in answer to the same Aelfflaed,*
he made predictions about the life of King Ecgfrith
and about his own bishopric

On another occasion also the same most reverend Aelfflaed,
virgin and mother of the virgins of Christ, sent and asked the
man of God, adjuring him in the name of the Lord that he
would deign to visit her and talk over matters of importance.
He went on board a ship with the brethren and came to the
island which lies at the mouth of the river Coquet from which
it receives its name. It is famous for its companies of monks,
and it was here that this same abbess asked him to meet her.
Having got into conversation with him, and having heard
much from him on the matters about which she was asking
him, suddenly, in the midst of their talk, she fell at his feet and
adjured him by the terrible awe-inspiring name of the King
of Heaven and of His angels, that he would tell her how long
Ecgfrith her brother would live and rule over the kingdom of
the English. "For I know", she said, "that through the spirit
of prophecy in which you abound, you can also tell me this,
if you wish." But he, being sorely afraid at her adjuration and
yet not wishing openly to reveal the secret she was asking about,
said: "It is wonderful that you, a wise woman and learned in
the Holy Scriptures, should be willing to speak of the term of
human life as if it were long, when the Psalmist says that 'our
years are reckoned as a spider's web', and when Solomon warns
us that 'if a man live many years and rejoice in them all, yet
let him remember the days of darkness, for they shall be many;

22 conl... C_1VH.   23 Ecg... C_1P_1. c *above* V. Egc... HO_3.
24 *ins*. illius M.   25 propheciae O_4.   26 co VH.   27 habundas C_1VH.
28 ap. uol. C_1VHO$_4$.   29 *gloss above* scilicet est VH.   30–31 temp. uit.
hum. C_1VHP$_1O_4$.   32 humane C_3O_3.   33 uite O_3.   34 haranea C_1.
35–36 commoneat H.   37 hiis O_3.   38 laetus C_1VHO$_8O_4$.
39 temp. ten. O_4.

multorum qui cum uenerint, uanitatis arguuntur praeterita,
quanto magis is[1] cui unius solum anni uita superest
breui uidetur tempore uixisse, ubi mors astiterit[2] in
p. 74 ianuis? Haec[3] audiens illa, fusis lacri|mis praesagia[4] dira
deflebat[5], extersaque facie, rursus audacia[6] feminea adiurauit per maiestatem summae[7] diuinitatis, ut diceret quem
habiturus esset heredem regni, cum filiis careret et fratribus.
Qui parum silens, Ne [8]dicas inquit[10],[9] quia caret, habebit
enim successorem quem germana ut ipsum Egfridum[11]
dilectione complectaris[12]. At illa, Obsecro inquit[10] dicas
quibus in locis sit ille. Qui ait, Cernis hoc mare magnum
et spaciosum[13] quot abundet[14] insulis? Facile est Deo de
aliqua harum sibi prouidere quem regno[15] praeficiat[16]
Anglorum. Intellexit ergo quia de Aldfrido diceret, qui
ferebatur filius fuisse patris illius, et tunc in insulis Scot-
torum ob studium litterarum exulabat. Sciebat autem
quia Egfridus[17] proponeret[18] eum constituere episcopum,
uolensque dinoscere si propositum sequeretur effectus, ita
querendo[19] exorsa est, O quam uaria intentione diuiduntur
corda mortalium. Quidam adeptis gaudent diuitiis, alii
amantes[20] diuitias semper egent, tu gloriam mundi quamuis
offeratur respuis, etiamsi ad episcopatum pertingere possis
quo sullimius[21] apud[22] mortales nichil[23] est, tui claustra
p. 75 deserti huic gradui praeferes[24]? | At ille, Scio me inquit[10]
tanto gradu[25] dignum non esse, nec tamen iudicium
superni gubernatoris uspiam effugere queo[26]. Qui si[27]
tanto oneri[28] me[29] subiciendum disposuit, credo quia post
modicum liberum reddet[30], et fortasse non amplius quam
duobus annis exactis, solitam me meae[31] solitudinis re-
mittet[32] ad requiem[33]. Praecipio autem tibi in nomine
Domini et Saluatoris nostri, ne cui ante meum obitum
quae a me audiuisti[34] referas. Cunque[35] illi [36]haec[38] et[37]

---

1 *om.* C₁VH. hiis O₃.   2 adst... C₁VH. asst... O₄.   3 hec O₃.
4 pre... M.   5 flebat O₄.   6 audatia C₃O₈M.   7 summe O₃.
8–9 inq. dic. C₁VHO₄.   10 inquid O₃.   11 Ecg... C₁VP₁.
Egc... H.   12 conp... C₁VH.   13 spatiosum C₁VHP₁C₃O₄M.
14 hab... C₁VHP₁O₃. habundat C₃.   15 *om.* C₁. *ins. above* V.
16 prof... O₃.   17 *om.* C₁VHP₁O₄.   18 *ins.* Ecgfridus C₁VP₁
Egc... H. Eg... O₄.   19 quaerendo O₈.   20 respuentes P₁

when they come, the past is reckoned as vanity'; how much more does he, to whom only one year of life remains, seem to have lived a short time, when death stands at the gates?" When she heard this, she shed tears and wept over these dire prophecies; but drying her eyes, once again with womanly daring, she adjured him by the divine majesty to tell her whom her brother would have as heir to the kingdom, seeing he lacked both sons and brothers. After a short time he said: "Do not say that these are lacking; for he will have a successor whom you will embrace with as much sisterly affection as if he were Ecgfrith himself." She answered: "I beseech you, tell me where he is." He said: "You see how this great and spacious sea abounds in islands? It is easy for God to provide from any of these a man to place over the kingdom of the English." So she understood that he was speaking of Aldfrith, who was said to be the son of Ecgfrith's father, and was then in exile among the islands of the Irish, for the study of letters. Now she knew that Ecgfrith proposed to appoint Cuthbert bishop, and wishing to learn whether this proposal would be carried into effect, she began to ask him in this way: "How the hearts of mortal men differ in their several purposes! Some rejoice in the riches they have gained, others who love riches always lack them. You despise the glory of the world, although it is offered, and although you may attain to a bishopric, than which nothing is higher among mortal men, yet will you prefer the fastnesses of your desert place to that rank?" But he said: "I know that I am not worthy of such a rank; nevertheless I cannot escape anywhere from the decree of the Ruler of Heaven; yet if He has determined to subject me to so great a burden, I believe that after a short time He will set me free, and perhaps, after not more than two years, He will send me back to my accustomed rest and solitude. But I bid you in the name of our Lord and Saviour not to tell anyone before my death what you have heard from me!"

21 subl... C_1VHO_4. 22 aput H. 23 aliquid non $C_1P_1O_4$. aliquit non VH. 24 praefers VHP_1. praeferres O_4. 25 gradui C_1VH. 26 potero O_4. 27 *ins.* me O_4. 28 honeri C_1V. gradui P_1. 29 *om.* O_4. 30 reddat $C_1VHP_1O_4$. 31 mee O_3. 32 remittat $C_1VHP_1O_4$. 33 quietem $C_1VHP_1O_4$. 34 audisti $C_1VHP_1O_4$. 35 cumque $C_1VHO_8O_4M$. 36–37 *om.* $C_1VHP_1O_4$. 38 hec O_3.

multa[1] alia quae querebat[2] exponeret, atque eam de quibus opus habebat instrueret, reuersus ad insulam et monasterium suum, solitariam ut coeperat[3] agebat sedulus uitam. Nec multo post congregata sinodo[4] non parua sub praesentia piissimi ac Deo dilecti regis Egfridi[5], cui beatae[6] memoriae[7] Theodorus archiepiscopus praesidebat unanimo[8] omnium consensu ad episcopatum ecclesiae[9] Lindisfarnensis electus est. Qui cum multis legatariis[10] ac litteris ad se praemissis nequaquam suo loco posset erui, tandem rex ipse praefatus una cum sanctissimo antistite Trumwine[11] nec non et aliis quam plurimis religiosis ac potentibus uiris ad[12] insulam nauigauit, genuflectunt omnes, adiurant per Dominum, lacrimas fundunt,| obsecrant, donec ipsum quoque lacrimis plenum dulcibus extrahunt latebris, atque[13] ad sinodum[14] pertrahunt. Quo dum perueniret, quamuis multum renitens unanima[15] omnium uoluntate superatur, atque[13] ad suscipiendum episcopatus officium collum summittere[16] compellitur[17]. Nec tamen statim ordinatio[18], sed peracta[19] hieme quae imminebat expleta est, atque ut uerbis eius propheticis[20] per omnia satisfieret[21], Egfridus[22] post annum Pictorum gladio trucidatur, et Aldfridus in regnum frater eius nothus[23] substituitur, qui non paucis ante[24] temporibus in regionibus Scottorum[25] lectioni operam dabat, ibi[26] ob amorem sapientiae[27] spontaneum passus exilium.

p. 76 (margin)

XXV.   [28] Quod[30] electus ad episcopatum[29] seruum comitis languentem aqua[31] benedicta curauerit[32]

Dum[33] ergo electus ad episcopatum uir Domini Cuthbertus[34] suam remeasset ad insulam, atque[35] aliquantulum temporis | secretus[36] Domino solita deuotione militaret,

p. 77 (margin)

1 ins. et C_1VHO_4.   2 quaer... HO_8O_4.   3 caep... VP_1. cep... O_3M.   4 synodo C_1VH.   5 Ecg... C_1VP_1. Egc... H. 6 beate O_3.   7 memorie O_3.   8 unamina O_9. unianimo C_1. 9 aeccl... VHO_8O_4. om. P_1. ecclesie C_3O_3.   10 legatoriis V. 11 Trumuuine C_1VHO_4. Trumuuini P_1. Trumwyne O_3.   12 om. C_1VHO_4. in P_1.   13 adque C_1V.   14 synodum $C_1VHP_1C_3$. 15 unamina O_9. unanimo C_1.   16 mittere C_1V. sub above H. 17 conp... C_1VH.   18 ins. eius $C_3O_8O_3$.   19 peracto C_1VH.

When he had expounded to her these and many other things about which she asked and had given her instruction about such things as she needed, he returned to his island and monastery, and industriously continued the life of solitude, as he had begun it.

Not long afterwards, when no small synod had gathered together, in the presence of the most pious King Ecgfrith beloved of God over which Archbishop Theodore of blessed memory presided, he was elected to the bishopric of the church at Lindisfarne with the unanimous consent of all. And when he could by no means be dragged from his place by the many messengers and letters that were sent to him, at length this same king himself, together with the most holy Bishop Trumwine, as well as many other religious and powerful men, sailed to the island; they all knelt down and adjured him in the name of the Lord, with tears and prayers, until at last they drew him, also shedding many tears, from his sweet retirement and led him to the synod. When he had come, in spite of his reluctance he was overcome by the unanimous will of them all and compelled to submit his neck to the yoke of the bishopric. His consecration however was not carried out until after the end of that winter which was then beginning. And so that his prophetic words should in all respects be fulfilled, Ecgfrith, a year afterwards, was slain by the sword of the Picts and was succeeded in his kingdom by his bastard brother Aldfrith, who for some considerable time before this had been pursuing his studies in the regions of the Irish, suffering a self-imposed exile to gratify his love of wisdom.

CHAPTER XXV. *How, when he was elected to the bishopric, he cured the ailing servant of a gesith with holy water*

When therefore Cuthbert the man of God, after his election to the bishopric, had returned to his island and for a little time was fighting the good fight in secret with his wonted devotion

20 propheticus C_1.   21 satisficeret M.   22 Ecg... C_1VP_1. Egc... H. 23 *changed from* notus C_1.   24 antea $C_1VHP_1O_4$.   25 Scoctorum M. 26 ipse $C_1VHP_1O_4$. 27 sapiencie O_3. 28–29 quomodo O_4. 30 quomodo $C_3O_3O_8M$.   31 *ins.* per se $C_3O_8O_3$. 32 curauerat VH. 33 cum $P_1O_8O_4$. 34 Cudberhtus C_1V. Cuthberhtus H.   35 adque C_1.   36 *om.* P_1.

euocauit eum uenerabilis episcopus eius Eata[1], atque[2]
ad suum colloquium[3] Mailros uenire praecepit[4]. Quo
expleto colloquio[5] dum domum redire coepisset[6], occurrit
illi comes[7] quidam Egfridi[8] regis, [9]rogauitque obnixe[10]
ut [11]ad benedictionem dandam[12] in uillulam suam domum-
que diuerteret. Quo cum peruenisset et gratifico omnium
susceptus esset officio, indicauit ei uir de infirmitate famuli
sui, Deo inquiens gratias sanctissime pater quod nos uidere
nostramque domum intrare dignatus es, et uere credimus
quia maximum nobis lucrum et mentis et corporis[13]
praestet[14] aduentus tuus[15]. Est autem nobis famulus
pessima diutius infirmitate cruciatus, et in tantum doloris
hodie perductus, ut morienti similior quam languenti

Greg.
Dial.
IV. 40

pareat. *Extrema* namque[16] *corporis parte praemortua*, per
modicum ore et naribus flatum trahere uidetur. Qui
confestim benedixit aquam et dedit ministro comitis
nomine[17] Baldhelmo[18] qui nunc usque superest, et in
aecclesia[19] Lindisfarnensi[20] presbiterii[21] gradum officio
tenens moribus implet, uirtutesque uiri Dei cunctis scire
uolentibus[22] referre melle dulcius habet[23], qui et mihi[24]

p. 78

hoc ipsum quod refero miraculum narrauit. Huic | ergo
dans aquam benedictam[25] uir Dei, Uade inquit[26] et gustan-
dam praebe[27] languenti. Qui dictis parens attulit[28] aquam
aegrotanti[29]. Quam[30] dum tercio[31] ori eius infunderet,
continuo contra morem se quietum dimisit in soporem.
Erat enim iam uespera[32]. Qui etiam silentio transegit[33]
noctem, et uisitanti se domino suo saluus mane apparuit.

XXVI. *Qualiter in episcopatu uixerit*

Susceptum autem episcopatus ordinem uenerabilis uir
Domini Cuthbertus[34], iuxta praecepta et exempla apo-

---

1 Eatha O₃.   2 adque C₁.   3 conl... C₁VH.
4 praecaepit VO₄.   5 conl... C₁VH.   6 caep... C₁P₁. cep... V.
7 *in margin* Nomen comitis Sibca C₃. *in margin* Nomen comitis
Sibul O₃.   8 Ecg... C₁V. Egc... H.   9–10 rogans C₁VH.
11–12 *om.* C₁VH.   13 *ins.* tuus C₁VHP₁O₄.   14 pre... C₁H.
15 *om.* C₁VHP₁O₄.   16 nanque P₁O₄M.   17 *om.* O₄.
18 Baldelmo C₃.   19 eccl... C₁O₃.   20 Lindisfarnensis C₁P₁.

to the Lord, his venerable bishop Eata summoned him, bidding him come to Melrose to have converse with him. When their conversation had finished and he was beginning his homeward·· journey, a certain gesith of King Ecgfrith met him and begged him urgently that he would turn aside to give a blessing to his homestead and his house. When he came there and had been received with dutiful kindness by all, the man told him about the illness of one of his servants saying: "I thank God, most holy father, that you have deigned to visit us and to enter our house, and in truth we believe that your coming will prove the greatest gain to us both in mind and body. But there is a servant of ours who has long been tortured by a most evil disease, and to-day he suffers so much pain that he appears more like a dying than a sick man. For the extremities of his body are prematurely dead and he seems to draw but little breath through his mouth and nostrils." He immediately blessed some water and gave it to the servant of the gesith, a man named Bald-helm, who is still alive and holding by appointment the office of priest in the church of Lindisfarne adorns it by his character. He counts it sweeter than honey to relate the miracles of the man of God to all who wish to know about them; and it was he who told me of this very miracle which I relate. So then the man of God gave him the holy water saying: "Go and give it to the sick man to take." He obeyed his words and brought the water to the sick man. After he had poured it into his mouth for the third time, the sufferer straightway fell into a quiet sleep which was unusual for him. It was now evening time, and he passed a quiet night also, and when his master visited him in the morning, he was found to be cured.

CHAPTER XXVI. *Of his manner of life in his bishopric*

Now the venerable man of God, Cuthbert, adorned the rank of bishop which he had received, by his virtuous works, in accordance with the apostolic precepts and examples. For he

21 presbiteri O_4.   22 nol... O_3.   23 dulc. hab. melle O_4.
24 michi O_4.   25 *om.* O_4.   26 inquid O_3.   27 prebe HO_4M.
28 adt... C_1VH.   29 egr... C_1VHO_3M.   30 qua C_1.   31 tertio $C_1VHP_1O_4$.   32 uespertina hora C_1VHO_4. *ins.* et P_1.   33 *ins.* et C_1VHO_4.   34 Cudberhtus C_1. Cuthberhtus VH.

stolica uirtutum ornabat operibus. Commissam nanque[1]
sibi plebem et orationibus protegebat assiduis, et ammo-
nitionibus[2] saluberrimis ad coelestia[3] uocabat, et quod
maxime doctores[4] iuuat, ea quae agenda docebat, ipse
Psa. 34. 10 prius agendo praemonstrabat. *Eripiebat[5] inopem de manu*
p. 79 *fortioris eius, egenum et pauperem a rapi|entibus[6] eum.*
1 Thess. Tristes ac *pusillanimes consolari*, male autem gaudentes
5. 14 ad *tristiciam[7] quae secundum Deum est*, reuocare curabat.
2 Cor.
7. 10 Solitam sibi parsimoniam sedulus exercere, et inter frequentiam turbarum monachicae[8] uitae[9] rigorem sollicitus
obseruare gaudebat. Esurientibus alimenta, indumenta
praebebat[10] algentibus, caeterisque[11] uitae[9] pontificalis
insignibus rite decoratus incedebat. Cuius internis id
est animi[12] uirtutibus, ea quoque quibus foras[13] effulgebat
miraculorum signa testimonium dabant, ex quibus aliqua
breuiter memoriae[14] commendare curauimus[15].

XXVII. *Quomodo interitum Egfridi[16] regis [17]et militiae[19]*
ipsius quem praedixerat[18] [20]absens[22] [23]uiderit
in spiritu[25, 24, 21]

Igitur dum Egfridus[26] rex ausu temerario[27] exercitum in
p. 80 Pictos duceret, eorumque regna atroci | [28]ac feroci[29]
seuicia[30] deuastaret, sciens uir Domini Cuthbertus[31] adesse
tempus de quo anno praeterito[32] interroganti eius sorori
praedixerat[33], non eum amplius quam uno[34] anno[35] esse
uicturum, uenit ad Lugubaliam[36] ciuitatem quae a populis
Anglorum corrupte[37] Luel uocatur, ut alloqueretur reginam quae ibidem in monasterio suae[38] sororis euentum
belli expectare disposuit. Postera[39] autem die deducentibus
eum ciuibus ut uideret moenia[40] ciuitatis fontemque in

1 namque C₁VH.   2 adm... C₁VHC₃O₈O₃M.   3 cael... C₁V.
cel... C₃O₃.   4 doctori C₁V. *changed from* doctori H.   5 *om.* C₁.
ins. in different hand V.   6 diripientibus O₈.   7 tristitiam C₁VHP₁.
8 monachice O₃.   9 uite C₃O₃.   10 preb... HO₈.
11 cet... O₃M.   12 anime C₁. animae VH.   13 foris P₁.
14 memorie O₃.   15 curabimus O₄.   16 Ecgfridi V. Egc... H.
17-18 *om.* O₄.   19 milicie C₃O₃.   20-21 futurum absens corpore

guarded the people who had been committed to his charge
with his constant prayers, and called them to heavenly things
by his most wholesome admonitions, and—a thing which is
a great help to teachers—he taught what ought to be done,
after first showing them by his own example. He delivered
"the poor from him that was too strong for him, yea, the poor
and the needy from him that spoiled him". He sought to
"comfort" the sad and "faint-hearted", and to bring back
those who rejoiced in evil to "godly sorrow". Gladly and
diligently he practised his wonted frugality and, amid the
thronging crowds, rejoiced to preserve the rigours of monastic
life. He gave food to the hungry, clothing to the suffering, and
he was duly adorned with all else that should mark the life
of a bishop. And signs and miracles whereby he shone outwardly
gave witness to the inward virtues of his mind. It has been
our task briefly to commemorate some of these.

CHAPTER XXVII. *How, though absent, he saw in spirit the
destruction of King Ecgfrith and of his army, in accordance with
his own prediction*

Now when King Ecgfrith, rashly daring, had taken an army
against the Picts and was devastating their kingdoms with
cruel and savage ferocity, Cuthbert the man of God knew that
the time was at hand concerning which he had prophesied
a year before to the king's sister, declaring when she asked
him that he would not live more than another year. He came
therefore to the town of Lugubalia [Carlisle], which the English
people corruptly call Luel, to speak to the queen who had
arranged to await the issue of the war there in her sister's
monastery. On the next day, while the citizens were conducting
him to see the walls of the city and a marvellously constructed

uiderit in spiritu factum C_3.   22 futurum C_1VH.   23-24 in spir.
uid. VHO_4.   25 *ins.* absentem VH.   26 Ecg... C_1VH.
27 temerio P_1.   28-29 *om.* $C_1VHP_1O_4$.   30 seuitia $C_1HC_3O_4$. saeuitia V.
31 Cudberhtus C_1V.   32 pret... O_4.   33 pre... VH.
34 *ins.* solum C_1VHP_1.   35 *ins.* solum O_4.   36 Lucubaliam P_1.
37 correpte C_1.   38 sue O_3.   39 postero P_1.   40 *om.* P_1. menia C_3O_3M.

ea miro quondam Romanorum[1] opere extructum[2], repente turbatus spiritu ut stabat super baculum mestam faciem deflexit ad terram, rursumque se erigens[3] atque[4] ad coelum[5] oculos attollens[6], ingemuit grauiter et non grandi uoce ait, Forte modo discrimen factum est certaminis. At presbiter qui astabat[7] intelligens[8] de quo diceret, incauta uelocitate ductus, respondit et dixit, Unde scis? Nolens autem ille amplius de his[9] quae sibi erant reuelata patefacere, Nonne uidetis inquit[10] quam mire mutatus ac[11] turbatus sit aer? Et quis mortalium sufficit inuestigare iudicia Dei? Attamen[12] confestim intrauit ad reginam, et secreto eam alloquens, erat autem dies sabbati, Uide inquit[10] maturae[13] illucescente[14] secunda sabbati

p. 81 ascendas[15] | currum, quia die dominico curru ire non licet, uadasque[16] et[17] regiam ciuitatem[18] citissime introeas, ne forte occisus sit rex. Ego autem quia crastina die ad uicinum monasterium ob dedicandam ibi aecclesiam[19] uenire rogatus sum, expleta dedicatione te continuo subsequor. Veniente autem[20] die dominico[21] praedicans uerbum Dei fratribus eiusdem monasterii, finito sermone et fauentibus cunctis qui aderant, [22]rursus[24] ita[23] coepit[25], *Obsecro* dilec-

1 Cor. tissimi [26]iuxta apostoli monita[27] *uigiletis, stetis*[28] *in fide,*
16. 13, 15 *uiriliter agatis et confortemini*[29], ne forte superueniens aliqua temptatio[30] uos imparatos[31] inueniat, sed[32] memores

Matth. potius[33] semper[34] illius dominici praecepti, *uigilate et orate*
26. 41 *ne intretis in temptationem*[35]. Putabant autem quia non multo ante pestilentiae[36] clades[37] et eos et multos circunquaque[38] lata cede[39] strauerat, eum de huiusmodi plaga iam reditura fuisse locutum. At ipse rursus assumpto[40] sermone, Quondam inquit[10] cum adhuc in mea demorarer insula solitarius, uenerunt ad me quidam de fratribus die

---

1 *om.* P₁.   2 exstr... C₁VHO₃.   3 erig. se C₁VH.
4 adque C₁.   5 cael... C₁V. cel... C₃O₃.   6 adt... C₁VH.
7 adst... C₁VH. asst... P₁.   8 intellegens C₁VH.   9 hiis O₃.
10 inquid O₃.   11 et O₄.   12 adt... C₁.   13 mature
C₁VHO₈O₃O₄M.   14 inl... C₁VH.   15 acc... O₉. *gloss above* id
est ut VH.   16 *om.* que C₁V. *gloss above* id est ut VH.
17 ad C₁VHO₄.   18 *ins.* ibique O₄.   19 eccl... C₁O₃.
20 *om.* C₁. *above* V.   21 *ins.* autem C₁.   22–23 ita rursus O₈.
24 *gloss in margin* scilicet loqui VH.   25 cepit C₃O₃.   26–27 *om.* O₄.

fountain of Roman workmanship, he was suddenly troubled
in spirit, and as he stood leaning on his staff he turned his face
sadly towards the ground; and again, standing upright and
lifting his eyes towards heaven, he sighed deeply and said in
a low voice: "Perhaps even now the issue of the battle is
decided." But a priest who was standing by, knowing of
whom he spoke, answered with incautious haste and said:
"How do you know?" Cuthbert, being unwilling to disclose
more of what had been revealed to him, said: "Do you not
see how greatly changed and disturbed the weather is? and
what mortal man is sufficient to enquire into the judgments of
God?" But he immediately went to the queen, and secretly
addressing her, it being Saturday, said: "See that you mount
your chariot early on Monday—for it is not lawful to travel
by chariot on the Lord's Day—and go and enter the royal
city quickly, lest perchance the king has been slain. But since
I have been asked to go to-morrow to a neighbouring monastery to dedicate a church there, I will follow you at once, as
soon as the dedication is completed."

Now when Sunday had come, he was preaching the word of
God to the brethren of the same monastery, and when the
sermon was over and all those present were approving, he
began again in this way: "Beloved, I beseech you to watch,
in accordance with the warnings of the Apostle, 'stand fast
in the faith, quit you like men, be strong', lest perchance some
temptation coming upon you may find you unprepared; but
rather be always mindful of that command of the Lord, 'Watch
and pray, lest ye enter into temptation'." His listeners thought
that he said this because a devastating pestilence had not long
before laid low both them and many others on every hand with
widespread destruction, and that he was prophesying a return
of this scourge. But continuing he said: "Once, when I was
still living alone in my island, some of the brethren came to

28 *om.* C₁VH.   29 conuertimini C₁VH. *ins.* iuxta apostoli monita O₄.
30 tribulatio C₁VH. temptacio C₃. tribulationis temptatio O₄.   31 inp...
C₁VH.   32 set O₃.   33 pocius C₃.   34 *ins.* estote O₄.
35 temptacionem C₃.   36 pestilenciae C₃.   37 cladis C₁VH.
38 circum... C₁VHP₁M.   39 caede P₁O₄.   40 ads... C₁VH.

sancto dominicae natiuitatis, rogabantque ut de mea casula
et mansione egrediens, solennem[1] cum eis et laetum[2]
diem tantae[3] ue..erationis transigerem. Quorum ego[4] |

p. 82 precibus[5] deuotis adquiescens[6] egrediebar[7], et consedi-
mus ad epulas[8]. At in media forte refectione dixi ad eos,
Obsecro fratres caute agamus[9] et uigilanter, ne per in-
curiam forte et securitatem inducamur in temptationem[10].
At illi responderunt, Obsecramus hodie laetum[11] agamus
diem[12], quia natale[13] est Domini nostri Iesu Christi. Et
ego, Sic inquam faciamus. Cunque[14] post haec aliquandiu
epulis[15] exultationi[16], ac fabulis indulgeremus, rursus ad-
monere[17] coepi[18] ut solliciti existeremus [19]in orationibus[21]
et uigiliis[20], atque ad omnes temptationum[22] incursus
parati. [23]Et illi[24], Bene inquiunt et optime doces, sed tamen
quia abundant[25] dies ieiuniorum, orationis et uigiliarum,
hodie gaudeamus in Domino, nam et angelus nascente

Luke 2. 10 Domino *euangeliz*abat[26] pastoribus *gaudium magnum, quod*
esset *omni populo* caelebrandum[27]. Et ego, Bene inquam
faciamus sic. Sed[28] cum epulantibus[15] nobis et diem
laetum[29] ducentibus tercio[30] eiusdem ammonitionis[31]
uerba repeterem, intellexere illi quia[32] non frustra haec[33]
tam studiose suggererem[34], et[35] expauescentes[36] dicebant[37],
Faciamus ut doces, quia necessitas magna nobis incumbit

p. 83 ut contra insidias diaboli et omnia | temptamenta semper
accincti spiritualiter[38] uigilemus. Haec[39] dicens, ego nescie-
bam sicut nec illi aliquid nobis occursurum nouae[40]
temptationis, sed[41] tantum instinctu[42] mentis ammonitus[43]
sum aduersus subitas temptationum procellas, statum
cordis semper esse muniendum. Sed[44] ubi reuersi a me
mane ad suum id est[45] Lindisfarnense monasterium redie-
runt, ecce quendam de suis morbo pestilentiae[46] obisse
repperierunt[47]. Et crescente ac seuiente per dies immo

---

1 sollemnem C₁VHM. sollennem P₁. sollempnem O₈O₃. 2 letum
C₃O₃.   3 tante P₁C₃O₃.   4 *om.* C₁VHP₁O₄.   5 praec... H.
6 acq... O₄.   7 egredior P₁O₄.   8 aep... O₄.   9 *ins.* nos
C₁VHP₁O₄.   10 temptacionem C₃.   11 letum C₃O₃.
12 diem ag. O₄.   13 nathale O₃.   14 cumque C₁VHO₄M.
15 aep... O₄. 16 exultatione C₁VH. exultationis P₁. exultacioni C₃.
17 amm... P₁O₄.   18 caepi C₁V. cepi C₃O₃.   19–20 *om.* P₁.
21 oracionibus C₃.   22 temptacionum C₃.   23–24 *om.* P₁.

me on the holy day of the Lord's nativity, and asked me to go out of the hut, my dwelling-place, that I might spend with them this holy day so sacred and yet so joyful; I yielded to their earnest prayers and went out, and we sat down to our feast. But it happened that, in the middle of the repast, I said to them: 'I beseech you, brethren, let us be cautious and watchful, lest by recklessness and carelessness we be led into temptation.' But they answered: 'We beseech you, let us be joyful to-day, because it is the birthday of our Lord Jesus Christ.' And I said: 'So be it.' And a little time after, while we were indulging in feasting, rejoicing and story-telling, I again began to warn them that we should earnestly engage in prayers and vigils and be ready for the approach of any temptation. They said: 'You give us good, yea excellent, instruction, but nevertheless, because the days of fastings, prayer and vigils abound, to-day let us rejoice in the Lord. For the angel, when the Lord was born, gave the shepherds glad tidings of the great joy which was to be observed by all the people.' I answered: 'Well, so be it.' But when, while we were feasting and spending the day joyfully, I repeated these words of admonition for a third time, they understood that it was not in vain that I made the suggestion so anxiously, and, being afraid, they said: 'Let us do as you tell us, for a great compulsion is upon us that we should watch against the snares of the devil and against all temptations, girding up the loins of the mind.' When I said this, I did not know, nor did they, that any new temptation would attack us, but I was only warned by the instinct of my mind that the heart should always be in a state of defence against any sudden storms of temptations. But when they left me in the morning and went back to their monastery, that is Lindisfarne, they found that one of their number had died of the pestilence; and as it grew and became worse from day to day,

25 hab... C_3O_3. 26 euuang... VH. ewang... O_3. 27 cel... $P_1C_3O_8O_3O_4M$. 28 set O_3. 29 letum C_3O_3. 30 tertio C_1VHP_1. 31 *ins.* die cum P_1. admonicionis C_3. 32 quod P_1. 33 hec O_3. 34 suggerem O_4. 35 *om.* C_1VH. 36 expauentes C_1V. pauentes P_1O_4. 37 dixerunt P_1. 38 spiritaliter C_1VH. 39 hec O_3. 40 noue O_3. 41 set O_3. 42 instructu M. 43 adm... $C_1VHP_1C_3O_4$. 44 at $C_1VHP_1O_4$. set O_3. 45 *ins.* in P_1. 46 pestilencie O_3. 47 reppererunt $C_1VHP_1O_3O_4$.

etiam per menses et annum pene[1] totum eadem clade,
nobilissimus ille patrum fratrumque coetus[2] spiritualium[3]
pene[1] uniuersus migrauit ad Dominum. Et nunc ergo
fratres uigilate et uos in orationibus, ut si quid uobis
tribulationis ingruerit, uos iam paratos inueniat. Haec[4]
dicente uenerabili antistite Cuthberto[5] rebantur[6] ut praefatus[7] sum quia[8] de reditu pestilentiae diceret. Sed[9]
post unum diem adueniens qui fugerat e bello, occulta
uiri[10] Dei uaticinia[11] miseris exponebat eloquiis. Proba-
tumque est ipsa die eademque hora qua uiro Dei iuxta
puteum stanti reuelatum est, cesis[12] circum tutoribus,
regem hostili gladio fuisse prostratum.

XXVIII. [13]*Quomodo Hereberto*[15] *anachoritae*[16] *obitum suum*
praedixerit[17], *comitatumque illius a Domino precibus*
obtinuerit [18]*sine mora*[19,14] |

p. 84 Non multo post tempore[20] idem famulus Domini Cuthbertus[21] ad eandem Lugubaliam ciuitatem rogatus aduenit,
quatinus[22] ibidem sacerdotes consecrare, sed et ipsam
reginam[23] dato habitu sanctae[24] conuersationis benedicere
deberet. Erat autem presbiter uitae[25] uenerabilis nomine
Herebertus[26] iamdudum uiro Dei Cuthberto[27] spiritualis[28]
amicitiae[29] foedere[30] copulatus, qui in insula stagni illius
pergrandis de quo Deoruuentionis[31] fluuii primordia
erumpunt uitam solitariam ducens, annis singulis ad eum
uenire, et monita ab eo perpetuae[32] salutis accipere consueuerat. Hic cum audisset eum illa in ciuitate demoratum,
uenit ex more cupiens salutaribus eius exhortationibus
ad superna desideria magis magisque inflammari[33]. Qui
dum sese alterutrum coelestis[34] sapientiae[35] poculis de-
p. 85 briarent, dixit inter alia Cuthbertus[36], Memen|to frater

1 paene C₁VO₈.   2 caetus C₁. cetus C₃O₈O₃.   3 spiritalium C₁VH.
4 hec C₃O₃.   5 Cudberhto C₁V. Cuthberhto H. Cutberto P₁.
6 reuertebantur O₉.   7 pre... O₄.   8 quod P₁.   9 set O₃.
10 *om.* M.   11 *ins.* uiri M.   12 caesis C₁P₁O₈M.   13-14 Quomodo obitus sui praescius Hereberti comitatum a Deo obtinuerit O₄.
15 Hereberchto VH.   16 anchoritae V. anachorite O₃.   17 pre...
VO₈.   18-19 *om.* VH.   20 *gloss above* id est post modico tempore VH.
21 Cudberhtus C₁V. Cuthberhtus H.   22 quatenus V.   23 data

yea and from month to month, and almost throughout the
whole year, nearly the whole of that renowned congregation
of spiritual fathers and brethren departed to be with the Lord in
that pestilence. Now therefore, brethren, do you also watch
and pray, so that if any tribulation come upon you it may find
you already prepared." When the venerable Bishop Cuthbert
had said these words, they thought, as I said before, that he
was speaking about the return of the pestilence. But the day
afterwards, one arrived who had fled from the fight and explained
by his sad story the mysterious prophecies of the man of God.
And it was proved that on the very day and at the very hour
when it was revealed to the man of God, standing by the
fountain, the king was laid low by the sword of the enemy and
his bodyguard slain around him.

CHAPTER XXVIII. *How he predicted his own death to Hereberht
the hermit and straightway obtained this man's company
from the Lord by his prayers*

Not long afterwards the same servant of the Lord, Cuthbert,
came by invitation to that same city of Carlisle, in order
that he might ordain some priests there, and might also
confer upon the queen herself the garb of the consecrated life,
and bless her. Now there was a priest of reverend life named
Hereberht who had long been bound to Cuthbert the man of
God by the bonds of spiritual friendship. He had been living
a solitary life in an island of that large mere from which rise
the sources of the river Derwent. He used to come to Cuthbert
every year and receive teaching from him concerning his
everlasting salvation. When he heard that Cuthbert was staying
in that city, he came according to his custom, wishing to be
aroused more and more by his salutary exhortations to heavenly
desires. When they had refreshed one another with draughts
of heavenly wisdom, Cuthbert said, amongst other things:

gloss above uel reginam H.   24 sancte O_3.   25 uite O_3.   26 Hereberhtus C_1VHO_4.   27 Cudberhto C_1V. Cuthberhto H.   28 spiritalis
C_1VH.   29 amiciciae O_9.   30 federe O_3.   31 Dioruuentionis VH.
Deruuentionis P_1. Deorwentionis O_8M. Deorwencionis O_3.   32 perpetue
C_3O_3.   33 flammari C_1. in- *added in margin* V.   34 cael... C_1V.
cel... C_3O_3.   35 sapiencie O_3.   36 Cudberhtus C_1V. Cuthberhtus H.

Hereberte[1] ut modo quicquid opus habes me interroges, mecumque loquaris, quia postquam ab inuicem digressi fuerimus, non ultra nos inuicem in hoc saeculo[2] carneis[3] oculis uidebimus. Certus sum enim quia *tempus meae*[4] *resolutionis instat*, et uelox est depositio tabernaculi mei. Qui haec[5] audiens prouolutus eius pedibus, fusisque[6] cum gemitu lacrimis, Obsecro inquit[7] per Dominum ne me derelinquas, sed[8] tui sodalis[9] memineris, rogesque supernam pietatem[10] ut cui pariter in terris seruiuimus[11], ad eius uidendam[12] claritatem[13] pariter transeamus ad coelos[14]. Nosti enim quia ad tui oris imperium semper uiuere studui, et quicquid ignorantia uel fragilitate deliqui, aeque[15] ad tuae[16] uoluntatis arbitrium castigare curaui. Incubuit precibus episcopus, statimque[17] edoctus in spiritu impetrasse se[18] quod petierat a Domino, Surge inquit[19] frater mi et noli plorare, sed gaudio gaude, quia donauit nobis superna clementia quod rogauimus eam[20]. Cuius promissi[21] et prophetiae[22] ueritatem sequens rerum finis astruxit[23], quia et[24] digredientes ab inuicem non amplius se corporaliter uiderunt, et[25] unius eiusdemque[26] momento temporis[27] egredientes e corpore spiritus eorum, mox beata inuicem uisione coniuncti sunt, atque[28] angelico ministerio pariter ad regnum[29] coeleste[31] translati[30]. Sed[32] Herebertus[33] | diutina prius infirmitate decoquitur[34], illa fortassis dispensatione dominicae pietatis, ut si quid minus haberet meriti a beato Cuthberto[35] suppleret dolor continuus longae[36] egritudinis[37], quatinus equatus[38] gratia[39] suo[40] intercessori[41] sicut[42] uno eodemque[43] tempore cum eo de corpore egredi, ita etiam una atque indissimili sede perpetuae[44] beatitudinis mereretur recipi.

(margin: 2 Tim. 4. 6)
(margin: p. 86)

---

1 Hereberhte C_1VH.   2 sec... O_3O_4.   3 carnalibus O_4.
4 mee O_3.   5 hec C_3O_3.   6 *om.* que C_1VHP_1O_4.   7 inquid O_3.
8 set O_3.   9 sodal. tui O_4.   10 piaet... V.   11 seru. in terr. O_4.
12 uiuendam C_1.   13 beatitudinem P_1O_4.   14 cael... C_1V.
cel... C_3O_3.   15 eque C_3O_3.   16 tue C_3O_3.   17 et statim P_1.
18 *om.* C_1. *ins. above* V.   19 inquid O_8O_3.   20 eum C_1VH.
21 promissionem C_1VHO_4.   22 prophecie O_3.   23 ass... V.

"Remember, brother Hereberht, to ask me now whatever you
need and to speak with me about it, because, after we have parted
from one another, we shall nevermore see one another in this
world with the eyes of the flesh. For I am certain that the time
of my 'departure' and of laying aside my earthly tabernacle
'is at hand'." When Hereberht heard this, he fell at his feet and
with sighs and tears he said: "I beseech you by the Lord not
to leave me but to remember your companion and ask the
merciful God that as we have served Him together upon earth,
we may journey together to the skies to see His glory. For
you know that I have always sought to live in accordance with
the commands of your mouth, and whatever I have done
amiss through ignorance and weakness, I have taken equal care
to correct in accordance with your judgment and will." The
bishop gave himself up to prayer and forthwith having learned
in spirit that he had gained what he sought from the Lord, he
said: "Rise up, my brother, and do not weep, but rejoice
greatly, because the clemency of Heaven has granted us what
we asked of it." And the issue of events confirmed the truth
of his promise and his prophecy; for after they had separated,
they did not see one another any more in the flesh, but they
departed from the body at the same moment of time and their
spirits were straightway united in the presence of the blessed
vision and together they were borne to the heavenly kingdom
by the ministry of angels. But Hereberht was first consumed
by a long illness, perhaps by the dispensation of the Lord's
grace, so that though he had less merit than the blessed Cuthbert,
the continual pain of a long illness would make up for it, and
being made equal in grace to his intercessor, he might be
counted worthy to depart from the body with him at one and
the same hour and also to be received into one and the same
dwelling of perpetual bliss.

24 om. C_1VHO_4.   25 ex C_1. sed P_1.   26-27 tempore diei C_1VH.
28 adque C_1.   29-30 trans. coel. M.   31 cael... C_1V. cel... C_3O_3.
32 set O_3.   33 Hereberhtus C_1VH.   34 dequoquitur C_1.   35 Cudberhto
C_1V. Cuthberhto H.   36 longe $C_3O_3O_4M$.   37 aegr... O_8O_4.
38 aeq... C_1VHO_8M. om. O_4.   39 ins. above Dei O_4.   40 ins. above
aequatus O_4.   41 intercessoris VH.   42 gloss above scilicet merebatur VH.
43 ins. diei C_1VHO_4.   44 perpetue O_3.

XXIX. *Quomodo uxorem comitis[1] per presbiterum*
suum[2] aqua benedicta sanauerit

Quadam autem[3] die dum parrochiam[4] suam circuiens
monita salutis omnibus ruris[5] casis, et uiculis largiretur,
nec non[6] etiam nuper baptizatis ad accipiendam spiritus
sancti gratiam manum imponeret[7], deuenit ad uillulam
cuiusdam comitis cuius uxor male habens quasi proxima
morti[8] iacebat. Cui iam uenienti occurrens ipse cómes[9]

p. 87 flexis genibus|gratias egit Domino de aduentu illius, et
introducens illum[10] benigno recepit[11] hospicio[12]. Cunque[13]
lotis more hospitalitatis manibus et[14] pedibus resedisset
antistes[15], coepit[16] referre illi[17] uir de languore coniugis
desperatae[18], obsecrans ut ad spargendam[19] eam aquam
benediceret, Credo inquit[20] quia mox aut sanitati Deo
donante restituatur, aut si moritura est, perpetuam de
morte transeat ad uitam, citiusque[21] moriendo com-
pendium[22] tam miserabilis ac[23] diutinae[24] uexationis ac-
cipiat. Annuit[25] deprecanti uir Dei et allatam[26] benedicens[27]
aquam dedit presbitero, praecipiens[28] ut super languidam
aspergeret. Qui introgressus[29] cubiculum in quo illa
exanimi simillima iacebat, aspersit illam[30] et lectulum eius,
sed et os illius aperiens gustum salutiferi haustus immisit[31].

Greg. *Res mira[32] et uehementer stupenda, mox ut eam aqua benedicta*
Dial. I. 10 *tetigit[33]* languentem, et quid erga eam ageretur[34] prorsus
ignorantem, ita plenam et mentis[35] et corporis sanitatem
recepit[36], ut confestim resipiscens benediceret Dominum,
gratiasque referret ei qui tales tantosque hospites ad se
uisitandam curandamque destinare dignatus sit[37]. Nec
mora exurgens[38], ipsis suae[39] sanitatis ministris ministerium
sana praebuit[40], pulchroque[41] spectaculo ipsa prima de|

1 com. ux. O₄. *ins.* missa O₄.   2 *om.* O₄.   3 *om.* VH.
4 par... O₉.   5 ruribus C₁VHO₄.   6 *om.* P₁.   7 inp... C₁VH.
gloss above scilicet et dum VH.   8 mort. prox. C₁VHP₁O₄.   9 *in*
margin Nomen loci Hintis. Nomen comitis Hemni C₃O₃.   10 eum
C₁VHP₁O₄.   11 recaepit C₁VO₄.   12 hospitio C₁VHO₄M.
13 cumque C₁VHO₄.   14 ac C₁VHP₁.   15 antestis VH.   16 caep...
C₁. cep... C₃O₃.   17 ei P₁.   18 desperate O₃.   19 aspergendam
C₁VHP₁.   20 inquid O₃.   21 ciciusque O₉O₃.   22 *gloss in margin* id
est breuitatem V (*above* H).   23 et O₄.   24 diutine P₁O₃.   25 adn...

CHAPTER XXIX. *How through his priest he cured the wife of a gesith with holy water*

Now on a certain day, while he was going round his diocese dispensing words of salvation in all the houses and villages of the countryside, and was also laying his hand on those who had been lately baptized, so that they might receive the grace of the Holy Spirit, he came to the house of a certain gesith whose wife was lying very ill and apparently at the point of death. The gesith himself came to meet him and, on bended knee, gave thanks to the Lord for his coming, and bringing him in, received him with kind hospitality. The bishop, when his hands and feet had been washed in accordance with the custom of hospitality, sat down again, and the man began to tell him about his wife's desperate illness, praying him that he would bless some water to sprinkle upon her. "I believe", he said, "that she will either be speedily restored to health by the grace of God, or that, if she is to die, she will pass from death to everlasting life, and, by dying, more quickly reach the end of her wretched and long-lasting affliction." The man of God granted his petition, and blessing the water which was brought to him, gave it to a priest, bidding him sprinkle it over the sick woman. He entered the sleeping chamber in which she lay like one dead, sprinkled her and her bed and, opening her mouth, poured in a portion of the health-giving draught. A wonderful and exceedingly amazing thing happened—as soon as the blessed water touched the sick woman, though it was done without her knowledge, she yet received full healing of mind and body, so that she immediately recovered her senses and blessed the Lord, giving thanks to Him who had deigned to bring such honourable guests to visit and cure her. Without delay she rose up whole and ministered to those who had themselves ministered to her health; and it was a fair sight to see how she

C₁VH. *gloss in margin* id est consensit V (*above* H).   26 adl... C₁VH.
27 *om.* P₁.   28 pre... O₈.   29 introgrediens O₄.   30 ipsam C₁VHO₄.
31 inm... C₁VH.   32 *gloss above* scilicet factum est VH.   33 contigit
C₁VHP₁O₄.   34 gereretur C₁VHP₁.   35 meritis C₁.   36 recaepit VO₄.
37 est C₁VH.   38 exsur... C₁VH.   39 sue O₃.   40 praeberet C₁VH.
gloss above scilicet et ut VH. praebet P₁. prebebat O₄.   41 pulcroque O₃.

p. 88 tota tanti uiri familia episcopo potum refectionis obtulit,
quae per ipsius[1] benedictionem poculum mortis euasit,
secuta exemplum *socrus* apostoli Petri, quae curata a
Luke 4.39 febribus per Dominum, *continuo surgens ministrabat illi*
ac[2] discipulis eius.

XXX. *Quomodo puellam [3] oleo perunctam a dolore capitis laterisque[4] curauerit*

Neque huic dissimile[5] sanitatis miraculum a uenerabili
antistite Cuthberto[6] factum multi qui praesentes fuere
testati sunt. E quibus est religiosus presbiter Ediluualdus[7]
tunc minister uiri Dei, nunc autem abbas coenobii[8]
Mailrosensis[9]. Dum enim more suo pertransiret uniuersos
docendo, deuenit in uicum[10] quendam in quo erant feminae[11] sanctimoniales non multae[12], quibus timore barbarici[13]
exercitus a monasterio suo profugis ibidem manendi sedem
p. 89 uir Domini paulo ante donauerat. Quarum | una quae
erat cognata praefati sacerdotis Edilwaldi[14] grauissimo
tenebatur languore depressa, per integrum namque[15]
annum intolerabili[16] capitis et totius[17] lateris alterius dolore
uexata, funditus a medicis erat desperata[18]. Indicantibus
autem de illa uiro Dei, et pro sanatione eius obsecrantibus
his[19] qui uenerant cum eo, miseratus ille[20] miseram[21]
unxit oleo benedicto. Quae[22] ab illa mox hora meliorari
incipiens, post dies paucos plena sospitate conualuit.

XXXI. *Quomodo per panem ab eo benedictum [23] infirmus sit[24] sanatus[25]*

Nec silentio praetereundum[26] arbitramur miraculum,
quod eiusdem uiri uenerabilis uirtute quamuis ipso absente

---

1 illius O₄.   2 et C₁VH.   3–4 a capitis et lateris dolore oleo curauerit O₄.   5 diss. huic C₁H.   6 Cudberhto C₁V. Cuthberhto H.
7 Aediluuald C₁VH. Ethiluuald P₁.   8 caen... V. cen... C₃O₃M.
9 Maillrosensis H.   10 *in margin* Nomen loci Bædesfelth C₃. *in
margin* Nomen loci Bedesfelth O₃.   11 femine C₁O₃.   12 multe
C₃O₃.   13 barbaricae C₁.   14 Aediluualdi C₁VH. Ethiluualdi P₁.

who had escaped the cup of death by the bishop's blessing, was the first of all the household of so great a man to offer him the cup of refreshment. She thus followed the example of the mother-in-law of the Apostle Peter, who, when she was cured of a fever by the Lord, forthwith rose and ministered to Him and to His disciples.

CHAPTER XXX. *How he cured a girl of pains in the head and the side by anointing her with oil*

There are many who have borne witness to a miracle of healing wrought in their presence by the venerable Bishop Cuthbert not unlike this last one; among these witnesses is the pious priest Aethilwald, then a servant of the man of God, but now the abbot of the monastery at Melrose. For while according to his custom he was going through all the villages teaching, he came to a certain village in which there were a few nuns to whom he, the man of God, had a short time before given a place of abode in that village, when they had fled from their own monastery through fear of the barbarian army. One of these, a kinswoman of the same priest Aethilwald, was afflicted by a very severe illness; for all through the year she had been troubled with an intolerable pain in the head and in the whole of one side, and had been entirely given up by the physicians. When those who had come with him told the man of God about her and prayed for her restoration, he had pity on her and anointed the wretched woman with holy oil. She began to get better from that very hour and after a few days was restored to complete health.

CHAPTER XXXI. *How a sick man was healed with bread which he had blessed*

Nor do we consider that we ought to pass over in silence a miracle which, as we have learned, was performed by the

Ediluualdi C_3O_4. Edilwoldi O_3.   15 nanque O_8O_4M.   16 intollerabili C_1. *altered from* intollerabili V. intolerabilis $O_9C_3O_8$.   17 tocius C_3O_3. 18 disperata C_1.   19 hiis O_3.   20 *gloss above* scilicet Cuthberhtus VH. 21 *gloss above* scilicet cognatam VH.   22 que C_3O_3.   23-24 sit inf. VC_3.   23-25 infirmus curabatur O_4.   26 preter... O_8.

patratum cognouimus[1]. Meminimus supra[2] Hildmeri praefecti, cuius uxorem uir Dei ab immundo[3] spiritu liberauerit. Idem ergo[4] praefectus[5] postea decidit [6]in

p. 90 lectum[7], grauissima[8] [9]pressus infirmi|tate[10], adeo ut crescente molestia[11] per dies[12], iamiamque uideretur[13] esse moriturus. Aderant multi amicorum qui ad consolandum uenerant languentem. Cunque[14] lecto iacentis assiderent[15], repente unus eorum intulit[16] quia secum haberet panem quem sibi nuper uir[17] Domini Cuthbertus[18] benedictionis gratia dedisset[19], Et[20] credo inquit[21] quia huius gustu possit, si tamen fidei nostrae[22] tarditas non obsistit medelam recipere salutis. Erant autem [23]laici[25] omnes[24] sed religiosi. Conuersi igitur ad inuicem, confitebantur singuli quia absque ulla dubietate crederent per eiusdem benedicti panis communionem eum posse sanari. ˊImplentesque[26] calicem aqua[27], immiserunt[28] pauxillulum[29] panis illius, et dederunt ei bibere. Cuius statim ut uiscera gustus ille aquae[30] per panem sanctificatus attigit, fugit dolor interaneorum omnis[31], fugit exteriorum tabitudo membrorum[32]. Nec mora expeditum a languore uirum salus subsecuta confirmauit, atque ad laudandam[33] famuli Christi sanctitatem, et[34] admirandam[35] fidei non fictae uirtutem, merito et ipsum et omnes qui celeritatem tam inopinatae salutis[36] uidere uel audiere sustulit.

XXXII. Qualiter [37]oblatum sibi iñ itinere[38] iuuenem [39]moriturum orando reuocauerit[41] ad [42]sospitatem uitae[43,40]

p. 91 Quodam quoque tempore dum sanctissimus gregis dominici pastor, sua lustrando [44]circuiret[46] ouilia[45], deuenit in montana et agrestia loca, ubi multi erant de circumpositis

1 cognouisse C₁. ins. namque VH.   2 supradicti P₁.   3 inm... C₁VH.
4 autem C₁VH.   5 pre... O₄.   6–7 infirmitatem C₁. in infirmitatem VHP₁O₄.   8 grauissimam C₁VHP₁O₄.   9–10 om. C₁VHP₁O₄.
11 om. C₁VHP₁.   12 ins. molestia sterneretur in lectum et C₁VHP₁O₄.   13 uid. iam. C₁VHP₁O₄.   14 cumque C₁VHO₄M.   15 ads... C₁VH.   16 gloss above pretulit VH.   17 uir nup. C₁VH.   18 Cudberhtus C₁V. Cuthberhtus H.   19 daret C₁VHO₄.   20 ex C₁.   21 inquid O₃.

virtue of the same venerable man, though he himself was
absent. We have already mentioned the reeve Hildmer whose
wife the man of God freed from an unclean spirit. Now this
same reeve afterwards took to his bed with a most serious illness,
and, as his affliction grew from day to day, he seemed already
to be at the point of death. Many of his friends came to
console the afflicted man. And as they sat by the bed in which
he lay, suddenly one of them recalled that he had some bread
with him, which Cuthbert, the man of the Lord, had recently
blessed and given to him. "And I believe", he said, "that
Hildmer by tasting this can receive healing, if only the slowness
of our faith does not hinder." Now they were all laymen, but
devout. So turning to each other, they confessed one by
one that they believed without any doubt that he could be
healed by partaking of this blessed bread. They filled a cup
with water and put in a very little of the bread, and gave it
to him to drink. No sooner had the draught of water, sanctified
by the bread, reached his stomach, than all the inward pain
disappeared as well as the outward wasting of his limbs. His
health returned without delay, and brought strength back to
the man who had thus been set free from affliction, deservedly
stirring him and all who saw or heard of the swiftness of so
unexpected a cure, to praise the holiness of the servant of God
and to wonder at the power of true faith.

CHAPTER XXXII. *How, by his prayers, he recalled to life
a dying youth who was brought to him when he
was on a journey*

Once, too, as the most holy shepherd of the Lord's flock was
going round visiting his sheepfolds, he came to mountainous
and wild regions where there were many gathered together

22 nostre O_3.   23-24 omn. lai. O_4.   25 *changed from* laci C_1.
26 inp... VH.   27 aq. cal. C_1HP_1.   28 inm... C_1VH. miserunt P_1.
29 pauxillulam C_1.   30 aque O_3.   31 languoris C_1VH.
32 menb... O_4.   33 lauandam C_1.   34 ad P_1O_4.   35 amm...
$C_1VHP_1O_4$.   36 sanationis $C_1VHP_1O_4$.   37-38 *om.* O_4.
39-40 a grauissima molestia curauit O_4.   41 reuocaret VHO_8.
42-43 uitam VH. uitam sine omni mora O_8O_3M.   44-45 ou. circ. P_1.
46 circumiret C_3O_4. circuieret O_8.

late uillulis[1] quibus manus erat imponenda[2]. Nec tamen in montibus ecclesia[3] [4]uel locus inueniri potuit[5] aptus, qui pontificem cum suo comitatu susciperet. Tetenderunt ergo ei tentoria in uia, et caesis[6] de uicina silua ramusculis, sibi quique tabernacula ad manendum qualia potuere fixerunt. Ubi dum[7] confluentibus ad se turbis uir Dei uerbum biduo predicaret[8], ac spiritus sancti gratiam nuper regeneratis[9] in Christo per manus impositionem[10] ministraret, ecce subito apparuerunt[11] mulieres ferentes in grabato[12] iuuenem longae[13] egritudinis[14] acerbitate[15] tabefactum. Ponentesque in exitu siluae[16], miserunt ad epis-

p. 92 copum|rogantes ut ad[17] accipiendam benedictionem ad se hunc afferri[18] permitteret. Quem cum ad se perductum acerrime uexatum[19] conspiceret, iussit omnes secedere

Vit. Ant. longius. Et *ad solita* orationis arma *confugiens*, data bene-
c. 27 dictione pepulit pestem, quam[20] sollicita medicorum manus pigmentorum[21] compositione nequiuerat. Denique eadem hora surgens, et accepto cibo[22] confortatus, reddita Deo gratiarum actione[23], regressus est [24]ad eas[25] quae se portauerant[26] feminas. Sicque factum est ut quae eum illo tristes [27]languidum[29] aduexerant[28], cum eis inde gaudentibus et ipse sospes ac[30] laetabundus[31] domum rediret.

XXXIII. *Quomodo* [32]*tempore mortalitatis*[33] *morientem puerum* [34]*matri sanum restituerit*[35]

Eodem tempore pestilentia subito exorta illis in partibus grauissima nece incubuit, ita ut in[36] magnis quondam re-
p. 93 fertisque habitatoribus[37]|uillis ac possessionibus uix paruae[38] raraeque[39] reliquiae[40] et interdum nullae[41] residerent[42].

---

1 *ins.* congregati C_1VHO_4.   2 inp... C_1VH.   3 aecclaesia V. aecclesia $HP_1O_8O_4M$.   4–5 pot. inu. uel loc. O_4.   6 cesis C_3O_3M. 7 cum C_1VH.   8 prae... O_8O_4.   9 baptizatis O_4.   10 inp... C_1VH. inposicionem C_3.   11 apparuere C_1VH.   12 grabbato P_1O_4. 13 longe C_1O_3.   14 aeg... O_8O_4.   15 aceruitate C_1.   16 silue O_3. 17 *om.* C_1. *ins. above* V.   18 adf... C_1VH. afferre C_3.   19 uexari O_4. 20 *gloss above* pestem V. *gloss above* scilicet pestem H.   21 picmen-

from the widely scattered villages, on whom he was to lay his hands. But in the mountains no church could be found, nor any place fit to receive the bishop and his retinue. So they pitched tents for him by the wayside and, cutting down branches from the neighbouring wood, they made every man for himself booths to dwell in as best they could. There the man of God had been preaching the word for two days to the crowds who flocked to hear him, and by the laying on of hands had ministered the grace of the Holy Spirit to those who had lately been regenerated in Christ, when suddenly there appeared some women bearing upon a pallet a youth, wasted with a long and grievous sickness. Placing him on the edge of the wood, they sent to the bishop, praying that he would allow him to be brought to him to receive his blessing. When the youth had been brought to Cuthbert and he saw his terrible affliction, he bade them all go farther off. And turning to his wonted weapon of prayer, he gave his blessing and drove away the plague which the careful hands of the doctors could not expel with their compounds and drugs. Thereupon the youth rose up the same hour, received food and was strengthened and, giving thanks to God, he returned to the women who had carried him. And so it came to pass that he returned home well and joyful, amid the rejoicings of the same women who had sorrowfully conveyed him thither when he was sick.

CHAPTER XXXIII. *How, during the time of the plague, he restored a dying boy in sound health to his mother*

At the same time there suddenly arose in those parts a most grievous pestilence, and brought with it destruction so severe that in some large villages and estates once crowded with inhabitants, only a small and scattered remnant, and sometimes

torum P_1.   22 cybo H.   23 *ins.* ad eas O_4.   24–25 *om.* O_4. 26 portarant C_1VH.   27–28 adu. lang. O_4.   29 *ins.* rediret O_9. 30 et O_4.   31 let... C_3O_3.   32–33 iam O_4.   34–35 osculo sanatum matri reddidit O_4.   36 *om.* C_1VH.   37 habitatore P_1.   38 parue C_1O_3. 39 rare O_3.   40 reliquie $C_1C_3O_3$.   41 nulle O_8O_3.   42 *gloss above* id est remanerent VH.

Unde sanctissimus pater Cuthbertus[1] diligentissime suam
lustrans parrochiam, eisdem paruissimis quae[2] superfuere
reliquiis ministerium uerbi et necessariae[3] consolationis
opem ferre non desiit. Adueniens autem in uiculum[4]
quendam, ibidemque omnibus[5] quos inuenerat auxilio
exhortationis[6] adhibito, dixit ad presbiterum[7] suum,
Putasne superest quispiam his[8] in locis cui[9] nostra uisitatione[10] et allocutione opus sit. An cunctis qui male
habebant uisis iam ad alios transire[11] licet? Qui circumspiciens omnia, uidit mulierem eminus stantem, quae
extincto paulo ante filio fratrem eius iam morti proximum
tenebat in manibus, lacrimisque faciem rigantibus[12] prae-
teritam pariter et praesentem testabatur erumnam[13]. Quam
cum uiro Dei ostenderet, nil moratus[14] accessit ad eam
et benedicens dedit osculum puero, dixitque ad matrem,
Ne[15] timeas[16] nec mesta sis, saluabitur[17] enim et uiuet
infans[18], neque ullus[19] ultra de domu[20] tua[21] hac mortalitatis
peste deficiet. Cuius prophetiae ueritati ipsa cum filio
mater multo exinde tempore uiuens testimonium dabat.

XXXIV. Quomodo[22] animam cuiusdam qui [23]de arbore[24] cadendo mortuus est[25] ad coelum[26] ferri conspexerit|

p. 94   Interea[27] dum praescius[28] uicini sui obitus[29] uir Domini
Cuthbertus[30] iam decreuisset animo deposita cura pastoralis
officii solitariam redire ad uitam, quatinus excussa sollici-
tudine externa inter libera orationum et psalmodiae[31]
studia[32] diem mortis uel potius uitae[33] coelestis[34] prae-
stolaretur[35] ingressum, uoluit prius non solum [36]sua[38]
circuita[39,37] parrochia[40], sed et aliis circa fidelium man-
sionibus uisitatis, cunctos necessario exhortationis[41] uerbo

1 Cudberhtus C₁V. Cuthberhtus H. . 2 que O₃. 3 necessarie O₃.
4 *in margin* Nomen uiculi Medeluong O₃. 5 hominibus P₁.
6 exortacionis C₃. 7 *in margin* Nomen presbiteri Tydi O₃.
8 hiis O₃. 9 *ins.* in C₁VH. 10 uisitacione C₃. 11 trans. ad al.
C₁VH. 12 riganti C₁. ...bus *above* V. 13 erumpnam C₃O₃.
14 *ins.* ille C₁VHP₁O₄. 15 nec M. 16 metuas C₁P₁C₃O₈O₃O₄M.
17 sanabitur *changed from* sabitur C₁. sanabitur VHP₁O₄. 18 inf. et

none at all, remained. So the most holy father Cuthbert, diligently traversing his diocese, did not cease to bring the ministry of the word and the help of much-needed consolation to the poor few who remained. Coming to one village and having helped by his exhortations all whom he found, he said to his priest: "Do you think that anyone is left in these parts who needs to be visited and exhorted by us; or have we seen all who are in trouble and can we now pass on to others?" The priest, looking round everywhere, saw a woman standing at a distance who, having lost one son a little while before, was now holding his brother in her arms at the point of death; her eyes, streaming with tears, bore witness both to her past and her present troubles. The priest pointed her out to the man of God, who did not delay but, approaching her and giving her his blessing, kissed the boy and said to the mother: "Do not fear nor be sad; for your infant will be healed and will live, nor will anyone else be missing from your home through this plague." The mother herself and her son lived long afterwards to bear testimony to the truth of this prophecy.

CHAPTER XXXIV. *How he beheld the soul of a certain man, who was killed by falling from a tree, being carried to heaven*

Meanwhile Cuthbert, the man of God, being aware that his death was approaching, had now decided in his mind to lay aside the cares of the pastoral office and to return to a solitary life, so that, freed from outside anxieties, he might await the day of his death, or rather of his entrance into heavenly life, in the undisturbed practice of prayers and psalm-singing; but first he wished not only to go round his own diocese, but to visit the other dwellings of the faithful in the neighbourhood and to strengthen them all with the needful word of exhortation;

uiu. O_4.   19 *om.* O_4.   20 domo $P_1O_8O_3O_4M$.   21 *ins. above* aliquis O_4. 22 qualiter VHO_8O_4M.   23–24 *om.* O_4.   25 erat O_4.   26 cel... O_8O_3. 27 *chapter number and capital missing* C_1.   28 pre... HO_4.   29 ob. sui O_4. 30 Cudberhtus C_1V. Cuthberhtus H.   31 psalmodie O_3.   32 studio C_1. *changed from* studio V.   33 uite C_3O_3.   34 cael... C_1V. cel... C_3O_3. 35 pre... O_8O_4.   36–37 circuita sua M.   38 suam VH.   39 circuire C_1VH.   40 parrochiam VH.   41 exhortacionis C_3. exort... O_3.

confirmare, ac sic ipse desideratae[1] solitudinis gaudio refoueri. Quod dum ageret, rogatus a nobilissima et sanctissima uirgine Christi Elffledae[2] abbatissa cuius superius memoriam feci, uenit ad possessionem[3] monasterii ipsius, quatinus ibidem et ipsam uidere atque[4] alloqui et aecclesiam[5] dedicare deberet. Nam et ipsa p. 95 possessio non|pauco famulorum Christi examine pollebat. Ubi dum hora refectionis ad mensam consedissent, subito [6]uenerabilis pater[7] Cuthbertus[8] auersam a carnalibus epulis[9] mentem ad spiritualia[10] contemplanda contulit[11]. Unde lassatis ab officio suo membris corporis, mutato colore faciei[12] et quasi attonitis[13] contra morem oculis, cultellus quoque quem tenebat decidit in mensam. Quod dum presbiter[14] eius qui astabat[15] et ministrabat aspiceret[16], inclinatus ad abbatissam dixit silentio, Interroga episcopum quid uiderit[17]. Scio enim quia non sine causa manus eius tremefacta cultellum deseruit, uultusque mutatur illius, sed[18] uidit aliquid spirituale[19] quod nos[20] caeteri[21] uidere nequiuimus[22]. At illa statim conuersa ad eum, Obsecro inquit[23] domine mi episcope dicas quid uideris modo[24], neque enim frustra lassata[25] tua dextera[26] cultellum quem tenebat amisit. Qui dissimulare conatus uidisse se quippiam[27] secreti, iocose respondit, Num tota die manducare ualebam? Iam aliquando quiescere debui. Illa autem diligentius adiurante ac flagitante ut exponeret uisionem, Uidi inquit[23] animam cuiusdam sancti manibus angelicis[28] ad gaudia[29] regni coelestis[30] ferri. Rursus illa, De quo inquit[23] loco assumpta[31] est? Respondit, De tuo monas- p. 96 terio. Adiecit nomen|inquirere. Et ille, Tu mihi[32] inquit[23] die crastino missas celebranti[33] nomen eius indicabis. Haec[34] audiens illa, confestim misit ad maius[35] suum monasterium, uidere qui[36] nuper raptus esset e corpore.

1 desiderate O₃.   2 Aelfflaede C₁V. Aelflaede H. Aelfleda P₁.
Elfledae C₃. Aelflede O₈. Elflede O₃M. Aelfflede O₄.   3 *in margin*
Nomen loci Osingædun C₃.   4 adque C₁. et O₄.   5 eccl...
C₁O₃O₄M.   6–7 *om.* C₁VHP₁O₄.   8 Cudberhtus C₁V.
Cuthberhtus H.   9 aep... O₄.   10 spiritalia C₁VH.
11 sustulit C₁VHP₁O₄.   12 facies C₁.   13 adt... C₁V.
14 *in margin* Nomen presbiteri Bæda C₃. *in margin* Nomen presbiteri
Baeda O₃.   15 adst... C₁VH. ass... O₄.   16 aspexit C₁VH.

and, having done this, to be refreshed by the joy of the solitude
he longed for. While he was thus engaged, at the request of
the most noble and holy virgin of Christ, the abbess Aelfflaed,
whom I have mentioned above, he came to an estate belonging
to her monastery, in order that he might see and have conversation with her and also dedicate a church. For the estate contained
no small number of the servants of Christ. When they had
taken their seats at the table at meal-time, the venerable father
Cuthbert suddenly turned his mind from the carnal banquet
to contemplate spiritual things. The limbs of his body relaxed
and lost their function, the colour of his face changed, and his
eyes were fixed against their wont as if in amazement, while
the knife which he was holding fell to the table. When his
priest, who was standing by and serving, saw this, he bent
towards the abbess, and said quietly: "Ask the bishop what he
has seen; for I know that not without cause has his trembling
hand loosed the knife, and his countenance changed; but he
has seen something spiritual which the rest of us have not been
able to see." She immediately turned to him and said: "I
beseech you, my lord bishop, tell me what you have just seen;
for not for nothing did your hand relax and loose the knife it
held." He attempted to hide the fact that he had seen anything
secret, and answered jestingly: "Can I eat all day? I must rest
sometimes." But when she adjured him and importuned him
more earnestly to reveal his vision, he said: "I have seen the
soul of a certain holy man being carried by the hands of angels
to the joys of the heavenly kingdom." Again she said: "From
what place was it taken?" He answered: "From your estate."
Then she enquired after his name. He said: "You will tell
me his name when I am celebrating mass to-morrow." When
she heard this, she immediately sent to her larger monastery
to see who had recently been summoned from the body. But

17 *ins.* modo C₁VHP₁O₄.   18 set O₃.   19 spiritale C₁VH.
20 *om.* C₁VHP₁.   21 ceteri O₃M.   22 non quiuimus C₁VH.
23 inquid O₈O₃.   24 *ins.* dicas M.   25 lassa O₄.   26 dextra P₁.
27 aliquid P₁.   28 angelorum O₄.   29 *om.* C₁VHP₁O₄.
30 *ins.* gaudia C₁VHP₁O₄. cael... C₁V. cel... C₃O₃.   31 ads...
C₁VH.   32 michi O₈O₄.   33 cael... O₈.   34 hec C₃O₃.
35 Mailros (*in different hand* V) H.   36 quis VH.

At nuntius[1] omnes ibidem saluos incolumesque repperiens, postquam mane facto reuerti ad dominam coepit[2],
obuios[3] habuit eos qui corpus defuncti fratris[4] sepelien-
dum in carro deferrent[5]. Interrogansque quis[6] esset,
didicit quia quidam de pastoribus bonae[7] actionis uir
incautius in arborem ascendens deciderat deorsum, et
contrito corpore ipsa hora spiritum exalauit[8], qua hunc uir
Domini ad coelestia[9] ductum uidebat. Quod dum rediens
abbatissae[10] referret, statim illa ingressa ad episcopum
iam tunc dedicantem aecclesiam[11], stupore femineo quasi
nouum aliquid[12] incertumque nuntiatura[13], Precor inquit[14]
domine mi episcope memineris ad missas Haduualdi[15]
mei, hoc enim uiro erat nomen, quia heri cadendo de
arbore defunctus est. Tunc liquido omnibus patuit, quia
multiformis prophetiae[16] spiritus uiri sancti praecordiis
inerat, qui et in praesenti[17] occultum[18] animae raptum
uidere[19], et quid sibi in futuro ab aliis indicandum esset,
potuit praeuidere.

XXXV[20]. *Quomodo aquam gustando in uini*
saporem conuerterit |

p. 97 Inde peragratis ex ordine superioribus locis, uenit ad
monasterium uirginum quod non longe ab hostio[21] Tini
fluminis situm supra docuimus, ubi a religiosa[22] et ad
saeculum[23] quoque nobilissima [24]famula Christi[25] Uerca
abbatissa magnifice susceptus[26], postquam de meridiana
quiete surrexerunt, sitire se dicens ut biberet [27]rogauit.
Querebant[29] quid bibere uellet, rogantes[30] ut uinum siue
ceruisam[31] afferri[32] liceret, Aquam inquit[33] date mihi[34].
Qui haustam de fonte aquam obtulerunt[35] ei. At ille data
benedictione ubi paululum gustauit, dedit astanti[36] presbitero[37] suo, qui reddidit ministro. Et minister accepto

1 nuncius O₄. 2 caep... C₁V. cep... C₃O₃. 3 obuiam O₈.
4 *ins.* ad (*above* V) H. 5 deferebant P₁. 6 quid P₁. qui
C₃O₈O₃M. 7 bone O₃. 8 exhalauit C₁O₄. 9 cael... C₁V.
cel... C₃O₃. 10 abbatisse O₈O₃. 11 eccl... C₁. aecclaesiam V.
12 al. quas. nou. P₁. 13 nunciatura C₃O₄M. 14 inquid O₃.
15 Aδuuualdi C₁. Hadwaldi C₃O₈O₃M. 16 gratiae C₁VH. prophetie O₃. 17 presenti O₈. 18 *om.* O₄. 19 *ins.* occultum O₄.

the messenger found that all there were safe and sound, and on
the following morning was preparing to return to his mistress,
when he met some men bearing the body of a dead brother to
burial on a cart. On asking who it was, he learned that one of
the shepherds, a man of good life, climbing a tree too incautiously
had fallen down, and his body was so injured that he breathed
forth his spirit at the very hour in which the man of God had
seen it carried to heaven. On his return, he told the abbess
and she immediately went to the bishop who was then dedicating the church; with woman-like astonishment, as if she were
announcing something new and doubtful, she said: "I pray
you, my lord bishop, remember at mass my Hadwald"—for
that was the man's name—"who died yesterday through falling
from a tree." Then it was clear to all how manifold was the
spirit of prophecy in the breast of the holy man, who could not
only see the secret removal of a soul in the present, but could
also foresee what would be told him by others in the future.

CHAPTER XXXV. *How, by tasting water, he gave
it the flavour of wine*

Having passed through the upper districts in turn, he came to
the monastery of virgins which, as we have explained above,
is situated not far from the mouth of the river Tyne; here he
was magnificently received by a devout and also—so far as
this world is concerned—a most noble handmaiden of Christ,
the abbess Verca. After they had risen from their midday rest,
he asked for something to drink, saying that he was thirsty.
They asked what he wished to drink and prayed that they
might be allowed to bring him wine or beer. "Give me
water!" he said. So they brought him water drawn from the
well. Having blessed it and drunk a little of it, he gave it to
his priest who was standing by, who gave it to a servant.

20 *From this point on, chapter numbers in* C₁ *are one less than in text.*   21 ostio
VH.   22 relegiosa C₁.   23 saecula VH. seculum O₃.   24–25 *om.* P₁.
26 *ins.* est VH.   27–28* (p. 266) *om.* C₁VH.   29 quaer...
P₁O₄.   30 rogabantque O₄.   31 ceruisiam O₃O₄.   32 afferre
P₁O₄.   33 inquid P₁O₃.   34 michi O₄.   35 optulerunt O₃.
36 ass... O₄.   37 *in margin* Nomen presbiteri Bædæ C₃. *in margin*
Nomen presbiteri Beda O₃.

poculo, Licet inquit mihi[1] bibere de potu de quo bibit
episcopus? Respondit, Etiam. Quare non liceat? Erat
autem et ille presbiter[2] eiusdem monasterii. Bibit ergo,
et uisa est ei aqua[3] quasi in saporem uini[4] conuersa,
tantique sibi testem uolens adhibere miraculi fratrem[5]

p. 98 qui | proxime astabat, porrexit ei poculum. Qui cum et
ipse biberet[28*], eius quoque palato pro aqua uinum sapiebat.
Aspectabant autem mirantes ad inuicem. Et ubi uacuum[6]
tempus ad loquendum acceperunt[7], confitebantur alterutrum quia uideretur[8] sibi [9]nunquam[11] melius[10] uinum
bibisse, sicut unus[12] ex ipsis[13] postea in nostro monasterio
quod est ad hostium[14] Wiri[15] fluminis non paruo tempore
demoratus, ibidemque nunc placida quiete sepultus, sua
mihi[16] relatione[17] testatus est.

XXXVI. *Quomodo inoboedientes[18] [19]ei quosdam[20] fratres tempestas maris[21] obsederit*

Duobus[22] igitur annis in regimine episcopali transactis,
sciens in spiritu uir Domini Cuthbertus[23] appropinquare[24]
diem sui transitus[25], abiecit pondus curae[26] pastoralis,
atque ad dilectum heremiticae[27] conuersationis agonem
quamtotius[28] remeare curauit, quatinus inolita sibi sollici-

p. 99 tudinis mundanae[29] spi|neta[30] liberior priscae[31] compunc-
tionis[32] flamma consumeret. Quo tempore, sepius[33]
ad uisitantes se[34] fratres de mansione sua egredi, eosque
praesens solebat alloqui[35]. Libet autem referre quoddam
tunc ab eo factum miraculum, quo clarius elucescat
quantum uiris sanctis obtemperandum sit etiam in his[36]
quae negligentius[37] imperare uidentur. Quadam die dum
uenissent quidam[38], egressusque ille exhortatorio[39] illos[40]

---

1 michi inq. O₄.   2 *in margin* Nomen presbiteri Betuald C₃O₃.
3 *om.* P₁O₄. aquam C₁VH.   4 *ins.* aqua P₁O₄. 5 *in margin* Nomen
fratris Fridumundus O₃.   6 *ins.* hic P₁.   7 receperunt C₁VHP₁O₄.
8 uiderentur C₁VHP₁O₄.   9–10 melius numquam C₁.
11 numquam C₁VH.   12 *in margin* Nomen fratris Fridumund C₃.
13 eis C₁VHP₁O₄.   14 ostium HO₈.   15 Uuiri C₁VHP₁O₄.
16 michi O₄.   17 reuelatione C₁VH.   18 inobed... O₈O₃M.
19–20 *om.* O₄.   21 *ins.* per septem dies O₈O₃M.   22 *note in margin*
De sancto Cuthberhto I V.   23 Cudberhtus C₁V. Cuthberhtus H.

When the servant had taken the cup, he said: "May I drink from the cup from which the bishop has drunk?" He answered: "Yes, why not?" Now this man also was a priest of the same monastery. So he drank, and it seemed to him as if the water had acquired the flavour of wine, and wishing to make a brother who was standing by a witness of so great a miracle, he handed him the cup; and when he too had drunk, he also tasted wine on his palate instead of water. They gazed at each other in wonder and when they had an opportunity to speak together, they confessed to each other that it seemed to them that they had never drunk better wine. One of these related it to me himself, for he dwelt some considerable time in our monastery which is at the mouth of the river Wear, and he now lies peacefully buried in the same place.

CHAPTER XXXVI. *How a storm at sea detained certain brethren who were disobedient to him*

So, having spent two years in episcopal rule, Cuthbert the man of God, knowing in his spirit that the day of his departure was at hand, threw aside the burden of his pastoral care and determined to return to the strife of a hermit's life which he loved so well, and that as soon as possible, so that the flame of his old contrition might consume more easily the implanted thorns of worldly cares. At that time he was wont to go out of his dwelling-place frequently, to meet the brothers who visited him and to speak with them in person. It is well to narrate a certain miracle wrought by him, so that it may be more evident how obedient we ought to be to holy men, even in those matters about which they seem to give very casual commands. On a certain day some of them had come and he went out to refresh them with words of exhortation; after

24 adp... C_1VH. 25 trans. sui O_4. 26 cure C_3O_3. 27 heremitice O_3C_3. 28 quantotius $C_1P_1C_3$. quantocius VH. 29 mundane O_3. 30 spinaeta VH. 31 prisce C_3O_3. 32 conp... C_1VH. 33 *om.* O_4. 34 *ins.* sepius O_4. 35 adl... C_1. *changed from* adl... V. *note in margin* læt her 7 foh on þone oþerne capitel V. 36 hiis O_3. 37 neglegentius C_1VH. 38 *ins. above* fratrum O_4. 39 exhoratorio C_1. ex ortatorio (*first* t *above*) V. exhortatoria H. ex oratorio *changed to* ex oratorio O_3. 40 eos $C_1VHP_1O_4$.

sermone reficeret, post admonitionem[1] completam[2] sub-
iunxit[3] dicens, Iam hora est, ut ad mansionem meam
regrediar, uos autem quia proficisci disponitis, primo
sumite cibos[4], et aucam illam, [5]pendebat enim auca[6]
in pariete, coquite et comedite, et sic in nomine Domini
nauem ascendite, ac domum[7] redite. Dixerat haec, et
data oratione[8] et[9] benedictione suam mansionem in-
troiuit[10]. Illi autem ut praeceperat sumpsere[11] cibos[12],
sed[13] quia abundabant[14] cibis[15] quos secum attulerant[16],
aucam de qua praeceperat[17] tangere non curabant. At[18]
cum refecti nauiculam uellent ascendere, exorta[19] subito
tempestas fera omnem eis nauigandi facultatem abstulit.
Factumque est ut septem diebus feruente unda conclusi
tristes in insula resident, nec[20] tamen culpam inoboedientiae[21], pro qua huiusmodi carcerem patiebantur[22] ad
p. 100   memoriam reuocarent. | Qui cum sedulo ad patris col-
loquium reuersi, ac de reditus sui dispendio conquesti,
pacientiae[23] ab illo monita perciperent[24], septima tandem
die egressus ipse ad eos uolebat mesticiam[25] eorum gratia
suae[26] uisitationis[27] et consolationis piae[28] uerbo lenire.
Ingressus autem domum in qua manebant, ut uidit aucam
non fuisse comestam[29], placido uultu et laeto[30] potius[31]
sermone redarguit eorum[32] inoboedientiam[33], Nonne inquiens incomesta adhuc pendet auca? Et quid mirum
si uos mare non sinit[34] abire? Citissime[35] ergo mittite
eam in caldariam, coquite et comedite, ut possit mare
quiescere, et uos domum remittere. Fecerunt statim ut
iusserat, contigitque miro ordine ut cum ad praeceptum
uiri Dei coctura in caldaria[36] foco agente feruere coepisset[37],
eadem hora unda in mari cessantibus uentis suo a feruore
quiesceret[38]. Expleta itaque refectione uidentes mare placidum ascenderunt nauem[39], et secundis flatibus cum gaudio

1 amm... C₁VHO₄.   2 conp... C₁VH.   3 subiuxit O₉.
4 cybos H.   5–6 quae enim pendet VH.   7 *ins*. uestram P₁.
8 oracione C₃.   9 ac C₁VHP₁O₄.   10 introiit C₁VHP₁.
11 sumsere O₄.   12 cybos H.   13 set O₃.   14 hab... C₁VHO₃.
15 cybis H.   16 adt... C₁VH.   17 pre... V.   18 et P₁.
19 exhorta C₁.   20 naec V.   21 inobed... C₁VP₁O₃.   22 pacie-
bantur C₃O₈.   23 patientiae C₁VHO₄M.   24 perceperunt C₁VH.

he had finished his admonition, he added these words: "It is now time for me to return to my dwelling and you, as you are disposed to start, first take some food; and that goose"—for there was a goose hanging on the wall—"cook it and eat it, and so in the name of the Lord go on board your vessel and return home." Having said these words and given them his blessing, he entered his dwelling. They took food as he had bidden; but because they had brought plenty of food with them, they did not trouble to take the goose as he had commanded them. When, after the meal, they wished to go on board their boat, suddenly a fierce tempest arose and entirely prevented them from setting sail. And it happened that for seven days they remained miserably on the island, shut in by the raging seas; nor did they realise that it was for the sin of disobedience that they were suffering imprisonment of this sort. When they had anxiously returned to speak with the father and complained about the delay in their return, they received from him exhortations to patience. However, on the seventh day, he went out to them of his own accord, wishing to alleviate their sadness by graciously visiting them and by words of pious consolation. As soon as he had entered the house in which they were and saw that the goose had not been eaten, with unruffled mien and even with joyful words, he convicted them of disobedience. "Does not the goose hang there still unconsumed," he said, "then why marvel that the sea does not permit you to depart? Put it quickly therefore into the pot; cook it and eat it in order that the sea may quieten and let you go home." They did at once as he commanded; and it happened in a wonderful way that when the goose which was to be cooked at the bidding of the man of God had begun to boil in the pot over the fire, at that same hour the waves of the sea ceased from their fury and the winds fell. And so when the meal was finished, they saw that the sea was calm and went on board their ship and with favourable

gloss above uel perciperent VH.   25 mestitiam C_1VHP$_1$.   26 sue O_3.
27 uisitacionis C_3O_3.   28 pie O_3.   29 commestam O_8.   30 leto C_3O_3.
31 pocius C_3O_3.   32 eos P_1O_4.   33 inobedientiae P_1O_4.
inobedienciam O_3.   34 siuit C_1VHP$_1$M.   35 certissime O_9.
36 caldario C_1VH.   37 caep... C_1V. cep... $P_1C_3O_3$.   38 quiescere
$O_9C_3O_3$M.   39 nauim VH.

simul et pudore domum remeauerunt[1]. Pudebat nanque[2] eos inoboedientiae[3] et sensus tardioris, quo uetebantur[4] suum etiam inter flagella conditoris dinoscere et emendare

p. 101   reatum. Gaudebant[5] quia in|tellexere tantam fuisse Deo curam de fideli suo famulo, ut contemptum eius etiam per elementa uindicaret. Gaudebant[6] quia uidere[7] tantam suimet curam suo[8] fuisse creatori, ut etiam manifesto miraculo ipsorum errata corrigeret. Hoc sane quod retuli miraculum, non quolibet auctore[9], sed uno eorum qui interfuere narrante cognoui, uitae uidelicet uenerabilis monacho et presbitero eiusdem monasterii[10] Cynimundo[11], qui plurimis late[12] fidelium longeuitatis[13] et uitae[14] gratia iam notus existit.

XXXVII.   [15]*Quanta egrotus temptamenta pertulerit,*
[16]*quidue de sepultura sua*[18] *mandauerit migraturus*[19, 17]

Repetiit autem insulam mansionemque suam uir Domini[20] Cuthbertus[21] mox peracto[22] die solenni[23] natiuitatis domi-nicae[24]. Cunque[25] eum[26] nauem[27] ascensurum caterua fratrum circumstaret, interrogauit unus ex eis ueteranus et uenerabilis uitae[28] monachus[29], fortis quidem fide sed

p. 102   dissenteriae[30] morbo corpore iam factus imbecillis[31], | Dic nobis inquiens domine episcope quando reditum tuum sperare debeamus. At ille simpliciter interroganti sim-pliciter et ipse quod uerum nouerat pandens, Quando inquit[32] meum corpus[33] huc referetis[34]. Qui[35] cum duos ferme menses in magna repetitae[36] suae[37] quietis[38] exulta-tione transigeret[39], multo consuetae[40] districtionis rigore corpus mentemque constringeret, arreptus infirmitate subita, temporalis igne doloris ad perpetuae[41] coepit[42] beatitudinis gaudia praeparari[43]. Cuius obitum libet uerbis

1 remearunt C₁VHP₁O₄.   2 namque C₁VH.   3 inobed... P₁O₃. 4 uetabantur C₁VHO₃. *above* uel uetabantur O₈. uerebantur P₁. 5 *ins.* uero O₄.   6 *ins.* quoque O₄.   7 uiderent P₁.   8 sui C₁. 9 *ins.* dubio O₄.   10 *ins.* nomine O₄.   11 Cynemundo C₁VH. 12 latae C₁VH.   13 long. fid. M.   14 uite O₃.   15 *ins.* De transitu beatissimi presulis Cuthberti O₄.   16–17 et quid de sepul-tura praeceperit O₄.   18 sua sep. VHO₈M.   19 *om.* VHO₈O₃M. 20 Dei P₁O₈O₃O₄.   21 *om.* C₁VH.   22 peracta C₁VH.   23 sollemni

winds returned home with feelings both of joy and shame. For they were ashamed of their disobedience and of their slowness to perceive, whereby they were hindered from recognising and correcting their faults, notwithstanding the chastisement of the Creator. They rejoiced because they saw that God took such care of His faithful servant that He even punished, by means of the elements, those who esteemed His servant lightly. And they rejoiced because their Creator took such care of themselves that He corrected their errors even by a manifest miracle. This miracle which I have related, I learned not from any chance source, but from the account of one of those who were present, namely from Cynimund, a monk and priest of reverend life of the same monastery, who is still alive and well-known far and wide to many of the faithful, on account of his great age and of his manner of life.

CHAPTER XXXVII. *What trials he endured while sick and what he commanded concerning his burial, when about to depart this life*

Now Cuthbert the man of God sought his island dwelling-place once more, as soon as ever the holy day of the nativity of the Lord was past. And when a crowd of brethren stood round him as he was about to go aboard his ship, one of them, an aged monk of venerable life, strong in the faith but now weakened in body by dysentery, said: "Tell us, lord bishop, when we may hope for your return." And the bishop, who knew the truth, gave a plain answer to this plain question, saying: "When you bring my body back here." He had passed almost two months greatly rejoicing in his refound quiet, keeping under both mind and body by the rigours of his accustomed strictness, when he was attacked by a sudden illness and began to be prepared by the fires of temporal pain for the joys of perpetual bliss. His death let me describe in

C₁VHM. sollenni P₁. sollempni O₃.   24 dominice O₃.   25 cumque C₁VHO₄M.   26 illum VH.   27 nauim VH.   28 uite O₃. 29 monacus C₃.   30 distenteriae C₁. dissentyriae H. dissenterie O₃. 31 inb... C₁VH.   32 inquid O₃.   33 corp. me. M.   34 refertis C₁O₄. *changed from* refertis V.   35 II *in margin* V.   36 repetite O₃.   37 sue O₃. 38 quiaet... V.   39 transieret, n *above* C₁.   40 consuaete C₁. consuete O₃. 41 perpetue O₃.   42 caep... C₁V. cep... C₂O₃.   43 prep... VHP₁.

illius cuius relatione didici describere, Herefridi uidelicet
deuotae[1] religionis presbiteri, qui etiam tunc Lindisfarnensi[2] monasterio abbatis iure praefuit[3]. Tribus inquit[4]
ebdomadibus continuis infirmitate decoctus, sic ad extrema
peruenit. Si quidem quarta feria coepit[5] aegrotare[6], et
rursus quarta feria finita aegritudine[7] migrauit ad Dominum. At[8] cum[9] mane primo inchoatae[10] infirmitatis[11]
uenirem, nam et[12] ante triduum cum fratribus insulam
adieram, cupiens solitae[13] benedictionis et exhortationis[14]
ab eo solatia[15] percipere, ut dato iuxta morem signo me
aduenisse prodidi, processit ad fenestram, et salutanti se
mihi[16] suspirium pro responso reddidit. Cui ego, Quid
habes inquam domine mi episcope, an forte nocte hac
p. 103   tuus te | languor tetigit? At ille, Etiam inquit[17] languor me
tetigit nocte hac[18]. Putabam quia de ueteri[19] sua infirmitate
cuius cotidiana pene molestia consueuerat excoqui, non
autem de noua et insolita diceret. Nec plura interrogans,
Da inquam benedictionem nobis, quia iam tempus nauigandi, ac domum remeandi[20] adest[21]. Facite inquit[22] ut
dicis[23], ascendite nauem[24] ac domum salui redite. Cum
autem Deus susceperit animam meam, sepelite me in
hac mansione iuxta oratorium meum ad meridiem contra
orientalem plagam sanctae[25] crucis quam ibidem erexi.
Est autem ad aquilonalem[26] eiusdem oratorii partem
sarcofagum[27] terrae[28] cespite abditum, quod olim mihi[16]
Cudda uenerabilis abbas donauit. In hoc corpus meum[29]
reponite, inuoluentes in sindone quam inuenietis istic.
Nolui quidem ea uiuens indui, sed pro amore dilectae[30]
Deo feminae[31], quae[32] hanc michi[33] misit, Uercae[34] uidelicet
abbatissae[35] ad obuoluendum[36] corpus meum reseruare
curaui. [37]Haec[39] ego[38] audiens[40], Obsecro inquam pater
quia infirmantem et moriturum te audio aliquos de
fratribus hic ad ministrandum tibi remanere permittas.

---

1 deuote O₃.   2 Lindisfarnensis C₁. *altered from* Lindisfarnensis V.
3 pref... V.   4 *ins.* namque *above* H. praefuit O₃.   5 caep... C₁V.
cep... C₃O₃. 6 egrotari C₁VH. egr...M. 7 egr... C₁VHP₁C₃O₃M.
8 ad quem P₁O₄.   9 dum O₄.   10 incoatae P₁. inchoate O₃.
11 infirmitate O₃.   12 *om.* P₁O₄.   13 solite O₈O₃.   14 exortacionis
C₃. exortat... M.   15 solacia C₁VHP₁C₃O₃.   16 michi O₄.

the words of him from whom I heard about it, namely Herefrith, a devoutly religious priest who also at that time presided over the monastery at Lindisfarne as abbot.

"After having been weakened", he said, "by three weeks of continuous sickness, he came to his end thus. For he was taken ill on a Wednesday and again on a Wednesday his illness came to an end and he went to be with the Lord. On the morning when his illness first began (for I had come to the island with the brethren three days previously) I came to him and gave warning of my approach by means of the usual signal, desiring to receive the comfort of his accustomed benediction and exhortation. He came to the window and answered my greeting with a sigh. I said to him: 'What is the matter, my lord bishop? Perhaps your illness has attacked you during the night?' He said: 'Yes, illness has attacked me during the night.' I thought that he was speaking of his old complaint which used to afflict him almost daily, and not of some new and unusual complaint. Without asking any further questions, I said: 'Give me your blessing, for it is time to set sail and to return home.' 'Do as you say,' he said, 'get on board your vessel, and return home safe and sound. And when God has taken my spirit, bury me in this dwelling near my oratory towards the south, on the eastern side of the holy cross which I have erected there. Now there is on the north side of this same oratory a sarcophagus hidden under the turf, which the venerable abbot Cudda once gave me. Place my body in this, wrapping it in the cloth which you will find there. I was unwilling to wear the cloth while alive but, out of affection for the abbess Verca, a woman beloved of God, who sent it to me, I have taken care to keep it to wrap my body in.' When I heard this I said: 'I beseech you, father, since I hear that you are ill and like to die, that you will allow some of the brethren to remain here and

17 inquid O₃.   18 hac nocte P₁.   19 uetere P₁.   20 repetendi C₁VHO₄. petendi P₁.   21 III *in margin* V.   22 *ins.* Cuthberhtus *above* V. inquid O₃.   23 dicitis P₁.   24 nauim VH.   25 sancte O₃. 26 aquilonem C₁VO₈.   27 sargofagum C₃.   28 terre O₃. 29 meum corp. C₁VHP₁O₄.   30 dilecte O₈O₃.   31 femine C₁O₃. 32 que O₃.   33 mihi C₁VHP₁C₃O₃.   34 Uerce O₃M. 35 abbatisse C₃O₃.   36 abuoluendam C₁.   37-38 *om.* C₁VHP₁O₄. 39 bᵉᶜ.O₂.   40 *ins.* haec C₁VHP₁O₄.

At[1] ille, Ite inquit[2] modo, tempore autem oportuno[3]

p. 104 redite. Cunque[4] diligen|tius obsecrans ut ministrum sus-
ciperet[5] nequaquam impetrare ualerem, tandem interro-
gaui quando deberemus reuerti. Qui ait, Quando Deus
uoluerit, et ipse uobis ostenderit. Fecimus ut iusserat,
conuocatisque mox in aecclesiam[6] fratribus cunctis, iussi
orationem fieri sine intermissione pro eo, quia Uidetur
inquiens mihi[7] ex quibusdam uerbis illius appropinquare[8]
diem quo sit exiturus ad Dominum[9]. Eram autem
sollicitus de reditu propter infirmitatem eius[10], sed quinque
diebus obstitit tempestas ne redire possemus. Quod

Gen. 41. diuinitus dispensatum fuisse *rei probauit euentus.* Ut enim
13 omnipotens Deus famulum suum ab omni labe mundanae[11]
fragilitatis ad purum castigaret, utque aduersariis eius
quam[12] nichil[13] contra fidei uirtutem[14] ualerent ostenderet,
uoluit eum tanto tempore segregatum ab hominibus[15]
et suae[16] carnis dolore et antiqui hostis acriori certamine
probari. Ut autem reddita tranquillitate insulam repe-
tiuimus, inuenimus eum suo monasterio egressum sedere
in domo[17] in qua nos manere solebamus. Et quia necessitas
quaedam poscebat fratres qui mecum uenerant renauigare
ad proximum litus, ipse remanens in insula confestim[18]

p. 105 patri ministerium praebere[19] | curaui. Siquidem calefaciens
aquam abluebam pedem[20] eius, qui[21] gratia diutini[22]
tumoris[23] iam tunc ulcus habebat[24], ac profluente[25] sanie[26]
cura indigebat. Sed et uinum calefaciens attuli[27], eumque
gustare rogaui. Uidebam nanque[28] in facie eius, quia
multum inedia simul et languore erat defessus. Completa
curatione resedit quietus in stratu[29], resedi et ego iuxta
eum. Cunque[30] sileret, dixi, Uideo domine episcope quia
multum uexatus es ab infirmitate postquam recessimus[31]
a te, et mirum quare nolueris ut aliquos nostrum qui tibi

---

1 ad C₁.   2 inquid O₃.   3 opp... C₃O₃.   4 cumque C₁VHM.
5 *ins.* sed P₁.   6 ecčl... C₁C₃O₃. aecclaes... V.   7 michi O₄
8 adp... C₁VH.   9 Deum C₁VHP₁O₄. IIII *in margin* V
10 uiri Dei *above* V.   11 mundane O₃.   12 quo (*changed to* V) H
13 nihil C₁VHP₁.   14 fortitudinem C₁VHP₁O₄.   15 ab hom
seg. O₄.   16 sue O₃.   17 domum C₁. domu VH.   18 *om.* O₄
19 pre... HP₁O₄.   20 pedes VHP₁.   21 *gloss above* scilicet pedes H

minister to you.' But he said: 'Go now and return at the proper time.' And though I besought him very diligently to accept a servant, I could by no means gain my request. At length I asked him when we ought to return. He said: 'When God wills and when He himself shall direct you.' We did as he commanded, and, immediately calling all the brethren to the church, I commanded that prayer should be made without intermission for him. 'For', I added, 'it seems to me from certain words of his, that the day is approaching when he will depart to be with the Lord.' Now I was anxious about returning on account of his infirmity, but for five days a tempest hindered us; however, as events proved, this was a divine dispensation. For in order that Almighty God might, by chastisement, purify His servant from all blemish of worldly weakness and in order that He might show his adversaries that they could avail nothing against the strength of his faith, He wished to test him by bodily pain and by a still fiercer contest with the ancient foe, cutting him off from mankind for that space of time. But when calm weather was restored and we returned to the island, we found that he had gone out of his monastery and was sitting in the dwelling in which we used to stay. And because some urgent matter compelled the brethren who came with me to return to the neighbouring shore, I myself remained on the island and immediately set about ministering to the father. So I warmed some water and bathed his foot which, owing to a long-standing swelling, now had an ulcer on it and, as it was suppurating, required treatment. I also warmed some wine and brought it and asked him to taste it; for I saw by his face that he was greatly wearied both by lack of food and by disease. When I had finished my ministrations, he sat down quietly again on the couch and I sat near him. Since he was silent, I said: 'I see, my lord bishop, that you have been greatly afflicted by illness since we left you; and I marvel that you would not suffer us, when we went away, to leave some of our brethren here to

22 diutinis O₄.
to V) H.
27 adt... C₁VH.
30 cumque C₁VHO₄M.

23 *changed from* timoris V.
25 profluenti C₁VHP₁.
28 namque C₁VH.
31 secessimus P₁.

24 habebant (*changed to* V) H.
26 saniae C₁VH.
29 strato C₁VHP₁.

ministrarent hic dimitteremus abeuntes. At ille, Dei inquit[1] prouidentia et uoluntate gestum est, ut[2] praesentia[3] et[4] auxilio destitutus humano, aliquo[5] paterer aduersa. Postquam enim a me[6] digressi estis, continuo coepit[7] languor[8] ingrauascere[9]. Ideoque de mea mansione egrediens huc intraui, ut quicunque[10] uestrum michi[11] ministraturi aduenirent, hic me possent inuenire[12], nec meam mansionem necesse haberent ingredi. [13]Ex quo autem ingrediens[14] hac in sede membra composui[15], non moui me hinc, sed quinque diebus his[16] et noctibus hic quietus permansi. Cui ego, Et quomodo inquam domine mi episcope sic uiuere potuisti? Num absque cibi[17]|perceptione tanto tempore mansisti? Tum ille retecto[18] lectisternio cui supersedebat, ostendit ibi[19] caepas[20] quinque reconditas et ait, Hic mihi[21] uictus erat his[16] quinque[22] diebus. Quotienscunque[23] enim os ariditate ac siti nimia [24]aruit et[25] ardebat, haec[26] gustando me recreare ac refrigerare[27] curaui. Uidebatur autem una[28] de caepis[29], minus quam dimidia parte corrosa[30]. Insuper ait[31], Et concertatores mei[32] nunquam[33] per omne tempus ex quo in hac insula conuersari coepi[34], tot mihi[35] persecutiones[36] quot in his quinque diebus intulere[37]. Non audebam interrogare quae essent temptationes[38] de quibus[39] dixerat, tantum rogaui, ut ministros susciperet. Annuit[40] ille, et quosdam nostrum secum retinuit, in quibus erat maior Beda presbiter qui ministerio eius familiariter semper adesse consueuerat, ideoque donationum acceptationumque[41] eius omnium conscius erat indubius. Quem ob id maxime secum manere[42] uoluit, ut si cuiuslibet acceptis muneribus digna recompensatione[43] non respondisset, illius admonitione[44] recoleret, et priusquam obiret, sua cuique restitueret. Sed et alium quendam de fratribus[45]

p. 106

---

1 inquid O_3.   2 *ins.* in P_1.   3 presenti P_1. pre... O_4.   4 *om.* P_1. 5 aliqua $VHP_1O_3O_4M$. V *in margin* V.   6 *ins. above* beatus pater inquit V.   7 caep... C_1V. cep... C_3O_3.   8 *om.* $C_1VHP_1O_4$. 9 ingrauescere $C_1VHP_1O_4$. *ins.* languor $C_1VHP_1O_4$.   10 quicumque C_1VH.   11 mihi $C_1VHP_1C_3O_8$.   12 inu. poss. C_1VH.   13–14 *om.* C_1VH.   15 conp... C_1VH.   16 hiis O_3.   17 cybi H.   18 resecto C_1. reiecto (*changed to* V) H.   19 eibi O_9.   20 cepas C_3O_3. 21 michi O_4.   22 *om.* $C_1VHP_1O_4$.   23 quotiescumque C_1VH.

minister to you.' But he said: 'It happened through the providence and will of God that, destitute of human society and help, I should suffer some afflictions. For after you departed from me, my sickness immediately began to grow worse; and so I left my dwelling-place and came in here in order that those of you who came to minister to me could find me here and not be compelled to enter my dwelling. And since I came hither and composed my limbs on this couch, I have not stirred from here, but for five days and nights I have remained in this place without moving.' I said to him: 'And how, my lord bishop, could you live thus? Surely you have not been so long without taking food?' Then he drew back the coverlet of the bed on which he was seated and showed me five onions concealed below and said: 'This was my food during these five days; for as often as my mouth was parched and burned through excess of dryness and thirst, I sought to refresh and cool myself by tasting these.' And indeed somewhat less than half of one of the onions seemed to have been nibbled away. And furthermore he added: 'My adversaries have never persecuted me so frequently, during all the time I have been living on this island, as during these five days.' I did not dare to ask what were the temptations of which he spoke. I only asked him to allow some of us to wait on him. He consented and kept with him some of our brethren, amongst whom was the priest Beda the elder, who was always accustomed to render him intimate service, and so knew all about all the gifts he had given and the presents he had received; for this reason Cuthbert greatly desired him to remain with him, in order that, if he had not made a fitting return for any gifts he had received, Beda might remind him of it, so that, before he died, he might restore to each one his own. Moreover he specially named another

quotiescunque P_1O_4.   24–25 *om.* $C_1VHP_1O_4$.   26 hec C_3O_3.
27 ref. ac rec. $C_1VHP_1O_4$.   28 *om.* C_1VHP_1.   29 cepis P_1O_3.
30 conrosa VH.   31 *om.* $C_1VHP_1O_4$.   32 *ins.* inquit O_4.
33 numquam C_1VH.   34 caepi C_1V. cepi C_3O_3.   35 michi O_4M.
36 persecuciones C_3.   37 VI *in margin* V.   38 temptaciones C_3.
39 *ins. above* sanctus V.   40 adn... C_1VH. *gloss above* id est permittet H.
41 acceptionumque $O_9P_1C_3O_8$.   42 retinere O_4.   43 conp... C_1.
reconp... VH.   44 amm... O_4.   45 *in margin* Nomen fratris
Ualchstod C_3. *in margin* Nomen fratris Walchstod O_3.

p. 107 specialiter ut inter ministros sibi adesset designauit. |Qui
longo quidem uentris fluxu grauiter quidem[1] aegrotabat[2],
neque a medicis poterat curari, sed merito religionis,
prudentiae[3], et grauitatis dignus extiterat, qui[4] testis esset
uerborum quae[5] uir Dei ultima diceret, uel quo ordine
[6]ad Dominum migraret[8,7]. Interea rediens domum
narrabam fratribus quia uenerabilis pater in sua[9] se insula
sepeliri iuberet, Et uidetur inquam mihi[10] iustius esse multo
et dignius impetrare ab eo, quatinus[11] huc transferri corpus
suum, et iuxta honorem congruum [12]in aecclesia[14] condi[13]
permittat. Placuerunt illis quae[15] dixeram, et uenientes
ad episcopum rogabamus dicentes, Non ausi sumus
domine episcope contempnere iussionem tuam qua te hic
tumulari mandasti, et[16] tamen rogandum uidebatur nobis
ut te ad nos transferre et nobiscum habere mereamur[17].
At ille, Et[18] meae[19] inquit[20] uoluntatis erat hic requiescere
corpore ubi quantulumcunque[21] pro Domino *certamen*
2 Tim. *certaui*, ubi *cursum consumma*re desidero, unde ad *coronam*
4. 7, 8 *iusticiae*[22] subleuandum[23] me a pio *iudice* spero. Sed[24] et
uobis quoque commodius esse arbitror ut hic requiescam,
propter incursionem profugorum uel noxiorum quorum-
libet. Qui cum ad corpus meum forte confugerint[25]
p. 108 quia qualiscunque[26] sum[27], fama tamen exiit[28]|de me
quia famulus Christi sim, necesse habetis sepius pro talibus
apud potentes saeculi[29] intercedere, atque ideo de praesentia[30] corporis mei multum tolerare[31] laborem. At nobis
multum diu precantibus[32] laboremque modi[33] huius gratum
nobis ac leuem fore asseuerantibus, tandem cum consilio
locutus uir Domini, Si meam inquit[34] dispositionem
[35]superare et meum[36] corpus illo reducere uultis, uidetur
mihi[37] optimum ut in[38] interioribus basilicae[39] uestrae[40]

1 *om.* C₁VHP₁O₄.   2 egr... C₁VHP₁O₈O₃M.   3 prudencie O₃.
4 *gloss above* uel quo H.   5 que O₃.   6–7 mig. ad
Dom. C₁VHP₁O₄.   8 VII *in margin* V.   9 a *above* C₁.
10 michi O₃O₄M.   11 quatenus C₁. *changed from* quatenus V.
12–13 cond. in aeccl. O₄.   14 aecclaes... V. eccles... C₁C₃O₃.
15 qui O₃.   16 sed O₄.   17 mer. hab. C₁VHO₄.
18 VIII *in margin* V.   19 mee O₃.   20 *ins. above* Cuth-
berthus V.   21 quantulumcumque C₁VHP₁.   22 iustitiae C₁VH.

brother to be amongst his servants. This man had long been very ill with diarrhoea and could not be cured by the physicians; but was worthy, by merit of his piety, prudence and seriousness, to be a witness of the last words that the man of God should speak and of the manner in which he departed to be with the Lord. Meanwhile, having returned home, I told the brethren that the venerable father had ordered that he should be buried in his own island. 'But', I said, 'it seems to me much more proper and worthy that we should win his permission to bring his body here and bury it with fitting honour in the church.' My words pleased them and we came to the bishop and asked him, saying: 'We did not dare, my lord bishop, to despise your commands in bidding us bury you here; nevertheless it seemed right to us to ask you to consider us worthy to bring you to ourselves and to have you with us.' He said: 'It was my desire that my body should rest here where, to some small extent, I have fought my fight for the Lord, where I desire to finish my course, and where I hope that I shall be raised up to receive the crown of righteousness from the righteous Judge. But I also think that it will be more expedient for you that I should remain here, on account of the influx of fugitives and guilty men of every sort, who will perhaps flee to my body because, unworthy as I am, reports about me as a servant of God have nevertheless gone forth; and you will be compelled very frequently to intercede with the powers of this world on behalf of such men, and so will be put to much trouble on account of the presence of my body.' But after we had pleaded with him earnestly and long, and had declared that labour of this kind would be pleasing and light to us, at length the man of God spoke words of counsel. 'If', he said, 'you wish to set aside my plans and to take my body back there, it seems best that you entomb it in the interior of your church, so that while

23 sull... P_1C_3.   24 set O_3.   25 confugerunt C_1.   26 qualiscumque C_1VHO_4.   27 sim P_1.   28 exibit O_9. exiuit $C_3O_8O_3M$.   29 seculi O_3O_4.   30 pre... HO_4.   31 tollerare C_1. 32 prae... HO_8.   33 eius modi C_1V.   34 inquid C_1O_3. 35–36 om. C_1. in margin V.   37 michi O_4.   38 in above C_1. 39 basilice O_3.   40 uestre O_3.

illud tumuletis, quatinus et ipsi cum uultis meum sepulchrum[1] uisitare possitis, et in potestate sit uestra[2] an aliqui illo de aduenientibus accedant. Gratias egimus permissioni[3] et consilio illius flexis in terra[4] genibus, ac domum redeuntes, frequentius illum exinde uisitare non destitimus.

XXXVIII. *Quomodo ministrum suum a profluuio uentris [5]ipse aegrotus[6] sanauerit[7]* |

p. 109
2 Tim.
4. 6

Cunque[8] increscente languore uideret *tempus* suae *resolutionis insta*re, praecepit[9] se in suam mansiunculam atque oratorium referri[10]. Erat autem hora diei tercia[11]. Portauimus ergo illum, quia prae molestia languoris ipse non ualebat ingredi. At ubi ad portam peruenimus, rogabamus ut alicui[12] nostrum liceret ad ministrandum ei pariter intrare. Non enim per annos plurimos quispiam illuc[13] praeter[14] ipsum intrauerat. Qui circumspectis omnibus, uidit fratrem cuius supra memini[15] uentris fluxu languentem, et ait, Walchstod[16] ingrediatur mecum. Hoc enim erat nomen fratris[17]. Qui cum ad nonam usque horam intus cum illo maneret, sic egrediens uocauit me, Episcopus inquiens te iussit ad se intrare[18]. Possum autem tibi rem referre[19] nouam permirabilem, quia ex quo ingrediens illuc tetigi episcopum deducturus eum ad oratorium, continuo sensi me omni illa longe infirmitatis molestia carere. Non[20] autem dubitandum supernae[21] pietatis hoc dispensatione[22] procuratum[23], ut qui multos antea sospes adhuc ualensque curauerat, hunc quoque moriturus curaret

p. 110

quatinus hoc quoque indicio pateret etiam corpore | infirmatus uir sanctus quantum spiritu ualeret. In qua profecto curatione sequebatur exemplum sanctissimi et reuerentissimi patris Aurelii Augustini[24] episcopi. Qui dum pressus

---

1 sepulcrum O₃.   2 uest. sit C₁VH.   3 permisioni O₄.
4 terram C₃O₈O₃M.   5–6 *om*. VHC₃O₈O₃M.   5–7 sanauit ipse
aegrotus O₄.   7 *ins*. egrotum VH. *ins*. egrotus uir beatus C₃O₈O₃M.
8 cumque C₁VHO₃O₄M. X *in margin* V. *in margin* In deposicione
eiusdem O₃.   9 pre... O₈O₃.   10 referre C₁P₁O₄.   11 tertia
C₁VHP₁.   12 *add* que C₁VH.   13 illic C₁P₁. *changed from* illic V.

you yourselves can visit my sepulchre when you wish, it may be in your power to decide whether any of those who come thither should approach it.' We gave him thanks on our bended knees for his permission and his counsel and, returning home, we did not cease from that time forth to visit him very frequently."

CHAPTER XXXVIII. *How though sick himself he healed his attendant of diarrhoea*

"And when his illness increased and he saw that the time of his departure was at hand, he commanded that he should be carried back to his little dwelling-place and oratory; it was now the third hour of the day. So we carried him thither because, owing to the pain of his disease, he could not walk. But when we came to the door, we asked him that he would allow one of us to enter with him to minister to him; although for many years no one except himself had entered it. And looking round us all, he saw the brother whom I mentioned before, who suffered from diarrhoea, and he said: 'Let Walhstod' (for that was the brother's name) 'enter with me.' He remained inside with him until the ninth hour, and then he came out and called me saying: 'The bishop has commanded you to enter. And I can tell you some very wonderful news, for since I went in there and touched the bishop when about to take him into the oratory, I forthwith felt that all my affliction and long-standing infirmity had left me.' Nor can it be doubted that this was brought about by the dispensation of the heavenly grace, so that he who had healed many before this, while he was well and strong, should when at the point of death also cure this man in order that by this sign too it might be plain how strong the holy man was in spirit, though he was weak in body. And in this cure truly he followed the example of the most holy and most reverend father and bishop, Aurelius Augustinus; for when he was afflicted by the disease from which

14 preter O₈O₄.   15 meminimus O₄.   16 Uualhstod C₁VH. Uualch-stod P₁. Walcstod C₃.   17 fratri C₁VHO₄.   18 intr. ad se C₁VHP₁O₄.
19 ferre C₁. re *above* V.   20 *gloss above* scilicet est H.   21 superne O₃.
22 dispensacione C₃.   23 *gloss above* scilicet esse H.   24 Agustini C₁VH.

S. Augus-
tini Vita
auctore
S. Possidio
c. 29

infirmitate qua et mortuus est[1] decumberet, *uen*it quidam *cum suo aegroto*[2] *rogans ut*[3] *eidem manum imponeret*[4] *quo sanus esse posset.* At ille, *Si* inquit *aliquid in his*[5] *possem, mihi*[6] *hoc utique primitus praestitissem*[7]. Rursus is[5] qui uenerat, Te inquit[8] *uisi*tare praeceptus[9] sum, siquidem in *somnis*[10] *dictum* accepi, *Uade ad Augustinum*[11] episcopum *ut eidem*[12] *manum imponat*[13], *et saluus erit*[14]. Quo ille audito, mox aegrotanti[15] manum benedicens[16] imposuit[17], nec mora sanatum ad propria remisit.

XXXIX. [18]*Quae ultima fratribus mandata dederit, et ut percepto uiatico*[19] *inter uerba orationis spiritum reddiderit*[20] |

p. 111 Intraui[21] autem inquit ad eum circa horam diei circiter nonam, inuenique eum recumbentem in angulo sui oratorii contra altare, assidere[22] coepi[23] et ipse. Nec multa loquebatur, quia pondus aegritudinis[24] facilitatem loquendi minorauerat. Uerum me diligentius inquirente quem hereditarium sermonem, quod ultimum uale[25] fratribus relinqueret, coepit[26] disserere pauca sed[27] fortia de pace et humilitate, cauendisque eis qui his[28] obluctari quam oblectari mallent. Pacem inquit[29] inter uos semper et caritatem custodite diuinam, et cum de uestro statu consilium uos agere necessitas poposcerit, uidete attentius[30] ut unanimes existatis in consiliis. Sed et cum aliis Christi seruis[31] mutuam habetote concordiam, nec uenientes ad uos hospitalitatis gratia domesticos fidei habeatis contemtui[32], sed familiariter ac benigne tales suscipere, tenere, ac dimittere curate, nequaquam uos meliores arbitrantes caeteris[33] eiusdem fidei [34] et uitae[36, 35] consortibus[37]. Cum

---

1 *ins.* in lecto C₁VH (*in margin* P₁) O₄.   2 egr... C₁VHC₃O₃M.
3 quo O₄.   4 inp... C₁VH.   5 hiis O₃.   6 michi O₄.
7 prest... C₁VHP₁C₃O₈O₄.   8 inquid O₃.   9 iussus O₄.
10 sompnis O₃.   11 Agustinum VH.   12 ille tibi C₁VH. tibi P₁.
13 inp... C₁VH.   14 eris C₁VHP₁.   15 egr... C₁VHC₃O₃M.
16 *om.* O₄.   17 inp... C₁VH.   18–19 Quomodo percepto uiatico O₄.

he died and was lying on his bed, there came a certain man bearing a sick friend, who asked him to lay his hands on him in order that he might be healed. But the bishop said: 'If I could do anything in these matters, I should surely have done something for myself first of all.' The man who had come said again: 'I have been bidden to visit you for I received a command in my sleep: "Go to Bishop Augustine in order that he may place his hand upon him and he shall be made whole".' When Augustine heard this, he forthwith placed his hand upon the sick man and blessed him, and without delay sent the man back healed to his own home.'"

CHAPTER XXXIX. *Of his last commands to his brethren and how, when he had received the viaticum, he yielded up his spirit in prayer*

"Now", he said, "I entered in to him about the ninth hour of the day and I found him lying in a corner of his oratory, opposite to the altar; so I sat down by him. He did not say much because the weight of his affliction had lessened his power of speech. But when I asked him very earnestly what words he would bequeath and what last farewell he would leave the brethren, he began to utter a few weighty words about peace and humility, and about being on our guard against those who would rather fight such things than delight in them. He said: 'Always keep peace and divine charity amongst yourselves; and when necessity compels you to take counsel about your affairs, see to it most earnestly that you are unanimous in your counsels. But also have mutual agreement with other servants of Christ and do not despise those of the household of faith who come to you for the sake of hospitality, but see that you receive such, keep them, and send them away with friendly kindness, by no means thinking yourselves better than others who are your fellows in the same faith and manner of life.

20 *ins.* coelis O_8M. *ins.* celis O_3. emiserit O_4.   21 XI *in margin* V. 22 ads... C_1VH.   23 caepi C_1V. cepi $P_1C_3O_3$M.   24 egr... C_1VHC$_3O_3$M.   25 *gloss above* scilicet uale dicens H.   26 caep... C_1V. cepit C_3O_3.   27 set P_1O_3.   28 hiis O_3.   29 inquid O_3.   30 adt... C_1VH.   31 famulis C_1VHP$_1O_4$.   32 contemptui C_1VHC$_3O_3O_4$M. 33 cet... C_3O_3M.   34–35 *om.* O_4.   36 uite O_3.   37 XII *in margin* V.

illis autem[1] qui ab unitate [2]catholicae[4] pacis[3] uel pascha non suo tempore celebrando[5], uel peruerse[6] uiuendo aberrant, uobis sit nulla communio. Sciatisque et[7] memoria retineatis, quia si uos unum e duobus aduersis|

p. 112 eligere necessitas coegerit, multo plus diligo ut eruentes de tumulo tollentesque uobiscum mea ossa recedatis ab his[8] locis, et ubicunque[9] Deus[10] prouiderit incole[11] maneatis, quam ut[12] ulla ratione consentientes iniquitati, scismaticorum iugo colla subdatis. Catholica patrum statuta diligentissime [13]discere atque[14] obseruare contendite, ea quoque quae per meum ministerium uobis [15]diuina pietas instituta uitae[17] regularis[16] dare dignata est, exercete solliciti. Scio enim quia etsi quibusdam contemptibilis[18] uixi, post meum tamen obitum[19] qualis fuerim[20], quam mea doctrina non sit contempnenda[21] uidebitis. Haec[22] et his[8] similia uir Domini per interualla locutus, quia uis ut diximus infirmitatis possibilitatem loquendi ademerat[23], quietum expectatione[24] futurae[25] beatitudinis diem duxit ad uesperam, cui etiam peruigilem quietis[26] in precibus continuauit et noctem. At ubi consuetum nocturnae[27] orationis tempus aderat, acceptis a me

Greg. sacramentis salutaribus *exitum suum* quem iam uenisse
Dial. II. 37 cognouit *dominici corporis et sanguinis* communione *muniuit, atque* eleuatis *ad coelum*[28] oculis, extensisque in altum *manibus*, intentam supernis laudibus animam ad gaudia regni coelestis[29] emisit. |

p. 113 **XL.** *Quomodo iuxta prophetiam psalmi quem*[30] *eo moriente* [31]*cantauerunt, Lindisfarnenses*[33] *sint impugnati*[34]*, sed Domino iuuante*[35] *protecti*[32]

At ego statim[36] egressus nuntiaui[37] obitum eius fratribus, qui et ipsi noctem uigilando atque orando transegerant,

1 *ins. above* inquit V.   2–3 pac. cath. O₄.   4 cahtolice C₃.
5 cael... C₁VH.   6 peruersae O₉C₁O₄M.   7 *ins.* in P₁.
8 hiis O₃.   9 ubicumque C₁VH.   10 *om.* C₁.   11 incolae
P₁O₄M.   12 et C₁.   13–14 *om.* P₁.   15–16 inst. uit. reg. diu.
pie. O₄.   17 uite C₃O₃.   18 contemtibilis P₁.   19 *ins.* apertius
C₁VHP₁O₄.   20 *ins.* et C₁VHO₄.   21 contemnenda C₁P₁.

But have no communion with those who depart from the unity of the catholic peace, either in not celebrating Easter at the proper time or in evil living. And you are to know and remember that if necessity compels you to choose one of two evils, I would much rather you should take my bones from the tomb, carry them with you and departing from this place dwell wherever God may ordain, than that in any way you should consent to iniquity and put your necks under the yoke of schismatics. Strive to learn and to observe most diligently the catholic statutes of the fathers; and practise with zeal those rules of regular discipline which the divine mercy has deigned to give you through my ministry. For I know that, although I seemed contemptible to some while I lived, yet, after my death, you will see what I was and how my teaching is not to be despised.' These and like words the man of God said at intervals, because, as we have said, the stress of his sickness took from him the power of speaking much. He passed a quiet day in the expectation of his future bliss, until the evening; and he also continued quietly in prayer through a night of watching. But when the accustomed time of nightly prayer arrived, he received from me the sacraments of salvation and fortified himself for his death, which he knew had now come, by the communion of the Lord's body and blood; and, raising his eyes to heaven and stretching out his hands aloft, he sent forth his spirit in the very act of praising God to the joys of the heavenly Kingdom."

CHAPTER XL. *How, in accordance with the prophecy of the psalm which they had been singing when he died, the Lindisfarne brethren were attacked, but, with the help of the Lord, were protected*

"I immediately went out and announced his death to the brethren who had passed the night in watching and prayers,

22 hec O₃.   23 adimerat VH.   24 expectacione C₃.   25 future C₃O₃.
26 quietus C₁VH.   27 nocturne O₃.   28 cael...C₁V. cel... C₃O₃.
29 cael... C₁VHP₁O₄. cel... C₃O₃.   30 *om.* O₄.   31–32 cantati Lindisfarnenses impugnati sunt O₄.   33 Lindispharnenses VH.   34 inp... VH.
35 *ins.* iterum O₈O₃.   36 saltim O₃.   37 nunciaui C₃O₃M.

et tunc forte sub ordine nocturnae[1] laudis dicebant psalmum quinquagesimum nonum cuius initium[2] est,

Psa. 59. 3 *Deus reppulisti[3] nos et destruxisti nos, iratus es, et misertus es nobis.* Nec mora currens unus ex eis accendit duas candelas, et utraque tenens manu ascendit eminentiorem locum ad ostendendum fratribus qui in Lindisfarnensi monasterio manebant, quia [4]sancta illa[5] anima iam migrasset ad Dominum. Tale namque[6] inter se signum |

p. 114 sanctissimi eius obitus condixerant. Quod cum uideret frater qui in specula Lindisfarnensis[7] insulae[8] longe de[9] contra euentus eiusdem peruigil expectauerat horam, cucurrit citius[10] ad aecclesiam[11] ubi collectus omnis fratrum coetus[12] nocturnae[13] psalmodie[14] solennia[15] celebrabat[16]. Contigitque ut ipsi quoque intrante illo praefatum canerent psalmum, quod superna dispensatione procuratum rerum exitus ostendit. Siquidem sepulto uiro Dei tanta aecclesiam[17] illam temptationis[18] aura concussit, ut plures e fratribus loco magis cedere[19], quam talibus uellent interesse periculis. Attamen post annum ordinato in episcopatum Eadberto[20] magnarum uirtutum uiro[21], et in scripturis nobiliter erudito, maximeque[22] elemosinarum operibus dedito, fugatis perturbationum[23] procellis, ut scripturae[24]

Psa. 146. uerbis loquar, *aedificauit[25] Ierusalem[26]* id est uisionem
2, 3 pacis *Dominus, et dispersiones Israel congregauit. Sanauit contritos corde et alligauit contritiones[27] eorum,* ut palam daretur intelligi[28] quid significauerit psalmus cum cognita beati uiri morte cantatus, quia uidelicet post eius[29] obitum[30] repellendi ac destruendi essent eius ciues[31], sed[32] post ostensionem irae[33] minantis, coelesti[34] protinus miseratione

p. 115 refouendi. | Cuius sequentia quoque psalmi eidem sensui

1 nocturne C₃O₃.   2 inicium O₈O₃M.   3 repu... C₁VO₃O₄.
4–5 *om.* P₁.   6 nanque O₈O₄M.   7 Lyndisfarnensis O₃.
8 insule O₃.   9 e O₉.   10 cicius O₉.
11 eccl... C₁C₃O₃. aecclaes... V.   12 caetus V. cetus C₃O₃.
13 nocturne O₃.   14 psalmodiae C₁VHO₄M.   15 sollennia
C₁VHM. sollennia P₁. sollempnia O₈O₃.   16 cael... C₁O₈.
17 eccl... C₁C₃O₃.   18 temptacionis C₃.   19 caed... O₈.

and then were by chance, according to the order of lauds, singing the fifty-ninth psalm, which begins, 'O God, thou hast cast us off and hast broken us down; thou hast been angry and hast had compassion on us.' Without delay one of them ran out and lit two torches: and holding one in each hand, he went on to some higher ground to show the brethren who were in the Lindisfarne monastery that his holy soul had gone to be with the Lord: for this was the sign they had agreed upon amongst themselves to notify his most holy death. When the brother had seen it, who had been keeping watch and awaiting the hour of this event far away in the watch-tower of the island of Lindisfarne opposite, he quickly ran to the church where the whole assembly of the brethren were gathered together celebrating the office of the nightly psalm-singing; and it happened that they also, when he entered, were singing the above-mentioned psalm. This indeed was ordained by divine providence, as the event showed. For after the man of God was buried, so great a blast of trial beat upon that church that many of the brethren chose to depart from the place rather than be in the midst of such dangers. But after a year, when Eadberht had been ordained to the bishopric, a man of great virtues and wonderfully learned in the scriptures, and greatly given to works of charity, the storms and disturbances were driven away; then if I may use the words of Scripture, 'The Lord did build up Jerusalem'—that is the vision of peace—'and gathered together the outcast of Israel. He healed the broken in heart and bound up their wounds', so that it was then given to them openly to understand what the psalm meant which they were singing when they heard of the death of the blessed man—namely that, after his death, his fellow-citizens were to be cast off and broken down, but after the manifestation of the wrath that threatened them, they would forthwith be revived by the divine mercy. And he who examines it again will see how well the rest of the psalm agrees with the same sense.

20 Eadberhto C_1VHO$_4$. Eadberchto P$_1$.   21 uir. uirt. O$_4$.
22 maximaeque C$_1$.   23 perturbationis M.   24 scripture O$_3$.
25 edif... C$_3$O$_3$.   26 Hier... C$_1$VH.   27 contriciones O$_8$.
28 intellegi C$_1$VH.   29 *om.* O$_3$O$_4$.   30 *ins.* eius O$_4$.   31 ciues eius
C$_1$VHP$_1$O$_4$.   32 set O$_3$.   33 ire C$_3$O$_3$.   34 cael... C$_1$V. cel... C$_3$O$_3$.

concordare qui retractat intelligit[1]. Impositum[2] autem
naui uenerabile corpus[3] patris, ad insulam Lindisfarnensium retulimus[4]. Quod magno occurrentium agmine,
chorisque canentium susceptum est, atque[5] in aecclesia[6]
beati apostoli Petri ad[7] dexteram[8] altaris petrino in
sarcophago[9] repositum.

XLI. *Quomodo puer demoniacus* [10]*sit humo cui lauacrum*[12] *corporis*[13] *infusum est in aquam*[14] *missa*[15] *sanatus*[11]

Sed[16] nec defuncto ac tumulato Christi famulo signa
sanitatum quae uiuens exercuerat, cessare potuerunt. Contigit nanque[17] puerum quendam in territorio Lindisfarnensium atrocissimo demone[18] uexari, ita ut sensu rationis
p. 116 funditus amisso clamaret, | eiularet[19], et uel sua membra uel
quicquid[20] attingere posset, morsibus dilaniare niteretur.
Missus est ad energuminum presbiter[21] de monasterio.
Qui cum solitus fuisset[22] per exorcismi gratiam immundos[23]
fugare spiritus, huic tamen obsesso prodesse nil prorsus
ualebat. Unde dedit consilium patri illius, ut impositum[24]
carro puerum ad monasterium deferret, atque ad reliquias
beatorum martirum[25] quae ibi sunt, Dominum pro illo
precaretur[26]. Fecit ut monuerat, sed noluere sancti Dei
martires[27] ei petitam reddere sanitatem, ut quam celsum
inter se locum Cuthbertus[28] haberet ostenderent. Cum
ergo insanus ululando, ingemiscendo[29] [30]et [32]frendendo[31]
dentibus[33] nimio cunctorum uisus et auditus[34] horrore
concuteret, nec esset qui aliquod[35] remedii genus excogi-
tare quiuisset, tunc[36] ecce quidam de[37] presbiteris[38] edoctus
in spiritu per opitulationem beati patris Cuthberti[39] illum
posse sanari[40], uenit clanculo ad locum ubi nouerat
effusam fuisse aquam[41], qua corpus eius defunctum fuerat

1 intellegit C₁VH.   2 inp... C₁VHP₁C₃.   3 corp. uen. C₁VHP₁O₄.
4 *gloss above* relatum est H.   5 adque C₁.   6 eccl... C₁C₃O₃.
aecclaes... V.   7 in C₁VHO₄.   8 dextera C₁VHO₄. *ins.* parte
C₁VHO₄.   9 sarcofago C₁VHP₁C₃O₄.   10–11 humo de loco
lauacri corporis eius sumpta sit sanatus O₄.   12 lauachrum C₃.
13 *ins.* eius VHO₈O₃.   14 aqua VH.   15 misso VH.
16 set O₃.   17 namque C₁VHO₃.   18 daem... O₄.
19 heiularet C₁VH.   20 quicquit C₃O₃.   21 *in margin* Nomen

We placed the body of the venerable father on the ship, and bore it to the island of Lindisfarne. It was received by a great company who came to meet it and by choirs of singers, and placed in a stone sarcophagus in the church of the blessed apostle Peter on the right side of the altar."

CHAPTER XLI. *How a demoniac boy was healed by an infusion of some of that soil on which was poured the water wherein his body had been bathed*

But not even when the servant of Christ was dead and buried, did miracles of healing cease, such as he had wrought when he was alive. For it happened that a certain boy on the Lindisfarne estate was vexed by a most cruel demon, so that he had completely lost his reason, and cried out, howled and tried to tear in pieces with his teeth both his own limbs and whatever he could reach. A priest was sent from the monastery to the demoniac boy; and although he had been accustomed to put impure spirits to flight by the grace of exorcism, he could nevertheless do nothing to help the possessed boy; so he counselled the boy's father to put him on a cart and bear him to the monastery and to pray to the Lord for him at the relics of the blessed martyrs which are there. The father did as he was advised; but the holy martyrs of God would not grant him the cure that was sought, in order that they might show what a high place Cuthbert held amongst them. When, therefore, the insane boy horrified all who saw and heard him by howling, groaning and gnashing his teeth, and there was no one who could think of any kind of remedy, then one of the priests, being instructed in spirit that he could be healed by the help of the blessed father Cuthbert, came secretly to the place in which he knew that the water had been poured wherein his

presbiteri Tydi C₃O₃.   22 esset O₄.   23 inm... C₁VH.
24 inp... C₁VH.   25 martyrum HP₁C₃O₈.   26 deprec... O₃.
27 martyres HP₁O₈M.   28 Cudberhtus C₁V. Cuthberhtus H.
29 ingemescendo C₁VH.   30-31 *om.* C₁.   32-33 dent. frend. O₄.
34 audito O₃.   35 aliquid O₈.   36 tum C₁VHO₄.   37 e O₄.
38 *in margin* Nomen presbiteri Cinimund C₃O₃.   39 Cudberhti C₁V.
Cuthberhti H.   40 san. posse P₁.   41 aquam fu. C₃.

lotum, tollensque inde modicam humi particulam immisit[1] in aquam. Quam deferens ad patientem[2] infudit in ore eius. Quo horribiliter hiante, uoces diras ac flebiles

p. 117 emittebat. Statim autem ut attigit aquam, continu|it clamorem[3], clausit os, clausit et[4] oculos qui sanguinei et furibundi patebant, caput[5] et corpus totum[6] reclinauit [7]in requiem[8]. Qui etiam placido sopore noctem transegit, et mane de somno[9] simul et uesania consurgens, liberatum se a demonio[10] quo premebatur[11] beati Cuthberti[12] meritis et intercessione cognouit. Mirandum et bonis omnibus delectabile spectaculum, cum uideres filium cum patre sospitem loca sancta[13] circuire[14], sanctorum auxilio gratias sanissima mente referre, qui pridie prae[15] insania mentis nec se ipsum quis[16] esset uel ubi esset poterat agnoscere. Qui ubi tota fratrum[17] caterua astante[18], uidente, et congratulante ad reliquias martirum[19] genibus flexis dedit laudem Deo Domino et Saluatori nostro Iesu Christo, iam et ab hostis uerbere liberatus, et in fide firmior quam fuerat effectus, ad propria rediit. Ostenditur usque hodie fossa illa cui memorabile infusum est lauacrum quadrato scemate facta, ligno undique circundata[20], et lapillis intus impleta. Est autem iuxta aecclesiam[21] in qua corpus eius requiescit, ad partem meridianam. Factumque est ex eo tempore, ut plures sanitatum operationes per eosdem lapides uel eandem terram Domino donante fierent. |

p. 118   XLII. *Quomodo corpus ipsius post undecim[22] annos[23] [24]sine corruptione sit[26] repertum[25]*

Volens autem latius monstrare diuina dispensatio quanta in gloria uir sanctus post mortem uiueret, cuius ante[27] mortem[28] uita sullimis[29] crebris etiam miraculorum patebat

---

1 inm... C₁VHP₁.   2 pacientem C₃.   3 clamores C₁VHP₁O₄.
4 *om.* C₁VHO₄.   5 capud C₁C₃. *add* que P₁.   6 *ins.* in quietem O₄.
7-8 *om.* C₁VHO₄.   ·   9 sompno O₃.   10 daem... O₈O₄.
11 praem... O₈.   12 Cudberhti C₁V. Cuthberhti H.   13 san. loc. M.   14 *ins.* ac VH.   15 pre O₈.   16 qui C₁P₁C₃O₈O₃M. *changed from* qui V.   17 frat. tota O₃.   18 ads... C₁VH. ıss... P₁O₄.   19 martyrum HP₁O₈M.   20 circum... C₁VHO₄.

dead body had been washed. Taking a small particle of the earth, he put it in water and brought it to the patient, pouring it into his mouth, which was gaping wide in a horrible manner, and uttering fearful and lamentable cries. But as soon as he touched the water, he restrained his cries, shut his mouth and his eyes which before were wide open, bloodshot and furious, while his head and his whole body sank into repose. He also passed the night in quiet sleep, and in the morning awoke from both sleep and madness, realising that he had been freed from the demon by which he was oppressed through the merits and the intercession of the blessed Cuthbert. It was a wonderful and delightful spectacle for all good men, to see the son sound in health going round the holy places with his father and returning thanks with sound mind for the help of the saints, when the day before, on account of his insanity, he did not know who he was or where he was. And with the whole company of the brethren standing by, looking on and congratulating him, he gave praises to our Lord God and Saviour Jesus Christ as he knelt at the relics of the martyrs and, being freed from the scourge of the enemy and at length made stronger in faith than he was before, he returned home. The pit is still shown to-day into which that memorable bath of water was poured—it is in the form of a square with a border of wood on all sides and filled up with pebbles; and it is moreover near the church in which his body rests, on the south side. And it happened from that time, by God's permission, that many miracles of healing took place by means of those same stones or with some of that earth.

CHAPTER XLII. *How his body was found incorrupt eleven years afterwards*

But the divine Providence wished to show still further in what glory the holy man lived after his death, whose sublime life had been attested before his death by frequent signs and miracles;

21 eccl... $C_1C_3O_3$.   22 *ins.* sit VH. xi O_4. xi O_8.   23 *ins.* sit O_8O_3M.   24–25 incorruptum repertum est O_4.   26 *om.* VHO_8O_3M. 27 *om.* C_1.   28 *om.* VH. *ins. in margin ante* mortem H. 29 subl... $C_1VHC_3O_4M$.

indiciis, transactis sepulturae[1] eius annis undecim immisit[2] in animo fratrum[3] ut tollerent ossa illius, quae more mortuorum consumpto iam et in puluerem redacto corpore reliquo sicca inuenienda rebantur[4], atque in leui arca[5] recondita[6] in eodem quidem loco sed supra pauimentum dignae[7] uenerationis gratia locarent. Quod dum sibi placuisse Eadberto[8] antistiti[9] suo medio ferme quadragesimae[10] tempore referrent, annuit[11] consilio eorum,

p. 119 iussitque ut|die depositionis eius quae est tercia decima[12] kalendarum Aprilium hoc facere meminissent. Fecerunt autem ita. Et aperientes sepulchrum[13] inuenerunt corpus totum quasi adhuc uiueret integrum, et flexibilibus artuum compagibus multo dormienti quam mortuo similius. Sed et uestimenta omnia quibus indutum erat non solum intemerata, uerum etiam prisca nouitate et claritudine miranda parebant. Quod ubi uiderunt[14], nimio mox timore sunt et tremore perculsi, adeo ut uix aliquid loqui, uix auderent intueri miraculum quod parebat, uix ipsi quid agerent nossent[15]. Extremam autem indumentorum eius partem pro ostendendo incorruptionis signo tollentes, [16]nam quae[17] carni illius proxima aderant prorsus[18] tangere timebant, festinarunt referre antistiti[19] quod inuenerant, qui tum forte in remotiore a monasterio loco refluis undique maris fluctibus cincto solitarius manebat. In hoc etenim semper quadragesimae[20] tempus agere, in hoc quadraginta ante dominicum natale[21] dies in magna continentiae[22], orationis, et lacrimarum deuotione ducere consueuerat. In quo etiam uenerabilis praecessor eius Cuthbertus[23], priusquam Farne peteret sicut et supra

p. 120 docuimus,|aliquandiu[24] secretus Domino militabat. Attulerunt[25] autem et partem indumentorum, quae[26] corpus sanctum ambierant. Quae[26] cum ille et munera gratanter acciperet[27] et miracula libenter audiret, nam et ipsa indumenta quasi patris adhuc corpori circundata[28] miro

---

1 sepulture O₈O₃.   2 inm... C₁VHP₁.   3 *ins.* Dominus C₁H.
4 *gloss above* id est putabant H.   5 archa O₃.   6 *gloss above* id est recondenda VH.   7 digne C₁VO₃.   8 Eadberhto C₁VH.
9 antestiti VH.   10 quadragesime P₁C₃O₃.   11 adn... C₁VH.
12 xiii C₁VH. tertio decimo P₁. tertia decima O₈.   13 *ins.*

so He put it into the hearts of the brethren, eleven years after his burial, to take his bones—which they expected to find quite dry, the rest of the body, as is usual with the dead, having decayed away and turned to dust—and to put them in a light chest in the same place, but above the floor, so that they might be worthily venerated. When they reported their decision to Eadberht their bishop, about the middle of Lent, he consented to their plan and ordered them that they should remember to do it on the day of his burial, which is the 20th of March. They did so; and opening the sepulchre, they found the body intact and whole, as if it were still alive, and the joints of the limbs flexible, and much more like a sleeping than a dead man. Moreover all his garments, in which he had been clothed, were not only undefiled but seemed to be perfectly new and wondrously bright. When they saw this, they were struck with great fear and trembling, so that they hardly dared to say anything or even to look upon the miracle which was revealed, and scarcely knew what to do. But they took away the outer garments to show the miracle of his incorruption, for they did not dare to touch what was nearest the skin; and they hastened to relate to the bishop what they had found. He happened to be in solitude in a place remote from the monastery, surrounded on every hand by the sea at flood tide. Here he always used to spend the time of Lent as well as forty days before the Lord's birthday, in deep devotion, with abstinence, prayers and tears. In this place also his venerable predecessor Cuthbert, before he went to Farne, as we have explained above, for a while fought for the Lord in solitude. So they brought him part of the clothes that had enwrapped the holy body. He joyfully received these gifts and gladly listened to the story of the miracles, kissing the garments with great affection, as though they were still wrapped round the father's body; and he said: "Put fresh

eius C_3. sepulcrum O_3.   14 *ins.* fratres C_1VHO_4.   15 *gloss above* scilicet aut V.   16–17 namque C_1O_3.   18 prossus C_3. 19 antestiti VH.   20 quadragesime C_3O_3.   21 nathale O_3. 22 continencie O_3.   23 Cudberhtus C_1V. Cuthberhtus H.   24 aliquam-diu O_3.   25 adt... C_1.   26 que C_3O_3.   27 sus... O_4. 28 circum... C_1VHO_4.

deosculabatur affectu, Noua inquit[1] indumenta corpori
pro his[2] quae tulistis circundate[3], et sic reponite in thecam[4]
quam parastis. Scio autem certissime quia non diu uacuus
remanebit locus, qui tanta coelestis[5] miraculi uirtute
consecratus est. Et beatus est multum, cui in eo[6] sedem[7]
quiescendi Dominus uerae[8] beatitudinis auctor atque
largitor concedere dignatur. Adiecitque mirando quae[9]
quondam uersibus dixi, et ait,

Quis Domini expediet coelestia[10] munera dictis?
Uel paradisiacas quae capit auris opes?
Dum[11] pius infesti dirupto[12] pondere loeti[13],
Uiuere siderea[14] semper in arce dabit,
Mortua nunc tanto qui membra decorat honore,
Pulchroque[15] perpetuae[16] pignore[17] prestat opis[18],
Quamque beata[19] domus[20] sub tantoque[21] hospite[22] fulges,
Nescia quae[23] neui[24] lumine laeta[25] micas.
Nec[26] tibi difficile omnipotens mandare[27] sub aruo,
Ne deposta[28] uoret funera[29] labes[30] edax,
Qui triduo seruas coeti[31] sub[32] uiscere uatem[33], |

Lucis iter pandens, mortis[34] ab ore tuo,
Qui ignibus in mediis insontia membra[35] tueris[36],
Ne Hebreum[37] noceat Chaldea flamma decus,
[38]Dena quater renouas[39] per frigora plebis amictum,
Quae Fariam[40] fugiens inuia[41] seruat humum,
Qui rediuiua leuem formas[42] in membra fauillam,
Cum tremet angelicis, mundus ab axe tubis.

Haec[43] ubi multis cum lacrimis ac magna compunctione[44]
pontifex tremente lingua compleuit[44], fecerunt fratres ut
iusserat, et inuolutum nouo amictu corpus leuique in
theca reconditum supra pauimentum sanctuarii com-
posuerunt[44].

---

1 inquid O_3. 2 hiis C_3O_3. 3 circum... C_1VHO_4.
4 theca $C_1VHP_1O_4$. 5 cael... C_1V. cel... C_3O_3. 6 om. in eo O_3.
7 ins. in eo O_3. 8 uere O_3M. 9 que O_3. 10 cael... C_1VO_4.
cel... C_3P_1M. 11 cum O_8M. 12 disrupto C_1VH. 13 leti
P_1O_3. 14 syderia M. 15 gloss above scilicet qui H. pulcroque C_3.
pulchraque $P_1O_8O_4$. pulcraque O_3M. 16 perpetuas (s above V) H.
perpetue O_3. 17 pignora C_3M. 18 opes C_1VH. 19 gloss above
scilicet es H. 20 gloss above scilicet o H. 21 tanto quae $P_1O_8O_4M$.
22 cespite C_1. 23 gloss above scilicet et H. 24 gloss above id est
maculae VH. 25 leta O_3. 26 gloss above scilicet est H

garments around the body instead of those which you have taken away, and then replace it in the chest which you have prepared. For I know most assuredly that the place which has been consecrated by the virtue of so great a heavenly miracle will not long remain empty. And greatly blessed is he to whom the Lord, the author and giver of true blessedness, shall deign to grant a place of rest therein. And as he marvelled, he added words which I once put into verse, saying:

> What tongue the heavenly gifts of God can tell?
>   What ear the joys of Paradise can hear,
> Until within heaven's starry citadel
>   The Lord in mercy grants us to appear,
> Who now adorns these lifeless limbs with grace,
>   Fair pledges of good things that know no end?
> Blest home! how great a guest shines in this place,
>   Free from all stain, where joy and glory blend!
> With ease, Omnipotent, his blest remains,
>   Thou bidst corruption's gnawing tooth to spare—
> Thou, who couldst keep thy prophet in the reins
>   Of the great whale three days, then to the air
> Open a path to light, even from death's jaws—
>   Couldst save fair Hebrews from Chaldean flame,
> Or, forty years, fleeing from Egypt, cause
>   Thy people's robes to be renewed; the same
> Who, when the angelic trumpets shake this earth,
>   Shall from our ashes give our limbs rebirth."

When the bishop had finished saying these things with many tears and great emotion, the brethren did as he had commanded: they wrapped the body in a new garment and, putting it in a light chest, they placed it on the floor of the sanctuary.

27 *gloss above* id est imperari H.   28 depasta C₁VH. *gloss above* id est comesta VH. deposita P₁.   29 *gloss above* id est corpora mortua VH. 30 labis C₁P₁O₄.   31 caeti V. ceti O₃.   32 *gloss above* pro in H.   33 *gloss above* id est Ionam H.   34 *gloss above* scilicet et H.   35 *gloss above* id est trium puerorum VH.   36 *gloss above* id est defendebas VH.   37 Ebreum C₁VHP₁. Hebreorum M.   38–39 denaque terrae nouas C₁. *changed from* denaque terrae nouas V. *gloss above* scilicet et qui H.   40 uariam C₁VH. *gloss above* scilicet plebs hebreorum VH.   41 *gloss above* id est de uia VH. 42 *gloss above* id est futuri temporis H.   43 *ins.* et huiusmodi plura C₁VHO₄. hec O₃.   44 conp... C₁VH.

XLIII.   *Quomodo corpus Eadberti*[1] *in tumulo*[2] *uiri Dei*[4]
ponentes, sarcophagum[5] *illius desuper posuerunt*[6,][3]

Interea Deo dilectus antistes[7] Eadbertus[8] morbo corripitur
acerbo[9], et crescente per dies multumque | ingrauascente[10]
ardore languoris non multo post, id est pridie nonas Maias
etiam ipse migrauit ad Dominum, impetrato[11] ab eo
munere quod diligentissime[12] petierat, uidelicet ut non
repentina morte sed longa excoctus aegritudine[13] transiret
e corpore. Cuius corpus in sepulchro[14] beati patris
Cuthberti[15] ponentes, apposuerunt[16] desuper arcam[17] in
qua incorrupta eiusdem patris membra locauerant. Ubi
nunc usque si petentium fides exigat[18], *miraculo*rum signa
fieri non desinunt. Sed[19] et indumenta quae[20] sanctissimum
corpus eius uel uiuum uel sepultum uestierant a gratia
curandi non uacant.

p. 122

Greg.
Dial. II. 38

XLIV.   *Qualiter*[21] *aegrotus*[23] *ad tumbam eius*
[24] *orando sit*[25,][22] *curatus*[26]

Denique[27] adueniens transmarinis e partibus clericus qui-
dam reuerentissimi et sanctissimi | Wilbrordi[28] Clementis
Fresonum[29] gentis episcopi, dum aliquot[30] dies ibidem[31]
hospes moraretur, decidit in infirmitatem grauissimam,
ita ut inualescente per longum tempus aegritudine[32] iam
desperatus iaceret. Qui cum uictus dolore uideretur sibi
nec mori nec uiuere posse, inuento salubri consilio dixit
ministro suo, Obsecro perducas me hodie post celebratas[33]
missas, adorare ad corpus sacratissimum uiri Dei, erat
enim dies dominica[34], spero per gratiam intercessionis eius
his[35] cruciatibus eripiar, et uel sanatus ad praesentem[36]
uitam redeam, uel defunctus[37] perueniam ad aeternam[38].

p. 123

1 Eadberhti VH. *ins.* episcopi VHC₃O₃O₄M.   2–3 ipsius posuerunt O₄.   4 sancti O₉.   5 sarcofagum VH.
sarchophagum C₃.   6 posuerint VH.   7 antestis VH.
8 Eadberhtus C₁VH.   9 aceruo C₁.   10 ingrauescente
C₁VHP₁O₄M.   11 inp... C₁.   12 diligentisse O₉.   13 egr...
C₁VHP₁C₃O₃M.   14 sepulcro O₃.   15 Cudberhti C₁V. Cuthberhti H. Cutberti P₁.   16 adp... C₁VH.   17 archam O₃.

CHAPTER XLIII. *How the body of Eadberht was placed in the tomb of the man of God, and the sarcophagus of the saint placed upon it*

Meanwhile Bishop Eadberht, beloved of God, was attacked by a fell disease and, as the violence of the illness increased from day to day, he himself not long afterwards, that is on the sixth of May, went to be with the Lord: and thus he won from Him the boon that he sought most earnestly, namely, that he might depart from the body not by sudden death, but worn out by a long sickness. His body was placed in the sepulchre of the blessed father Cuthbert and they placed over it the chest in which they had put the incorrupt limbs of the same father; and there even now signs and miracles are not wanting, if an importunate faith seeks for them. Even the garments which covered his most holy body, whether in life or death, do not lack the grace of healing.

CHAPTER XLIV. *How a sick man was cured by praying at his tomb*

Now one of the clergy of the most reverend and holy Willibrord Clement, the bishop of the Frisians, who had come from across the sea, after staying there for some days as a guest, fell grievously ill so that his affliction increased for a long time and he lay in a hopeless condition. Overcome by the pain, he seemed as though he could neither live nor die, until, thinking of a profitable plan, he said to his servant: "I beseech you, lead me to-day, after mass has been celebrated, to worship at the most sacred body of the man of God"—for it was Sunday—"for I hope by virtue of his intercession to be freed from these tortures, so that either I may be restored to health in this present life, or else I may die and attain to eternal life." He did as he

18 *gloss above* id est retardat H.   19 set O_3.   20 que O_3.
21–22 ei. ad tum. aeg. or. sit O_4.   23 egrotus VHO_3M.   24–25 sit or. VH.
26 sanatus $C_3O_8O_3O_4M$.   27 *om*. C_1VH.   28 Uuilbrordi $C_1VHP_1O_4$.
29 Fresiorum P_1.   30 aliquod C_1H. *ins*. ibidem O_4.   31 *om*. O_4.
32 molestia $C_1VHP_1O_4$. egr... C_3O_3M.   33 cael... C_1.   34 dom.
dies O_8.   35 hiis O_3.   36 pre... O_4.   37 defuntus C_1.
38 eternam O_3. eterno C_3.

Fecit ille ut rogauerat[1], baculoque innitentem aegrotum[2] in aecclesiam[3] non paruo cum labore perduxit. Qui cum ad[4] sanctissimi ac Deo dilecti patris sepulchrum[5] genua curuaret, caput[6] in terram dimitteret[7], pro sua sospitate rogaret, tantas continuo uires suum corpus de incorrupto illius corpore accepisse persensit, ut absque labore[8] ipse ab oratione resurgeret, absque adminiculo uel ministri ducentis, uel baculi sustentantis ad hospicium[9] rediret. Qui post dies paucos roborata ad integrum uirtute, uiam qua[10] disposuerat peregit.

XLV.   *Quomodo paraliticus sit[11] per eius calciamenta[12] sanatus[13]* |

p. 124
Greg.
Dial.
IV. 16

Erat in monasterio quodam non procul inde posito[14] adolescens, *ea quam Greci paralisin[15] uocant* infirmitate, *omni membrorum officio destitut*us. Unde abbas ipsius sciens in monasterio Lindisfarnensi[16] medicos esse peritissimos, misit eum illo, rogans infirmanti si quid possent curationis conferrent. Qui cum suo quoque abbate et episcopo iubentibus diligenter illi assisterent[17], et quicquid nossent erga eum industriae[18] medicinalis impenderent[19], nichil[20] omnino proficere ualebant, quin potius[21] crescebat cotidie morbus et paulatim in deteriora uergebat[22], adeo ut excepto ore nullum [23]pene[25] membrum[24] posset loco

p. 125
mouere. Cunque[26]|a carnalibus medicis diu frustra laborantibus desperatus ac desertus iaceret, confugit ad diuinum[27] [28]medici coelestis[30,][29] auxilium[31], qui in ueritate petitus

Psa. 102. 3
propitius[32] fit omnibus iniquitatibus nostris[33], qui sanat[34] omnes languores nostros. Rogauit nanque[35] ministrum suum ut aliquam sibi portiunculam[36] de incorruptibilibus[37] sacri corporis afferret[38] exuuiis[39], quia crederet per huius se uirtutem ad gratiam sanitatis Domino largiente reuersurum. Qui consulto abbate attulit[40] calciamenta quae

1 rogatus fuerat O_4.   2 egr... $C_1VHP_1C_3O_3M$.   3 eccl... $C_1C_3O_3$.   4 *ins.* sepulchrum $C_1VHP_1O_4$.   5 *om.* $C_1VHP_1O_4$. sepulcrum O_3. 6 capud C_1. 7 demitteret O_3. 8 *om.* absque lab. M. 9 hospitium $C_1VHP_1C_3O_4M$.   10 quam VHO_4M.   11 *om.* $C_3O_8O_3O_4M$. 12 *ins.* sit $C_3O_8O_3O_4M$. 13 sanitatem receperit O_4. 14 positum C_1.   15 paralysin C_1V.   16 Lindisfarnensium C_1VHO_4. Lindisfarnensis M.   17 ads... C_1VH. asisterent P_1.

had asked and with no small effort led the sick man, leaning on his staff, into the church. He bent his knees at the sepulchre of the most holy father, beloved of God, and with head bowed to the ground he prayed for recovery; forthwith he felt that his body had received such strength from that incorrupt body, that he rose from prayer without any effort and, without the help of the servant who had led him or of the staff that had supported him, he returned to the guesthouse. After a few days, when his strength was completely restored, he set out on his intended journey.

CHAPTER XLV. *How a paralytic was healed by his shoes*

There was, in a certain monastery not far away, a youth who was deprived of all use of his limbs by the disease which the Greeks call paralysis. And his abbot, knowing that there were some very skilled physicians in the monastery at Lindisfarne, sent him there, asking whether they would if they could provide some cure for the sick man. On the command of both the abbot and the bishop, they diligently came to his aid and applied all the medical skill they possessed, yet they availed nothing at all; but rather his disease daily grew worse and gradually he became weaker, until he could hardly move a limb but only his mouth. But when he lay despaired of and deserted by the carnal physicians who had long laboured in vain, he fled to the divine aid of the heavenly Physician, Who, when sought in truth, "pardoneth all our iniquities and healeth all our diseases". He therefore asked his servant to bring him some portion of the incorruptible relics of the sacred body because he believed that, by the bounty of the Lord, he might return to the grace of health through its virtues. And having consulted the abbot, the servant brought the shoes which had been

18 industrie C_3O_3.   19 inp... C_1VH.   20 nihil C_1VH. nil P_1.
21 pocius C_3.   22 uertebat C_1VH.   23–24 memb. pene C_3. membrorum C_1M.   25 paene O_8.   26 cumque C_1VHO$_4$M.
27 auxilium C_1VHP$_1$O$_4$.   28–29 coelestis medici O_4.   30 cael... C_1V. cel... O_3.   31 *om.* C_1VHP$_1$O$_4$.   32 propicius P_1C_3.   33 *ins.* et C_1VHO$_4$.   34 nanat C_1.   35 namque C_1VHO$_3$.   36 portionem C_1VHP$_1$O$_4$.   37 incorrept... C_1.   38 adf... C_1VH.   39 *gloss above* id est spoliis uel uestimentis H.   40 adt... C_1V.

uiri Dei in sepulchro[1] pedes induerant, et ea pedibus dissolutis aegroti[2] circundedit[3]. Siquidem primo a pedibus eum paralisis[4] apprehenderat[5]. Fecit autem hoc noctis initio[6], cum tempus requiescendi adesset. Statimque ille

Kings
3. 20

placidum dimissus in soporem, procedente *intempestae*[7] *noctis silentio* coepit[8] alternis palpitare pedibus, ut palam qui uigilabant et uidebant ministri animaduerterent, quia donata per reliquias uiri sancti uirtute medicandi, sanitas optata a planta pedum per[9] caetera membra esset[10] transitura. At ubi consuetum in monasterio nocturnae[11] orationis signum insonuit, excitatus[12] sonitu resedit ipse. Nec mora solidatis interna uirtute neruis artuumque compagibus uniuersis, et[13] dolore fugato sanatum se esse

p. 126

intelligens[14] surrexit, et in[15] gratiarum|actionem[16] Domino omne nocturnae[11] siue matutinae[17] psalmodiae[18] tempus[19] stando persoluit. Mane autem iam facto processit ad aecclesiam[20] uidentibusque et congratulantibus uniuersis circuiuit[21] loca sancta orando, et suo saluatori sacrificium laudis offerendo. [22]Factum nanque[23] est ut pulcherrima rerum conuersione is qui dissolutus toto corpore illuc[24] in uehiculo perlatus fuerat[25], inde strictis firmatisque membris

Vergil
Aen. I,
203
Psa. 76.11

omnibus domum per se rediret incolumis. Unde *meminisse iuuat*, quia *haec*[26] est *inmutatio*[27] *dexterae*[28] *excelsi*, cuius memoranda ab initio[29] mirabilia mundo fulgere non cessant.

XLVI.   [30]*Qualiter anachorita Felgildus*[32] *operimento*[33]
parietis eius[34] [35]*a uultus tumore est*[37, 36] *mundatus*[38, 31]

Nec praetereundum[39] arbitror quid miraculi coelestis[40]

p. 127

etiam per reliquias sanctissimi oratorii in | quo pater uenerabilis solitarius Domino militare consueuerat, diuina pietas ostenderit. Quod tamen utrum meritis eiusdem

1 sepulcro O₃.   2 egr... C₁VHP₁C₃O₃M.   3 circum... C₁VHP₁O₄. 4 paralysis C₁V. 5 adp... C₁VH. 6 inicio C₃O₈M. 7 intempeste C₃O₃.   8 caep... C₁V. cep... C₃O₃M. cet... O₃. 9 in C₁VHP₁O₄.   10 ess. memb. C₁VHP₁.   11 nocturne O₃. 12 concitus C₁VH.   13 ac C₁VHP₁O₄.   14 intellegens C₁VH. 15 *om.* C₁VH.   16 actione P₁O₈.   17 matutine O₃.   18 psalmodie VO₃.   19 munus P₁. *above* uel munus O₈.   20 eccl... C₁C₃O₃.

upon the feet of the man of God in the sepulchre and put them upon the nerveless feet of the sick man—for the paralysis had first seized him in his feet. He did this at the beginning of the night when the time for rest had come; immediately the sick man fell into a calm sleep and, as the silence of the dead of night came on, first one and then the other foot began to twitch, so that the servants, who were awake and watching, clearly perceived that the desired restoration had been given by means of the healing powers of the saint's relics, and that it would pass from the soles of his feet throughout his other limbs. And when the accustomed signal for the nightly prayer sounded through the monastery, he was aroused by the sound and sat up. Without delay the sinews and all the joints of his limbs were strengthened with inward power, the pain was banished, and he rose up realising that he had been healed, and spent the whole time of the nightly psalm-singing, or mattins, standing up and giving thanks to the Lord. When morning came he went to the church and, with everyone watching and congratulating him, he went round the holy places praying and offering the sacrifice of praise to his Saviour. And it came to pass, by a most happy turn of events, that he who had been carried there on a cart with all his body paralysed, returned home by himself safe and sound, with all his limbs under control and strong. Hence it is profitable to remember that this is the unchanging right hand of the Most High, whose wonders, memorable from of old, cease not to shine in the world.

CHAPTER XLVI. *How the hermit Felgild was cured of a swelling in the face by the covering of his wall*

I think that I ought not to pass over a certain heavenly miracle which the divine mercy showed by means of the fragments of the most holy oratory in which the venerable father used to fight in solitude for the Lord. But whether this ought to be

21 circuit C_IVH. circumit O_4.   22–23 factumque C_IVHP$_I$O$_4$.   24 *om*. M.
25 erat C_IVHP$_I$.   26 hec P_IO$_3$.   27 imm... P_IO$_4$M. immutacio C_3.
28 dextere O_3.   29 inicio C_3O$_8$M.   30–31 Quomodo Felgildus operimento parietis eius sanatus sit O_4.   32 Felgeldus VHC$_3$.   33 *ins*. eius M.
34 *ins*. sit VH. *om*. eius M.   35–36 in uultu sit O$_8$O$_3$M.   37 *om*. C$_I$VHC$_3$.
38 *ins*. sit C$_3$.   39 preter... VHO$_8$O$_4$M.   40 cael... C$_I$V. cel... O$_3$C$_3$.

beati patris Cuthberti[1], an successoris eius Edilwaldi[2] uiri aeque[3] Deo dediti ascribendum[4] sit, internus arbiter[5] nouerit. Neque[6] aliqua ratio uetat utriusque merito factum credi, comitante etiam fide reuerentissimi patris Felgildi[7], per quem et in quo miraculum ipsum quod refero sanationis completum est. Ipse est qui tercius[8] eiusdem loci et militiae[9] spiritualis[10] heres hodie maior septuagenario in magno uitae[11] futurae[12] desiderio terminum praesentis[13] expectat. Cum ergo uiro Domini Cuthberto[14] ad coelestia[15] translato Edilwaldus[16] eiusdem insulae[17] et monasterii colonus existere coepisset[18], qui et ipse multos antea per annos in monachica[19] conuersatione probatus rite gradum anachoreticae[20] sullimitatis[21] ascenderat[22], repperit quia parietes praefati oratorii qui tabulis minus diligenter[23] coaptatis erant compositi, longa essent uetustate[24] dissoluti, et separatis ab inuicem tabulis facilem turbinibus praebuissent[25] ingressum. Sed[26] uir uenerabilis qui coelestis[27] aedificii[28] magis quam terreni decorem quaerebat[29], sumpto foeno[30] uel argilla uel quicquid

p. 128 huiusmodi materiae[31] repperisset[32], stipaue|rat[33] rimulas, ne cotidianis[34] imbrium siue uentorum iniuriis ab orandi retardaretur instantia. Cum haec[35] igitur Edilwaldus[36] ingressus locum uidisset, postulauit a frequentantibus se fratribus pelliculam uituli[37], eamque illo[38] in angulo quo et ipse et praedecessor[39] eius Cuthbertus[40] sepius orans stare uel genuflectere solebat, clauis affixam[41] uiolentiis[42] procellarum opposuit[43]. At postquam ipse quoque expletis ibi[44] duodecim[45] continuis annis gaudium supernae[46] beatitudinis intrauit, ac tercius[47] locum eundem Felgildus[48] incolere[49] coepit[50], placuit reuerentissimo Lindisfarnensis

---

1 Cudberhti C₁V. Cuthberhti H. Cutberti P₁. Cuthberthi M.
2 Aediluualdi C₁VH. Adeluuoldi P₁. Eadiluualdi O₄.   3 eque O₃.
4 ads... C₁VHC₃. ass... O₄.   5 arbitrer C₁.   6 nec O₃.   7 Felgeldi
C₁VH.   8 tertius C₁VHP₁O₄M.   9 milicie O₃M.   10 spiritalis
C₁VH.   11 uite C₃O₃.   12 future C₃O₃.   13 pre... O₄.
14 Cudberhto C₁V. Cuthberhto H. Chutberto P₁.   15 cael... C₁V.
cel... C₃O₃. ins. regna C₁VHP₁O₄.   16 Aediluualdus C₁VH.
Oetheluualdus P₁. Ediluualdus C₃. Eadiluualdus O₄.   17 insule C₃O₃.
18 caep... C₁V. cep... P₁C₃O₃.   19 monacica C₃.   20 anachoretice
O₃.   21 subl... C₁VHC₃O₄.   22 ascendebat C₁VHP₁O₄.

ascribed to the merits of the same blessed father Cuthbert or
of his successor Aethilwald, a man equally devoted to God,
He knows who judges the heart. Nor does any reason forbid
us to believe that it was wrought by the merits of both,
accompanied also by the faith of the most reverend father
Felgild, through whom and in whom the miracle of healing,
to which I refer, was wrought. He is the third heir of that
dwelling and of that spiritual warfare and to-day, more than
seventy years of age, he awaits the end of the present life,
eagerly longing for the life to come. Now when Cuthbert
the man of God had been translated to the heavenly kingdom,
Aethilwald began to inhabit the island and the hermitage, after
having for many years previously been tested by the monastic life, and having duly risen to the heights of the hermit life.
He found that the walls of that same oratory which had been
made of planks not too carefully joined together, had been
loosened through age, and the planks had come apart and
allowed easy access to stormy winds. But the venerable
Cuthbert who sought the splendour of a heavenly mansion
rather than of any earthly habitation, used to take straw or
clay or whatever material of that kind he could find and stuff
up the cracks, so that he might not be hindered from the
fervour of his prayers by the daily violence of rain or wind.
When therefore Aethilwald entered the place and saw this,
he asked the brethren who used to visit him for the skin of
a calf, and fixed it with nails in the corner in which he and his
predecessor Cuthbert used most often to stand or kneel in
prayer; and so he kept out the violence of the storms. But after
he had spent twelve years there continuously and had entered
upon the joy of heavenly bliss, and Felgild the third hermit had
begun to inhabit this place, Eadfrith the most reverend bishop

23 O_4 breaks off here.   24 ins. et C_1VH.   25 pre... O_8.   26 set O_3.
27 cael... C_1V. cel... O_3.   28 edi... C_3O_3M.   29 quer... C_1O_3.
30 feno C_3O_3.   31 materie C_3O_3.   32 repperiret C_1VHP$_1$.   33 stipasset
C_1VHP$_1$.   34 cotidianas C_1.   35 om. P$_1$. hec O_3.   36 Aediluualdus C_1VH.
Oidilualdus P$_1$. Ediluualdus C_3.   37 uitulae C_1.   38 om. P$_1$.   39 prode...
C_1VH.   40 Cudberhtus C_1V. Cuthberhtus H. Cutbertus P$_1$.   41 adf...
C_1VH.   42 uiolentus $O_9C_3P_1$.   43 obp... C_1VH.   44 sibi M.
45 xii C_1VH. x̄ī P$_1O_8$.   46 superne O_3.   47 tertius C_1VHP$_1$.
48 Felgeldus C_1VH.   49 incolare C_1VH.   50 caep... C_1V. cep... C_3O_3.

aecclesiae[1] pontifici Eadfrido[2] dissolutum uetustate oratorium illud a fundamentis restaurare. Quod dum esset opus expletum, et multi deuota religione a beato Christi athleta Felgildo[3] postularent, quatinus aliquam illis particulam de reliquiis sancti ac Deo dilecti patris Cuthberti[4] siue successoris eius Edilwaldi[5] dare debuisset, uisum est illi diuisam particulatim memoratam pelliculam petentibus dandam, sed daturus eam aliis prius in se ipse quid haec[6] uirtutis haberet expertus est. Habebat nanque[7] uultum deformi rubore simul et tumore perfusum, cuius quidem

p. 129 futuri in eo languoris | et prius cum adhuc communi inter fratres uita degeret aspicientibus in facie eius signa patebant. At cum in solitudine remotus minorem corpori cultum[8], maiorem adhiberet continentiam, et quasi diutino carcere inclusus, rarius uel fotu[9] solis uel aeris uteretur[10] afflatu, excreuit languor in maius, faciemque totam tumenti ardore repleuit. Timens ergo ne forte magnitudine huiusmodi infirmitatis solitariam deserere uitam, et communem necesse esset conuersationem repetere, fideli usus est praesumptione, sperauitque se illorum ope curandum, quorum se mansionem tenere, et uitam gaudebat imitari. Mittens enim praefatae partem pelliculae[11] in aquam, ipsa aqua lauit faciem suam[12], statimque tumor omnis qui hanc obsederat et scabies foeda[13] recessit, iuxta quod mihi[14] et primo religiosus quidam presbiter[15] huius monasterii Gyruensis[16] indicauit, qui se uultum illius et prius tumentem ac deformem nosse, et postea mundatum[17] per fenestram manu palpasse referebat, et ipse postmodum Felgildus[18] retulit, astruens quia res ipsa ita ut presbiter narrauerat esset completa[19], et[20] quod ex eo tempore cum inclusus per multa annorum curricula maneret ut prius immunem[21] ab huiusmodi molestia uultum semper

---

1 eccl... $C_1C_3O_3$.   2 Eafrido M.   3 Felgeldo C_1VH.
4 Cudberhti C_1V. Cuthberhti H. Cutberti P_1.   5 Aediluualdi
C_1VH. Oidilualdi P_1. Ediluualdi C_3.   6 hec C_3O_3.   7 namque
C_1VHP$_1O_3$.   8 *gloss above* scilicet et VH.   9 potu C_1.

of the church at Lindisfarne decided to restore the oratory from
its foundations, since it was falling to pieces through age.
When the work was finished, many devout persons asked
Felgild, the blessed warrior of Christ, to give them some portion
of the relics of the holy father Cuthbert beloved of God, or of
his successor Aethilwald. He determined to give this same skin
to those who asked him, dividing it in pieces. But before he
gave it to others, he first tried upon himself what virtue it had.
Now his face was covered with a disfiguring redness and swelling, and even before, when he had lived a communal life
among the brethren, the symptoms of this illness were clearly
seen upon his face. But when he went into solitude he practised
greater abstinence and took less care of his body, and being
shut up as it were in long captivity, he enjoyed more rarely
the warmth of the sun and the breath of the wind; thus his
affliction increased, and the inflamed swelling covered the whole
of his face. And fearing lest perhaps, owing to the heaviness
of his affliction, he would have to give up his solitary life and
take to communal life again, he hoped with the boldness of
faith to be cured by the aid of those whose dwelling he rejoiced
to inhabit, and whose manner of life he rejoiced to imitate. So
he put a part of this same skin into water and washed his face
with it, and immediately all the swelling which had covered
it and the loathsome scab departed. This was first told me
by a certain devout priest of this monastery at Jarrow who
affirmed that he first knew Felgild's face in its swollen and
deformed state, and afterwards had felt it with his hands
through the window after it was healed. And Felgild himself
related it afterwards, adding that it took place as the priest
had narrated, and that from that time although he remained
shut up as before for many years, his face had always been

10 *gloss above* scilicet cum VH. 11 pellicule O8O3. 12 suam fac.
C1VHP1. 13 feda C1VP1C3O3. 14 michi M. 15 *in margin*
Nomen presbiteri Ceolberct C3. *in margin* Nomen presbiteri Ceolbercht O3.
16 Gyruuensis C1VH. Giruensis P1O3. 17 mundatam C1VH. 18 Felgeldus C1VH. 19 expleta C1VHP1O8O3M. 20 ex C1. 21 inm... C1VH.

p. 130 haberet, agente | gratia Dei omnipotentis, quae et in praesenti multos et in futuro[1] cordis et corporis nostri *languores sanare* consueuit, satiansque[2] *in bonis desiderium* nostrum, sua nos *in* perpetuum *misericordia et miseratione coronat*[3].

Psa. 102.
4, 5

[4]Explicit liber de uita et miraculis sancti[6] Cudberhti[7] Lindisfarnensis aecclesiae[8] episcopi feliciter. Amen[9, 5].

1 *ins.* omnes C₁VHP₁.   2 sac... C₃O₃M.   3 *ins.* Amen C₁VH.
4-5 *om.* O₉O₄.   6 beatissimi patris C₃O₈O₃M.   7 Cuth-

free from this affliction, through the grace of Almighty God who, in this present age, is wont to heal many, and, in time to come, will heal our diseases of mind and body; for he satisfies our desire with good things and crowns us for ever "with lovingkindness and tender mercies".

End of the book of the life and miracles of St Cuthbert, Bishop of Lindisfarne. Amen.

berhti VH. Cuthberti P₁C₃O₃M.   8 eccl... O₃.   9 *om.* C₃O₈O₃M.

NOTES

NOTES TO THE ANONYMOUS LIFE

✠

BOOK I

CHAPTER I (p. 60)

Prologue. The Prologue follows the regular pattern of the saints' lives written on the Antonian model. The writer expresses his unworthiness and incapacity to write the life of the holy man, but undertakes to do it at the express command of some superior. The tradition goes back finally to Athanasius' *Life of Antony* freely translated from the Greek into Latin by Evagrius, presbyter and later bishop of Antioch in the late fourth century, and to the *Life of St Martin* by Sulpicius Severus of about the same date. These lives, together with Jerome's *Life of St Paul*, became models for later lives of saints for several centuries, all over Western Europe. Thus Paulinus, in his prologue to the *Life of St Ambrose*, declares that he has been asked to write it in the style in which Athanasius and Jerome wrote the *Lives of St Antony and St Paul*, and in which Severus wrote the *Life of St Martin* (*Sancti Ambrosii Opera*, ed. Ballerini, Milan, 1883, vol. VI, col. 885).

The Prologue is a literary curiosity. Chapters 1 and 2 are simply a mosaic of borrowings of which, except for the proper names, not a word is original. For sources of borrowings see text. The greater part of the Prologue was afterwards borrowed by Eddius in his prologue to the *Life of St Wilfrid* (W. Levison, *Script. rerum Merov.* VI, pp. 181 f.; *Eddius*, p. 150).

The use of the *Epistola Victorii* is interesting. This letter is the introduction to Victorius' Paschal Cycle, which was used by the Roman church for fixing the date of Easter until the improved cycle of Dionysius Exiguus came into use. It shows that this cycle was known in the north fairly early, and there is some evidence of its use in the Celtic church at a much earlier date (cf. *O.E.N.* pp. 24 n. and 48 n.). The whole preface is an interesting illustration of Levison's statement that the historical learning of the seventh century in Northumbria sprang from two roots—chronology and hagiography (*Bede, L.T.W.* p. 112).

Eadfrith. Eadfrith became bishop of Lindisfarne in 698 after the death of Eadberht. Symeon describes him as a pious and worthy bishop (Symeon, *H.D.E.* vol. I, p. 38). He was greatly devoted to the memory of Cuthbert, for it was he, too, who encouraged Bede to write the *V.P.* and to whom the Prologue is addressed. He restored Cuthbert's oratory on Farne Island (*V.P.* c. 46). His name is also associated with the famous Lindisfarne Gospels (B.M. Cott. Nero D.iv), for in the tenth-century colophon which purports to be written by the priest Aldred, we read that Eadfrith wrote this book, and there seems little doubt that if he did he must have done the illumination too (*A.E.E.* vol. v, pp. 341 ff. and J. Brønsted, *Early English Ornament*, London, 1924, p. 92 n.). If this is so, Eadfrith must have been a very remarkable calligraphist (but see R. A. S. Macalister, *The Colophon of the Lindisfarne Gospels*, Essays and Studies presented to William Ridgeway, Cambridge, 1913, pp. 299–305). St Columba too was writing a psalter when he died; he had also made a copy of Finnian's gospel secretly, which is said to have led to his leaving Ireland (*Vit. Col.* Reeves, III, c. 23, pp. 233 and 248 ff.). He had also written a gospel with his own hand which he left to St Berach (*L.I.S.* II, p. 39). When Eadfrith died in 721 he was buried near St Cuthbert, and his body, together with that of Eadberht, the bones of Aidan, or rather such as had been left by Colman, the head of Oswald and various other relics were taken with the body of St Cuthbert in its wanderings through Northumbria after 875 (see *V.P.* c. 39n. p. 357). In 1104, when Cuthbert's body was translated to the Chapel of the Nine Altars, Durham, Eadfrith's remains were placed in another part of the church (Symeon, *H.D.E.* I, pp. 57, 252; see also *D.N.B. s.v.* Eadfrith).

CHAPTER III (p. 64)

V.P. c. 1, *V.M.* c. 1.

Tumma or **Trumwine.** Tumma or, as he is called in the *V.P.*, Trumwine was bishop of the Picts with his seat apparently in the monastery at Abercorn. After Ecgfrith, king of Northumbria, was defeated by the Picts at Nechtansmere in 685, Trumwine had to retire to Whitby (*V.P.* c. 30n. p. 353), where he lived on for a long time as a simple monk and where he died and was buried (*H.E.* IV, 26). This was presumably some time before the *V.A.* was written (i.e. 705 at the latest), as the phrase "sanctae memoriae" shows (though occasionally this phrase is used of a living person, cf. *Eddius*, pp. 46, 122, 140, 167). He accompanied King Ecgfrith on a special journey to Farne in 684 to persuade the unwilling Cuthbert to accept the office of bishop (*V.A.* IV, 1; *V.P.* c. 24). It may be as Plummer suggests (II, p. 268) that it was on this occasion that Trumwine heard the story told in this chapter. On the subject of eyewitnesses, see Introduction, pp. 12 f. Tumma is a hypocoristic or intimate form of the name Trumwine (Redin, p. 72).

Elias. Bede does not mention this Lindisfarne priest. The name does not occur in the Liber Vitae. Judging by the latter and by the *Ecclesiastical History*, Scripture names seem to have been very sparingly used in the north at this time, with the single exception of the name John.

Games. St Wulfstan was also good at games, and it was while playing games that he was called to a life of greater devotion (*Vita Wulfstani*, ed. R. R. Darlington, R.H.S. 1928, p. 6).

Early prophecy of bishopric. The early prophecy of how a saintly child is in due course to become a bishop is fairly common in hagiographical writings. It was prophesied of St Samson of Dol in his youth (*St Samson of Dol*, p. 16). Cf. also *Vita Eligii*, I, 2 (*Script. rerum Merov.* IV, p. 670) and Anso, *Vita Ursmari* (*ibid.* VI, p. 454). Rufinus (*Historia Ecclesiastica*, X, 15, ed. T. Mommsen and E. Schwartz. *Eusebius, Werke* II, Leipzig, 1908, p. 90) tells how Athanasius was recognised as a bishop, while still a boy, by some of his playmates.

CHAPTER IV (p. 66)

V.P. c. 2, *V.M.* c. 2.

Cuthbert's knee. Cuthbert was apparently suffering from synovitis or water on the knee, due perhaps to some injury. Poulticing would be the usual remedy a doctor would still recommend. But for another explanation see note on *V.P.* c. 37, p. 355.

Angelic ministrations. The angels in the Egyptian deserts helped the anchorites while they were alive, warned them of the approach of death, and received their souls after death (cf. *H.L.* cc. 8, 29, 34, 71). St Martin too was frequently visited by angels (Sulp. Sev. *Dial.* II, 13; Halm, p. 196). St Antony was caught up to the third heaven by angels (*Vit. Ant.* c. 37; Migne, LXXIII, col. 155) and the same tradition is found in the Irish lives too, where stories of angelic assistance abound. We read, for instance, that Mochuda of Rahen had a convent whose number was "seven and seven score and seven hundred, and every third man among them conversed with angels" (*L.I.S.* II, p. 300). In Adamnan's *Life of Columba* a whole section is devoted to angelic ministrations. Angels play an important part in the life of Cuthbert. He saw angels taking the soul of Aidan and of Hadwald to heaven (I, 5; IV, 10); he received an angel into the monastery at Ripon and was fed with angelic food (II, 2); he was assisted to build his hut on Farne by angels (*V.P.* c. 17); and they ministered to him during his last days on Farne Island. Plummer (*V.S.H.* I, p. clxxxi) points out that in the Irish legends it is clear that angels have taken the place of the fairies of the older religion. It may be true to a lesser extent in the English lives, though the literary influences are probably enough to account for most of the stories of angelic ministrations.

CHAPTER V (p. 68)

V.P. c. 4, *V.M.* c. 4.

Feeding flocks. Many saints kept sheep in their youth, such as Patrick, Walaricus, Simeon Stylites and Coemgen. It does not necessarily follow that Cuthbert was of peasant extraction (see *V.P.* c. 6n. p. 344).

The soul of Aidan. Visions of souls being carried to heaven by angels are common in the lives of the saints. A priest in Ireland saw the soul of Cedd, with a company of angels, taking the soul of Chad to heaven (*H.E.* IV, 3; for other instances, see *H.E.* III, 8; IV, 9). A whole series of visions of this sort is related in Adamnan's *Life of Columba*, and in almost every case these visions are of the same type. The soul of the dead or dying person is surrounded by a band of angels and is often enclosed in a globe of fire, as here, while the one to whom the vision is revealed is invariably absent at a greater or less distance from the death-bed (see further *Bede, L.T.W.* pp. 213 ff.). Perhaps the prototype is the vision seen by Antony of the death of Amon, related in the Evagrian *Life of Antony* (*Vit. Ant.* c. 32; Migne, LXXIII, col. 153). Antony learns almost immediately of the death of Amon. Bede says that Cuthbert heard the next morning, while the *V.A.* makes it a few days afterwards. In the similar story told by Gregory of Tours concerning the vision granted to Bishop Severinus of Cologne of the death of St Martin, the death occurred "the same day and hour" as Severinus heard the heavenly choir (Gregory of Tours, *Virtutes Martini*, I, 4; *Script. rerum Merov.* I, p. 590). The story occurs very often in MSS after Sulpicius Severus' *Life of St Martin* and forms part of the collection known as the Martinelli (*B.H.L.* II, 5621). See H. Delehaye, *Anal. Boll.* XXXVIII, 1920, pp. 11 ff.

Aidan. Aidan was the first bishop of Lindisfarne. Bede gives us practically all the information we possess about this wise and gentle saint. He was a monk of Iona (*H.E.* III, 3) and was sent at the request of King Oswald to reconvert Northumbria after the disastrous invasion of Penda. He was consecrated bishop probably in 635. He fixed his see at Lindisfarne, probably because of its likeness to Iona and the fondness of the Irish missionaries for out-of-the-way sites (*H.E.* II, p. 126), and also because he did not wish to associate his mission with that of Paulinus by placing his seat at York. His teaching was most successful. He became the close friend of the saintly King Oswald and, after the death of the latter in 642, he continued to be friendly with Oswini, king of Deira. Oswini was murdered with the connivance of Oswald's brother Oswiu, king of Bernicia. Aidan survived his patron only twelve days, dying on August 31st, 651, at Bamburgh (*H.E.* III, 3, 5, 6, 16, 17). It is interesting to note that Aidan was accustomed to retire to the island of Farne for meditation, so that Cuthbert was following the tradition of the earlier saint. Bede speaks in the highest terms of Aidan's beauty of person and character and of his wonderful humility. He was buried at Lindisfarne, his body being translated to the right side of the altar, that is, presumably, the south side, when the larger church was built. Part of his relics were carried away by Colman after the Synod of Whitby in 664. Part of them afterwards accompanied the body of St Cuthbert in its wanderings and finally reached Durham in 995 (see note to *V.P.* c. 39, p. 357). *Aidanus* is equivalent to the Irish name *Aedhán*, the diminutive of *Aedh*.

R. Leader. Bede does not mention the scene of the incident. The Leader falls into the Tweed two miles below Melrose (cf. W. J. Watson, *Celtic Place-Names of Scotland*, Edinburgh, 1926, p. 471).

In populari uita. The same phrase occurs in Bede's *Epistle to Ecgbert*, par. 5. "Popularis" comes from "populus" in the sense of "lay" or "secular", just as λαϊκός comes from λαός (*H.E.* II, p. 380). Compare also the Irish term "tuatha" = "lay", derived from "tuath", a division of land.

CHAPTER VI (p. 70)

V.P. c. 5, *V.M.* c. 6.

Chester-le-Street, "Kuncacester". (See other forms in the text and cf. Mawer, pp. 43–4.) The name occurs in *V.A.* only. A mistaken reading of the Bollandists made earlier editors guess Lanchester as the scene of the miracle, though it is only fair to note that C. J. Bates had seen the Trier and Arras MSS (T and A) and had given the correct forms of all the place-names in the *V.A.* in an article entitled, "The Names of Persons and Places mentioned in the early Lives of St Cuthbert" (*Arch. Ael.* N.S. XVI, 1894, pp. 81 ff.). This story emphasises the fact that a large part of County Durham was deserted country until well on into the Anglo-Saxon period. The rarity of Anglian pagan burials in the county emphasises the same fact. The writer of the *Vita S. Oswaldi* in the eleventh century declares that the land between the Tees and the Tyne was in the sixth century one vast deserted region and haunt of wild beasts (*Vita S. Oswaldi*, c. 1; Symeon, *H.D.E.* I, p. 339). Cuthbert was doubtless travelling along the Roman road.

Miraculous food. The simple story told by the Lindisfarne monk is much heightened in the corresponding account in the *V.P.* Here he is merely weather-bound; in the *V.P.* he is being specially honoured by God for his insistence on observing the Friday fast. The story is reminiscent of one told by Sulpicius Severus (*Dial.* I, 11; Halm, p. 163) of the Egyptian abbot who went to visit a recluse near the Nile, and on going into his cell found a basket of palm branches, divinely provided, full of warm bread, hanging fixed to the door post. The story belongs to a type which may be called the miraculous provision of food. Other examples in the life of Cuthbert are the provision of food by the angel at Ripon (II, 2), of dolphin flesh (II, 4) and of the fish provided by the eagle (II, 5). All these miracles are most likely reminiscences of such scriptural stories as the food provided for Elijah by the ravens, or the feeding of the multitudes, or the angels ministering to our Lord in the desert. For other possible sources see *Bede, L.T.W.* p. 210.

Shepherds' dwellings. Stevenson in his note on this passage (Stevenson, *C.H.* p. 554) very appositely quotes Camden on the subject of these shepherds' huts: "All over the Wasts, as they call them, as well as in Gillesland, you see as it were the ancient Nomades; a Martial sort of people, that from April to August lye in little Hutts (which they call Sheals or Shealings) here and there dispers'd among their flocks" (Camden's *Britannia*, ed. E. Gibson, London, 1695, col. 851).

CHAPTER VII (p. 72)

Wearying the reader. It was the custom in writing saints' lives to apologise for not relating the whole of the miracles of the saint on the plea that the hearer or reader might be wearied. Sulpicius, for instance, does so in the passage our author has borrowed in I, 2. In the first preface to Adamnan's *Life of St Columba* a similar plea is put forward. (Cf. also John 21. 25.)

Military service. This is the only reference in the *V.A.* to Cuthbert's military service. We learn nothing of it in Bede nor of his vision of the reeve's soul carried to heaven. It makes it highly probable that Cuthbert did not enter the monastery until he had reached at least the age of seventeen. He was perhaps fighting in Oswiu's army against Penda.

BOOK II

CHAPTER I (p. 74)

Cuthbert's asceticism. This description of Cuthbert's asceticism is borrowed verbally from the Evagrian *Life of Antony*. It need not therefore be taken too seriously. But, as other incidents in Cuthbert's life show, he was given to asceticism, though not to the wilder forms common among the Egyptian hermits, and described in the *Vitae Patrum* or the *Lausiac History* of Palladius. These ascetic excesses were also prevalent in the Irish monasteries through the influence of Lérins and the Gallo-Roman foundations of St Martin. Fasting was carried to excess amongst the Egyptians. St Antony took food every two or four days only (*Vit. Ant.* c. 3; Migne, LXXIII, col. 128). On the other hand, judging by other passages in the same life (e.g. cc. 25, 27), the saint seems to have been aware of the dangers of protracted fasting and to have warned his followers against it. Another form of asceticism consisted in going without sleep. Macarius of Alexandria tried to do without sleep altogether and only gave it up when he began to go mad (*H.L.* c. 18). The same hermit spent six months in a marsh infested by mosquitoes. He looked so hideous on his return that he was recognised by his voice only (*loc. cit.*). Eustathius' body was so dried up that the sun shone through his bones.

In Ireland fasts were prolonged for two, three or four days (Gougaud, *C.C.L.* p. 98 and n.). Adamnan of Coldingham abstained from food and drink except on Sundays and Thursdays (*H.E.* IV, 25). Other forms of austerity were praying, standing up to the neck in water (II, 3 and n. p. 319), while some allowed worms to devour their flesh (*V.S.H.* Introd. p. xcvi, n. 14). Finnchua of Bri Gobann remained suspended on iron hooks for seven years (Ryan, *Monast.* p. 400). The crown of martyrdom was denied to the Irish saints until the Norse incursions at the end of the eighth century. But, instead, they sought to win the martyr's crown by extreme asceticism. In a seventh-century Irish homily, the writer describes three kinds of martyrdom: white martyrdom, which implies abandoning everything for God's sake; blue martyrdom, freeing oneself from evil desires by means of fasting and labour; and red martyrdom, enduring death for Christ's sake (Ryan, *Monast.* p. 197; see also A. Wilmart, "Analecta Reginensia", *Studi e Testi*, LIX, Rome, 1933, pp. 56, 78). Gregory also makes the distinction between those who suffered outward and those who suffered inward martyrdom (Greg. *Dial.* III, 26, p. 197. See further W. Levison, "Die echte und die verfälschte Gestalt von Rimberts Vita Anskarii", *Zeitschrift des Vereins für Hamburgische*

Geschichte, XXIII, 1919, p. 114 and n. 1). Perhaps this is why our author twice refers to the saint after his death as martyr (IV, 15; IV, 17). It is interesting to note that in Wales, the form Merthyr (martyr) is often found in place-names dedicated to saints who were not martyrs such as Merthyr Cynog, Merthyr Tydfil. See also L. Gougaud, *Devotional and Ascetic Practices in the Middle Ages,* London, 1927, pp. 147 ff., 159 ff., 205 ff.

But the gradual introduction of the rule of St Benedict into the monasteries of Northumbria, during the seventh century, discouraged all the more spectacular forms of asceticism. "In place of rivalry in ascetic achievement, St Benedict established a common mode of life...common prayer, work and reading; and the sanctification of the monk was to be found in living the life of the community" (Cuthbert Butler, *Benedictine Monachism,* London, 1919, p. 45).

Cuthbert's virtues. This description of St Cuthbert's virtues which is a verbal borrowing from the *Actus Silvestri,* a life of St Sylvester not yet edited in full, and found among other places in Li (see p. 33), occurs again at the beginning of Adamnan's Life of St Columba. Levison has collected other instances in which the same description is used for other saints (W. Levison, "Sigolena", *Neues Archiv,* XXXV, 1910, pp. 227 f. and "Konstantinische Schenkung und Silvester-Legende", *Studi e Testi,* XXXVIII, Rome, 1924, pp. 213 f.). The text of the *Actus* used by the author is what Levison calls "Text B".

CHAPTER II (p. 76)

V.P. c. 7, *V.M.* c. 7.

Tonsure. The passage "postquam...susceperat" is quoted by Amalarius (*De ecclesiasticis officiis,* Lib. IV, c. 39; Migne, CV, col. 1234. I owe this reference to Dr Levison). The passage is also quoted by Eddius in his *Life of Wilfrid* (c. 6).

The different forms of tonsure were one of the subjects of controversy between the Roman and Celtic Churches. The Celtic form is generally supposed to have been a shaving of the hair to a line from ear to ear behind which the hair was grown. In the *Hákonar Saga,* St Columba appears to King Alexander III of Scotland in a dream and he is described as being *mjǫk fram-snoðinn,* "very bald in front" (*Hákonar Saga,* ed. G. Vigfusson, Rolls Series, 1887, p. 260. I owe this reference to Prof. Bruce Dickins). There is some reason for believing that the Celtic tonsure was of Druidic origin (*V.S.H.* p. clxvi, n. 1; *Vit.Tr.* p. 509; also Gougaud, *C.C.L.* pp. 201 ff. and references).

The shape of the tonsure, the formula used in baptism and, most of all, the date of Easter, were the three main points of difference between the Roman and the Celtic churches. It is curious to notice that, although Cuthbert is said to have received the Petrine or Roman tonsure, nevertheless shortly afterwards (as appears from *V.P.* cc. 7, 8 compared with *H.E.* v, 19) he and Abbot Eata and the rest of the brethren were driven out of Ripon and back to Melrose because they refused to accept the Roman Easter.

Monastic vows. In the *V.P.* Cuthbert is said to have taken monastic vows at Melrose. Here it is implied that he took them at Ripon. The former is much more probable, especially in view of the detailed and circumstantial account which Bede gives, based on what he had learned from the eyewitness Sigfrith.

Guest-master. We are told in the *V.P.* account (p. 176) that he was elected "suscipiendorum officio praepositus hospitum", corresponding to the "fertigis" of an Irish monastery. As this officer was in touch with the outside world, no brother would be chosen for this post unless he were a man of great tact and virtue (cf. *H.E.* i, p. xxviiin.).

Guests. In the Celtic monasteries, as also in the Egyptian and Gallo-Roman monasteries, guests were received with great enthusiasm. Warm water was fetched in a footbath and the duty of foot-washing was performed by the abbot or one of the monks. St Martin always did it himself. On a fast day, the fast might be relaxed and the brethren permitted to share the guests' food. A separate building was provided for them as the story here shows. See also *Regula S. Benedicti,* c. 53, pp. 96 ff.

Wintry weather. We learn from the *V.M.* that the incident happened in December.

Meals. The Benedictine and Columban rules only permitted one meal a day and that towards evening. But in Columban monasteries it is clear that a meal was taken about 3 p.m. while in Benedictine monasteries the meal came to be taken about midday and there was sometimes extra supper in the evening between Easter and Pentecost. But the Columban rule allowed travellers, even penitents, to eat at the third hour and reserve something for the journey's end (Ryan, *Monast.* p. 386, n. 5). It is clearly some such permission that Cuthbert has in mind, when he offers him food (cf. also *V.P.* c. 5 and n. p. 344). The food for the day's meal of the monastery is in course of preparation and only a few scraps of yesterday's meal are available for the guests.

Similar miracle. This miracle like many others has a scriptural precedent which the author refers to in the earlier part of the chapter, namely Abraham entertaining angels unawares (Gen. 18) (cf. *Bede, L.T.W.* pp. 207ff.). The prototype of the provision of warm bread is perhaps the story of the Egyptian abbot quoted above (i, 6n. p. 314).

CHAPTER III (p. 78)

V.P. c. 10, *V.M.* c. 8.

Plecgils. The name *Plegils* comes second in the Liber Vitae on f. 19 under the heading of *presbyteri.* It is possibly the same man. The name *Plectgils* occurs in the list of clerics on f. 30 and *Plecgils* in the list of monks on f. 35. Nothing is known of this man beyond what we learn here.

Aebbe or Ebba. Sister of St Oswald and Oswiu and aunt of King Ecgfrith. For further details about her see *D.N.B.* and *D.C.B. s.v.* Eonfled. She has given her name to St Abb's Head. Ebchester, Co. Durham, is also according to Ekwall (*Oxford Dictionary of Place Names*, Oxford, 1936, p. 152) the "Chester" of Ebba or Ebbe (see Mawer, p. 71). As the parish church in Ebchester is dedicated to St Ebba, it is quite possible that the tradition may be true that her brother Oswiu gave her the Roman site there to found a monastery inside a disused fort, just as her monastery at Coldingham was probably inside a disused fort (cf. Fursey's monastery at Burgh Castle, Bassa's at Reculver or Cedd's at Othona). For the date of her death see below. Her remains were brought to Durham in the eleventh century by the arch-relic-hunter Aelfred Westou (*Bede, L.T.W.* pp. 105 ff. and IV, 14n. p. 339).

Coldingham. In County Berwick. There are still traces of a mediaeval monastery near by. But on St Abb's Head itself there are traces of an ancient fort with buildings inside, and it is quite possible that here we have the site of Aebbe's monastery inside the disused fort. The description of the place in the fuller account given in *V.P.* c. 10 fits in well with this site. See *Antiquity*, VIII, 1934, pp. 202 ff. for photographs and further details, in a note by O. G. S. Crawford. The date of the foundation by Aidan is uncertain. Aethilthryth (St Audrey) entered this monastery after she left her husband Ecgfrith to take the veil at Wilfrid's instigation in 672 (*H.E.* IV, 19).

Double monasteries. The monastery here was one of the double monasteries which seem to have arisen in Gaul in the seventh century and thence to have passed to England. They consisted of monks and nuns under the supervision of an abbess usually of royal or noble birth. Symeon tells us, speaking of Coldingham, that they consisted of congregations of monks and nuns residing in the same place but in different dwellings (Symeon, *H.D.E.* I, p. 59). The most famous of them was that at Whitby under Hilda. We read in Bede of other similar double monasteries at Hartlepool, Barking, Ely, and Bardney (*H.E.* II, p. 150). There were others at Repton, Wimborne, Minster (Thanet) and Wenlock (cf. P. Stephanus Hilpisch, "Die Doppelklöster: Entstehung und Organisation", *Beiträge zur Geschichte des alten Mönchtums und des Benediktinerordens herausgegeben von Ildefons Herwegen*, XV, Münster in Westf., 1928, pp. 44 ff.). We do not hear of scandals at any except at Coldingham. Bede tells us (*H.E.* IV, 25) that it was consumed with fire as a punishment for the wickedness and corruption that existed there. The *A.S.C.* dates the fire in 679. Symeon on the other hand declares that the fire took place during the period of St Cuthbert's episcopate 685–7 (Symeon, *loc. cit.*). This fits in better with the traditional date of Aebbe's death (683) for Symeon distinctly declares that Cuthbert, shocked by the immorality at Coldingham, forbade women to enter his church at Lindisfarne and gives some examples of the awful retribution which fell upon those who sought to enter his church at Durham (Symeon, *loc. cit.*).

Cuthbert's attitude to women. Cuthbert's attitude to women is always represented both in *V.A.* and *V.P.* as being of the friendliest. He

pays a visit to Aebbe here, he is deeply devoted to his fostermother Kenswith
(II, 7), he visits Aelfflaed twice (III, 6; IV, 10) and answers her questions,
he is on friendly terms with Iurminburg, wife of Ecgfrith (IV, 8), he stays
at the monastery of the Abbess Verca (*V.P.* c. 35) and receives from her
a linen cloth in which he is wrapped after his death (*V.P.* c. 37). The position
of women generally was high in Anglo-Saxon times, as the appointment
of a woman over the double monasteries shows (cf. G. F. Browne, *The
Importance of Women in Anglo-Saxon Times*, London, 1919, pp. 11 ff.). But
when the Normans came over and the Continental belief in the inferiority
and impurity of women was introduced, this fear and dislike of women came
to be attributed, very unfairly, to the saint, and attempts were made to
explain his dislike. Symeon's excuse was the most popular. The "Irish"
Life tells three different stories to explain this dislike (*Arch. Ael.* Ser. IV, 6,
1921, pp. 88 ff.). In Ireland, though the saints of the primitive period were
on friendly terms with women, the Irish saints of the second order (second
half of the sixth century) had all the Egyptian dislike of them. An amusing
story is told of the childhood of St Brendan when a little girl, wishing
to play with him, jumped into the chariot in which he was seated reading
his psalms, he showed his incipient saintliness by flogging her severely with
the reins and driving her away in tears (Ryan, *Monast.* p. 249). It was an
Irish saint who said on seeing a sheep: "In hoc loco, non ero; ubi enim ovis,
ibi mulier; ubi mulier, ibi peccatum" (*V.S.H.* I, p. 250).

Immersion. This was a regular form of asceticism among the Irish,
Welsh, Breton and Scottish saints, St Patrick and St Coemgen among their
number (*Vit.Tr.* p. 485; *L.I.S.* II, p. 123). The saints stood immersed in
cold water, generally during the night, reciting psalms and prayers. Other
Anglo-Saxon saints who indulged in ascetic practices of this nature were
Drihthelm of Melrose, Wilfrid, and Aldhelm (Gougaud, *C.C.L.* p. 95).

Sea animals. Aelfric in the Anglo-Saxon homily on the life of St
Cuthbert describes the creatures as seals (Wyatt, *Anglo-Saxon Reader*,
Cambridge, 1925, p. 82). Bede calls them otters. Probably the story was
originally told of otters, for the otter in Ireland was supposed to have magical
properties, and several stories are told of their friendliness to the saints in
the Irish lives. An otter used to bring St Coemgen a salmon every day
to supply his monastery, while on another occasion, when the same saint
dropped a psalter into a lake, an otter dived for it and brought it up
unharmed (*L.I.S.* II, pp. 123, 125).

Spies. A similar story is told of the spy who followed St Fintan by
night to see where he was praying and found him surrounded by heavenly
light. The saint rebuked the spy and warned him not to repeat the offence
(*V.S.H.* II, 102). Another similar story is that of the brother who spied
upon St Columba's tryst with the angels. In this instance, too, the spy is most
strictly forbidden to say anything about the incident until after the death of
the saint (*Vit. Col.* Reeves, III, 16, p. 217). It is extremely common for
a saint to forbid those who have witnessed a miracle to make any mention
of it until after his death. Compare Chad's injunction to Owini, the brother

who witnessed the angelic visitors who came to warn him of his approaching death (*H.E.* IV, 3). The prohibition probably derives from our Lord's command to His disciples on the Mount of Transfiguration (Matth. 17. 9), a passage which Bede quotes in relating this same miracle (*V.P.* c. 10). But, in addition, the spy forms a valuable witness as the saga of the saint grows rapidly in the years after his death. The prohibition also helps to explain why nothing was heard of the miracle at the time of its happening, a difficulty which might otherwise arise in the minds of his contemporaries who outlived him and witnessed the gradual development of the saga. And, in addition to all this, one must not forget the widespread folklore belief that a wonderworker does not like to be spied upon by unauthorised persons. This dislike is found in the Irish saints' lives and in the secular stories, and is preserved in modern fairy-tales. Cf. the story of Wayland Smith as described by Scott in *Kenilworth* (c. 10). Cf. also the story of St Ciaran and the eavesdropper whose eye was plucked out by a pet crane (*St Ciaran, Irish Life*, c. 24).

Animals and birds. Cuthbert's friendliness with animals and birds is in both the Egyptian and the Irish tradition. Miss Waddell has collected the best stories of both traditions in her book called *Beasts and Saints* (London, 1934). She has also included the Cuthbert stories. The tradition of Cuthbert's affection for the eider ducks, that still breed plentifully on the Farne Islands, is preserved in the name of "St Cuthbert's birds" by which they are still known. In the "Irish" life a story is told of a seal which rescued a psalter which Cuthbert had dropped into the sea. For other illustrations of the friendliness of the Irish saints to beasts and birds see *V.S.H.* I, pp. cxliiff. Bede in *V.P.* c. 21 (see note p. 350) attempts to interpret these stories by explaining that we lose our dominion over the animal world by neglecting to serve the Lord and Creator of all things. In the *V.A.* and *V.P.* we learn how Cuthbert was provided with food by his horse (I, 6), how the sea animals at Coldingham ministered to him (II, 3), how an eagle provided him with food (II, 5), how the birds departed from his crops at his command (*V.P.* c. 20) and how the ravens brought him lard for his boots (III, 5). And in every case Cuthbert's attitude towards the animals and birds is uniformly kind and thoughtful. Note particularly Bede's account of the horse finding the bread and meat in the shepherd's hut (*V.P.* c. 5).

CHAPTER IV (p. 82)

V.P. c. 11, *V.M.* c. 9.

Niuduera regio. This region, which is equivalent to Bede's Niduari (*V.P.* c. 11), is of course the region of the Nid people. Professor Max Förster maintains that the original form must have been *Nuid-* rather than *Niud-*, but all the available MSS of the *V.A.* agree in the form *Niud-* (cf. Max Förster, "Zur i-Epenthese im Altenglischen", *Anglia*, LIX, 1935, p. 297). It is usually supposed that it refers to a Pictish settlement near the R. Nith in Dumfriesshire, but Professor Watson considers it most improbable that the Picts in question lived in the south-west of Scotland (W. J. Watson, *Celtic Place-Names of Scotland*, Edinburgh, 1926, pp. 175 ff.). Nor does the account here and in *V.P.* c. 11 fit in well with such a situation. There may quite well have been another river of the same name on the east coast of Scotland. Bates ("The Names of Persons and Places mentioned in the early Lives of St Cuthbert", *Arch. Ael.* N.S. XVI, 1894, pp. 81 ff.) associates Kirkcudbright (that is the cell of St Cuthbert) with this incident, but there is another Kirkcudbright in Ayrshire which is certainly not connected with it.

Epiphany. That is, January 6th. This day was in very early times the feast both of the Nativity and of the Baptism. But in the west it came to be associated chiefly with the visit of the Magi to Bethlehem, though the connection with the Baptism was never entirely forgotten. In addition, the feast of the turning of the water into wine was also celebrated on this day. Possibly this miracle became connected with it owing to the rite of the "Blessing of the Waters", which in ancient times took place on this day. Water drawn on the day and stored acquired special merit, and according to some traditions was turned into wine (*E.R.E. s.v.* Epiphany). Augustine in a sermon on the Epiphany (Sermo CXXXVI*a*; Migne, XXXIX, col. 2014) draws attention to these three feasts celebrated on the day of Epiphany and adds that the feast of the feeding of the five thousand was also celebrated on the same day. The writer of the gloss which was afterwards inserted in the text of H, T, B and P had this sermon in mind.

Dolphin flesh. The dolphin was long considered to be a fish (not a mammal as it really is), and so the church permitted it to be eaten during Lent. It was until recently considered a great delicacy in parts of France.

Tydi. The priest Tydi as we gather from this incident belonged to Melrose and was also responsible for the story of the miraculous food provided by the eagle (II, 5). Later on he tells the story of the child cured at *Medilwong* (IV, 6) and of the demoniac cured at Lindisfarne (IV, 15). It is fairly clear therefore that he was transferred from Melrose to Lindisfarne, perhaps at the same time as St Cuthbert. He was a contemporary of the writer of the Life, and is possibly the priest of that name mentioned in the Liber Vitae in the list of priests on f. 19*b*. The name Tidi occurs in a list of clerics on f. 26. Nothing further is known of him. For the form of the name see Redin, p. 128.

The gift of prophecy. The gift of prophecy was a sign of increasing spiritual power, as we see in the Life of Antony (*Vit. Ant.* c. 38; Migne, LXXIII, col. 156) and in the life of Benedict. In fact, the words used by Gregory to describe Benedict's spiritual growth in this direction are borrowed verbally by Bede to describe Cuthbert's experience (*V.P.* c. 11; see text). After this incident an increasing number of instances of his prophetic powers is given. Macarius of Egypt, when he was forty years old, received grace to contend against evil spirits both by healing and by forecasting the future (*H.L.* c. 17). St Martin too acquired prophetic gifts and the power of foreseeing events

(Sulp. Sev. c. 21; Halm, p. 131). St Columba was so greatly endowed with prophetic gifts that Adamnan devotes the first book of his life of the saint to describing examples of them.

CHAPTER V (p. 84)

V.P. c. 12, *V.M.* c. 10.

R. Teviot. The form *Tesgeta* which occurs in all the MSS is due to a misreading of *Tefgeta*, caused by the easy confusion between an *s* and an *f* in the insular script. The same mistake occurs apparently in IV, 10 where *Ofingadun* becomes *Osingadun*. The Teviot is a Roxburghshire river, the largest tributary of the Tweed (cf. J. B. Johnston, *Place-names of Scotland*, 3rd ed., London, 1934, p. 308).

Eagle. This would be the white-tailed eagle—*Haliaëtus albicilla*—which lives mostly on fish. It is the eagle described in the Anglo-Saxon poem on the battle of Brunanburh as "earn æftan hwit" (*Anglo-Saxon and Norse Poems*, ed. N. Kershaw, Cambridge, 1922, p. 70). Until recently it occasionally appeared in England in the autumn.

CHAPTER VI (p. 86)

V.P. c. 13, *V.M.* c. 11.

Illusory fire. A similar story of an illusory fire occurs in Gregory's Life of St Benedict (Greg. *Dial.* II, 10, p. 97). A bronze idol is thrown on to the kitchen fire and immediately the whole kitchen seems to be ablaze, but the saint prays and the fire departs, leaving the kitchen unharmed. Bede refers to this incident in *V.P.* c. 14. There are Irish instances of illusory fires of much the same kind. Once when St Fintan and his brethren were eating, the refectory seemed to be ablaze, but the saint drove away the illusory fire by his prayers (*V.S.H.* II, p. 99). In these cases it is the work of the devil; but sometimes, like the burning bush, it is a divine sign. The house in which St Wilfrid was being born seemed to be on fire (*Eddius*, pp. 4, 151), and a similar story is told of the birth of St Fechin (*V.S.H.* II, p. 77).

CHAPTER VII (p. 88)

V.P. c. 14, *V.M.* c. 12.

Kenswith or **Coenswith.** The system of fosterage, which was extremely widespread in Ireland and Scandinavia, seems to have been common in England also (for examples see *E.R.E. s.v.* Fosterage). In Ireland and Wales, and probably in England too, it was mostly confined to children of noble birth (cf. Giraldus Cambrensis, *Descriptio Cambriae*, II, 4 and 9, ed. J. F. Dimock, Rolls Series, 1868, VI, pp. 211, 225; *V.P.* c. 6n. p. 344). Fosterage in Ireland ended at the age of 17, and at this age too the youth had to decide whether he would enter a monastery, though he might decide two years earlier (Ryan, *Monast.* p. 213 n.). According to *V.P.* c. 4 it was his vision of the death of Aidan which led Cuthbert to make up his mind to take to the monastic life. Aidan died in 651. If the age of decision was the same in the north of England, as is highly probable, then Cuthbert would be born about 634. It could hardly have been later, as he had seen some military service before he entered the monastery (I, 7 and n. p. 315). It may possibly have been a year or two earlier. Cuthbert would therefore be something more than 53 years old, when he died in 687.

Hruringaham. This place has not been identified. Judging from I, 5 it must be somewhere near the River Leader and the Lammermuir Hills and in the neighbourhood of Melrose. For various guesses about this and other unidentified places in the lives see Bates' article mentioned above (*Arch. Ael.* N.S. XVI, 1894, pp. 81 ff.). See also *Antiquity*, VIII, 1934, pp. 97 ff.

Fire extinguished. Many saints are said to have put out fires by their prayers. Bede mentions Marcellinus of Ancona (*V.P.* c. 14 and n. p. 347). Another instance is to be found in the *Life of St Martin* (Sulp. Sev. c. 15; Halm, p. 124).

CHAPTER VIII (p. 90)

V.P. c. 15, *V.M.* c. 13.

A devil cast out. It is not clear why our author should have put this incident here, before he tells us about the removal of St Cuthbert to Lindisfarne. He takes the trouble to explain that Cuthbert was prior of "our church" and it is clear from III, 1 and IV, 1 that by "our church" he means Lindisfarne. Bede in both *V.M.* and *V.P.* preserves the same order, though in *V.M.* he states emphatically that

> Tempore namque fuit Lindisfarnensis in illo
> Praepositus cellae

and he is equally emphatic in *V.P.* c. 16 (see n. p. 348).

Hildmer. We learn from *V.P.* that he was a reeve of King Ecgfrith. Nothing more is known of him except that Bede in *V.P.* c. 31 describes how he was healed of a very serious illness by means of bread which the saint had blessed.

Travelling on horseback. It was the custom of the Celtic monks to travel on foot, probably for purposes of mortification and also out of humility (see *V.P.* c. 6 n. p. 344). We know for instance that Aidan, Chad, Kentigern and Malachy generally travelled thus. Even Wilfrid, anti-Celtic though he was in his sympathies, nevertheless did his last journey to Rome on foot as an old man of seventy for purposes of mortification (*Eddius*, c. 50; Gougaud, *C.C.L.* pp. 175 f.). But Cuthbert seems to have had no qualms about riding on horseback. Bede tells us (*V.P.* c. 9) that he sometimes travelled on horseback but more often on foot when preaching in the surrounding villages.

BOOK III

CHAPTER I (p. 94)

V.P. cc. 16 and 17, *V.M.* cc. 14 and 15.

Adcides. This curious form, which as a glance at the variant readings will show, has been a stumbling-block to the scribes, may possibly be a misreading of the name of some tribe or place whither Cuthbert went after leaving Melrose and going to Lindisfarne. It is just possible that it might be a reference to an earlier attempt on the part of Cuthbert to live the life of an anchorite. There are two caves in Northumberland traditionally associated with Cuthbert, both known as Cuddy's or St Cuthbert's cave. One is near Doddington where there is also a Cuddy's well. The other is in the Kyloe Hills near Holburn and fairly close to Lindisfarne. On the other hand *adcides* may simply be a misreading of *abscedēs*, i.e. *abscedens*.

Eata. Eata was a pupil of St Aidan and abbot of Melrose when Cuthbert entered the monastery. He afterwards went to Ripon, taking Cuthbert with him. He left, together with Cuthbert, rather than accept the Roman Easter. Evidently in the intervening period both he and Cuthbert must have accepted the Roman practice, for when Colman left Lindisfarne after the Synod of Whitby, because he could not accept the Roman rule, Eata was chosen to take his place as abbot of Lindisfarne, while still remaining abbot of Melrose. When Wilfrid's great diocese of Northumbria was divided in 678, Eata became bishop of Bernicia. In 681 this Bernician diocese was further divided. He remained at Lindisfarne while Tunberht succeeded him at Hexham. When Cuthbert was elected bishop in 685, the latter was allowed to remain at Lindisfarne while Eata went to Hexham. Eata died of dysentery (*V.P.* c. 8) about 686 (*D.N.B. s.v.* and *H.E.* II, p. 193).

The Lindisfarne rule. We gather from Bede that discipline was somewhat lax at Lindisfarne when Cuthbert arrived. It is clear from this passage that it was not merely the Benedictine rule which Cuthbert introduced. *Regula* is probably used here rather to signify the ascetic teaching of the saint or else the "traditional not codified observance of a monastery" (Gougaud, *C.C.L.* p. 79). There were moreover many Gaulish monasteries which adopted the rule of Columban together with that of St Benedict. The more practical as well as the more moderate Benedictine rule was added to that of Columban as early as the seventh century and finally supplanted it. It is therefore very possible that the traditional rule of St Cuthbert, probably that also in use at Melrose and Ripon (*V.P.* c. 9), was observed, together with the Benedictine rule, tending to make the latter stricter and more ascetic than was the original intention of the founder (cf. W. Levison, "Die Iren und die Fränkische Kirche", *Historische Zeitschrift*, CIX, 1912, pp. 7f.).

Contemplative and active life. The distinction between the two types of life, the active and contemplative, seems to have been first definitely formulated by St Gregory (*Homilies on Ezechiel*, II, ii, 7, 8; Migne, LXXVI, cols. 952, 953, quoted by Cuthbert Butler, *Benedictine Monachism*, p. 96). The theory was accepted in Ireland and the same division between the "vita theorica" or "contemplativa" and the "vita actualis" is found in the earliest Irish writings. The superiority of the contemplative over the active life was an accepted doctrine throughout the church all through the Middle Ages, and held by Bede as firmly as the rest (*H.E.* II, pp. 68 ff.; see also *V.P.* c. 17 and n. p. 349).

Hermits. In Ireland the third order of Irish saints at the beginning of the seventh century are described as anchorites who dwelt in desert places. This desire for the desert, reminiscent of the Egyptian hermits, was found in England too. Fursey spent the latter part of his life in seclusion (*H.E.* III, 19). Wihtberht had lived a hermit life in Ireland (*H.E.* V, 12). Drihthelm lived a solitary life near Melrose (*H.E.* V, 12), and Haemgils went to Ireland to live a solitary life (*H.E.* V, 12). It will be seen that all these except Drihthelm had a close connection with Ireland.

Devils. Much less emphasis is laid on the devils in the *V.A.* than in the *V.M.* or *V.P.* (cf. *V.P.* cc. 17, 22, 37), though even in these there is not a great deal. In the saints' lives of the strict Antonian model the fight with devils was an integral part of the warfare carried on by the Christian soldier. Contrast the large part played by devils in the *Life of St Martin* or Felix's *Life of St Guthlac* (cf. Kurtz, pp. 108 ff.). Stones were also thrown by devils at St Dunstan (Stubbs, *Dunstan*, pp. 15, 28).

Farne. Our author does not mention the first period of Cuthbert's retirement when he made his way to a retreat only a short distance from the monastery. The Farne Islands are a series of rocky islands and reefs off the coast of Northumberland. Farne, the largest of them, is about sixteen acres in area, with precipitous rocks on the west side, but the rest of the coast is fairly low. It is about one and a half miles from the mainland near Bamburgh and about seven miles from Lindisfarne. The remains of the fourteenth-century medieval chapel doubtless mark the site of Cuthbert's hermitage. Farne had already been used by Aidan as a place of retreat and in Bede's time his solitary cell was still to be seen (*H.E.* III, 16). After Cuthbert's death his successors were Aethilwald and Felgild and, later on, Aelric, Aelwine, Bartholomew, and Thomas an ex-prior of Durham (see *D.C.B. s.nn.*). Soon after the death of Bartholomew, the convent at Durham decided that Farne should henceforth be inhabited by at least two monks, one the *magister* or *custos*, the other his *socius* (J. Raine, *North Durham*, London, 1852, pp. 341 ff.). For an excellent and detailed account of the island as it was in 1848, see Eyre, *St Cuthbert*, pp. 32 ff. In the same place Eyre quotes a twelfth-century account of the island.

An island was often chosen by hermits or small communities of monks, and to-day their beehive-shaped cells are still to be seen in a ruined condition in Ireland on Inishmurray, Skellig Michael, Ardoilean and elsewhere (Lord Dunraven, *Notes on Irish Architecture*, ed. by Margaret Stokes, I, London,

1875, pp. 27 ff.). In Scotland they are found amongst other places on an island in Loch Columcille, on Eilean na Naoimh, and on the Brough of Deerness and the Brough of Bissay in Orkney (J. Anderson, *Scotland in Early Christian Times*, Edinburgh, 1881, pp. 94 ff. and *Proceedings of the Society of Antiquaries of Scotland*, 1921-2, p. 67). We have literary references in Adamnan and elsewhere to journeys made by the Celtic monks in search of an island solitude (*Vit. Col.* I, 20; II, 42; see also *V.S.H.* I, p. cxxii). Hereberht (IV, 9) lived on an island in Derwentwater still known as St Herbert's Isle. There was an island near Llantwit too on which a hermit lived (*St Samson of Dol*, p. 26). Cf. also T. D. Kendrick, *The Druids*, London, 1927, pp. 138 ff.

Almost no one. The author seems to imply here that others had attempted to live on Farne as well as Cuthbert. For Aidan's residence in Farne see above, p. 325.

Cuthbert's dwelling. These huts that Cuthbert made for himself are, as we see from the fuller account in the *V.P.* and *V.M.* and in *H.E.* IV, 28, of the same type as those used by the hermits in Egypt. Amon for instance made himself two round huts (*H.L.* c. 8), while John of Lycopolis made himself three round cells in one of which he worked and ate, in one he prayed and the other was for his bodily needs (*H.L.* c. 35). The cashel or wall around it also goes back to the old tradition; the high wall enclosing the separate buildings is still the regular plan of the Coptic monasteries of Upper Egypt (E. H. Sawyer, "The First Monasteries", *Antiquity*, IV, 1930, pp. 316 ff.). Such was the arrangement of John of Beverley's retreat near Hexham and such too was the regular plan of Irish monasteries, as can still be seen at Skellig Michael and elsewhere. The round dwelling with a dug-out floor may be a development of the pre-Christian type of Anglo-Saxon dwellings such as are occasionally found round in shape and with a dug-out floor (T. D. Kendrick and C. F. C. Hawkes, *Archaeology in England and Wales*, 1914-1931, London, 1932, pp. 320 ff.). But the use of great stones seems to point rather to that "megalithic feeling" in early Anglo-Saxon architecture which Baldwin Brown attributes to Irish influences (*A.E.E.* II, p. 46).

cubitum uiri. Compare Rev. 21. 17: "cubitorum mensura hominis" and Irish *fer chubat*.

CHAPTER II (p. 96)

V.P. c. 17, *V.M.* c. 15.

Large stones. See note on angelic ministrations (I, 4, p. 312). A precisely similar incident is recorded of St Benedict when he was building his own cell (Greg. *Dial.* II, 9, pp. 96-7).

Mirabilis Deus, etc. This quotation from Psa. 67. 36 (Vulg.) is extremely familiar in saints' lives. "Sanctis suis" of course means "holy places", but it was naturally taken to refer to the saints.

CHAPTER III (p. 98)

V.P. c. 18, *V.M.* c. 16.

Fountains and wells. A similar incident is related of Antony (*Vit. Ant.* c. 27; Migne, LXXIII, col. 150); and of Benedict (Greg. *Dial.* II, 5, pp. 88–9) to which Bede refers in *V.P.* c. 19. The production of fountains of water by a saint is common enough, especially in the Irish lives. Generally speaking the fountains are not produced by what Plummer calls the "more prosaic process of digging", but by the saint's crozier or bell, by a touch of the horse's hoofs, or from a saint's blood or tears. But St Colman, St Fechin and St Maedoc all produced wells in the way described here (*V.S.H.* I, 272; II, 77, 151). The numerous holy wells associated with the name of a saint (cf. Cuddy's well near Doddington, Northumberland) show how the pagan cult of fountains had been given a Christian veneer and, as Plummer says (*V.S.H.* I, c), doubtless these stories of the miraculous production of fountains and wells are a sign of this; but one must not, on the other hand, overlook the obvious Scriptural analogues and their influence on these stories, such as Moses striking the rock or the verses quoted by Bede in telling the same story in the *V.P.* (see *V.P.* c. 18, text). There are still two shallow wells on Farne, one inside Prior Castell's tower and the other close to the landing, near the site of the guest-house.

CHAPTER IV (p. 98)

V.P. c. 21, *V.M.* c. 19.

Timber. The timber was to be used as a foundation for a building over a small hollow or chasm in the rocks for his "daily necessities". There is still a chasm in the rocks near the site of his dwelling, known as "St Cuthbert's gut". It was probably over this hollow that St Cuthbert put up his little closet, using the piece of timber as a sort of bridge foundation. The story has an obvious didactic intention, which Bede makes full use of in his account. The brethren had failed in holy obedience and the forces of nature are called in to make up for their deficiencies. See also *V.P.* c. 36 and n. (p. 354).

CHAPTER V (p. 100)

V.P. c. 20, *V.M.* c. 18.

Ravens. The mediaeval tradition of this story describes the birds as crows, as for instance in the Cuthbert paintings on the Carlisle stalls (about 1500) and the Metrical Middle English Life. Aelfric in his homily on Cuthbert calls them ravens (Wyatt, *Anglo-Saxon Reader*, p. 85). Fowler points out that there are no trees on Farne on which crows would build, though rooks do occasionally build elsewhere. His opinion is that the birds were probably jackdaws which abound there now (*Metr. Life*, p. 69).

Manual labour. Manual labour was encouraged among the monkish communities in Egypt and Ireland. Bede had strong views on the importance of manual labour in the life of the community, as well as to the individual (see *H.E.* I, p. xxv). Antony set the example for hermits in the story quoted by Bede in *V.P.* c. 20 (*Vit. Ant.* c. 25; Migne, LXXIII, col. 149). Fursey also worked with his hands during his hermit life (*H.E.* III, 19). Manual labour was also ordained by the Rule of St Benedict (*Regula Benedicti*, c. 48, pp. 88 ff.).

Clausus. This was a still greater advance in the rigour of a hermit's life. Gradually the hermit became more and more devoted to the contemplative life and weaned from the active life as Bede's comments show (*V.P.* c. 17; cf. also Homilia 35 (*Opp.* v, p. 263) and *H.E.* I, p. xxxin. and II, p. 69). John of Lycopolis spent thirty years entirely confined to his little cells, receiving only the necessaries of life through a window just as St Cuthbert did (*H.L.* c. 35).

Penitent ravens. Compare the charming story of the penitent she-wolf who had stolen the hermit's food (Sulp. Sev. *Dial.* I, 14; Halm, p. 166), and of the grateful lioness who brought the hermit the gift of an animal's skin (*loc. cit.* c. 15; Halm, pp. 167 f.).

CHAPTER VI (p. 102)

V.P. c. 24, *V.M.* c. 21.

Aelfflaed. Aelfflaed was half-sister of Aldfrith and daughter of Oswiu and Eanfled. She was dedicated to the service of God by her father after his victory over Penda in 655. She was sent to Hilda first at Hartlepool and then at Whitby, where she must have been when the great Synod of 664 took place. She succeeded Hilda as abbess in 680. Her name follows those of Eanfled and Iurminburg in the list of queens and abbesses in the Liber Vitae, f. 13. The date of her death is uncertain (see *D.C.B. s.v.*).

The nine orders of angels. The angels were distributed into three hierarchies of three orders each, according to the early tradition of the Church—the first order consisting of cherubim, seraphim and thrones; the second of dominions, virtues and powers; the third of principalities, archangels and angels. This arrangement of hierarchies appeared first in its fully developed form in the treatise περὶ τῆς οὐρανίας ἱεραρχίας ascribed to Dionysius the Areopagite (Migne, *Patrologia Graeca*, III, coll. 119 ff.).

Coquet Island. This island, which lies opposite the mouth of the R. Coquet, would form a convenient meeting place between Farne and Whitby. It was, according to Bede (*V.P.* c. 24), already celebrated for its companies of monks. Several pre-Conquest objects have been found on the island, particularly a ring bearing the inscription OWI in runes. At the beginning of the twelfth century it was the scene of the hermitage of the Dane known as St Henry of Coquet (*A History of Northumberland*, v, Newcastle-upon-Tyne, 1899, p. 315).

Ecgfrith. Ecgfrith was the second son of Oswiu whom he succeeded as king of Northumbria in 670 or 671 (cf. *H.E.* II, p. 211). His first wife was the saintly Aethilthryth, daughter of Anna, king of the East Angles. She is better known as St Audrey. She left Ecgfrith before the consummation of their marriage to take the veil and so Ecgfrith married again as he had a right to do according to canon law, this time marrying Iurminburg. He was slain by the Picts in 685 at the disastrous battle of Nechtansmere. It was Ecgfrith who helped Benedict Biscop to found the monasteries of Wearmouth and Jarrow; his name is on the contemporary dedication stone still preserved in the church at Jarrow. See also note on IV, 8 pp. 334 ff. and *D.C.B. s.v.*

Aldfrith. Aldfrith succeeded to the throne after the death of Ecgfrith. He was an illegitimate son of Oswiu and an Irish princess. This fact explains Aelfflaed's apparent temporary forgetfulness of his existence. Aldfrith was well known in Ireland where he was known as Flann Fina, his mother's name according to Irish authorities being Fina. He lived in exile during his brother Ecgfrith's life, in Ireland according to William of Malmesbury (*Gesta Regum*, ed. W. Stubbs, Rolls Series, 1887, p. 57), but in Iona according to the *V.A.*, probably in both. Aldhelm dedicated his work on metres to him and also wrote another letter, which still survives, to a certain Ehfridus usually identified with Aldfrith (though Ehwald does not accept the identification) on his return from Ireland. He congratulates him in florid style on his return from a six years' stay in Ireland and reminds him that, thanks to Adrian, Theodore, and other scholars, England can supply equally good instruction (*Aldhelmi Opera*, ed. R. Ehwald, *M.G. Auctores Antiquissimi*, xv, 1919, pp. 486 ff.). Aldfrith had a considerable reputation in Ireland as a teacher and a learned man, though none of his writings has survived, the poems attributed to him being much later in date. His court seems to have been a centre of learning and a connecting link between Irish and Northumbrian culture during the late seventh century. Both A. S. Cook and F. Liebermann have suggested that the court of Aldfrith may well have been the place where the Anglo-Saxon poem *Beowulf* originated (R. W. Chambers, *Beowulf. An Introduction*, 2nd ed. Cambridge, 1932, p. 489; see also *Vit. Col.* Reeves, p. 185 n.). The reference here to the fact that Aldfrith is still living gives a *terminus ad quem* for the date of the *V.A.* Aldfrith died in 705. The reference to the raising of the relics of Cuthbert in 698 and the miracles which happened at least a year afterwards point to a date between 699 and 705 for the life (see Introduction, p. 13).

Prophecies about rulers. These prophecies about kings and rulers form a class by themselves in the stories of prophetic powers related of the saints. Aidan prophesied the death of King Oswini (*H.E.* III, 14). Cedd predicted the death of Sigeberht of Essex (*H.E.* III, 22). Columba prophesied concerning the successor of King Aidan just as Cuthbert does here, and about Aengus son of Aedh Comman (*Vit. Col.* Reeves, I, 9, p. 35; I, 13, p. 42). Benedict also predicted the future of King Totila (Greg. *Dial.* II, 15, pp. 102–3). The Chadwicks see in this incident of Aelfflaed, affinities with Celtic mantic literature (H. M. and N. K. Chadwick, *The Growth of Literature*, I, Cambridge, 1932, p. 472).

BOOK IV

CHAPTER I (p. 110)

V.P. c. 24, *V.M.* c. 21.

Cuthbert becomes bishop. Cuthbert's reluctance to accept a bishopric is only in accordance with the attitude of a large number of saints who were made bishops under protest, including Martin, Ambrose, Augustine, Chad, Wilfrid and Dunstan. The most extraordinary example is perhaps that of Ammonius who cut off part of his ear to avoid being made a bishop, and even threatened to cut out his own tongue, so they left him to his life of contemplation (*H.L.* c. 11). It is in fact a constantly recurring hagiological feature and whenever the hero of a saint's life is made a bishop, one may almost take it for granted that he will at first refuse, either on the ground of unworthiness or, like Cuthbert, so that he may not have to forsake the contemplative for the active life.

Council. This *senatus* is presumably the gathering of the king's officials and personal retainers. Bede refers to the gathering as a *synodus* (as does the *V.A.* chapter title) and declares that Theodore presided over it (*V.P.* c. 24).

Saxons. It was the habit of the fifth-century inhabitants of Britain to call all the invaders Saxons, whether they were Angles, Saxons or Jutes, or any other nationality. Today the Celtic races speak of the English as Saesneg or Sassenach. One may compare the way in which the later ninth-century invaders were all classed as Danes, no matter to which of the Scandinavian families they actually belonged. The Latin writers of the seventh century in Northumbria, even though they were Angles, seem to have adopted the same nomenclature. Even Bede who draws attention to the distinction between Angles, Saxons and Jutes did not draw the distinction when writing in Latin. Bede quotes Hwaetberht as saying that Monkwearmouth is in Saxonia, while Bede himself, in the very chapter in which he makes the distinction mentioned above, refers to the "Anglorum sive Saxonum gens" (*H.E.* I, 15; *H.E.* II, p. 368). Wilfrid speaks of himself as "episcopus Saxoniae" and elsewhere calls the Mercians "Saxones" (*Eddius*, cc. 21, 30). For further discussion of the subject see J. N. L. Myres in Collingwood and Myres, *Roman Britain and the English Settlements*, Oxford, 1936, pp. 343 ff. and R. H. Hodgkin, *A History of the Anglo-Saxons*, I, Oxford, 1935, pp. 157 ff.

Tumma. See note to I, 3, p. 311.

Bosa. Bosa, who is stated in four of the MSS to have accompanied Trumwine, was a pupil of Hilda at Whitby and was made bishop of Deira with his seat at York when Wilfrid was driven out by King Ecgfrith in 678, and his diocese divided. When Wilfrid was restored in 686, Bosa was expelled from the see, only to be restored when Aldfrith again expelled Wilfrid in 691 or 692. He died in 704 or 705 (see *D.C.B. s.v.* For the form of the name see Redin, p. 86).

Theodore. When, on the death of Deusdedit, Wighard was chosen primate with the consent of the church of the English nation (*H.E.* III, 29), he was sent to Rome to receive the pallium from Pope Vitalian, but died of the plague in Rome in 667. The Pope thereupon appointed Theodore of Tarsus, giving him as colleague and adviser Abbot Adrian, an African and abbot of a monastery near Naples. After various hindrances they arrived in Canterbury together with Benedict Biscop in 668. Though a man of nearly 67, Theodore threw himself into the work of the province with enthusiasm. His influence not only as an administrator but as a patron and encourager of arts and letters cannot well be overestimated. He died in 690, aged 88 (*H.E.* v, 8; *D.C.B. s.v.* and Bright, pp. 256ff.).

Cuthbert's virtues. This account of Cuthbert's virtues as a bishop has been copied word for word by Eddius to describe Wilfrid (*Eddius*, c. 11). It is borrowed from Isidore of Seville's description of a bishop's qualifications, *De ecclesiasticis officiis*, II, c. 5; Migne, LXXXIII, cols 785–6. I am indebted to Dr Levison for the reference.

quid, cui, quando, quomodo. A series of indirect questions introduced by *quid, cui, quando, quomodo*, etc. was a common rhetorical device in Late Latin writers. For a collection of such passages see C. Weyman, *Beiträge zur Geschichte der christlich-lateinischen Poesie*, München, 1926, pp. 267, 296.

canones. The term *canon* is used in the sense of a Testament in the Life of St Cainnech: "Cum sanctus Kainnicus utrumque canonem legisset" (*V.S.H.* I, p. 53), i.e. the Old and New Testaments. The Egyptian tradition of learning large portions of the Scriptures, especially the Psalter, by heart was preserved in the Celtic Church. Aidan's disciples employed themselves in reading the Scriptures and learning the psalms (*H.E.* III, 5), while Wilfrid learned the whole Psalter by heart in his youth (*Eddius*, c. 3).

CHAPTER III (p. 114)

V.P. c. 29, *V.M.* c. 23.

Wife of a gesith healed. This story is very similar to one told of John of Beverley by Bede (*H.E.* v, 4). For a discussion of the type of miracle to which this belongs see *Bede, L.T.W.* p. 209. For the meaning of the term 'gesith' see H. M. Chadwick, *Studies in Anglo-Saxon Institutions*, Cambridge, 1905, pp. 325ff.

Hemma. The name occurs twice in the Liber Vitae in the list of priests on f. 18 *b*. It is scarcely likely that either of these can be this man. For the form of the name see Redin, p. 76.

Kintis. This place or district has not been identified.

Beta. Four of the MSS read "Beda". If this is the correct reading it is probably the same person as the "maior Beda presbiter" referred to in *V.P.* c. 37 (and see n. p. 355). Glosses in two of the MSS of the *V.M.* (P and K) attribute the incident to Aethilwald, probably through confusion with the Aethilwald mentioned in the next chapter (Jaager, p. 101 n.). The name Beta may be a short form of some compound with Bet-, such as Betwald, Betfrith, Betgils (Redin, p. 44).

CHAPTER IV (p. 116)

V.P. c. 30, *V.M.* c. 24.

Aethilwald. As we learn from the *V.P.*, Aethilwald was at this time acting as servant of Cuthbert, the task of a young novice, just as Wilfrid in his youth acted as servant to Cudda (*Eddius*, c. 2). He was prior of Melrose at the time that the *V.A.* was written, while at the time of the writing of the *V.P.* he was abbot of the same monastery. He was consecrated bishop of Lindisfarne, apparently, in 721. It was he who caused an elaborate case to be made for the Lindisfarne Gospels, and also a cross in memory of Cuthbert. The cross bore Aethilwald's name and shared in the wanderings of the saint's body, being erected finally in Durham churchyard (*H.E.* II, p. 297; Symeon, *H.D.E.* I, p. 39). It has long since disappeared. This Aethilwald must not be confused, as he often is, with the hermit who followed Cuthbert on Farne (*V.P.* c. 46 and n. p. 359).

Bedesfeld. This place has not been identified.

Similar miracle. St Martin similarly cured a paralytic woman with holy oil (Sulp. Sev. *Vita Mart.* c. 16; Halm, p. 125).

CHAPTER V (p. 116)

V.P. c. 32, *V.M.* c. 26.

Penna. Nothing is known of this man. Owing to a slip of the Bollandists the name has always hitherto been printed as Henna. It may be a hypocoristic form of some compound in Pen-, such as Penheard, Penweald, Penwealh.

Carlisle. Cf. Symeon, *H.D.E.* I, p. 53: "Luel quod nunc Carleol appellatur."

Ahse. The only guess that has been made as to the identity of this region, between Hexham and Carlisle, is that of Cadwallader Bates (*Arch. Ael.* N.S. XVI, 1894, pp. 81ff.), who suggested Aesica or Great Chesters, a station on the Roman Wall. One objection to this is that Ahse is stated to be a region.

Tents. St Patrick also used tents when journeying (*Vit. Tr.* pp. 41, 184, 278; *H.E.* II, p. 240). "Tabernaculo", says Bede, "solemus in itinere uel in bello uti" (*Expositio in II Epist. Petri*, cap. 1; *Opp.* XII, 249). Referring to the period between 875 and 883 when St Cuthbert's body was being carried about from place to place, Reginald of Durham says that "when no house afforded him an hospitable roof, he remained under the covering of tents" (c. 14; Eyre, *St Cuthbert*, p. 101).

Putting us forth. This scriptural trait, derived of course from the story of the raising of Jairus' daughter, occurs again and again in the saints' lives. Thus in the *Life of St Martin* there are two stories of his raising the dead, and in each case he began by putting out all the people (Sulp. Sev. *Vita Mart.* cc. 7 and 8; Halm, pp. 117, 118). Columba when raising a boy from the dead drove away the multitudes from the scene of the miracle (*Vit. Col.* II, 32). St Samson of Dol also sent away all the other brethren except one, when he restored a brother almost dead at Llantwit (*St Samson of Dol*, p. 19). Cf. also *loc. cit.* p. 33 and the *Life of St Germanus of Auxerre*, c. 38 (*Script. rerum Merov.* VII, p. 279, 1).

CHAPTER VI (p. 118)

V.P. c. 33, *V.M.* c. 27.

Tydi. See note on II, 4 (p. 321).

Medilwong. This place has not been identified; Symeon of Durham mentions Mediluong as the scene of the murder of Oswulf, king of Northumbria (Symeon, *H.D.E.* II, 41, 376). It probably means "middle field" rather than "field of discussion", as Stevenson and others suggest (*Opp. Min.* p. 278). Craster has suggested that it is the original name of one of the Middletons in Ilderton, though it might equally well be the one in Belford (cf. Mawer, p. 142).

Epidemics. There were several visitations of the plague in the seventh century, one of the worst being in the year of the Synod of Whitby, 664. It seems to have raged on and off throughout the second half of the seventh century (*Vit. Col.* Reeves, p. 182n.). It can hardly have been typhus, as Plummer suggests (*H.E.* II, p. 196), that Boisil at any rate died of, judging from the symptoms described by Bede in *V.P.* c. 8, but rather the bubonic plague. On the other hand, the fact that the Irish and Welsh names for it mean "yellow sickness", from the yellow colour of the patient, would point to some disease other than plague, of which jaundice was one of the symptoms. Perhaps more than one epidemic disease was raging.

CHAPTER VII (p. 120)

V.P. c. 25, not in *V.M.*

A priest. Three of the MSS give the name of the priest as Baldhelm. Bede names Baldhelm as his source and describes him as a Lindisfarne monk (*V.P.* c. 25). He was fond of singing the praises of Cuthbert. The name occurs three times in the Liber Vitae; once on f. 15 third in the list of anchorites, once in the list of clerics on f. 24, and once in the list of monks on f. 36 b.

tarda molimina, etc. The quotation is from St Ambrose (*Expositio evangelii secundum Lucam*, II, 19, ed. C. Schenkl, Vienna Corpus, XXXII, pars 4 (1902), 52). The same quotation appears in part in *Eddius*, c. 19: "tarda molimina nesciens." Compare also "Dialogus de Scaccario" I, 7 (*Stubbs, Select Charters*, ed. H. W. C. Davis, 9th ed., Oxford, 1913, p. 216; ed. A. Hughes, C. G. Crump, C. Johnson, Oxford, 1902, p. 90 and cf. p. 187). I am indebted to Dr Levison for this information.

Sibba. Nothing further is known of this man. Sibba is the name o a bishop of Elmham in the early ninth century, and it occurs occasionally in place-names such as Sibton, Suffolk, and the Sibfords in Oxfordshire. It is probably a hypocoristic form of Sigeberht (but see Redin, p. 78).

CHAPTER VIII (p. 122)

V.P. c. 27, *V.M.* c. 29.

Ecgfrith's death. Ecgfrith was apparently supreme over some part of the Pictish land; but it was clearly an uneasy rule. We read in *Eddius* (c. 19) of a victory gained over them somewhere about 672 with the help of Beornhaeth. Ecgfrith had undertaken the expedition into Forfarshire against the advice of his friends, including Cuthbert. From the time of this overwhelming defeat Northumbria's strength began to grow less (*H.E.* IV, 26). He was slain on Saturday, May 20th, 685, at Nechtansmere, having been trapped into the mountains by the Picts. According to Symeon he was buried at Iona (Symeon, *H.D.E.* I, p. 32; see also III, 6n. p. 329).

Roman remains. This is an interesting reference to Roman work. The impression made by the Roman remains upon the Angles and Saxons was considerable. It is clear from this passage that the true origin of these Roman buildings and structures was known to the more educated Anglo-Saxons as far back as the seventh century, but the phrase often used to describe them in Anglo-Saxon literature is *eald enta geweorc*, the old work of giants. An Anglo-Saxon poem "The Ruin" describes the ruins at Bath in some detail (*Anglo-Saxon and Norse Poems*, ed. N. Kershaw, Cambridge, 1922, pp. 54–5). The Roman cities to a large extent seem to have been left severely alone as places of habitation by the Saxon peasants who regarded towns as "tombs surrounded by nets" (Ammianus Marcellinus, XVI, 2, 12, quoted by Myres in *Roman Britain and the English Settlements*, p. 439). But occasionally a Roman city seems to have been taken over at a comparatively early date. Thus Canterbury became the seat of the kings of Kent; we hear of a reeve of the city of Lincoln about 628, who was converted by the preaching of Paulinus (*H.E.* II, 16); and we read here of the reeve of Carlisle. But the archaeological evidence for a continuous survival of any of the Roman cities, including London, is very slight (Myres, *op. cit.* pp. 425 ff.). William of Malmesbury refers to Roman ruins existing in his time at Carlisle (*Gesta Pontificum*, ed. N. E. S. A. Hamilton, Rolls Series, 1870, p. 208; for a further discussion of antiquarian learning in Anglo-Saxon times see H. M. and N. K. Chadwick, *The Growth of Literature*, I, Cambridge, 1932, pp. 295 ff.).

The queen. Iurminburg was the second wife of Ecgfrith, whom he married after Aethilthryth had left him to enter a monastery. Iurminburg seems to have been very hostile to Wilfrid and to have plotted against him (*Eddius*, c. 24). After her husband's death she took the veil and, to quote Eddius, "from being a she-wolf she was changed into a lamb of God, a perfect abbess and an excellent mother of the community". Her name occurs in the Liber Vitae (f. 13) in the list of queens and abbesses between Eanfled and Aelfflaed.

Second sight. A very similar instance of second sight is the story told by Palladius of Didymus of Alexandria who saw in a trance the death of the Emperor Julian at the exact moment when the event happened (*H.L.* c. 4).

CHAPTER IX (p. 124)

V.P. c. 28, *V.M.* c. 30.

St Herbert's Isle. The island of Derwentwater on which Herbert lived his hermit's life is still called St Herbert's Isle. His name appears in the list of anchorites on f. 15 of the Liber Vitae. This visit to Carlisle took place after the incidents related in the previous chapter, when Cuthbert was in Carlisle in order to bestow the veil on Iurminburg and ordain priests (*V.P.* c. 28).

Maris. Here used in the sense of a mere.

Similar miracle. St Fintan is also related to have gained permission for two brothers to die together. One of them had to be recalled to life so that this could happen (*V.S.H.* II, p. 105).

Foreknowledge of death. A large number of saints from St Antony onwards were permitted to know the date of their death. This is the most common type of prophetic vision. Bede relates several instances where angelic visitors brought a warning: to Chad (*H.E.* IV, 3), to Earcongota (*H.E.* III, 8), to Sebbi king of Essex (*H.E.* IV, 11), to Wilfrid at Meaux (*H.E.* IV, 11; cf. *Eddius*, c. 56). Cuthbert, we are told, was warned by a divine oracle, though its exact nature is not described. Boisil and Caedmon also knew of their coming departure, though we are not told how the knowledge came to them. This form of foreknowledge perhaps owes its conception to the story of Hezekiah who was promised fifteen years of life by the word of the Lord (Isaiah, c. 38). Eddius quotes this passage in connection with Wilfrid's vision at Meaux. It was doubtless due to the fear of sudden death (cf. Eadberht's prayer, *V.P.* c. 43), which lasted all through the mediaeval period and of which an echo occurs in the Litany. The saint who was forewarned was given time to prepare himself and fortify himself for his departure by his last communion (see further Bede, *L.T.W.* pp. 211 ff.).

CHAPTER X (p. 126)

V.P. c. 34, *V.M.* c. 31.

Aelfflaed. See III, 6 and n. (p. 328).

Osingadun. Osingadun is possibly a misreading of Ofingadun. The confusion of the insular *s* and *f* has already been seen in the form *Tesgeta* in II, 5. Bede tells us the place referred to was an estate belonging to Aelfflaed's monastery, that is Whitby. There is an Ovington which lies on the southern slope of the north bank of the Tyne, a mile west of Ovingham. There is Anglo-Saxon work in the church at Ovingham and he might have been consecrating a church there. But there seem to be no traces of any Anglo-Saxon connections with Ovington. Furthermore Bede in the *V.P.* account describes how Aelfflaed made inquiries at the "larger monastery", presumably Whitby, and the news of the death of Hadwald was brought next morning. This would make the identification with Ovington, Northumberland, still less likely. On the other hand, the incident is related immediately after the account of Cuthbert's visit to Carlisle, and Ovington, Northumberland, would be on his way between Carlisle and Lindisfarne. It cannot be the Ovington in North Riding as the earlier forms show. Ovenden near Halifax was in the possession of the church at Durham in the twelfth century, but apart from that there seems no reason for identifying it with the place mentioned here.

We are told definitely in the *V.A.* that *Osingadun* was in Cuthbert's see, but in the *V.P.* account (c. 34) Bede seems to imply that the place was outside his diocese. Carlisle was within his jurisdiction because the king gave him the site on the occasion of his consecration at York in 685, as we learn from the *Historia de Sancto Cuthberto* (Symeon, *H.D.E.* I, p. 199). The *Historia* also states that Cuthbert founded a congregation of nuns and placed an abbess there and founded schools.

Fodder from trees. The reason given in the *V.M.* for Hadwald's fall is that he was climbing a tree to get fodder for his flock. Sir James Frazer in his edition of Ovid's *Fasti* (*Publii Ovidii Nasonis Fastorum Libri Sex*, III, London, 1929, p. 358) has collected some references to this custom of using the branches of trees for fodder, from Hesiod, Theocritus, and Vergil. He quotes Paley as saying that in countries where grass is less plentiful than with us, sheep, goats and cattle are still fed in great measure on the foliage and succulent twigs of trees.

Hadwald. Nothing further is known of Hadwald though the name Hadwald occurs four times in the Liber Vitae (ff. 23, 26*b*, 27, 31*b*). It is hardly likely to be this man in any case.

Similar miracle. A similar story of how Antony saw in a trance the ecclesiastical troubles caused by the Arians in 339 at Alexandria is found in *Vit. Ant.* c. 51 (Migne, LXXIII, col. 162).

The mass. The mass was a dedication mass for the church. The point at which Aelfflaed burst into the church was some time during the canon of the mass. It would have been more appropriate if she had arrived at the point where commemoration is made of the faithful departed. But it is the commemoration of the living, at an earlier point in the canon, which begins with "Memento, Domine, famulorum famularumque"; the commemoration of the departed begins with "Memento *etiam*, Domine". It is just possible, of course, that in the original version of the story Aelfflaed did enter at this point.

CHAPTER XI (p. 128)

V.P. c. 36, *V.M.* c. 32.

Cuthbert's return to Farne. Before accusing Cuthbert of lightly throwing up his episcopal duties, as is so often done, one must remember that he had had a warning that the day of his death was approaching. Apart altogether from any supernatural warnings, Cuthbert probably knew well enough that his end was not far off, and he felt that the effort of making these constant episcopal journeys was too much for a body already worn out by asceticism.

CHAPTER XII (p. 128)

V.P. c. 38, *V.M.* c. 35.

Walhstod. When Bede is giving his account of England in 731, at the end of *H.E.* (v, 23), he mentions a Walchstod, bishop of Hereford. It is possible but not likely that it is the same man. The Walchstod mentioned by Bede was bishop some time between 727 and 736. The name Ualchstod appears in the Liber Vitae in the list of priests on f. 19*b* and in the list of clerics on f. 26 and twice on f. 27.

CHAPTER XIII (p. 130)

V.P. cc. 39 and 40, *V.M.* cc. 36 and 37.

Cuthbert's death. The brief account here of Cuthbert's death and burial contrasts strongly with the long account in *V.P.* of Cuthbert's last days with which Bede was furnished by Herefrith. The washing of the dead body was part of the ritual preparation for burial. Wilfrid's body was washed twice before its burial (*Eddius*, c. 66).

His burial. The custom of placing the unconsecrated host on the dead body is mentioned in the miracles of St Otmar by Iso Magister, I, 3 (Migne, CXXI, col. 782). It is possible that this took the place of the consecrated host which was once put into the mouth of the dead but had been forbidden by the Church. There is an instance in Gregory's *Life of Benedict* where the saint orders the consecrated host to be placed on the breast of a young monk who had been buried but whom the earth had previously refused to receive (Greg. *Dial.* II, 24, pp. 116–17). Plummer compares the shoes placed upon the feet of the dead with the "hell-shoon" with which in heathen Scandinavia it was the custom to bind the feet of a corpse (*H.E.* II, p. 270). The whole of the passage from "Postquam... gaudentem" is quoted by Amalarius in his *De eccl. offic.* (Migne, CV, col. 1236).

Wrappings. The wrapping was waxed presumably with the object of keeping out the air. When the coffin was reopened in 1104 the inner coffin itself was covered with a linen cloth of a coarse texture dipped in wax (Symeon,

H.D.E. I, p. 255). Reginald of Durham in describing the examination of the body at the translation in 1104 says that it was everywhere enveloped with a very thinly woven sheet of linen next to the body. This he described as the winding sheet which the Abbess Verca gave Cuthbert (*V.P.* c. 37). He was clothed then in an alb, amice, mitre, gold fillet, stole and fanon, tunic, dalmatic and episcopal shoes. Next to the dalmatic were robes of silk and three covering robes above. In the place of these covering robes there were put in 1104 three costly robes, two of silk and the third and outer one of the finest linen. When the coffin was opened in 1827, the remains of five silken robes were found (Raine, *St Cuthbert*, p. 193). Four of these are still to be seen in the chapter library at Durham (see C. F. Battiscombe, "The Relics of St Cuthbert", *Transactions of the Architectural and Archaeological Society of Durham and Northumberland*, VIII, pt I, 1937, 43–79).

Stone coffin. This stone coffin was given to the saint by Cudda (*V.P.* c. 37 and n. p. 355).

CHAPTER XIV (p. 130)

V.P. c. 42, *V.M.* c. 38.

The incorrupt body. The phenomenon of the undecayed body has been known from earliest times. References to it are found in the classical authors (e.g. Quintus Curtius, x, 10; Pausanias, v, 20). Saintyves quotes several modern examples of corpses preserved in a mummified form such as those still to be seen in the crypt of St Michel at Bordeaux or in the catacomb of the Capuchins at Palermo. (For a discussion of the whole subject see P. Saintyves, *En marge de la Légende dorée*, Paris, 1930, pp. 284 ff.) Bede refers to four saints whose bodies were found incorrupt after death: Aethilberg (*H.E.* III, 8), Fursey (*H.E.* III, 19), Aethilthryth (*H.E.* IV, 19), and Cuthbert. In addition we may add Oswald's relics (*H.E.* III, 6), while it is implied that the body of Earcongota was also incorrupt. Aelfric in his Homily on St Edmund (Thorpe, *Analecta Saxonica*, London, 1846, p. 125) mentions also St Edmund and St Withburga, Aethilthryth's sister, while William of Malmesbury adds Aelfheah also (W. Stubbs, *Willelmi Malmesbiriensis Gesta Regum*, I, Rolls Series, 1887, p. 260). In the *Acta Sanctorum* it is recorded of a very large number of saints and martyrs that their bodies were found incorrupt after periods varying from a few days to hundreds of years. It was regarded, as Bede points out, as a sign of purity of life that the body should remain incorrupt after death. It is curious that an incorrupt body on the other hand is often regarded in popular tradition with the greatest suspicion. There was a lingering belief that the bodies of excommunicated people would not perish in the grave (Saintyves, *op. cit.* p. 286), while witches and wizards like Michael Scot were preserved in the same way (cf. Scott, *Lay of the Last Minstrel*, canto 2, st. 19; *Bede*, *L.T.W.* pp. 221 ff.; also William of Newburgh, Bk v, cc. 22–4, *Chronicles of the Reign of Stephen*, ed. R. Howlett, Rolls Series, 1885, pp. 474–82).

The body of Cuthbert was still alleged to be incorrupt in the early eleventh century when it was often seen by Aelfred Westou the sacrist. There is a long anonymous account of the translation and the opening of the coffin in 1104 which appears frequently among the sets of miracles attached to many MSS of the *V.P.* such as O₃, O₆, Ar₂, H₁, H₂, Ad₁, Ad₂, Dj₁, Dj₂, Du, Va, etc. (printed in Symeon, *H.D.E.* I, pp. 247ff.; see also p. 49 above). In this account there is a circumstantial description of the examination of the incorrupt body. In 1537 Henry VIII's commissioners visiting the monastery are said to have found the body in the same condition (*Rites of Durham*, Surtees Soc. CVII, p. 102). The tomb was opened again in 1827 when a mere heap of bones was found. There are some who maintain that the incorrupt body was removed in 1538 to another part of the church and that another body was substituted. The incorrupt body still remains, it is asserted, in a secret place in the Cathedral known only to three Benedictines. For a full, though biased, account of the incorrupt body, see J. Raine, *St Cuthbert*, Durham, 1828; see also C. F. Battiscombe, *loc. cit.*

Decani. According to the Benedictine rule, certain monks of good testimony and holy conversation in a monastery were given the charge of ten younger monks for disciplinary purposes, in order to lighten the abbot's burden. Sometimes more than ten were placed under this *decanus* (*Regula Benedicti*, c. 21, p. 56). This arrangement goes back to pre-Benedictine times as one of St Jerome's epistles shows (St Jerome, *Epistle* p. 22, 35, ed. I. Hilberg, Vienna Corpus, LIV, 1910, p. 197). For later uses of the word see Stubbs, *Dunstan*, Introduction, p. xiv.

Eadberht. After the death of Cuthbert, Wilfrid held the see for a year. Eadberht who had been a monk at Lindisfarne was then appointed bishop. Bede (*H.E.* IV, 29) tells us that he was famous for his knowledge of the scriptures and for his almsgiving. He was careful to give tithes of all he possessed to the poor. He also replaced the thatched roof of the Lindisfarne church by a roof of lead. The permission of the bishop had to be obtained for the elevation of the relics, for this elevation was the equivalent of the canonisation of the saint (H. Delehaye, *Sanctus*, Brussels, 1927, pp. 184ff.).

Relics. From earliest times, a saint's tomb became a place of sanctity and acquired miraculous powers together with anything which had been in contact with it. The bodies of the saints in Europe were at first protected from the many translations and dismemberments which they afterwards suffered, and representative relics such as these here described had to suffice. It was customary to deposit relics in a church at its dedication and the crypts at Ripon and Hexham, the places made by Wilfrid for the deposition of the relics he had brought from Rome and elsewhere, still remain. Gregory the Great ordered Mellitus not to destroy the temples of the idols but, having destroyed the idols themselves, to sprinkle the temple with holy water, erect altars and place relics therein (*H.E.* I, p. 30). For the extent to which the rage for relics, especially the bones of saints, grew, one has only to note the story of Aelfred Westou, sacrist of Durham about 1020, who gathered together the bones of Bede, Aidan, Boisil, Aebbe, Eadberht, Eadfrith, Aethilwald and several other saints connected with Cuthbert and placed them all together in the shrine of the latter at Durham (Symeon, *H.D.E.* I, pp. 88, 221).

CHAPTER XV (p. 132)

V.P. c. 41, *V.M.* c. 40.

Martyr. Cuthbert is twice referred to as martyr in the *V.A.*, here and in IV, 17. He is looked upon as having obtained the equivalent of martyrdom. In IV, 16 he is twice called confessor, that is, one who has confessed his religion in face of great danger without necessarily having suffered death for it. See note to II, 1 (pp. 315 f.).

Similar miracle. A very similar miracle is recorded of Wilfrid and the water with which the body was washed (*Eddius*, c. 66). For further examples of miracles connected with the relics of saints, especially healing drinks, etc., made by steeping some holy relic in water, see *Bede, L.T.W.* pp. 217 ff.

CHAPTER XVI (p. 134)

V.P. c. 44, *V.M.* c. 41.

Willibrord. Willibrord Clement, as Bede calls him, was educated under Wilfrid at Ripon and afterwards in Ireland (Alcuin, *Vita Willibrordi*, cc. 3, 4). He set out for Frisia in 690 with eleven companions. He obtained the help of Pippin, duke of the Franks, and won many converts. Pope Sergius consecrated him archbishop of the Frisians and gave him the name of Clement, with his seat at Utrecht. He died in 739 at the monastery of Echternach which he had founded (*H.E.* V, 10, 11 and *Script. rerum Merov.* VII, 134, n. 1).

CHAPTER XVII (p. 136)

V.P. c. 45, *V.M.* c. 43.

Monastic doctors. In the same way we read that sick people came to Iona for medical attention (*Vit. Col.* I, 27, Reeves, pp. 55 ff.).

CHAPTER XVIII (p. 138)

Other miracles. For the miracle of the holy bread, see *V.P.* c. 31 and for the miracle of water changed into wine, *V.P.* c. 35.

Winfrith. Winfrith can hardly be the famous Boniface for the latter was not ordained bishop until 722. It might be Winfrith, bishop of Mercia, in succession to St Chad (*H.E.* IV, 3), though he was deposed by Theodore for disobedience, soon after the Council of Hertford, somewhere about 676. I know of no other Winfrith.

NOTES TO BEDE'S PROSE LIFE

PROLOGUE (p. 142)

Bede's method. Bede's method of working is very clearly illustrated by this Prologue. His first draft is verified by Herefrith and others who had known Cuthbert personally, while a fair copy is sent to Lindisfarne for general approval. Compare also his method of writing the *H.E.* as described in his Preface to that work. It is typical of Bede's carefulness that he omits the names of the witnesses given by the author of the *V.A.* but where he has any fresh information to give, or where he has himself heard the story from some other source, then, as he tells us in the Preface, he is careful to name his witnesses, adopting the principle he had learned from his favourite author Gregory (Greg. *Dial.* Preface to Bk 1, p. 16). He also distinguishes between witnesses who saw the incidents themselves and those who heard them from another (cf. cc. 5, 6 and 23). He does not in fact mention the *V.A.* at all in this place, though he mentions it as a source in the Preface to the *H.E.* He is attempting to write a life which shall be more attractive and fuller than the very concise, but none the less readable, little life by the anonymous monk of Lindisfarne. Perhaps, as Levison suggests (*Bede, L.T.W.* p. 127 n. 1), this is why he does not mention his source, out of delicacy, not wishing to hurt the feelings of the author who had written the briefer life.

Herefrith. Herefrith was an abbot of Lindisfarne, but by the time that Bede wrote the *V.P.* had apparently resigned the office. He was at one time in the monastery at Melrose, for he tells the story of Cuthbert's illness there, when the plague attacked the monastery carrying off Boisil among others (*V.P.* c. 8). Later on he attended the saint in his last illness and gave the full and complete account of his death which Bede incorporated in his *V.P.* in cc. 37–40. It is probably his name which appears in the Liber Vitae under the list of anchorites on f. 15, where he appears as "Herefrid presbyter". If it is the same man, it probably means that he gave up the office of abbot of the monastery in order to take to the hermit life.

It has been suggested by H. Hahn (*Bonifaz und Lul*, Leipzig, 1883, pp. 175 ff.) that Herefrith may have been the author of the *V.A.*, but it seems very improbable that one who gave Bede such an affecting account of the saint's last days should have written the very perfunctory chapter which the anonymous author devotes to Cuthbert's death; an even more convincing proof that it was not Herefrith is that the author of the *V.A.* was under the impression that Cuthbert took monastic vows at Ripon. Bede tells us, what is certainly correct, that it was at Melrose that he took them. Herefrith, who had himself been at Melrose in Boisil's time, must have known this fact (cf. also Introduction, p. 12 and cc. 8 n. and 23 n. pp. 346, 351).

Guthfrith. Guthfrith afterwards became abbot of the monastery at Lindisfarne. It is he who told Bede the story of the calming of the sea by Aethilwald, Cuthbert's successor as hermit on Farne Island (*H.E.* v, 1). Guthfrith was apparently dead when Bede wrote the *H.E.*, that is about 731. The name Cuthfrith occurs in the Liber Vitae (f. 15*b*) in the list of abbots of the rank of priest. The name Guthfrith appears on f. 18*b* under the heading of priest.

Mansionarius. The office of *mansionarius* is defined by Du Cange as "custos et conservator aedis sacrae, aedituus". It is evident that his duties were connected with the care and upkeep of the church including the altar, so that the entry of Bede's name in the album of the church would be part of his duty.

Album. The "album congregationis" would be the Liber Vitae or its predecessor, a list of names both of the living and the dead, for whom prayers were offered during the celebration of mass. In its earliest form it was a diptych, or two-leaved tablet, on which the names of the dead members of the community were written on the left-hand side, and the living on the right. These names were read out after the mementos of the dead and of the living in the canon of the mass. These diptychs were often made of ivory—hence perhaps the name "album". But at a later stage, as the list grew, the diptych was enlarged by the insertion of extra leaves and was gradually replaced by a Liber Vitae. The Liber Vitae of Lindisfarne and Durham has been preserved in the British Museum (MS Cott. Domit. VII). It was composed in the ninth century at Lindisfarne, presumably on the basis of the older album, and contains lists of benefactors as well as members of the community. The name of Bede appears five times in the Liber Vitae, see c. 37 n. p. 355. Plummer in his introduction to *H.E.* (I, pp. xxvii f.) gives examples of the habit of formal agreement or confraternity between monasteries for mutual prayer and examples of individuals requesting to be placed on such lists. Alcuin enjoyed a similar privilege with regard to Wearmouth and Jarrow. For further information, see A. Ebner, *Die klösterlichen Gebetsverbrüderungen bis zum Ausgange des Karolingischen Zeitalters*, Regensburg, 1890; U. Berlière, *Revue liturgique et monastique*, XI, 1926, 134 ff.

CHAPTER III (p. 160)

The miracle of the rafts. This incident is omitted in the *V.A.* The monastery was declared by Smith to be that of Tynningham, situated on the river Tyne, which runs through Haddingtonshire. This site is certainly not far from the scenes of Cuthbert's early youth, but Tynningham is on the north side of the river and not the south, as Bede distinctly says here. Further on the three occasions when Bede mentions the river Tyne in the *H.E.* (v, 2; v, 6; v, 21), it is clear that he means the Tyne between Durham and Northumberland. Stevenson believes that it was this river Tyne, while Raine considers that it is Tynemouth monastery which is referred to. But again Tynemouth is on the wrong side of the river. The English Metrical

Life of Cuthbert (Surtees Soc. LXXXVII, p. 34) makes South Shields the scene of this incident. Canon Savage in a paper called "Abbess Hilda's first religious house" (*Arch. Ael.* N.S. XIX, 1898, pp. 47 ff.) makes out a very good case for believing that the monastery mentioned here is a monastery at South Shields, to which possibly St Hilda was first sent (but see Bright, Preface, p. x); it was this monastery over which Verca afterwards became abbess and where Cuthbert turned the water into wine (*V.P.* c. 35). A marginal gloss in Ar₂ in a late fifteenth-century hand reads "forte ubi iam est capella sancte Hilde". This miracle is referred to in the anonymous Vita Oswaldi to illustrate a somewhat similar miracle performed by St Oswald at Ramsey (*H.Y.* I, p. 448). For the comparison of the rafts with birds cf. *Beowulf*, l. 218. "flota..fugle gelicost".

The hostile onlookers. The remarks of the onlookers show how slow was the progress of Christianity in the more remote districts and in fact everywhere. St Gregory's letter to Mellitus quoted in *H.E.* (I, 30) shows how clearly that wise prelate realised that the progress from heathenism to Christianity was slow. We read later on in the *V.P.* of the incantations and amulets which the people used to ward off disease (*V.P.* c. 9 and n. p. 346). A striking example of this same mixture of heathenism and Christianity is to be found in Bede's account of Redwald, king of the East Saxons, who in the same temple had an altar to Christ and another one on which he offered up sacrifices to devils, that is to say to his pagan gods (*H.E.* II, 15; for other examples see *Bede, L.T.W.* pp. 202 ff.).

Witness. Notice how careful Bede is to state his authority when he is not depending on the *V.A.* A marginal gloss in C₃, O₃ and H₂ gives the name of the brother as Baella.

CHAPTER IV (p. 164)

News of Aidan's death. The *V.A.* says that Cuthbert heard of the death of Aidan after a few days. Aidan died at Bamburgh, so that it is unlikely that the news would reach Cuthbert on the banks of the river Leader, nearly fifty miles away, in a few hours, unless of course this is also to be treated as a miracle.

CHAPTER V (p. 168)

Food miraculously supplied. Bede's account of this miracle is greatly heightened when compared with the simple story in the *V.A.* There no mention is made of the woman who pressed him to eat, nor of any compulsory fast; the point is that the Lord provided him with food in a desert place. In the *V.P.* the point is that the Lord rewarded him for having refused to break his fast, even when travelling, until the ninth hour. According to the Columban rule, monastic travellers were allowed to eat at the third hour (see *V.A.* II, 2), and presumably the same rule would hold good for the faithful laity on a fast day. A marginal gloss in O₃ and H₂ gives the name of the place in which the widow lived as *Loedra* and the place in which the food was provided as *Aloent*, perhaps Alwent near Gainford, Co. Durham. The river Allen was originally called Alwent and Allendale was Alwentdale; see Mawer, s.v. *Allen* and *Alwent*.

Fasts. In the ancient church Wednesdays and Fridays were both fast days; the Jews set aside Mondays and Thursdays as fast days, and the early Christians, while adopting the Jewish custom, altered the fasting days to Wednesday and Friday (cf. Tertullian, *De Ieiuniis*, c. 14; Migne, II, col. 973). Bede tells us that Aidan observed both these days; in fact he uses the same words as here in describing Aidan's Friday fast (*H.E.* III, 5 and n.). Possibly Cuthbert observed the Wednesday fast too; indeed we learn in the next chapter that he found it difficult in his earlier years to fast for long periods, lest he should become unfitted for the labour required of him. It is worthy of notice that Cuthbert did not abstain from flesh on Friday. There was much variation in this matter of abstinence, especially among the laity, in the early mediaeval church (see Cabrol, *s.v.* Abstinence; also L. Gougaud, *Devotional and Ascetic Practices of the Middle Ages*, London, 1927, p. 148).

Ingwald. Nothing further is known of Ingwald. The name Inuald occurs in the Liber Vitae, f. 19 in the list of priests. It is not to be inferred from this passage that Bede was living at Wearmouth at the time. Wearmouth and Jarrow together formed one monastery (*H.E.* I, p. 393). Ingwald may have lived at Wearmouth, though Bede certainly was at Jarrow when he wrote this (cf. cc. 6 and 46).

CHAPTER VI (p. 172)

Melrose. Cuthbert's reception at Melrose is described by Bede only. The *V.A.* implies that he took his monastic vows at Ripon. It is much more likely, however, that it was at Melrose, for this place was close to the scene of his vision of Aidan and in the district in which he spent his youth. The site of the monastery was old Melrose, about two and a half miles east of the existing monastery ruins. The seventh-century buildings were burned down by Kenneth MacAlpin in 839.

Cuthbert's social position. Cuthbert is often said to have been of peasant extraction, presumably because he was keeping sheep when he saw the vision of Aidan. But it by no means follows. Cuthbert would probably not have been sent to foster-parents if he had not been of noble birth. We read of his long journey on horseback far from the scene of his childhood (*V.A.* I, 6 and *V.P.* c. 5); here we find him again mounted and carrying a spear. Riding on horseback at this time was the privilege of the noble classes in Ireland and almost certainly in Northumbria. That is why Aidan unless compelled by necessity refused to go on horseback (Ryan, *Monast.* p. 245). The servant is possibly the monastery servant though it may well be Cuthbert's own servant, just as it was the servants of his family who carried him out when his knee was diseased (*V.P.* c. 2). These things do not seem to fit in well with Cuthbert's supposed lowly origin.

Boisil. Boisil was prior of the monastery, a "priest of great virtues and of a prophetic spirit" (*H.E.* IV, 27). The town of St Boswell's is named after him. Bates (*Arch. Ael.* N.S. XVI, p. 86, quoted by Plummer, *H.E.* II, p. 266) states that the church at Tweedmouth is dedicated to St Boswell. This however seems to be an error. The church of Lessudden in Roxburghshire is apparently the only church dedicated to him (J. M. Mackinlay, *Ancient Church Dedications in Scotland*, Edinburgh, 1914, p. 242). The touching account of his death occurs in chapter 8 (see below). He twice appeared in a vision to a companion of the priest Ecgbert and a former disciple of his own, bidding Ecgbert not make his intended journey abroad to do missionary work on the Continent (*H.E.* V, 9). For the date of his death, see below.

Sigfrith. This Sigfrith cannot be the abbot of Wearmouth of the same name who died in 688 and had therefore long been dead when Bede wrote the *V.P.* The name occurs in the Liber Vitae under "Nomina clericorum" on f. 28, but it is a common name as a glance at the *Onomasticon Anglo-Saxonicum* (ed. W. G. Searle, Cambridge, 1897, pp. 417ff.) will show.

Intoxicants. Custom differed in monasteries and among the saints with regard to their attitude to intoxicating liquors. Palladius declared "that to drink wine with reason was better than to drink water with pride" (*H.L.* Prol.). Beer was drunk in the Columban monasteries and Cuthbert himself on one occasion drank water which had been miraculously turned into wine (*V.P.* c. 35; cf. also *V.A.* III, 3). In the *Life of St Samson of Dol* it is stated that "no one ever saw him drunk", though the writer adds that "never did he put away altogether from himself any drink" (*St Samson of Dol*, p. 22). In the *Vita S. Oswaldi*, c. 21 (Symeon, *H.D.E.* I, p. 361) we learn that after the arrival of King Ceolwulf, licence was given to the monks of the church at Lindisfarne to drink wine and beer; for previously they were in the habit of drinking only milk and water, according to the old tradition of St Aidan.

CHAPTER VII (p. 174)

Alhfrith. We learn from Bede (*H.E.* III, 25; III, 28; V, 19) that Alhfrith was king and reigning at the same time as his father Oswiu. Florence of Worcester (*an.* 664) describes him as under-king of Deira. He married Cyniburh, daughter of Penda of Mercia, who after her husband's death is said to have become abbess of a monastery at Castor near Peterborough (Hardy, I, pp. 370, 371). Alhfrith was greatly influenced by Wilfrid and it was largely owing to the latter's influence that he became a strong supporter of the Roman party. He even wished to accompany Benedict Biscop and Wilfrid to Rome in 653, but was forbidden by his father Oswiu. The monastery which he founded at Ripon and gave in the first instance to Eata, he afterwards gave to Wilfrid somewhere about 660, when Eata and his followers refused to accept the Roman Easter. He was present at the Synod of Whitby, in 664, strongly supporting the Roman party; after this he disappears from history. As we know that he rebelled against Oswiu

(*H.E.* III, 14), we can only conclude that he was either slain or exiled. The famous Bewcastle cross in Cumberland was perhaps put up in his memory. It has on its west side a long runic inscription in which have been read the names of certain people who put up the cross to Alhfrith. On the north side is the name CYNIBURUG (*A.E.E.* vol. v, passim).

Store-house. The *V.A.* calls this a "cubiculum"; Bede who is closely following the *V.A.* calls it a "conclaue". It seems therefore that it must have been some kind of room or dwelling used for storage. It is clear from both accounts that the guesthouse was a separate building.

CHAPTER VIII (p. 180)

Boisil's death. This long and beautiful account of Boisil's death is peculiar to the *V.P.* As it was Herefrith who related it to Bede, it makes it very unlikely that Herefrith can have been the author of the *V.A.* as has been suggested (see *V.P.* Prologue and notes p. 341). Boisil must have died some years before the Synod of Whitby, for very soon after that Cuthbert was transferred to Lindisfarne. Boisil's death took place after the expulsion of Eata from Ripon which was in 660 or 661. After his death Cuthbert acted "for some years" as prior of Melrose as the next chapter shows. His remains were brought to Durham about 1020 by Aelfred Westou.

The gospel. For Boisil's foreknowledge of the date of his death, see note on *V.A.* IV, 9, p. 335. The copy of the gospel of St John from which he was reading was long supposed to be the gospel of St John preserved in the library of the College of Stonyhurst in Lancashire. It is a small book measuring $5\frac{1}{4} \times 3\frac{1}{2}$ in. and has its original seventh-century binding. Baldwin Brown, however, in 1930, pointed out that this gospel has not seven, but eleven gatherings (*A.E.E.* VI, i, pp. 1 ff.). In the same place he puts forward other arguments to show that it is very improbable that this is the Boisil gospel. (For further description of this gospel, see G. D. Hobson, *English Binding before 1500*, Cambridge, 1929, pp. 1, 2 and plate I.)

CHAPTER IX (p. 184)

Incantations and amulets. For other examples of the use of these "ligaturae" or "fylacteria" as Bede calls them in *H.E.* IV, 28, see Plummer's note, *H.E.* II, p. 266. In one of the Canons of Clovesho (A.D. 747) we get a passage which is reminiscent of Bede's words. It is entitled "Ut omni anno episcopi parochias suas peragrent". It bids every bishop visit his see every year, teaching those who rarely hear the word of God and forbidding them to make use of pagan customs such as "divinos, sortilegos, auguria, auspicia, fylacteria, incantationes" and all such heathen errors (H. and S. III, pp. 363–4). It will be noticed that when Cuthbert became a bishop, as well as before his consecration, he considered it his duty to make the pastoral journeys which the Council of Clovesho laid down. The same magical observances are often referred to in the Penitentials and in the sermons based upon the model set by Caesarius of Arles (d. 542).

CHAPTER X (p. 188)

Appointed hour. Cuthbert would return in time for the mattin office, or lauds, which in Benedictine monasteries began immediately after mattins, at dawn ("incipiente luce", *Regula Benedicti*, c. 8, p. 41). In the *V.A.* (II, 3) he returns home at "cockcrow" to unite in prayer with the brethren.

CHAPTER XI (p. 192)

Bede's informant. The brother who afterwards became a priest was Tydi (*V.A.* II, 4).

CHAPTER XIV (p. 200)

Similar miracles. The miracle concerning Benedict referred to here is in St Gregory's *Dialogues* (II, 10, p. 97; see also note on *V.A.* II, 8, p. 323). So also is the story of Marcellinus Anconitanus (Greg. *Dial.* I, 6, p. 42).

CHAPTER XV (p. 202)

Reeve of King Ecgfrith. If Ecgfrith were actually king, then the incident must have happened after 671, the year in which Ecgfrith probably came to the throne. A marginal note in three MSS gives his wife's name as Eadswith (see p. 204 n. 7).

CHAPTER XVI (p. 206)

Arrangements at Lindisfarne. Bede gives two accounts of the arrangements in the Lindisfarne monastery, one here and one in *H.E.* IV, 25. By a comparison of the two, it is possible to deduce that the arrangements did not differ so much from those of an Irish monastery as is often supposed. In Ireland a bishop living in the monastery was subject to the abbot—the monastic bishop usually not being a diocesan. Aidan, as Bede tells us in *H.E.*, was the founder of the monastery and consequently its first abbot too. The other bishops who followed Aidan lived in the monastery, took part in the election of the abbot, and then, together with all the others in the monastery, were subject to his rule, or at least so Bede seems to imply in this place (but see *Bede, L.T.W.* p. 72).

Gregory's letter. Bede is quoting here from Gregory's reply to Augustine's questions. He inserted nearly the whole letter into his *Ecclesiastical History* (*H.E.* I, 27). Levison notes that some attempts have been made to prove that the letter is not genuine but was forged at some period between 721–31; he points out that its presence in this Life proves that it is at least earlier than 721 (*Bede, L.T.W.* p. 128, n. 2).

Wife of the reeve. Bede wishes to make it quite clear that although he has placed the story of the cure of the reeve's wife (following *V.A.*) in the Melrose series of miracles, it really belongs to the Lindisfarne period (see *V.A.* II, 8 and note p. 323; also *V.P.* c. 15n. p. 347).

Chapter. See note on *V.A.* III, 1, p. 324. The custom of reading a portion or chapter of the Rule each day led to the assembled body of monks being called the Chapter, and their meeting place the Chapter-house (*N.E.D.* s.v. Chapter).

Midday rest. There is another reference to this midday rest in *V.P.* c. 35. It was a feature of the Benedictine Rule that it permitted this rest during the summer months, and contrasts with Cuthbert's Irish asceticism with its traditional tendency to forego sleep as a means of mortification. In fact it is probable that the troubles we read of here are due to the clash between the less austere Benedictine customs which, through the growing Roman influence, were becoming more common even in Lindisfarne, and the more austere Irish customs which were partly traditional at Lindisfarne and partly strengthened by Cuthbert's arrival to act as provost under Eata, who was now abbot of both Melrose and Lindisfarne (see also Du Cange, s.v. meridiana and Plummer, *H.E.* I, xxvi, n. 5).

Tears. Bede says again in his Commentary on Exodus (XXX, 18; *Opp.* VII, p. 364) that tears are most fitting, especially when celebrating the Divine mysteries. The gift of tears was possessed by many saints, the most famous being St Dunstan (Stubbs, *Dunstan*, pp. 50, 379).

Who stood by. In the canon of the mass, in the "memento" of the living, the body of worshippers is described as "omnes circumstantes". All evidence goes to show that standing was the usual posture, and even kneeling at the consecration came later, possibly in the twelfth century with the elevation. There is some evidence, however, for prostration at the consecration at an early period in Ireland (Ryan, *Monast.* p. 349).

Sursum Corda. The Sursum Corda is of course part of that dialogue between priest and congregation which leads up to the canon of the mass. The reference to the lifting up of the voice is explained by the fact that at this point of the service there is an "ekphonesis", or raising of the tone of the voice, the preceding prayer having been said "secrete".

Dress. The simplicity of Bede's time would seem to have disappeared in Alcuin's day, for he warns the monks of Lindisfarne against glorying in the vanity of their dress (*Epist.* 20, *M.G. Epist.* IV, Berlin, 1895, pp. 57 and

58). A very similar account of Augustine's dress of which Bede is probably thinking is found in Possidius' *Life of St Augustine*, c. 22; cf. also Jerome, *Epistle*, 22, 27, ed. I. Hilberg, Vienna Corpus, LIV, 1910, p. 183: "Vestis nec satis munda nec sordida et nulla diversitate notabilis."

CHAPTER XVII (p. 214)

Contemplative life. The feeling was general and widespread in Egypt, in Gaul, and in Ireland, and, as we see by Bede's words in this chapter, in England too, that the life of the hermit, the life of divine contemplation, was more advanced than the cenobitic life (Ryan, *Monast.* pp. 258 ff.). As a result, in sixth-century Ireland the monks were ready to make for the desert, even against the wishes of their abbot, so greatly did they thirst for the life of contemplation. Bede is careful to state that Cuthbert entered on the hermit life with the full consent of his abbot. See also *Regula Benedicti*, c. I, p. 10 and III, 1n. p. 324.

Cuthbert's first cell. The first scene of his hermit life is supposed to be the rocky islet called St Cuthbert's Isle, about one hundred yards from Lindisfarne, and south-west of the priory. It is surrounded by water at high tide, but can be approached over a slippery ridge of stones at low tide. There are traces of an ancient chapel, still to be seen on the island, which used to be called the chapel of St Cuthbert in the Sea (J. Raine, *North Durham*, London, 1852, p. 146).

Rheuma. Bede also speaks of the "rheuma" in his *De Temporum ratione*, c. 29, and in *H.E.* V, 3. He owes the idea to Vegetius, *Epitoma rei militaris*, IV, 42, as C. W. Jones has shown (*Classical Review*, XLVI, 1932, pp. 248 ff.; cf. also G. Macdonald, *Classical Review*, XLVII, 1933, p. 124 and Levison in *Bede, L.T.W.* p. 118n.).

CHAPTER XVIII (p. 216)

Maundy Thursday. Maundy Thursday or Coena Domini was in Ireland a day specially devoted to the care of the person, when the monks washed their heads, had their hair cut and so forth. But the custom of bathing on this day in preparation for Easter was widespread. St Augustine refers to the practice in one of his letters (*Ep.* 54, 7, ed. A. Goldbacher, Vienna Corpus, XXXIV, pars II, 1888, p. 168). Ritual feet-washing was throughout the Middle Ages observed in every monastery on this day, when always the superior had to wash the feet of the inferior. The feet of subordinate priests, of the poor or of inferiors were washed by priests, bishops, nobles and sometimes even sovereigns (*E.R.E. s.v.* Feet-washing). Maundy Thursday was in fact called Skyre Thursday in the north of England, possibly from O.N. *skíra*, to purify. In the south of England it became Shere Thursday, and so arose an imaginary etymology from the cutting of the hair for Easter.

When Brendan reached the island of the Procurator, the latter speedily prepared a bath for Brendan and his men for it was the day of the Lord's Supper (*L.I.S.* II, p. 59).

Feet-washing. St Cuthbert in his scorn of washing seems to have been seeking to rival Antony, who neither bathed his body in water nor ever washed his feet, nor even endured so much as to put them into water unless compelled by necessity (*Vit. Ant.* c. 23; Migne, LXXIII, col. 147).

Genuflexions. Prayer amongst the Irish was accompanied by gestures of adoration, by prostrations and genuflexions, and the arms were often held outstretched to form a cross. An Irish gloss relates that James the Less used to make two hundred genuflexions in the day and two hundred in the night, on the bare flags of marble in the Temple at Jerusalem, so that his knees were as large as camel's knees. For this reason James the Less became very popular among the Irish ascetics (Gougaud, *C.C.L.* pp. 91–2). It is not quite clear why the callus at the junction of Cuthbert's feet and shins should have been caused by genuflexions. For another explanation, see note to chapter 37, p. 355.

CHAPTER XIX (p. 220)

The birds driven away. This story of the driving away of the birds is not found in *V.A.* The prototype of this miracle is obviously the story which Bede quotes of Antony driving away the wild asses from his little plot in the desert in which he had planted a few herbs (*Vit. Ant.* c. 25; Migne, LXXIII, col. 149). The reference to Benedict concerns the story of how the saint produced a well from a rock on the top of a mountain to save the monks in the three monasteries on the mountain coming down to the valley for their water (Greg. *Dial.* II, 5, p. 88).

CHAPTER XX (p. 222)

Similar miracle. The incident to which Bede refers here is the story of the raven who obeyed the commands of St Benedict and removed some poisoned bread beyond human reach (Greg. *Dial.* II, 8, pp. 91 ff.).

CHAPTER XXI (p. 224)

Cuthbert's power over animals. The idea of the dominion over the lower creation, originally given to man, having been lost by sin is common in the lives of saints. Liselotte Junge gives a collection of such passages in *Die Tierlegenden des Hl. Franz von Assisi*, Leipzig, 1932. Bede himself discusses the same subject in his *Commentarii in principium Genesis*, c. i (*Opp.* VII, p. 27).

CHAPTER XXII (p. 228)

Devils. The passage is reminiscent of the account in the Evagrian Life of the devils by whom Antony was tempted (*Vit. Ant. c.* 20; Migne, LXXIII, col. 144). See also *V.A.* III, 1 and note, p. 325.

Crowds. Crowds also resorted to Antony, and again Bede is obviously thinking of the chapter describing this in the Evagrian Life. It became a regular feature of the Lives based on the Antonian model to describe how crowds resorted to the saint. Felix in his *Life of Guthlac* closely models his account of the resort to the hermit on this account of Bede (Felix, *Vita Guthlaci*, IV, 31; see Kurtz, pp. 118 ff.).

CHAPTER XXIII (p. 230)

Herefrith. This story is peculiar to Bede and is again based on the testimony of Herefrith. See note to prologue p. 341.

CHAPTER XXIV (p. 234)

Synod. This was the synod held in the neighbourhood of the river Aln at a place called *Adtuifyrdi*, i.e. "at the double ford" (*H.E.* IV, 28 and n.). It was a mixed body of ecclesiastics and laics. Bright suggests that it was where the Aln is crossed by two fords near Whittingham (Bright, p. 373). Alnmouth has also been suggested.

CHAPTER XXV (p. 238)

Conference with Eata. This was probably the occasion when the arrangement was made whereby Eata became bishop of Hexham and Cuthbert became bishop of Lindisfarne. See note to *V.A.* III, 1 (p. 324).

CHAPTER XXVII (p. 242)

Sabbath. In the Celtic church the sabbath was strictly kept. The "Cain Domnaig" or Law of the Sunday, which was passed as a law in the ninth century but was probably much earlier, prohibits both riding and beginning a journey on Sunday. St Columba, for instance, refused to go to a monastery with Berach "on my feet to-night, for the eve of Sunday has begun". So Berach carried him (*L.I.S.* II, p. 38).

Chariot. A reproduction of a chariot such as the one here mentioned appeared on the sculptured stone at Meigle in Perthshire, which perished when the church was burnt down in 1869. It is pictured in J. R. Allen and J. Anderson, *Early Christian Monuments of Scotland*, Edinburgh, 1903, pt. III, p. 331. Chariots were widely employed in Northumbria and in Ireland. St Patrick and St Brigid and many other Irish saints used them, though they refused to ride on horseback (Ryan, *Monast.* pp. 244 ff.).

Royal city. Presumably Bamburgh. Bede on three occasions in the *H.E.* (III, 6, 12, 16) refers to Bamburgh as the "royal city".

Plague. The story of Cuthbert's foreknowledge of the coming of the plague is not told in the *V.A.* Plummer quotes the story to illustrate the hardness of monastic life in Northumbria at this time (*H.E.* I, p. xxx). It would appear from the story, too, that Cuthbert occasionally sought the company of his brethren at Lindisfarne on feast-days.

Story-telling. Possibly these stories would be prose sagas preserved by oral tradition and dealing with either secular or ecclesiastical subjects. It is likely, for instance, that some of the stories related by Bede in the *Ecclesiastical History* were derived from sagas handed down by oral tradition—such as the story of Gregory and the Angles (*H.E.* II, 1) or the debate in the Northumbrian Council (*H.E.* II, 13). And it is highly probable that many of the stories about St Cuthbert in the *V.A.* and *V.P.* are based on the sagas of the saint told at Lindisfarne and elsewhere. Occasionally apparently, secular themes were welcomed in the monasteries in the form of heroic poems. Alcuin in a letter to Hygebald, bishop of Lindisfarne, written in the year 797, warns him that, when priests dine together, it is fitting for them to listen to a reader and not to a harpist, to the discourses of the fathers, not to the poems of a heathen. "What", he adds, "has Ingeld to do with Christ? Strait is the house; it will not be able to hold them both." We are not told what was the subject or character of the songs referred to in the story of Caedmon (*H.E.* IV, 24), which is the earliest reference to the cultivation of poetry or minstrelsy in England (cf. H. M. Chadwick, *The Heroic Age*, Cambridge, 1912, pp. 41, 79; and H. M. and N. K. Chadwick, *The Growth of Literature*, I, Cambridge, 1932, pp. 335-7).

Ecgfrith's bodyguard. Ecgfrith's bodyguard or "comitatus" all died around their prince after the fashion of the Heroic Age. It was, as Tacitus tells us (*Germania*, c. 14), the greatest disgrace among the Teutonic nations for a *comes* to take to flight even when his lord had fallen. When Cynewulf, king of Wessex, had been slain by Cyneheard (*A.S.C. an.* 755) the king's men all refused the terms offered them and fought until all had been killed except one British hostage (see further *O.E.N.* pp. 166ff.).

CHAPTER XXVIII (p. 248)

Hereberht's illness. The *V.A.* account has nothing to say of the sufferings endured by Hereberht in order that he might be accounted worthy to die on the same day as Cuthbert.

CHAPTER XXX (p. 254)

Aethilwald. In the *V.A.* account (IV, 4) Aethilwald is described as prior of Melrose; here he is described as abbot. Unfortunately the date of Aethilwald's appointment as abbot of Melrose is unknown.

Bedesfeld. The village of *Bedesfeld* in which the nuns had taken refuge has not been identified; but we presume that their flight took place about 685, when Ecgfrith was killed by the Picts at Nechtansmere and when Trumwine had to leave his monastery and see at Abercorn, and flee to Whitby.

CHAPTER XXXI (p. 254)

Blessed bread. For the wide use of relics steeped in water, and the liquor given as a drink, see *Bede, L.T.W.* pp. 217 ff. and *V.A.* IV, 15 n. p. 340. This miracle is not told in full by the author of the *V.A.* but merely referred to in the last chapter in a list of miracles omitted.

CHAPTER XXXII (p. 256)

Church. It is interesting to note how the church was the natural place to look to for a night's shelter, as also in Iceland until very recently. For the many uses to which churches were put in mediaeval times, see *A.E.E.* I, pp. 346 ff.

CHAPTER XXXIII (p. 258)

The dying boy. In the *V.A.* (IV, 6) the mother and son are still alive. Whether Bede had any definite information or not we do not know, but here he presumes that they are dead.

CHAPTER XXXIV (p. 260)

The death of Hadwald. Bede has spoiled the simpler story in the *V.A.* (IV, 10). There the point is that Aelfflaed rushes breathlessly into church to tell him the name of the dead shepherd and arrives just as Cuthbert has reached the part of the mass where the faithful departed are remembered. It is longer but much less dramatic in Bede. Cf. Plummer, *H.E.* I, p. xlvi.

CHAPTER XXXV (p. 264)

Water changed to wine. Probably the monastery at South Shields. See note on *V.P.* c. 3, p. 343. This story is not told in the *V.A.* but merely referred to in the last chapter. It was Verca who gave him the linen sheet in which he was afterwards buried. Her name does not appear in the Liber Vitae. In marginal glosses in C_3, O_3 and H_2 the name of the priest is given as Beda, that of the servant as Betuald and that of the Jarrow brother as Fridumund (Fridmund H_3). The name Fridumund occurs under the list of abbots in the Liber Vitae, f. 17.

CHAPTER XXXVI (p. 266)

The uncooked goose. This story is not in the *V.A.* It illustrates well the duty of obedience; even though the cooking of the goose was unnecessary, yet the question of holy obedience was involved, and nature herself was at one with the saint in impressing the heinousness of his disciples' offence in disobeying his simplest command (see *Bede, L.T.W.* pp. 223 ff.). Bede's love of a picturesque incident doubtless led him to include this miracle.

Cynimund. The name Cynimund is a common one and occurs eleven times in the Liber Vitae, twice in the list of priests, once on f. 18 *b* and again on f. 19. The same name occurs also under "Nomina regum vel ducum" on f. 12. Nothing further is known of this priest. There is another Cynimund mentioned in *H.E.* III, 15, but Bede states that he was a monk of Jarrow or Monkwearmouth ("our church"). As the name is so common, it is highly improbable that it is the same man. The name also occurs in a marginal gloss to c. 41. See note below (p. 358).

CHAPTER XXXVII (p. 270)

Old complaint. In *V.P.* c. 8 we learn that after St Cuthbert recovered from the plague, he was left with some after effects which troubled him for the rest of his life. When St Cuthbert's tomb was opened in 1899 and the contents examined, it was found that the bones of the sternum and clavicle showed extensive signs of disease. Dr Selby Plummer, who examined the bones, was inclined to think that the disease was of tubercular origin and that the "imperfect diagnosis of those days might well confound a tubercular lesion coincident in one subject with the prevailing epidemic plague in others" (Dr Selby Plummer, "St Cuthbert. Notes on the examination of his remains", *Northumberland and Durham Medical Journal*, 1899, pp. 1–15).

Cross. There is a certain amount of early evidence for the setting up of free-standing crosses to mark a place of burial or for some other reason. We read of a cross by which Columba sat on his last walk before his death (*Vit. Col.* Reeves, III, 23, p. 231). There are numerous crosses mentioned in the documents connected with the life of St Patrick (*Vit. Tr.* pp. 72, 276, 325, 326). The Ruthwell and Bewcastle crosses are generally ascribed to the late seventh century, while the Acca cross, lately in Durham and now in Hexham, was probably one of the crosses mentioned by Symeon of Durham, placed at the head and the foot of Acca's grave (Symeon, *H.D.E.* II, p. 33). Further there is the cross associated with Cuthbert and put up by Aethilwald which is also mentioned by Symeon (I, 39) and which was afterwards brought to Durham. (For a full account of the early history of the cruciform monument, see *A.E.E.* v, c. 6.)

Dwelling. The dwelling is the house mentioned in *V.P.* c. 17 near the landing-place used for the reception of the brethren. It probably stood on the site near the landing-place, where a rough stone shelter now stands.

Cudda. This Cudda is possibly the same as the one mentioned in *Eddius*, c. 2. There he is described as "ex sodalibus regis", meaning, probably, one of the king's thegns. This man gave up secular life owing to a paralytic infirmity and became a monk at Lindisfarne. Wilfrid was sent to him as a young man by Queen Eanfled to act as his servant. The name appears second in the list of abbots in the Liber Vitae on f. 17 and again under the list of clerics on f. 24. It is a hypocoristic form of some name with the prefix Cuth-, such as Cuthbert, Cuthwine, etc. (Redin, pp. xxxvi, n. 2 and 62).

Ulcer. It is not clear whether the suppurating ulcer was on the front or the heel of the foot. If it were on the heel, it might be due to a bedsore brought on through neglect. Dr Selby Plummer (*loc. cit.*) connects it with the extensive callus at the junction of the feet and legs mentioned in c. 18. He points out that the illnesses from which Cuthbert suffered, the acrid tumour of the knee (c. 2), the tumour in the groin (c. 8), the callus at the junction of the foot and leg (c. 18) and this ulcer of the foot, are all to be associated with tubercular mischief. His appearance and temperament, his charm of manner, his hysterical tears (c. 16) and his tendency to go off into visions (c. 34, etc.) are all symptomatic, according to Dr Selby Plummer.

Onions. Raw onions are still used by travellers in hot countries and by others for the purpose of allaying thirst (see Fowler in *Metr. Life*, p. 103).

Beda. It is not known who Beda the elder was. The name of Beda appears five times in the Liber Vitae, twice in the list of priests and three times in the list of clerics (see Prologue, n. p. 342).

Cuthbert's gifts. Compare Bede's own anxiety when he was dying to divide his little possessions, his pepper, napkins and incense, among his fellow-monks (*H.E.* I, p. lxxvi). St Antony similarly divided up his garments on his death-bed between Athanasius and Serapion (*Vit. Ant.* c. 58; Migne, LXXIII, col. 167).

Cuthbert's burial place. Cuthbert's anxiety to have his body left in Farne is paralleled by Antony's anxiety to have his body buried in a place known to no one but his two faithful followers (*Vit. Ant.* c. 58; Migne, *loc. cit.*).

Flee to my body. The right of asylum was, as we learn from the Laws of Ine (c. 5) and the Laws of Alfred (c. 2), common to churches and monasteries during the Anglo-Saxon period (F. L. Attenborough, *The Laws of the Earliest English Kings*, Cambridge, 1922, pp. 39, 65). But some churches, especially those which possessed the body and relics of a famous saint, seem to have had special privileges in this respect. After the Conquest certain churches received special privileges by charter from the king (see *Cath. Enc. s.v.*

Asylum). Among these churches were Beverley, where the privilege was called the "Peace of St John of Beverley"; Hexham with its relics of Acca and Alhmund; Ripon where the bones of Wilfrid lay; and Tynemouth where St Oswin was buried and where the privilege of sanctuary was known as the "Peace of St Oswin". When St Cuthbert's body was brought to Durham, the right of sanctuary continued to be exercised there. All through the Middle Ages, right up to 1524, there are entries in the registers of the cathedral recording the names and crimes of those who sought sanctuary. Persons who took refuge fled to the north door and knocked for admission, using the large knocker which still survives. Over the north door were two chambers in which there were always two guardians who admitted fugitives at any hour of the day or night, and the Galilee bell was immediately tolled. The fugitives were then provided with a gown of black cloth which had a yellow St Cuthbert's cross on the left shoulder. They were given bedding and provision at the expense of the house for thirty-seven days.

Needless to say this right of sanctuary came, as Cuthbert foresaw, to be greatly abused, and all through the Middle Ages laws and regulations were made limiting these privileges. Finally, in the reign of James I, the privilege was entirely denied to criminals, though it was not until the reign of George I that the sanctuary of St Peter's at Westminster was abolished (*Sanctuarium Dunelmense et Sanctuarium Beverlacense*, Surtees Soc. v, 1837, pp. xviff.).

CHAPTER XXXVIII (p. 280)

Similar miracle.   Bede has taken the story of Augustine told here, with verbal borrowings, from the text of St Augustine's Life by Possidius, c. 29. See text, p. 282.

CHAPTER XXXIX (p. 282)

Cuthbert's farewell.   The farewell speech is again based on the Antonian model. One may compare Chad's farewell speech to his followers (*H.E.* IV, 3) or Columba's last words as described by Adamnan in *Vit. Col.* III, 23 (Reeves, p. 234). While Antony bids his followers beware of the heresies of the Meletians and Arians (*Vit. Ant.* c. 58; Migne, LXXIII, col. 167), Cuthbert bids his beware of the Celtic heretics. This seems inappropriate enough, coming from one who was so deeply influenced by the Irish tradition of Iona and Lindisfarne and who had left Ripon rather than accept the Roman Easter. Bede in his Life of Cuthbert follows the *V.A.* in carefully refraining from mentioning the reason for his and Eata's departure from Ripon, and these words which have been put into his mouth do not ring true. On the other hand, in the *H.E.* (III, 25) Bede clearly states the reason for their departure. Bede seems to have been influenced here partly by his literary model—the Evagrian Life of Antony—and partly by his desire to attribute his own Roman convictions to his favourite saint. Again the words in which he claims that they will recognise his true worth after his death, by no means fit in with the picture of the humble-minded saint which Bede gives us elsewhere, but remind us much more of the words that Tennyson puts into the mouth of St Simeon Stylites in his poem about that saint.

Cuthbert's body. Cuthbert's warnings about what they are to do with his body if trouble arises, seem to be connected with the troubles referred to vaguely in the next chapter as happening between the death of Cuthbert and the election of Eadberht at Lindisfarne. But Cuthbert was speaking more truly than he knew, for the day came when the monks of Lindisfarne had to follow their patron's instruction. After the fall of York in 867, the ravages of the Danes became so frightful that Bishop Eardulf in 875, hearing of the approach of Halfdene king of the Danes and his ravaging army, took up the body of the saint and departed from Lindisfarne. For seven years the saint's body was carried about into different parts of Northumbria, until in 883 peace was restored, and the saint rested at Chester-le-Street. Here it remained until 995 when once more, owing to political troubles, Bishop Aldhun took the body to Ripon and thence to Durham. Aldhun finished a church and shrine for it in 998. The present church was begun by Bishop William of St Carilef in 1093, and in Bishop Ranulf Flambard's time the work was sufficiently advanced to permit of the retranslation of the body in 1104 to the feretory behind the high altar.

Sacraments. The sacraments referred to are penance and extreme unction. The sacrament of extreme unction was given before the viaticum. Cuthbert then received holy communion, under both kinds, receiving it sitting, as we learn from the *V.M.* (Eyre, *St Cuthbert*, p. 79; J. Lingard, *History and Antiquities of the Anglo-Saxon Church*, II, London, 1845, pp. 44-6).

CHAPTER XL (p. 284)

The prophetic psalm. This psalm (Vulgate 59, A.V. 60) forms part of the office for mattins or lauds on Wednesday in both the Roman and Benedictine breviaries. The date of his death was Wednesday, March 20th, 687. It is difficult not to connect the troubles here vaguely referred to with Wilfrid, who was in charge of the diocese between the death of Cuthbert and the election of Eadberht in the following year. Wilfrid's dislike of the Celtic Church was well known. It is highly improbable that Bede, though he possibly disliked Wilfrid, would have mentioned his name even though he were the cause of the trouble. The troubles may well have been caused, as the Bollandists long ago suggested (*AA.SS. Mar.* III, pp. 114 f.), by Wilfrid's attempts to do away with the traditional rule of the monastery and to substitute the pure Benedictine rule; or alternatively it may have been his desire to exercise his authority over the monastery where until that time the bishop had either been abbot himself or had lived in subjection to the abbot. Jaager has shown clearly that it cannot refer to an attack of the Picts, as Bright suggests (Jaager, p. 120; see also Introduction, p. 9 above).

Visio Pacis. This, the usual mediaeval interpretation of "Jerusalem" goes back to St Jerome (Hieronymus, *Liber interpretationis Hebraicorum nominum,* ed. P. de Lagarde, Onomastica sacra, I, Göttingen, 1870, pp. 50, 9 and 62, 5). It is found in the sixth- or seventh-century hymn

> Urbs beata Hierusalem, dicta pacis visio,

and also in Cynewulf's Anglo-Saxon poem on Christ, lines 50–51:

> Eala, sibbe gesihð, Sancta Hierusalem,
> Cynestola cyst, Cristes burglond.

And again it is found in the M.E. poem "The Pearl", where in l. 952 Jerusalem is said to mean "Syȝt of pes".

Right side of the altar. The bones of Aidan had already been buried on the right (i.e. the south) side of the altar at Lindisfarne (*H.E.* III, 17). When Colman left Lindisfarne after the Synod of Whitby, he took some of Aidan's bones with him. Cedd was also buried on the right side of the altar in his church at Lastingham.

CHAPTER XLI (p. 288)

Relics. The relics of the blessed martyrs may possibly be some of those relics brought back in large numbers by both Benedict Biscoþ and by Wilfrid. For a discussion of the use of relics in the seventh century, see *Bede, L.T.W.* pp. 216ff. The author of the *V.A.* puts this miracle after the translation.

Cuthbert's superiority. This is the only example in Bede of the widespread type of relic miracle in which, other relics having been unsuccessful, the relic of some particular saint proves effective, thereby showing his superior virtues. The incident in both form and language closely resembles the healing of a cleric through the power of St Benedict when the relics of other martyrs were unavailing (Greg. *Dial.* II, 16, pp. 103 ff.). A marginal gloss in C_3, O_3 and H_2 gives the name of the priest who recommended Cuthbert's aid as Cinimund; cf. c. 36 above and note, p. 354.

CHAPTER XLII (p. 290)

Date of burial. The 20th of March was the day on which St Cuthbert died, so that he was buried on the day of his death. This was a regular custom, so that the festival of a saint is often called his "depositio" (Plummer, *H.E.* II, p. 240).

Lenten retreat. St Kentigern used to retire to a solitary place during Lent (*Lives of St Ninian and St Kentigern,* ed. Forbes, 1874, p. 188), and also Bishop Dubricius (*St Samson of Dol,* p. 37).

The new coffin. The chest referred to is undoubtedly the wooden coffin, many pieces of which were recovered when the tomb was opened in 1827 and are now preserved in the Chapter Library at Durham. Reginald of Durham (c. 43) refers to the coffin which was seen at the translation of

1104 and describes the carving on it. There is no doubt that the coffin he describes is the one found in fragments in 1827. The character of the carving, the runic and other inscriptions, all fit in with a seventh-century date. For a detailed description of it, see *A.E.E.* v, pp. 397ff., and Raine's *St Cuthbert*, pp. 188ff.

Will not long remain empty. It is clear from c. 43 that Eadberht is prophetically referring to his own place of burial.

Poem. This little poem may perhaps have belonged to Bede's "Librum epigrammatum heroico metro, sive elegiaco", which he mentions in his list of works at the end of the *H.E.* and which is now lost. It is not quite clear whether Bede put into verse words previously uttered by Eadberht or whether Eadberht is quoting a poem previously written by Bede. The author of the English Metrical Life understood it to mean the latter (*Metr. Life*, p. 116). Bede would be only twenty-four years old at the time, so that this is the less likely alternative. The English verse is a fairly free rendering of the original. "Fariam...humum" means Egypt. Cf. Lewis and Short's *Latin Dictionary s.v.* Pharius. Dr Levison suggests to me that Bede perhaps borrowed the expression from Lucan's *Pharsalia*.

CHAPTER XLIV (p. 296)

Sunday mass. Mass was celebrated by the Irish, as by others, on Sundays and other feast-days, such as Easter Day, Christmas, and the anniversary of certain saints (Ryan, *Monast.* p. 345). Presumably from this passage, Sunday mass was the custom at Lindisfarne, as also at Llantwit (*St Samson of Dol*, p. 24).

CHAPTER XLV (p. 298)

The paralytic cured. This miracle is a good deal heightened from the simple account in the *V.A.*

Mattins. That is, the mattin office which began at cockcrow (cf. c. 10n. p. 347). Lauds followed at dawn.

CHAPTER XLVI (p. 300)

Aethilwald. Aethilwald as we learn from *H.E.* (v, 1) was a monk at Ripon. Guthfrith relates the story of how he calmed the sea when a hermit on Farne. He died on the island in 699. His name, in the form Oediluald, comes first in the list of anchorites in the Liber Vitae, f. 15. This is also the form of the name in the *H.E.* (v, 1).

Felgild. The name Felgeld comes fourth in the list of anchorites in the Liber Vitae on f. 15. It is probably the same man. Nothing more is known of him. The name of the Jarrow monk is given in a marginal note in C_3, O_3 and H_2 as Ceolbercht, a name which occurs as that of an abbot of priestly rank in the Liber Vitae, f. 15b.

INDEX

Concordance of the three Lives of St Cuthbert

V.A.	V.P.	V.M.	V.A.	V.P.	V.M.
I. 1	Prol.	Prol.	III. —	23	—
2	Prol.	Prol.	6	24	21
3	1	1	7	—	—
4	2	2	IV. 1	24	21
—	3	3	2	26	22
5	4	4	3	29	23
—	—	5	4	30	24
6	5	6	—	31	25
7	—	—	5	32	26
II. 1	—	—	6	33	27
—	6	—	7	25	—
2	7	7	8	27	29
—	8	—	9	28	30
—	9	—	10	34	31
3	10	8	—	35	—
4	11	9	11	36	32
5	12	10	—	37	33, 34
6	13	11	12	38	35
7	14	12	13	39, 40	36, 37
8	15	13	14	42	38
III. 1	16, 17	14, 15	—	43	39
2	17	15	15	41	40
3	18	16	16	44	41
—	19	17	—	—	42
4	21	19	17	45	43
5	20	18	—	46	44, 45, 46
—	22	20	18	—	28

Addendum

Page 42. P. Paul Grosjean informs me that there is a transcript of the lost Utrecht MS of the V.P. used by the Bollandists in the Royal Library, Brussels. It is in MS 3196–3203, ff. 94–100 (J. Van den Gheyn, *Catalogue des manuscrits de la Bibliothèque royale de Belgique*, v, Brussels, 1905, p. 407). I have not been able to see it or get a copy of it owing to the war.